Something in the Woods is Taking People

Five Book Series

Stephen Young

Copyright © 2014 by Stephen Young

All rights reserved.

Table of Contents

Mysterious Things in the Woods	3
Something in the Woods is Taking People	89
Taken in the Woods	212
Predators in the Woods	389
Hunted in the Woods	458

Mysterious Things in the Woods...

Mysterious Disappearances, Missing People; *Sometimes* found...

Stephen Young

~~~

**Copyright © 2014 by Stephen Young.
All rights reserved.**

What really is out there in the woods?

Sometimes the scariest thing is evidence we can plainly see, but can't completely understand....

Table of Contents

Introduction 7
Chapter One: The Clapham Wood Mystery 9
Chapter Two: More mysterious forests 13
Chapter Three: The Bennington Triangle 17
Chapter Four: The Smiley Faced Killers 21
Chapter Five: Captured rural Serial Killers 28
Chapter Six: Other strange missing persons cases in rural areas 30
Chapter Seven: Missing hunters, accidents, natural causes? 39
Chapter Eight: Demons, The Collins elite, and child disappearances. 42
Chapter Nine: The Dalatov Pass Incident 47
Chapter Ten: Cattle & Human Mutilations 50
Chapter Eleven: Underground Bases? 56
Chapter Twelve: UFO reports in forests, woods and mountains? 60
Chapter Thirteen: Searching for more explanations. 64
Chapter Fourteen: Bigfoot? 66
Chapter Fifteen: The Dogman 72
Chapter Sixteen: Do Thunderbirds really exist? 76
Chapter Seventeen: Shape-shifters, and Skin walkers 80

Chapter Eighteen: Portals and different dimensions? 82
Conclusion 85

Introduction

Mysterious deaths in a forest said to be controlled by Satanists; Mountain climbers found inexplicably mutilated; Large numbers of college aged men found dead in creeks; a hiker walks over the top of a hill in front of the rest of the hiking party and has vanished by the time they crest the hill; the little boy who says he was taken by a 'shimmering woman' in the forest.

The village of native Inuits that 'disappeared'; hunters found dead in strange circumstances; experienced climbers disappearing, their bodies never found;

Missing bodies found, placed as though deliberately intended to be found.

No screams for help, no signs of the missing person; vanished into thin air. No trails or tracks left, no clothing found, no smoke, no shelters, no clues...

One only need search the internet briefly to come across the many disturbing cases of missing persons in forests and woods, that have been covered by both local and national newspapers for *decades*.

These and many other mysterious incidents in rural locations in America, Canada, Australia, England and indeed worldwide, have sparked debate by many into what could possibly be the cause.

There are many theories....and with these theories comes the visceral, primal fear that we humans may be victim to a predator; that in the blink of an eye, outsmarts us very easily.

Stalked as prey and snatched without warning... Never to be seen again. Or found, in the most horrible of circumstances....

Chapter One:
The Clapham Wood Mystery

The 'Clapham Woods Mystery' refers to a woodland area in West Sussex, England, where many believe satanic and alien activity has been occurring for a long time, causing the deaths of pets and even people.

The area is allegedly imbued with an eerie atmosphere, which can make those who visit it feel very unwell.

Fortean Times Magazine covered the story of how, since the 1960's, there have been reports of UFO sightings, and some people walking in the woods have had the sensation of being physically attacked while there, as well as a number of mysterious fatalities.

Reports exist from those who claim to have felt suddenly nauseous upon being in the forest; of being followed by someone or *something* unknown, and of being physically attacked by something, whilst others say their dogs have gone missing while out on walks there.

Policeman Peter Goldsmith's body was found hidden amongst the trees in 1972; a Vicar was found dead after disappearing in the forest; then, the body of Jill Matthews was discovered horribly murdered in 1981.

Paranormal and occult investigators Charles Walker and Toyne Newton detailed their own investigation of the place in a 1987 book, after they had carried out a comprehensive investigation into the believed use of the woods by a satanic cult, which they claimed was named 'Hecate,' after the goddess of magic and witchcraft.

Charles Walker has been quoted as stating that when investigating the strange area, he appealed for information from local people and met with a man in the woods who had contacted him. The man, who stood shrouded by the trees, masking his face, threatened serious repercussions should Walker continue his investigation; claiming that he had the support of some very powerful connections who 'would tolerate no interference' in their ritualistic slaughtering.

Walker says mysteriously, "The human disappearances, of which there were several, ended up as Open verdicts. Searches were made of the likely routes; paths these people were thought to have taken and nothing was found...then sometime later, bodies were found in areas known to have been extensively searched by the Police."

In other words, it would seem that the bodies were kept, either alive or dead, for some time, prior to them being placed back at a spot where they were most likely to be discovered.

Echoes of similarity are found in a number of mysterious disappearances in national parks in America and Canada, as well as in bodies of water across America, (more on which will be covered in the next two chapters on the Smiley Face killers, and Mysterious disappearances in National Parks.)

According to Toyne Newton, a skeptical investigator named Dave Stringer of *the Southern Paranormal Investigation Group*, visited the Clapham Woods with a Geiger counter in 1977, and it began to register at an alarmingly high level. Mr. Stringer stopped, looking around him with concern. He said that then, he suddenly saw a dark shape about 12 feet tall, which he could only describe as a 'black mass.'

Seconds later, he claimed a large white disk object shot out from the trees, disappearing fast into the sky. The dark mass subsequently then disappeared.

Extremely curious, Stinger allegedly retraced his last steps and found, at the spot where the form had manifested, an imprint of a four toed footprint.

Interestingly, several miles to the North of Clapham Woods, is Chanctonbury Ring, which is again thought to be the location of possible satanic worship. The infamous occultist Alistair Crowley believed it was a place of great dark power. Clapham Woods, Chanctonbury Ring and another nearby Iron Age hill fort known as Fissbury ring, are all said to be linked by a mystical triangle of Ley lines.

Chapter Two:
More mysterious forests

Do certain wilderness areas have more anomalies than others? Why do some forests and woods experience more unnatural incidents?

The Berwyn Mountains lie in North Wales. UFO reports are not new to this area. Local reports claim this peak region has been the location of many been unidentified objects in the skies.

Other sightings have included 'big cats' and 'hounds of hell.' A popular tourist destination for hikers, the mountains are also highly hazardous, with SAR teams called out almost daily.

It is believed by many UFO investigators that a craft crashed here in 1974. '*The Berwyn Incident*,' as it was called, became a hotbed of tales of alien body retrieval, hushed-up government activities, weapons testing, Men in Black, and disinformation tactics, the like of which drew comparisons to Rendlesham Forest and even Roswell.

Interestingly, prior to this incident, the area had been plagued by a large number of 'phantom helicopter' sightings, seen flying low at night, often over dangerous terrain and in terrible weather. '*Something*' was flying around, and many of the witnesses believed it seemed to be searching for something.

In 2010, U.K. Government files were released about the incident, with the official version explaining it as an earth tremor which came at the same time as a meteor, but according to the BBC, the Ministry of Defence's conclusions did not convince all those who witnessed it. Their files included a letter from one local witness, who wrote: *"Something" came down in the Berwyn Mountains on that night; I am certain."*

Another highly mysterious place is the Hoia-Baciu Forest, also known as the 'Bermuda Triangle of Transylvania.' Incidences in this forest include sightings of orbs, and unusual physiological sensations that many people have reported on their visits there, including sudden nausea, vomiting, headaches, anxiety and long-lasting insomnia; people have even returned with unexplainable scratches and burns on their skin.

The forest became most famous when back in the 1960s, several photographs were taken of a UFO shaped object in the sky, at low altitude, above the forest.

Multiple people have reportedly gone missing in the forest; faces, dark shadows and orbs that are not visible to the eye commonly appear in photographs; while people who visit this forest always feel like being watched.

In Cornwall, Connecticut, lies another highly mysterious forest. Within the area sits Dudley Town, a small old town which has the unfortunate name of 'The Village of the Damned.'

Founded in the 1740's, it was a popular place for tourists, as it was set in dense beautiful forest among Bald Mountain and Woodbury Mountain, but it started to be called 'The Dark Entry Forest,' after the nearby town residents started experiencing hallucinations of demons, who they said were tormenting them and telling them to commit suicide. Livestock would frequently go missing. Residents too went missing, and those that didn't frequently left the area, never to return to it because of the terrifying effect the area had on them.

Visitors say it is now strangely devoid of wildlife and eerily quiet. Orbs of light are often seen 'dancing' across their line of vision. Set on private land, the Dark Entry Forest is now said to be patrolled by a shadowy group who threaten anyone with trespass if they enter. No-one really knows why the area is so sinister and abundant with unexplained phenomena.

On the other side of the world, the Black Mountain region in Australia is also a site of supernatural events, with numerous accounts of mysterious disappearances of people and animals.

Over history there have been reports of people disappearing, never to be seen again. Police and trackers, who then set out looking for the missing, also disappear. There have been reports ranging from 'strange sounds', sightings of 'spirits' or human-like shadows, and disturbing air turbulences reported by pilots, giving Black Mountain the name 'Mountain of death'.

Alien researchers say it is a place with UFO activity. Some claim it was built by artificial means, and are the remnants of an ancient civilization dating back many thousands of years.

Chapter Three: The Bennington Triangle

The 'Bennington Triangle' was named as such by a New England author Joseph A. Citro during a radio programme in 1992, a play perhaps on the name 'Bermuda triangle,' to describe an area of the South-western region of Vermont, where a number of people went missing between 1920 and 1950.

Bennington was a small town near the mysterious Glastenbury Mountain. European settlers who founded their homes there began to tell of seeing unusual lights over the mountain. Tales of hairy 'wild men,' and other strange bigfoot-type beasts in the woods abounded.

The mystery deepened enormously however in 1945. Seventy-four year old Middie Rivers was familiar with the wilderness area. He was an experienced hunt and fishing guide. On November 12, 1945, he escorted a party of four hunters into the mountainous woodlands.

Leading the way back to their campsite, Rivers suddenly disappeared from view, and seemingly vanished, leaving only one clue. An extensive search was instigated, but investigators found only a single bullet beside a stream-bed. No trace of Rivers was ever found.

Middie Rivers disappearance was the first in a series of missing person's cases over the next five years. In December, 1946, a year later, Paula Weldon, a sophomore at Bennington College vanished while hiking along Glastenbury Mountain's 'Long Trail'. A couple who had been behind her told searchers that they had seen her turn a corner, but when they reached the corner, Paula was gone.

Although the search and rescue team called in the FBI, as they did in Middie Rivers' case, again, no trace of Paula Weldon was ever found.

On Columbus Day 1950, eight-year-old Paul Jepson disappeared from the family farm. No trace of the child or his bright red coat was ever found, although hundreds of volunteers combed the mountainside in search of him.

Then, just three weeks later, 53-year-old Frieda Langer slipped into a mountain stream while hiking with her cousin. Telling her cousin that she would catch up with him after changing into dry clothes, Frieda disappeared on the walk back to camp.

Subsequent search teams scoured the area on foot, and by helicopter, but found nothing. Another four more searches were then carried out, with more than 300 strong parties made up of the military, police, and volunteers, but all came up empty-handed.

Then, in May, her body was discovered in an open area where she could not have been missed during the search; in an area that had been thoroughly searched many times before in the attempts to find her.

Again, as in the Crawley Woods cases, there is the implication that her body was seemingly deliberately placed there to be found.

Oddly, the cause of her death was determined as 'unknown.' Shockingly, according to some sources, one witness stated that the body appeared fresh; as though Freida had died only moments earlier, and her face bore an expression of horror, "like she had died of fright."

The implication here again is that she had been kept somewhere by someone or 'something,' in all of the months between her disappearance and her body being found.

Rumours and theories abound about the location and the reason for people's fate in the mysterious location. Some believe a Bigfoot-like "Bennington Monster" is the perpetrator, while others cite that they are alien abductions. Others feel there is a portal in the area, which opens to another dimension. More believe it to have been a serial killer, while the more rational amongst speculators will say that accidents happen in such areas, due to the very nature of the great outdoors, and that in terms of numbers, this is a very tiny proportion of people, given the huge amount of visitors to national park and forest areas such as Bennington.

Can any of these answers explain why in Maddie's case, her body was found without any decomposition? Or where she had indeed been in the forest for the several months before she was suddenly found dead? Or why she was returned to the area where she disappeared, as though placed there?

Chapter Four:
The Smiley Faced Killers

Some observers of these cases, may wish to draw parallels with the strange and disturbing phenomenon of scores of young men, who since the mid '90's, have been vanishing without a trace, only for many of them to be found dead, weeks or months later, in rivers or creeks, in areas the search parties have thoroughly searched several times before. Their bodies as though placed there to be found.

The term 'The Smiley Faced Killers,' came about when it was discovered that many of the locations had smiley face graffiti near by. This has since however been ruled out as being tied to any of the missing persons.

Listing just a few of the cases, Chris Jenkins was a very popular student at the University of Minnesota, who was on the college swim team. He disappeared one night in 2003. When his body was discovered in the Mississippi river about four months after he had disappeared, to the police his death looked like an accidental fall after a night of drinking, however, rather disturbingly, his body was found encased in ice, with his hands folded over his chest, in a manner that was wholly inconsistent with the official verdict of drowning. His cause of death was eventually re-determined as homicide.

Tyler Blalock, 19, was found in Kraut Creek, on Sept. 29, 2012, in the rural Appalachian State University's southeast side of campus, with police saying it looked like he hit his head and fell in. His mother however, could not understand how her son, a lifeguard, could end up dead in a creek.

Honour student Jared Dion, again, like the other boys, a popular and athletic person, was discovered, five days after he disappeared, in the river near Wisconsin University in 2004. At a later autopsy, it was found that he had been moved ten hours prior to his death, and that because his body was still in rigor, he could not have been dead any longer than 72 hours, meaning he had been alive for some time prior to his death and had not died the day of his disappearance.

Todd Geib was last seen on June 12, 2005. When he was discovered in a remote bed of water, his death was ruled as drowning, however when a new autopsy was carried out, he was discovered to have been dead only 2-5 days, despite being missing for over three weeks. In other words, again, he had been somewhere, alive, for approximately two weeks prior to his death.

Up to one hundred young men, predominately in the Midwest, but state wide, have disappeared or drowned, all under very similar circumstances. Journalist Kristi Piehl was the first to link the cases together. Young, popular, athletic, white, college students go missing after a night out drinking with friends. Choosing to go home alone, instead of walking with friends or taking a cab, they disappear, only to be found some time later, drowned in nearby rivers or creeks.

Many will say they were simply drunk and disoriented and fell in the river. Others will ask why they would choose to walk to a river or creek, often in the mid of winter, rather than go straight home? Some will say inevitably, that the reason they are all of a similar victimology is because more young men than women would opt to walk off alone at night, they are popular college kids, letting off steam drinking and underestimating how much they have drunk, who then get into difficulty walking home. Interestingly, however, several of them were former lifeguards or very active sportsmen and active outdoorsmen; and most of them were not known to be particularly heavy drinkers.

Kristi Piehl, along with two former NY police detectives, some forensic examiners, and many of the victim's families, disagree that the young men have merely fallen prey to the outdoors and misadventure. Piehl and the detectives veer toward a much more sinister explanation; a group of killers, identities yet unknown, who deliberately target these men, for reasons not yet known.

Talking on Coast to Coast radio, Piehl was joined by forensic pathologist, Dr Michael Sikirica to discuss the tragic case of Todd Geib. The area where Geib was last seen was thoroughly searched three times. During one of the searches, as many as 1,500 volunteers searched the area. Nothing was found. Then on July 2, his body was found. Again, as in the Bennington case, and the Crawley woods case, it was almost as though his body was deliberately placed back in the location to be purposely found.

When Dr Sikirica was allowed access to the autopsy files, he concluded through forensic analysis that Todd had been dead only between two to five days; he had no water in his lungs and his body was not in the condition it would be expected to be in. He had not been in the water for the thirty days he had been missing; meaning that he had been held or kept somewhere for approximately three weeks, before being taken to the creek. Dr Sikirica's opinion was backed up by many other examiners, at an international convention of Medical Examiners.

This has echoes of Frieda Langer case, where she had been missing, alive, for longer than the time of her recent death.

Piehl says of the cases, "A lot of people have asked me, who is doing this? Whoever had Todd, is a sick individual. I think we're going to find a dark human being, of a kind we haven't met yet," said Piehl.

Unknown to Piehl, around this time, Kevin Gannon, and Anthony Duarte, retired NYPD detectives, were already investigating mysterious deaths of several college men from New York State. Each of the deaths had been ruled as accidental drownings. They then learned of more student drowning deaths in the Midwest. In all, the two detectives were able to connect unexplained drowning deaths of at least 40 male students across the whole country. The two detectives think that in each of these cases, the missing men were drugged, and their bodies then placed in water, in order to make it appear as if they had drowned.

The two detectives are of the opinion that these deaths are highly likely to be the work of more than one killer, because some of them have taken place on the same day, in separate geographical states. Speaking to CNN, Gannon says, "I believe these young men are being abducted by individuals, taken out, and held for a period of time before they're entered into the water." He believes the victims are mentally abused and sometimes physically, prior to being killed.

Professor Associate of Criminal Justice, Professor Lee Gilbertson of the organisation 'Nationwide Investigations', was quoted by NBC, as saying, "This is a nationwide organization."

At the time, both Senator Sensenbrenner of Wisconsin and U.S. Congressman McNulty of NY, submitted requests to the FBI for them to investigate the mounting number of disturbing cases occurring and to make efforts to stop them.

Patrick McNeill, was 21 when he walked out of a bar in New York City on a cold night in February 1997. He told his friends he was taking the subway back to Fordham University. His body was found near a Brooklyn pier nearly two months later. The Pathologist stated he was not drunk when he died of drowning.

Another renowned Forensic Pathologist , Dr. Cyril Wecht stated, "There's no way this man is accidentally going to fall into a body of water, (and) the fly larvae (found) have been laid in the groin area. It's an indoor fly—could not have been an outdoor fly. And the larvae were there, did not move ahead into the later stage. So we have a body that was already dead before it was placed in the water...I would call it a homicide, yes."

The larvae indicate clearly that McNeill was kept, alive, indoors, prior to his tragic death.

Kevin Gannon, NYPD homicide detective investigating the McNeill case since 1997, said, "He was stalked, abducted, held for an extended period of time, murdered, and disposed."

Some have commented that the victims clothes have been tampered with prior to being found, suggesting they were removed. Others have said that victims are being recovered with their clothes, wallets, and college ID cards, but that any religious necklaces, such as Crosses and St Christopher' they were wearing, were not recovered.

Former federal drug enforcement agent Jerry Snyder is the founder of a non-for-profit victim-search group called *Find Me*, composed of active and retired law enforcement officials and consultants. Together they've studied more than 200 of these drowning cases across the country. "Look at all the names here and we think we've only scratched the surface; that's what's really scary to me,' Snyder said.

Is it a cult, syndicate, or gang of serial killers that has criss-crossed America, travelling to rural college campuses in 25 different cities in a dozen different states in an ever increasing murder spree."

It is fair to say that young men are prone to misadventure after drinking, and there are tragically many documented cases of drowning worldwide; however, not necessarily in this number or in these particular ways. It would almost seem as though the men are being deliberately targeted. It is hard to believe that so many educated and sporty men would choose to walk toward rivers in the winter, alone, and jump in, or fall in. Worryingly, no-one has ever yet seen them being abducted, and there are never any witnesses to the crime.

Why are the bodies returned to the area previously searched? Is it abductor/abductors? Or is it something less easy to define?

Chapter Five: Captured rural Serial Killers

If the idea of serial killers seems too extreme, perhaps there should be some consideration of cases which have clearly involved the capture of a serial killer.

In 1999, a murderer was roaming the Yosemite national park. Three female tourists had vanished from their rooms at the Cedar Lodge. A few months later, they were found, brutally murdered in the Park.

Five months later, Joie Armstrong, 26, a naturalist at the Yosemite Institute, also went missing. Her truck was still parked in the driveway of her home at her cabin. Her body was found in the woods, not far from the cabin.

A park employee had noticed a car parked near her cabin on the night of her disappearance, and police issued an alert for the car. A few days later, police spotted the car parked up near Merced River Canyon. They came across a man wandering naked. He said his name was Cary Stayner and that he worked as a handyman at Cedar Lodge. After the encounter, investigators compared the car tires to tire tracks found at the crime scene, and they matched. The police found Stayner and arrested him. He confessed quickly and readily to all of the killings.

His own family history, astonishingly, also revealed a disturbing crime perpetrated against one of his brothers, and perhaps was something that so disturbed him, it shaped him into a killer too.

At the age of seven, his brother had disappeared without trace one afternoon in 1972, whilst walking home from school alone along the Yosemite Highway. Eight years later, Cary had heard an announcement on the radio that his brother had been found. It turned out that his brother had been abducted by a paedophile and former employee of the Yosemite Lodge, and kept prisoner for all of those years. Investigators wondered if Cary's homicidal behaviour had been caused perhaps by his own family's experience.

Chapter Six:
Other strange missing persons cases in rural areas

In 2012, former police office David Paulides published *Missing 411*, to nationwide astonishment in America, and his subsequent radio interviews were compelling and intriguing.

He detailed the number of people who have gone missing in the National Parks of America, over a time spanning decades. He puts the number to close to one thousand.

Ruling out the tragic number of people who fall victim to human error or natural accidents in the park and natural causes, he describes case after case of highly strange and seemingly inexplicable incidents of people going missing, sometimes found, sometimes never found.

And here lies the similarity in that in a lot of the cases of those persons found, he states that it would appear almost as if they have been placed back along the search route, as if purposely to be discovered, as in the Clapham Woods cases, and the college boys.

Paulides says in his many interviews that he was originally led to the phenomenon by two unnamed park service employees who approached him with their concerns. He undertook a thorough and comprehensive investigation, and it was from this that he discovered case after case of mysterious and frankly inexplicable stories.

There are no unsuccessful attempts, and very few witnesses to recall what happened to them; no cases known of someone *almost* being taken and being able to relate what *almost* happened to them. Who or What is it that is so successful at it? What do they do to be able to pull this off with this level of accuracy? Is it a satanic cult? Could a gang of kidnappers or a serial killer abduct people silently each time with no trace? Is it a natural predator, waiting, stalking and striking? Could an animal attack and abduct someone yet the victim not cry out or leave any sign of the attack? Is it a human predator? Or is it something unknown that we have never had the misfortune, unlike the victims, to yet encounter?

It seems that David Paulides however, is not the first to have noticed such strange things happening in forests in America. Veteran Cryptozoologist Loren Colemen noticed the phenomenon years ago.

In 2007, former parks employee Butch Farabee, published *Death in Yosemite*, in which there are descriptions of mysterious deaths and disappearances, and before this, Junitta Baldwin wrote *Unsolved Disappearances in the great Smokey Mountains*.

She says, "*This book began with a list of more than one hundred people who had met with some type of misfortune in the Great Smokey Mountains. Some of these persons vanished during daylight, from different locations, on different dates, but surrounded by other people.*"

One of the many listed cases in Baldwin's book is that of Thelma Melton, and her name is also listed in *The Charley Project*, which profiles over 9,000 missing people "cold cases" mainly in the United States.

Thelma was aged 58, when she was hiking with her friends, Trula, and Red. They were there as a group of families who'd leased a campground and lived there during the summer months, mostly retired folk.

Thelma, better known as 'Polly', Trula and Red set out that day in September 1981, at around 3pm, to hike Deep Creek Trail. Having reached the end of the trail, they had turned round and were heading back to the campground, when suddenly without explanation, Polly began to walk very fast, as if she intended to leave the other two behind. The other two friends grinned at each other, thinking with amusement that she would soon slow down. Polly was a tall lady, around 6 feet tall, a little overweight, and with high blood pressure for which she needed to take medication in order to control the nausea it caused her.

When she didn't slow down at all, her friends started to look at each other with incomprehension. She carried on at the same pace and they shouted out to her but she didn't slow down, and went over the top of a hill ahead of them, descending it. Her friends expected to see her sitting on one of the seats over the hill and resting after her speedy walk, but when they came over the crest, they could see no sign of their friend.

Polly had hiked the trail with them for the last twenty years, and she had never been known to venture off the path; her abiding fear of snakes would never have let her, but her friends could see no sign of her. She had vanished.

A search party was arranged and a search made for her, but to this day, she has never been found.

The Tri-City Herald covered another story back in March 8th 1963, when a Mrs Pankin took three of her children to look at a waterfall behind their camp site, at the Big Lake resort, at Deep Lake, Washington. Reaching the waterfall, Mrs Pankin told her 4 year old son, Bobby, to sit on the ground and wait for them as they walked ten feet away to get closer to the waterfall.

When she and her children walked back only a couple of minutes later, Bobby was no-where to be seen. He was wearing just his swimming shorts and no shoes. After spreading out and shouting for him, they returned to the camp site for help. Local sheriffs organised a search party. At midnight, a k9 tracked Bobby's scent for two miles until it came to a fork in a logging road and stopped. The dog refused to go any further.

The search lasted for a week, with over one thousand people on foot and horses looking for him; but no trace was ever found. The road was not fit for cars to drive down so it was not possible for him to have been taken by car. Dogs that could track bears were brought in, but they picked up no scent of bears and no visible signs were found of an animal attack. Some in the newspapers theorised a giant eagle could have picked the child up.

Talking to the Tri-City Herald, the father, Mr Pankin said, "*It's as if Bobby climbed up to the top of a tree and then kept going.*"

Set up in 1997, the Crater Lake Institute provides a chronology of strange incidents which have occurred at the Crater Lake National Park. Back in the 1970's, photographer Charles McCullar went there to photograph the picturesque winter scenery.

He disappeared; at least, until bits of his bones were found, scattered over a steep bank of the Creek drainage. But the mystery remains how it was possible for McCullar to have walked from the North Entrance, on top of 105 inches of new snow, for 14 miles into Bybee Creek, considering that he had no snow gear with him.

Unfortunately, there are seldom witnesses to account for what happened to these people. One rare case does have witnesses however; The McCloud Newspaper '*The Siskiyou Daily News*,' covered the story of the disappearance and search for a 3-year-old boy who went missing at a county campground located in the Mc-Cloud area in vicinity of the McCloud River. '*He was found cold and frightened but unharmed*,' they reported.

The strange details of what the boy said happened to him were then actually posted by the boy's grandmother herself, on the '*above top secret* forum;' a popular site for all things paranormal and conspiracy related.

She writes, 'Last fall my three and a half year old grandson was lost in the Shasta Forest for 5 hours. Thanks to volunteers and rescue personal he was found. My son said "He was here, then within a second he was gone." 'They thought he had been abducted by other campers. About 3 weeks after this happened, he was at my house, and out of the blue he announced, "*I don't like the other grandma Kappy*" (his name for me, Grandma Kathy).

'I said, "*What are you talking about buddy? I'm the only grandma Kappy,*" He said "*Don't you remember when I was lost in the woods? Well, the other grandma Kappy grabbed me and took me to a creepy place; she's really a robot.*"

'I was thinking he was telling a story, so I asked, "*What was creepy about it, and why do you think she was a robot?*"

He replied, "*It was a cave with spiders, and there was guns. I was too scared, so I didn't touch anything. But, when she climbed a ladder, the light made her look like a robot. There were other robots too. She made me lay down to look at my tummy. She told me that I am from outer space, and they put me in my mom's tummy. Then she took me back to the river and said to wait under the bush until someone found me.*"

As if his story is not disturbing enough, she continues, 'One of the reasons I am bothered by this story, is because I was camping in the same area the year before. And, I woke up one morning face down in the dirt, out of my tent and sleeping bag. I had a puncture wound in the back of my head. I'm a grandma in my 50's; I don't sleep in the dirt! I was violently ill. Too sick to even pack and go home. I thought it was a spider bite. It took me a very long time to feel normal. I had no emotions.'

More Unnatural Events

In the Spring 1983, in Devon, England, Eric Ley lost 30 sheep. The 'predator' struck at night, silently, and seemingly without causing any disturbance to the rest of the flock around its victim. The only evidence of the attack was the remains, usually skin, head and feet, according to Di Franci, who studied the phenomenon, producing *The Beast of Exmoor*.

So followed the largest 'man-hunt' ever mounted in England. The Marine commandos were called in to assist in capturing whatever was doing this, hunting with live ammunition, which was unheard of in England, in a remote yet public area.

Witness, bus driver, John Franks, interviewed by Francis, said he saw something "about 2 feet 6 inches to the shoulders, with powerful legs. I remember thinking, God but you're ugly. The head just didn't fit on the body."

The 'beast' was never captured, and livestock have continued to be killed at intervals since in the area, as well as prior to this, throughout the last two centuries.

Controversially, Francis believes whatever it was, may have been responsible for the fate of a missing girl. Genette Tate was 13 in August 1978, when she set off on her bike to do a Saturday newspaper round. On her way home, in Aylesbeare village, on the north side of the East Devon Pebbled Heathlands, she met two of her school friends, Margaret and Tracey, at a small bridge crossing a narrow stream. Genette dismounted to walk with them up a small hill, but when the ground flattened out, she said goodbye to her friends, got back on her bike and pedaled off, going round a bend in the small country road.

She was never seen again. Margaret and Tracey were behind her and as they rounded the bend too, just a couple of minutes later, and just 300 yards away, they found her bike lying on its side in the lane, the back wheel still spinning. There was no sign of a struggle.

At first the girls thought she was playing a joke on them, hiding behind the hedges ready to jump out on them. They called out to her and looked for her, finally going back to the village to tell people.

A search party was launched, including Marine commandos, helicopters and dog trackers, but the dogs could pick up no scent and they could find no clues to her disappearance; no tire tracks, no damage to the bike, no scream heard. It was a heartbreaking tragedy that badly affected her family.

Chapter Seven:
Missing hunters, accidents, natural causes?

The fact that there were 65,439 SAR rescues between 1992-2007, for example, displays just how easy it can be to become lost and disoriented in the wilderness, just in America alone. While there are usually large and often very populated trails inside of these areas , with good signage on display; if you were to step a couple of feet off the path, turn around a couple of times, or get distracted, you could be lost in seconds. It's that easy for people who do not hike everyday; and even those that do will testify to just how easy it is. For those who live in cities, parks are an unknown natural phenomenon that perhaps are seriously underestimated in terms of possible danger.

Moving through a dense forest filled with underbrush and trees can be truly disorientating. It is incredibly easy to get lost or separated form your group, in seconds. One slip in the woods can be fatal. You can hit your head on a rock, slip into a creek, break a leg, and die undiscovered.

Wild animals, scavengers then come across the body. Children and the elderly are obviously more inclined to fall behind or wander off. Those who wander off in such terrain are less easy to find, dead or alive, then less inhospitable terrains. Many of those who die on mountains like Everest, for example, do so after sitting down to rest, and end up freezing to death while asleep without even being aware they are in any danger.

Hypothermia can cause severe disorientation, loss of mental faculties, and it comes on fast. Confusion, delirium, semi-consciousness, drowsiness, and exhaustion set in; Hypothermia is also known to cause people to seek to burrow and hide, for survival. Thus it is possible they crawl into crevices and caves and between rocks, seeking any shelter they can find from the harsh elements. Therefore they are in effect hidden from search parties.

However, not all of the cases of strange disappearances occur in winter; and why would they not shout out for help when search parties approach? Additionally, not all of the cases of strange disappearances occur in winter, however. Many of the cases happen in the summer months, not the dead of winter.

Many of those who disappeared, like the school swim team and sports team members of the boys found in rivers, were highly experience outdoorsmen and hunters. According to Outdoor Life Magazine, between 1997-2003, 336 hunters were reported missing, according to records of the *Oregon Office of Emergency Management*.

SAR Search & Rescue teams found 12 dead; many others were not found.

With no centralised reporting it is hard to try to determine the numbers missing, and found; however, according to reporter and investigator Don Zaidle, the fate of many missing hunters is never discovered.

Zaidle describes another mysterious case that took place in Quebec, near the Caniapiscau River. In 2003, James Rambone, 51, an experienced outdoorsman, was hunting when he spotted a bull and took off after it, hoping to shoot it. Later, hunters in his party found his fluorescent vest and camera, but Mr Rambone seemed to have disappeared without trace; no clothing or any signs were left that showed the hunter had ever been there. He had seemingly vanished into thin air. Subsequent SAR searches with tracker dogs could not find any trace of him.

Interviewed at the time, his girlfriend, Pam Ruzzo, commented,

"A guide of thirty-five years told me, "They always find a person; dead or alive." Bears, Wolves, they don't eat clothing, and would not have eaten his gun! Something's just not right. You don't just vanish."

Chapter Eight: Demons, The Collins elite, and child disappearances.

Adding further to the mystery of the missing, and the search for possible explanations, is the very strange disappearance of children at the Cursed Devil's Gate Reservoir.

In August 1956, 13 year old Donald Baker, and his friend, 11 year old Brenda Howell went for a bicycle ride. When they didn't return, the police were called, and an all-out search for them began. Volunteers combed the area and frogmen went into the reservoir, but they could find only the children's bicycles.

Then, in 1957, 8 year old Tommy Bowman was hiking on a trail above Devil's Gate, just a few yards ahead of his family when he rounded a corner and vanished into thin air. The search party scoured the area for a week, with bloodhounds, helicopters and professional trackers. No trace was found. The search was eventually called off.

It wasn't until thirteen years later, that freeway employee Mack Edwards came forward and confessed to abducting and killing Donald and Brenda. Sentenced to death, he hung himself in his cell in 1970, but Tommy's disappearance remained unexplained. Then, another child, 6 year old Bruce Kremen disappeared 3 years later, while on a hike with his YMCA group. Again, there were no traces of his disappearance. This time, however, speculation was growing of a local man; the genius co-founder of Jet Propulsions, Jack Parsons, who was heavily involved in the US space program. He was also a top ranking occultist.

His mansion was alleged to be the location of magick ceremonies and rituals; with their purpose being an attempt to open a portal to hell. Some occult authors believe they were successful and that the portal is indeed in the Devil's Gate region. Rumours of drug taking orgies, and black magic sacrifices including children were rife; however police at the time gave them no credence.

Avid paranormal researcher and writer, Nick Redfern, however chronicles a strange episode in his own life which ties into this theory. While researching for a book, he was contacted by whistle-blowers of a secret sinister group within the US Government/Military, who called themselves 'the Collins Elite.'

Set up to investigate ufology and alien abductions from the 1940's onwards, the Collins Elite came to a conclusion that humans were at war with demon entities or aliens, that may be abducting or feeding off our souls. They believed there was a cold hearted intelligence of deceptive, demonic, non-human entities, who masqueraded as aliens.

Jack Parsons, grand master Aliester Crowley, wanted to make some sort of Faustian pact with these entities and utilise their powers of mind control. The Collins elite's projects were said to involve occult rituals in an attempt to open portals and harness the power of demonic entities to use for their own military purposes. These anonymous insider whistleblowers claimed that the Collins Elite were too afraid to go public with its findings, knowing that it would cause social and spiritual panic and hysteria; because it would be a revelation by the government that demons were real.

According to Thelemic legend, in 1918 Aleister Crowley summoned an inter-dimensional entity named Lam. From this encounter, some believe Crowley opened a portal, which allowed 'aliens' a path into our world. With their 'Babylon Working,' it was suggested that this portal may have then been even more fully opened by Jack Parsons and Ron L Hubbard. Interestingly, looking further into this, from *Occult World of Jack Parsons*, John Carter notes this was the era when Roswell and other incidents began...

Did Jack Parsons really open a portal to an inter-dimension world where demons, or aliens, now had free access to our world?

Carol Mack, with a Masters in religious studies, writes, in '*A field guide to Demons*,' of demons as shape-shifters, '*with preference for concealment, who hide in trees, wait in caves, protecting their natural habitats, awaiting the trespass of human travellers, expecting their usual tithes, and when ignored they can be vengeful.'*

Some demons, she believes, serve as portals to sacred ground, serving as guardian spirits watching over the sanctuary they protect, standing at the portal. As the traveller approaches in the woods or stands at the banks of rivers, these demonic protectors serve as warnings of entrance to something of a divine power beyond. The sacred nature of forests, water, mountains are guarded by these entities, she believes, perhaps from the destroying nature of man's attitude toward their environment, declaring these wilderness areas as forbidden and sacred.

Could demons really lurk in the wilderness? In what form could they manifest?

An interesting story comes from several centuries ago. The *Daily Mail* newspaper, on May 16th, 2014, reported on the archaeological discovery of a 7 foot dog in the grounds of an ancient Abbey in Suffolk, England, in the area where 500 years ago, a wild 'dog' or demon, allegedly went on a murderous rampage. A ferocious hell-hound with fiery eyes, which was reported to have caused the deaths of several people.

During a terrific thunderstorm in 1577, at Holy Trinity Church, Blythburgh, a sudden clap of thunder burst open the doors of the church, and a devil-dog entered, running wild and killing a man and a boy in the congregation, as the Church steeple crashed through the roof. Then, at St Mary's Church nearby, another two of the congregation were similarly killed, the Reverend describing it as a 'Satan-like Beast, in a visible form and shape,' that twisted the necks of the two worshippers as they knelt in prayer, in silence; no sound coming from its feet as it ran.

Chapter Nine:
The Dalatov Pass Incident

Perhaps the most disturbing or bewildering wilderness case, which has seen much debate and speculation in the years since it happened, is the Dyatlov Pass incident, of February 2nd, 1959, which took place in the Ural Mountains of Russia. Theories have ranged from it being murderous marauders, to the Yeti, to more the paranormal.

Nine hikers, 7 men and 2 women, from the Ural Polytechnic Institute, set out on a trek that was rated as 'most dangerous.' Igor Alekseievich Dylatov was the group's leader. All of them however were fairly experienced hikers.

When they did not return, a rescue party was launched. The remains of their tent was quite quickly located, pitched on the uppermost slope of the 'Mountain of the Dead', Kholat Syakhl, with a slash that had been made from the inside of the tent with a knife. Human tracks were found in the snow heading downhill, away from the tent. *Barefoot* human tracks.

Inside the tent were their boots, stacked in a neat row, and their dinner, frozen and uneaten. The climbers' bodies were discovered a mile or so away from their camp, scattered, half dressed, without their coats and without their shoes, and with severe injuries.

Curiously, their injuries included *crushed internal organs*, and three of the climbers died from blunt force trauma, not hypothermia. One of the women, Ludmila Dubinina was found with *her tongue removed*. On forensic examination, it was found that her stomach contained coagulated blood, which indicated that her heart was beating and that she was alive when her tongue was removed.

In other words, she was alive when it happened. Her eyes were also removed. How was this possible? Even more strangely, none of them were found to have any external wounds, not even scratching on the skin.

What phenomenon could have caused these climbers to flee the safety and shelter of their tent, without their shoes? What could have attacked them to cause such horrific internal injuries, and mutilations?

Speculation was rife in that cold war era, ranging from nuclear weapons testing, to aliens, to a band of prisoners from a gulag, or wild men (although bearing in mind they were at a very high altitude and in a completely inhospitable location). Others say they were fleeing an impending avalanche, though no recent snow was found on the tent.

Some say it was one or more Yeti's that caused the internal injuries; but no animal tracks were found. Others point to the rumour of strange lights seen in the sky during the time period, and of their injuries being consistent with a fall from a great height, clearly implying that they were victim of alien abduction and dropped back on the ground once they were of no more use.

Lev Ivanov, the lead investigator, concluded mysteriously, that all nine deaths had been caused by what he described as "*an unknown elemental force, which they were unable to overcome.*"

What could that possibly mean? And why would it have led to the removal of one victim's eyes and tongue?

Given the circumstances, this perplexing case leads perhaps to the need for a discussion about cattle mutilations, and the more recent and terrifying alleged phenomenon of *human mutilation*...

Chapter Ten:
Cattle & Human Mutilations

Alien or Satanic predators? As in the Dyatlov case, and the many recorded cases of cattle mutilations, who is behind this phenomenon? Both David Perkins, a Yale graduate and UFO researcher, and researcher Chris O'Brien, are experts in this particular field of high strangeness. Perkins writes of a curious case in the foreword to O'Brien's *Stalking the Herd*. He says he first became involved in this phenomenon when he was actually considered a suspect to a mutilation close to his home.

At a Conference he attended in Albuquerque back in 1979, authorities gathered to try to get to the bottom of what was going on. Because evidence of an occult ceremonial sacrificial site in Montana was presented as evidence, along with the findings from a laboratory at Oklahoma State University that the hallucogen mescaline, (an hallucogenic similar to LSD) had been found in the body of a mutilated cow, Perkins said the US Government decided to go with the satanic Cult theory, as opposed to any alien intervention in the mutilations happening, despite this satanic cult theory later being found to be behind only a very tiny minority of the mutilation cases.

An organisation called 'Aerial Phenomenon Research' had also come out with the statement, that "*a satanic organisation has plans of bringing a 100 year reign of terror and darkness,*" backing the Satanic theory. The UFO investigators however disagreed; they had evidence themselves that pointed to the mutilations being done by alien entities.

But the theory goes even deeper; not only did many feel that there were non-human's carrying out these abductions and mutilations; but behind these non-humans, were earth-bound puppet masters too.

Linda Molton Howe, an Emmy-winning journalist, who produced the film '*strange harvest*' on the subject of the cattle mutilations, posited that a shadow government had made a treaty with the aliens.

Greg Bishop, another investigator, claimed to have seen evidence from a New Mexico state patrolman, Gabe Valdez, of items left near mutilation sites- many *man-made* artefacts, such as a gas mask, radar chaff, parts of a laser; and he stated that livestock owners in the region had found listening devices installed on telephone lines and inside their homes.

Are their findings the answer to the mystery? Certainly there are many researchers who believe that Governments agreed with Alien races to allow the abduction of humans and animals for alien experimentation, in return for the exchange of advanced technology for Governments to utilize. So, perhaps this is the answer; however, curiously, this appears not to be a modern-day phenomenon.

In 1905, in Avon, England, sheep were the target of a very strange attack. A local police sergeant was quoted in the London *Daily Mail* newspaper at the time as saying, "I have seen them and say definitely that it's impossible for it to be the work of a dog. Dogs do not suck the blood out of sheep."

A year later, in 1906, near Guildford, England, fifty sheep were killed in the same night; their blood drained from their bodies and suffering mutilation.

At first, it seemed it was just cattle and other livestock that were being mutilated. However, in the most horrific revelation, Derek Gough, a journalist and investigator, who used to write for UFO magazine, investigated alleged UFO sightings in the remote Brecon Beacons of Wales, in the late 1990's, and claimed that he was contacted by military man who said he was part of a "fast response, find and secure" black ops group, under the command of NATO.

As a Special Forces soldier, the man claimed he was part of a team that would be dispatched to areas to search for human remains, and to undertake "clean-up" operations; sealing and securing an area and ensuring the remains of people were removed by the scientists with them, and to reclaim any UFO evidence that remained.

Horrifyingly, he explicitly said that humans were being snatched up while out alone in rural wilderness locations, experimented on by alien entities, and subsequently they died as a result. His job had been to find them and clear up their human remains.

Could this really be happening?

One of the best documented cases of human mutilation is the 1988 Guarapiranga Dam incident in Brazil. Gruesome photos of the victim and the autopsy report are readily accessible online. The case is gruesome to read, but amazingly similar to the methodology used each time for cattle mutilations. The victim's body was drained of blood, his eyes, ears, and tongue were taken; his digestive and reproductive organs were removed. Horrifically, it was determined that the man had been alive during his dismemberment, (just like the female climber at the Dyaltov Pass)

Strangely, although it was determined that the man had died 48 to 72 hours prior to his discovery, there were *no signs of decomposition or rigor mortis*, which is not the normal case in death, and, despite the rural location, there was no evidence of predators on the body.

How he had died was abundantly clear; but *who* had mutilated him was a mystery. Why his body was not in the usual state of decomposition was also a complete mystery.

There's also the infamous case of Sgt. Jonathan P Louette, who was stationed at White Sands Missile Test Range back in 1956, and whose mutilated body was found on the Range, three days after an Air Force major had witnessed him *being dragged off and lifted up into a "disk shaped" object*.

Butch Witkowski, a former police detective, has been studying accounts of human mutilations for many years now and is particularly outspoken about it.

"*30,000 people go missing each year and are never seen or heard from again.*"

He believes that the Government may be complicit in some of these disappearances, suspecting that a deal with extraterrestrials was brokered sometime ago in the 1950's to allow this to happen.

Shockingly, researcher Don Ecker, director of *UFO Magazine* and a retired law enforcement officer, describes talking to John Ford, (retired officer of the Federal Court System, and Chairman of the Long Island UFO network) who relayed to him a large number of cases that he knew of involving human disappearances, abductions, and *human mutilation*. It was his belief that there was a covert involvement by the Government.

Ford apparently carried out an investigation into the disappearance of a number of mostly young adults over the course of one year in areas that had a high number of reported UFO sightings. Ford's conclusion, having discussed the cases with many personal friends in the police forces of those local districts, was that the facts were being suppressed, so as '*not to panic the public.*'

Ecker describes one case, in 1989 in south-eastern Idaho, of two cattle owned by different ranchers, being found mutilated with their organs surgically removed. The Sheriffs determined that it was a cult killing; however, Ecker claims that *no human or animal tracks were found, nor any tyre marks on the ground*.

He also says that as a result of looking into this, he discovered that one of the investigators on the case had also been assigned to a case of *human mutilation*, when two hunters in Idaho in 1979 had come across the body of a man out in the middle of no-where, with all the classic injuries associated with mutilations.

Are there really a sinister rogue group of aliens coming down to perform their experiments on unsuspecting human beings? Could it really be true? It certainly seems one possibility, according to the alleged findings of many experts, and if this is the case, it is almost too disturbing to imagine.

Chapter Eleven: Underground Bases?

In Dulce, New Mexico, there is a top secret facility under ground, so say some people. It has aliens and some of the most genetically altered things possible. In Level 6 of the base there are reptilian-humanoids, caged giants, aliens, and human prisoners; row after row of drugged humans, humans in cages and vats, and curiously what is referred to as human 'varieties;' hybrids and mutations.

Dulce is not the only one. There are reportedly over 100 across the US and worldwide, in remote locations such as National Forests, due to the seclusion afforded by such locations allegedly.

'Witnesses' have come forward to claim they were 'employed' in such bases but to escape, after daily encounters with all types of beings, monsters, reptilians and 'greys', while working amongst the thousands of abducted human prisoners who are 'mind controlled' to be used in horrific genetic experiments.

These bases are said to be allegedly controlled by the Military, and financed by the massive and highly secretive 'black ops' budget.

Researcher Richard Sauder has been an outspoken critic in his belief of these deep underground military bases for many years now. He believes there has been a widespread construction program of underground and undersea bases; secret facilities built with highly sophisticated technology, by "shadow governments."

He alleges that the technology which powers these bases may in fact be associated with *dimensional portals* and *non-human intelligences*, and that this is the reason why these projects are kept so secret. The public would be horrified and panic at the revelation.

Others say that the information about these bases being full of aliens is 'leaked' as disinformation in order to distract from what the government itself is *really* doing. One such base, Sauder believes, lies in tunnels beneath Mt Shasta, and leads to a UFO base.

Philip Schneider, now deceased, and some believe murdered, was according to his own account, an explosives engineer who worked for the U.S. Government. In 1979, carrying high-level security clearance, he claims he participated in the building of the secret underground base, in Dulce.

He says that he became suspicious of the nature of the engineering project when he noticed the strong presence of Green Berets and Special Forces personnel. His fears were realized, he claims, when after drilling underground he came face-to-face with a 7-foot tall gray alien, and shot and killed it. He was saved, he said, by one of the Green Beret's who 'gave his life for him'. In all, 60 humans allegedly lost their lives that day at the infamous 'Alien-Human Battle of Dulce.'

He became a very outspoken whistle-blower, and while many decried his identity and said he was a phony, others believed when he died by suicide, it was actually foul play.

Another whistle-blower gives a different version to the battle. John Lear, whose father designed the Leer Jet, and whose own career involved being a pilot who apparently flew aircraft for a CIA linked company, said on record that there was no such 'fire fight;' What *did* happen instead, he said, was that deep in the underground base, a 'gray' was giving a science lecture to 40 human scientists, when a soldier walked in, accidently forgetting he had a 38 strapped to his belt; it was stipulated by the 'grays' that no firearms were allowed in the lecture room, and on seeing the gun, the alien instantly killed the soldier because of it.

Leer says that members of Delta force, who were watching the lecture by video-link in another part of the base, then went en-masse to the lecture room in search of retribution for their killed comrade, but when they got into the fight, the aliens then killed all of them.

Lear's belief was that the Government had made secret deals with the aliens to exchange humans for advanced technology that could be weaponised, but he claims that the aliens took advantage of this deal and took far more humans than had been agreed.

So, is this really what has happened? Are humans now the offering to ancient races, who dwell in secret underground ET/Military bases? Well, a counter-argument comes from a very interesting character. Billy Meier, now in his seventies, may not have been heard of by most people, but as well as being a simple farmer in Sweden, he is also known for the incredibly accurate prophesies that have been given to him, he says, by 'extraterrestrial humans,' from another planet, for the last 60 years.

As proof of his credibility, he patented and copyrighted his predictions when he received them from these non-humans. Some of his predictions, published *before* any of them occurred, include the 9/11 attacks, the Iran Hostage crisis, polar displacement and magnetic shifts, the Soviet invasion of Afghanistan in '79, and the terrorist hostage crisis at the Iranian embassy in London in 1980, all of which subsequently occurred. It would seem then that he quite possibly has somehow been receiving advanced information of future events, from this race of non-humans.

In his contacts with those who give him the predictions, he has said they have told him that no such underground military/alien bases exist.

Who is right?

Chapter Twelve:
UFO reports in forests, woods and mountains?

Travis Walton's abduction case is one of the most debated in Ufology. In Sitgreaves National Forest, back in November 1957, Travis and six others were working thinning trees with saws. After a long hard day, they were headed for home in a pick-up truck, when they spotted a bright light in the early evening dusk through the trees. As they came to a more open spot, what they allegedly saw amazed and terrified them.

Twenty feet off the ground a golden disc shaped object was hovering. It was hovering stationary below the tree tops, an estimated twenty feet in diameter. Seizing the opportunity of a life-time, and desperate to get closer, Travis left the truck and walked to the underneath the object. Suddenly, an incredibly bright ray shot down and he felt as though he had been electrocuted.

After that, he says, he fell into unconsciousness. The men in the truck, thinking he had been killed, fled as fast as possible. Their conscience got the better of them however, and later they returned to the area to see if Travis was ok; but his body was gone.

Travis said he found himself on board the spaceship. He re-appeared, five days later. No other

UFO case has perhaps received as much disagreement, with many claiming it was an elaborate hoax and that Travis failed a lie detector test. Others point to the two further lie detector tests he went on to pass.

In another case, the Mutual UFO network Journal of 1988, details an incident in Minastee National Forest, in which a school principal and teacher were at a camp with school children when a huge silent shimmering cylindrical object floated above the trees, moving slowly and almost transparently.

In fact, scores of UFO sightings have been reported at Great Sand Dunes National Park, where in the 1970's the area became rife with mutilation stories. A very perplexing case was reported in newspapers at the time. It occurred in October 1974, when hunter Carl Higdon was out elk hunting in the park. The *Rawlins Daily Times* covered the strange story.

The hunter Higdon claimed that as he pulled the trigger on his rifle, the bullet shot in slow motion, falling into the snow about fifty feet away. Going to retrieve the bullet, he found it strangely mangled. This bullet jacket was examined by a Dr. Walter Walker, a Consultant in Metallurgy, who could only say that it must have struck something incredibly hard and with great force to be in the state it was. How had it got so mangled?

As Higdon retrieved the bullet, he claimed he was overcome by a strange sensation throughout his body, and to his utter astonishment, he said came face to face with a humanoid being, over 6 feet tall in a black jumpsuit outfit. He said that the entity spoke to him, saying that if he took the pill he offered, he would not feel hungry for four days. Higdon duly swallowed the pill.

Higdon claimed it then felt as though he had entered another dimension; the elk he had been hunting stood stock still in a frozen state. Everything had gone silent. He was then told by the alien that they were travelling to his home planet, located some hundreds of thousands of light years away. In a flash, Higdon then arrived at that far-off location. He described these new surroundings as having extremely tall buildings, lit by a sun of incredible power, so bright that it hurt his eyes. Then the next thing he knew, he was back in the forest, over two hours later.

A sheriff, finding him in a state of shock and hysteria, took him to the nearest hospital, where blood tests showed he had highly elevated levels of vitamins in his body. Was this verification that he had indeed met with an ET and taken a pill from him?

Even more astonishingly, it was found that scars on his lungs following a bout of TB years ago, had completely disappeared.

The case was investigated by Dr. Leo Sprinkle, a Professor of Psychology at the University of Wyoming, who astonishingly concluded that it appeared to actually be a true story.

Chapter Thirteen:
Searching for more explanations.

Are animals & the natural environment to blame? Are some of the reported sightings, attacks, and mysterious disappearances in forests and woods simply caused by animals in their natural habitat?

Animals do attack people, bears particularly. Big cats sometimes play with their prey, without inflicting wounds with their teeth and claws, and then lose interest if not hungry. Cougar are fast and strong.

But can these natural predators leave no trace of their crime? Bear attacks happen, but wouldn't they always leave some evidence of the attack; blood, pieces of torn fabric? And while bear attacks do happen, these incidents are few and far between; additionally the incidences so far discussed here are frequently in areas where bears do not habituate.

Some advocate that animals can attack and almost nothing will be left, perhaps just rubber from a shoe, or an earring, whilst clothes may be found further away due to the victim being dragged; But, can they do all of that soundlessly, with the victim remaining silent throughout? And would they not at least leave a trail as the victim was dragged?

Mountain lions, cougars, go for the throat when they kill and kill where they attack rather than running off with a person. Would animals eat an entire body including the large bones?

Animals simply don't consume a whole body. Are there other 'animals' out there we don't know about?

Chapter Fourteen: Bigfoot?

Cryptologist Loni Strikler has looked into this mysterious field for many years; his interest first started in 1981, when he was fly-fishing in a woodland area, and he shockingly came across an 8 foot tall creature with dark matted hair, moving very fast in the bushes.

He also stated the very strange events that occurred afterward, when he reported it to the police, after it bit a nearby dog. He'd gone straight away to locate the nearest telephone to call the police, it being a time period before cell phones, and he found one in a bar. He then returned to the scene, where he was told to get back in his car and drive away. As well as there being several police cars there, when he returned again about an hour later, still very curious to know what was going on, he said that there were helicopters and many other official looking cars.

He subsequently tried for years afterwards to find out more information, but mysteriously he was always told the incident had not been reported and "had not happened."

Then, as his career as a cryptologist developed, one day he received a message from someone who told him that he had been one of the first responders on the scene that day, and that he had always thought it very peculiar himself, because they had closed the road down, and a government team arrived and told the police to leave, as unmarked helicopters flew over the area like they were looking for *something*. The man told him; it was a large scale 'man-hunt,' that the local police would not have been able to organise to that extent in that time. He wondered *how* the unusual team had been mobilized so quickly, and *why*.

A few years after that, Strikler says he met an old man while fishing again, who told him that he had seen a large skeleton, with no clothes around it, and on pulling out his fishing tape, he had measured the size of its bones. They were far too large to be human, and he said the skull was much bigger than a man's. He said that the police arrived on the scene, along with mysteries unmarked vehicles and unmarked helicopters began to circulate in the air again.

It's not just in America though that there have been reports in the parks and forests of Bigfoot creatures. Tony Healy and Paul Cropper's *In search of Australia's Bigfoot*, relate the incident of an Australian national park service ranger, Percy Window's encounter one day, as he was clearing some undergrowth in the national park, back in 1978.

Hearing grunting noises, he thought it might be a wild pig and went to investigate. Suddenly, he came within twelve feet of a big black hairy 'man-thing', with huge hands, one of which was wrapped round a branch. The ranger was close enough to it to see the hair on its fingers, which he described as 'human-like,' with a thick neck and a muscular, solid build. He said to those who interviewed him years later, "*Before, I might have agreed they were comic book-stuff- but no more. They exist all right, and I've never been so scared in my life.*"

He said that he was numb with fear, and indeed his widow stated that for two days afterwards, this hardened ranger spent two days in bed, recovering from the shock.

More recently, Dr Melba Ketchum, a veterinarian, has been carrying out DNA testing on samples found from an alleged Bigfoot. In November 2012, she listed a new species name for Bigfoot, 'Homo sapiens cognatus', with The International Commission on Zoological Nomenclature. She claims her study revealed that Bigfoot, as a result of her five year DNA study, is a *human relative* that first existed 15,000 years ago as a hybrid cross of modern Homo sapien, with an unknown primate species. Unfortunately, with so much hot debate and controversy surrounding the findings, it is difficult to understand whether the results stand up to full scrutiny.

In an interview with Coast to Coast am radio, she likened Bigfoot to '*special forces soldiers*' who cannot be seen unless they want to be, and that she sees them now as a '*tribe of people.*'

With reports of Bigfoot being a hybrid, and of strange cryptids, such as the Bray Road beast, or 'dogman', Lizard man, the Jersey devil, and others, is it possible that there has been tampering of our and animals dna? If so, has this been done by man, or alien species?

Others differ in their view of what Bigfoot is. Paranormal researcher Rob Riggs says of Bigfoot, "*I think we may be talking about creatures that have access to physical spaces that humans cannot perceive. They are three-dimensional physical creatures but they are able to go into spaces that lie outside our perception because they are outside our reality...somehow these creatures enter into spaces that we are not tuned into mentally.*"

Others believe that Bigfoot is not a biological entity at all, with one school of thought believing it is a shape-shifting entity, capable of 'inter-dimensional travel.'

Is this why no body has ever been found? No burial sites? Others feel it is an extraterrestrial hybrid, explaining that this would account for why it is so elusive. Many Bigfoot reported sightings do apparently coincide with ufo reports, and cattle mutilations are said to shortly afterward.

The 'Presque Incident' of 1966, involved witnesses seeing a strange craft descend into a wooded area, illuminating the woods, and coming out of the same area. Many reported seeing 'a dark featureless, gorilla-like humanoid.' It was a case that was well-documented and the witnesses have continued to corroborate their stories.

Another sighting, dubbed the 'Horizon City Monster incident,' includes the account of a Ms Montanez, who claims a Bigfoot creature near El Paso Texas, walked up a mound and simply disappeared in front of her. When she went closer to the spot, she found no cave or hole for which it to have been able to disappear into.

Edwards Air force base, in the Mojave Desert, was said by witnesses to have had so many reports of Bigfoot creatures walking around inside the base that military personnel were apparently told not to make it public knowledge, for fear of frightening the public.

With many believing that Bigfoot entities have the power to communicate telepathically, as many witnesses have claimed, are they able to lead people off without people realizing they are wandering off to another part of the woods?

There is also the Skunk Ape, an alleged 7 foot tall gorilla-like beast. Sightings of the brown-furred creature were their highest in the 1970's when hundreds of Floridian's reported seeing the beast amongst swamps and even roadsides. Supposedly closely resembling the believed appearance of Bigfoot, a State Representative even attempted to protect the species by trying to pass law that it not be harmed on capture. Researchers apparently collected hair samples, footprint casings, and even photographs of it.

Then there are the Native American legends of the "Mountain Devils", named 'Seeahtiks', who were according to Native American stories, believed to be able to stun their prey with hypnotic powers.

In England, on the national park Dartmoor, there have been reported sightings over the years of what some believe to be a wolverine, bear, or large cat species. Founder of the 'Big Cats' network, Mark Fraser, says, "*It looks like a wolverine or bear; or a large wild dog. It's a very strange animal. I've worked with dogs all my life and it's definitely not that. This is a lot bigger.*"

Chapter Fifteen: The Dogman

Do Wolf-men really exist?

Wolf-men, or dog-men; mysterious creatures, with reported elusive sightings, and sometimes very close-up encounters.

They are one of the most enigmatic creatures that supposedly prowl in the national parks, woodlands and swampy areas. Linda Godfrey is known as the leading expert in this field, having been drawn into the world of cryptozoolgy by reports of these entities, and having received some very sober and credible reports. 7 witnesses were polygraphed and were found to be displaying no deception in their testimonies.

A journalist in her native Wisconsin, she has been looking into the possibility of creatures that are described as looking like 'dogmen', or 'upright canines,' since 1991. Since then she says she has received reported sightings from all over the country.

Godfrey first became involved in researching the phenomenon while a reporter at the Walworth County Week, after hearing gossip about rumors of people spotting a creature that looked like a were-wolf.

What once was perhaps considered as belonging in ancient myths and lore, many believing perhaps these creatures were the manifestation of native American medicine men shape-shifting into spirit creatures, or some kind of inter-dimensional beings, came to the forefront of modern society in the small conservative town of Elkhorn, Wisconsin, in June 1992 when citizens began reporting sightings of a strange 6-7 foot tall creature.

She describes the sightings of the creatures reported as looking fully like a dog, but walking on its hind legs, across roads, at surprisingly fast speed, and using its forearms to carry dead deer and road kill.

Linda Godfrey wrote about the sightings in the local newspaper, completely skeptical and yet intrigued. Elkhorn was a small town not known for outlandish or strange claims; certainly not large strange creatures, whose appearance baffled and frightened them.

Beginning her investigation, the reporter found that the local animal control officer, John Fredrickson, actually had a full collection of alleged sightings already that had been reported to him. She duly began to contact some of those who had reported the incidents to him. She states that the witnesses varied in every demographic. Each of the reports describe the creature as at least 7 feet, and say it has a muscular build.

One lady, L. Endrizzi, came across the creature one night in 1989, while driving home after finishing work. It was dark, but she clearly saw a creature like a big dog, appear to be kneeling by the road side, with some form of prey held in its front paws. As to what she thought it was, she was reported as saying she believed it was satanic.

A high school student in 1991 told her that the creature actually chased her car, leaving scratch marks along the side. She said it was over 7 ft tall in her estimation, and ran upright. When Godfrey looked at the marks, they appeared to be those of a clawed creature.

The investigator says many Native Americans she has spoken with tend to feel there is a more supernatural explanation for its presence, believing they are spirit creatures from another place and members of a shape shifting skin-walker tribe.

What Godfrey discovered, during her questioning of many witnesses, was that a lot of the sightings occurred near water, and Native American landmarks, such as burial grounds.

Some of the reports were very odd, in terms of the creatures disappearing as though in a mist, or seen one moment, only to disappear before their eyes, or as though walking through a tree. A little like some of the reports of Bigfoot sightings, again lending to some people's theory that they are inter-dimensional beings. At least three of the witnesses she encountered referred to the creature as being demonic, or from hell.

Some witnesses said that as the creature stared at them, it was like it was able to send them telepathic messages; warning them to be frightened of it.

Are some of the encounters wildmen? A man who disappeared into the woods 27 years ago was finally found in 2013. He had been regarded as an urban legend, until police finally arrested him while attempting to steal food from a camp in Maine. The man, Chris Knight told the police, that the last time he'd spoken to another human being was back in the 1990s. He told them that he had lived in the woods and had survived by stealing food and supplies from campers.

Back in 1869, a wild man was reportedly spotted by at least 100 residents in Steuben County, according to the book 'In the Big Thicket;' a heavily forested areas in Southeast Texas, where according to some, '*the unknown makes appearances in what we understand to be our reality.*'

According to reports of the time, the 'wild man' made shrieking sounds as it tore through the forest areas. It was described as covered with matted, thick hair. The creature was described as "running while bent close to the ground."

Chapter Sixteen:
Do Thunderbirds really exist?

Could Thunderbirds be responsible for carrying off victims, leaving no footprints to track and no evidence of their presence?

In 2005, *Oregon Archaeological Society* were excavating when they found the bone of an ancient bird; a Teratorn. Teratorn bones have subsequently been found all across North America. The largest one found had a wingspan that was greater than 24 feet, and weighed over 170 pounds. A carnivore, it had a jaw designed to pick up and swallow small prey whole.

Back in the late 1960s and early 1970s, people living in southeast Washington began to report seeing a strange large bird, with a wingspan that they described as being the size of a small airplane. Then, in 2002, people in Alaska reported that they had seen a giant bird that had an estimated wingspan of over fourteen feet.

In 1980, *Boston Magazine* wrote an article that featured a Police Sergeant, who said he was driving home from work one night in the summer when he encountered a six-foot tall winged creature that was standing in the middle of the road.

In 1976 in Rio Grande Valley, hunters searched the area attempting to win a reward for the capture of a giant creature which it was said, had begun to terrorize the local residents. Reports flooded in of a bird with wings large enough to fold over its own body, that made a shrieking sound and looked, according to many witnesses, like a pteranodon, an extinct flying reptile.

Three teachers from San Antonio claimed to have seen a huge bird on Feb. 24, 1976. Tracey Lawson, 11, and her cousin Jackie Davies, 14, were out playing in Tracey's back yard when the bird appeared, about 100 yards away.

The Brownsville Herald printed the details told to them by a frightened man who encountered a strange "birdlike" creature outside his home. "*I was scared; it's got wings like a bird, but it's not a bird. That animal is not of this world.*"

The article noted that reports of seeing the bird started shortly after a number of cattle mutilations had occurred in the area. The paper commented that one eyewitness said he believed the bird was large enough to pick up a small child and take off with it.

How had this bird managed to survive in the wilderness and are there more of them? Some might say it was mistaken for a golden eagle, or condor, although the colouring doesn't seem to match either of these birds.

Could a 'thunderbird' scoop up a child or even an adult and carry it away a distance in a remote area?

The Harpy Eagle, (not a native of America) was discovered by scientists at Liverpool University, to have fed on Magabey monkeys, with their skulls being found in the eagles nests, carrying off animals weighing over 20lbs. Lead researcher, Susanne Schultz says this is evidence of birds being able to carry off animals more than twice their own body weight.

Then there's the consideration of another very strange creature, who again, could perhaps be considered as a suspect in the disappearance of people and animals.

Does the 'Jersey Devil' really exist? If so, where does it hide?

In the two thousand square miles of woods and marshland in south-eastern New Jersey, sightings of such an entity involved attacks on livestock and dogs. Over one hundred sightings alone were reported in 1909.

Even a respected councillor reported his own sighting which occurred outside his home, and on going outside to investigate, he reportedly found cloven footprints in the snow.

Many saw the creature flying. Mr Evans of Gloucester reported to the *Philadelphia press*, about a beast which he said was "3 ½ feet high with a dog-like head and a long neck, with wings about two feet long and back legs like those of a bird." Others described the creature as "7 feet tall and 'cave-man' in size."

The Philadelphia zoo even offered a $10,000 reward for its capture. Scientists at the Smithsonian at the time speculated that it was a prehistoric creature from the Jurassic period that had somehow managed to survive.

Chapter Seventeen: Shape-shifters, and Skin walkers

Many of those who reported encounters with the 'dogman,' and 'bigfoot,' felt that the entities were coming from another world rather than ours; that they were of a more spiritual form in origin, and that their origins could lie in the occult supernatural.

In Native American lore, a form of magic allows the Native American medicine man to take the physical form of a creature, and Teacher Hoss Lors recently wrote in *Skinwalker Shards Linger*, about his frightening experience while living on a Navajo reservation.

In his garage one evening, a rabid dog approached, and thinking to put the dog out of its misery and safeguard the children nearby, he hit the dog on the head, killing it.

Going inside his house for a moment or two, when he returned back outside, the body of the dog had disappeared, but there were no paw prints in the snow. Later that night, he said he began to fell very ill and was overcome with nausea and a high fever.

His wife and neighbour both said he must visit the medicine man or he would die, and although he was reluctant, they insisted. On reaching the Medicine man, he was given treatment, which the neighbour's boy witnessed and later said that he had seen a spirit form leaving Lors body; the medicine man confirmed that the dog had been a shape-shifter, and had entered Lors body with evil intent. The medicine man said if he had not come to him, he would have been dead within twenty four hours.

Lors went onto investigate the subject of shape-shifters and found it to be a strongly believed phenomenon amongst the Native Americans he encountered, though it was rarely openly spoken of. It was believed that mentioning the shape-shifter would cause it to be drawn to that person.

He found that through rituals, certain medicine men would choose the path of 'bad' magic in order to develop their powers, and were required to provide a human sacrifice in order to be given the power to shift into an animal form whenever desired.

Perhaps it's possible then that because whatever takes the missing people in remote woods and forests areas is never actually seen, it might be being done by a shape-shifter in animal form.

Chapter Eighteen:
Portals and different dimensions?

The Missing village of native Inuits.

This inexplicable case concerns the whereabouts of the over 30 men, women and children who allegedly vanished without a trace from an Inuit fishing village in the first half of the 20th Century.

In 1930, a Canadian fur trapper, Joe Labelle, arrived at the village on Canada's Lake Anjikuni. He had been there before, and yet this time he was surprised and then shocked to find the usual busy village seemingly completely empty of life.

Too frightened to stay there, he left hastily, in fear of whatever it was that had caused the disappearance of all of the villagers.

He found the Mounties, who set out to investigate the man's claims. They found no evidence of any kind of struggle or violence. They could also allegedly find no tracks in the snow.

Everyone was stumped as to what could possibly have happened, with some pointing the finger at the demonic entity 'Torngarsuk' who, according to Inuit legend, is a powerful sky deity who is the leader of a legion of malevolent spirits, said to be invisible to all but Inuit shamans and able to manifest in animal form.

Was their disappearance down to demonic activity, or had they somehow slipped into another different dimension? Was this also the cause of the same fate of two RAF airmen, Stewart and Day? In Iraq in 1924, the two pilots were flying over the desert, when they suddenly, inexplicably landed their plane on the desert floor safely, and left it.

Their water and any other necessities were left in the plane, and their footprints were seen for approximately 40 metres, before suddenly stopping. No trace, despite rigorous searching and speaking to local tribes, was ever found of the pair.

Wisconsin metaphysical investigator Mary Sutherland, says that some portal areas are heat sensitive, causing those that enter to become very warm, while others have a sudden drop in temperature. She believes they have an effect on emotional well-being too, causing some to feel exuberance, and other to feel severe depressive sensations. Judgement is liable to be impaired as a result. The body may absorb the negative energy of the portal or vortex area.

Crucially, she believes that while the portals are generally permanent; some may be unstable, manifesting for only brief moments in time. This would certainly help to explain the strange experiences and apparitions that are only seen by some, but not all, of the visitors to the remote areas. The ability to become confused, disoriented and lost, sometimes forever, along with strange feelings of physiological changes, would certainly hold true as an explanation for some people's disappearances.

'Dead Man's Hill' in Burlington was probably built on an ancient Native American burial mound. It was here that Sutherland carried out one of her investigations, to see if indeed any unusual experience would occur. Photographing strange lights, when they returned home, they found they had somehow 'lost time' whilst on their trip, with their watches showing an earlier time than the time it had been when they had been in the hill area.

If indeed it is accepted that there are areas where positive energy exists, in places like Glastonbury, and Sedona, and energy is found to run along Ley Lines, then why would it be strange to believe that the opposite of this can exist; places of negative energy?

Conclusion

Why can't we find a definitive answer to explain all of these mysterious anomalies, which sometimes, it seems, can be deadly?

We can't find an answer, because it would seem it is unknowable, for several factors.

Theories about what could cause disappearances and deaths in remote locations range, as has been outlined, from simple misadventure/accident, and indigenous animal attacks, to serial killer/s, kidnappers, satanic cults, to nefarious secret government underground bases, to the more elusive and possibly paranormal Bigfoot, ufo abductions, portals and time dimensions, demons, and ultimately to an unknown 'force' or 'intelligence.'

The very fields of cryptozoology and ufology are extremely controversial areas, where vehement debate and wildly differing opinions seem the norm. Combine this with the mass of disinformation that appears along with it, and it's easy to understand why getting to the heart of the matter can feel so hard to reach for so many. These are fields of study where it seems one struggles to find common ground and absolute proof. While Bigfoot experts will claim it is the cause of that hybrid animal; ufo experts will claim it is the cause of aliens. Those who believe the Government are conducting secret military operations will side on this argument. An array of conspiracy theories abound here. Others will say it is simply down to inexperience and underestimating the ferocity of the terrain into which people naively venture. Others will say that animals, and killers in the woods, are all the explanation necessary.

Others will point to the supernatural or occult, and there we are dealing with the unknown and the unprovable; esoteric beliefs and theories, the supernatural, the paranormal, and perhaps, as yet undiscovered laws of physics.

There may be no definitive answer; and there may be more than one cause.

Is there one cause? Is it a combination of causes? If more than one is responsible, are they, as some would suggest, playing off the methods used by others to confuse and hide their activities, throwing us off the scent? For example, many in the UFO field believe ET's deliberately display certain behaviours to purposely confuse people as to what is really happening.

It can feel a little like looking into murky water and hoping to find it clear. Probing the depths of the water merely stirs up the dark murkiness and provides elusive glimpses of shapes inside it that are impossible to identify.

Perhaps one should look to the respected but controversial likes of John Keel for an explanation. In his books such as *The Mothman Prophecies*, Keel coined the term 'ultra terrestrials,' to describe UFO and alien entities he believed to be non-human and capable of taking on whatever form they wanted to, like the Trickster of folklore.

Concepts such as demons, apparitions, and monsters, to him, were all inter-related, even the very same entities. Multiple paranormal or supernatural entities all formed of the same unknown origin. Termed 'Instrumentalism,' the theory postulated is that these entities or manifestations are all interchangeable, even determined perhaps by our own sub-conscious and manifesting to us according to our social consciousness.

Underlying this is the belief that there is not one answer, but a multitude of 'unknown,' answers of metaphysical substance behind these encounters and sightings. They defy logical scientific rational explanation, but this is not meant to undermine the truth that they exist. They are just not that easy to explain. Because they can not be given clear explanation yet, does not serve to lessen their existence.

They originate possibly from an alternate reality to our own reality, beings that exist in a different frequency to ours, but at times, enter our dimension;

possibly from another dimension, or spirit world, and enter ours to play with us, tease us, frighten us, and mystify us...

If 'the new physics' believes in time shifts, parallel dimensions, concurrent time lines, wormholes, intelligent quantum particles, then is it so difficult to believe in such anomalous phenomenon appearing in our world?

Whatever the answer truly is, people won't stop looking until they find it...

SOMETHING IN THE WOODS
IS TAKING PEOPLE

Stephen Young

Copyright 2014 Stephen Young

All Rights Reserved

Something in the Woods is taking people.

Something unknown that we cannot define; something that others have had the misfortune to encounter.

People snatched soundlessly, never to be seen again. Or returned; dead.

A strange and highly unusual predator. Highly intelligent. Very successful. And able to overpower someone in an instant.

This is a puzzle. An often deadly one.

Here follows some very troubling and disturbing accounts....

Table of Contents

Introduction	92
Chapter One: The Disappeared	94
Chapter Two: Hunting for Explanations. UFO and Alien Involvement?	102
Chapter Three: Invisible Assailants?	109
Chapter Four: Malevolent Spirits? The Djinn, Fairies	114
Chapter Five: Shadow People?	125
Chapter Six: Spirit Helpers?	137
Chapter Seven: Mysterious Cases of Children Going Missing	141
Chapter Eight: Snatched by Something Under the Ground?	151
Chapter Nine: Military Involvement in Disappearances?	166
Chapter Ten: The Work of Satanists?	173
Chapter Eleven: More Mysterious Disappearances	195
Conclusion	211

Introduction

Fatal accidents can happen very easily to even the most experienced climbers, and in the wilderness, hikers can get lost in an instant. A couple of wrong turns and they can be lost immediately. A slip on a rock or a trip near a crevice and death or serious accidents can come quickly.

Falling into a creek or down between a pile of rocks, a body; dead or injured, can be hidden from search parties quite easily. However, with highly trained tracker dogs and heat seeking infra-red equipment to detect a person's body heat, the mystery often remains as to why people are not found, or are found in the most unusual of circumstances.

Natural predators can lurk in the wilderness; bears, cougars, and occasionally a hiker will be victim to these wild animals. They feed where they kill, or drag their bloody victim to a nearby lair; they leave a trail that is obvious to searchers.

However, the victims in this book show no evidence of an animal attack.

For these victims, there is no logical explanation....only enigma and many questions...

Something in the Woods is taking people....

People taken; sometimes returned, but never the same again.

Stalked as prey and snatched without warning... Never to be seen again. Or found, in the most horrible of circumstances....

Chapter One: The Disappeared

As of writing this in June 2014, after days of thorough ground and air searches, rescuers still haven't been able to locate a fire-fighter and paramedic who disappeared while on an off-duty hiking trip with a friend in the Los Padres National Forest, Arizona.

Fit and athletic Mr Herdman had taken off barefoot one evening, chasing his dog when it had started running off from their camp. He hasn't been seen since.

His dog was later seen during the subsequent search. Search dogs were used in the area where Herdman's footprints were found, but it seems the tracker dogs have not been able to trace his scent any further than the immediate area he was last seen in.

(Author Update: Tragically, his body has since been found. After a substantive search that lasted two weeks, involving constant aerial and ground searches, using hundreds of SAR teams and volunteers, K9's, and heat-seeking equipment, he was found deceased lying on a steep ascent approximately 2,000 feet from where he had last been seen.

He'd suffered blunt force trauma. It was determined that he'd fallen, though when this occurred can't be determined beyond "a few days."

He was found in the same area in which searchers had been looking for him, night and day, for the last fourteen days.

Why was his scent not able to be picked up? How had it just stopped?

Why was he not seen? Though much of the area is dense in vegetation, he was only partially covered by brush and clearly visible on a rock surface.

How could he have been there all that time?

If he hadn't been there for that duration, where had he been?

"What's the chances someone barefoot, at night, would scale a mountain of 1200 feet?" said the Sheriff.

As to why he'd been attempting to climb a rock edge, the investigating Sheriff commented, "I'm not sure we'll get an answer."

The Sheriff stated that he did not appear to have been trapped and that he appeared to be lying over the ground.

It was then stated that the area where he'd been found had *not* been searched; yet we know over 50 square miles *had* been searched? It also still doesn't explain how the tracker dogs had not picked up a scent to lead them to where his body was located.

Why had he climbed a cliff? Is it possible he was fleeing something?

* * *

In July 2012, sixty-six-year-old Michael LeMaitre was the subject of a huge search effort in Alaska that was to last several days.

He'd completed many marathons and was competing in the Seward's Mount race. Last spotted by race organisers approaching the mid point of the race, on a busy main trail, they expected him back at the five kilometre finish shortly after. He was never seen again.

Despite thorough and intensive searching with tracker dogs, they could find no trace of him and no scent to follow. Thermal imaging equipment searched for signals of his body, yet none could be found.

Hundreds of volunteers took to the area, searching every possible crevice for over ten days.

How could he disappear in so small a spot they all wondered, running a planned round route of just 5k and surrounded by other runners? They were mystified by finding absolutely no trace of him.

He disappeared without trace. Every crevice was searched. He left no scent to track.

It's almost as though he was plucked into the air. He certainly wasn't on the ground anymore...

* * *

In July 2006, student Aju Iroaga was standing alone on a country road just by Lake Superior, having stormed off-site of a tree planting project.

He'd been told to re-do the trees he'd just planted and he was angry. He'd already re-done his work once, and he was exhausted. Now he was stuck there, in the middle of the forest, several kilometres from the company base. He'd been told if he was quitting, he'd have to wait for the team to finish and then he would be taken back to the base to get his belongings and leave.

He waited for nearly four hours, just standing there, and was last noticed still there at about quarter to four in the afternoon. At 6pm when the team finished however, he had disappeared.

Concerned, the supervisors and team looked around for him, two of them even staying there that night in case he turned up.

Police officers arrived at about 11 pm, and at dawn they began their search with helicopters and K9 units to pick up the students trail. However, the dogs could find no scent of him.

The police's original theory was that he'd decided to walk through the wilderness to the camp. They had nothing else to go on; but no footprints or scent to track either.

He was never seen again.

At one stage, the Ontario Police suggested that because he was a fit young man, he may have run an access road the length of over *60km* to the Trans Canada Highway to hitch a ride.

Despite how fit he was it seems a highly unlikely theory.

A website put together by the heartbroken family says, "That there is no evidence of foul play, and no evidence that he walked off, leaves an unacceptable mystery. People simply do not vanish."

The co-owner of the company he was there working for was quoted as saying, "He was certainly strong enough, both in will and physically to be able to take care of himself."

Where did he go? And what did he meet that was stronger than him?

* * *

In June 2013, the Reiger family from Oklahoma were on vacation in Ecuador. The family decided to take a short hike from their hotel, along a scenic trail. At some point along the hike, the two boys ran on ahead but only one of them returned.

The elder son it seemed had disappeared into thin air. The boys were close to each other on the hike, separated only momentarily when the elder had vanished.

"The really strange thing about it is," his father told newspapers, "that whatever happened to him was in the space of five minutes; we were right behind him. You couldn't get lost. The whole of the trail is visible. If he was hurt, he would have been seen."

Searchers could not seem to locate the boy's tracks, and indeed stated that they didn't detect any other tracks in the boy's vicinity either. No-one heard him shout or scream, no sounds of any thrashing in the undergrowth or of a fall, no blood, no scent.

Army troops were called in and the Soldiers rappelled down the ravines, tracker dogs, fire-fighters, and volunteers from the village below joined in.

Some have suggested, given that they could not find a body in the ravines, and that they couldn't detect his scent, that the most logical thing that could have happened was that he was suddenly 'lifted' from the ground by something. It's as though he was somehow 'disappeared' into invisibility.

"I could see; I was there. I don't know why they didn't find him. He would have been seen. I cannot come up with a scenario that makes any sense. Nothing makes any sense," says his Father.

* * *

'A hiker's disappearance adds to hundreds of others,' wrote an Oregon newspaper in 2013.

They'd discovered that an astonishing figure of two hundred and forty people were recorded as missing after going into the Oregon wilderness since the late nineties.

Highlighting just two of the cases, they related how a former member of the United States Coast Guards had disappeared in the Willamette National Forest in 2012.

His profession had depended on him being extremely fit and athletic, and he kept up his level of fitness after leaving with frequent hikes and cycling. However, once he entered the national park he was never seen again. Nor were any of his belongings, including an inflatable raft and his cell-phone. Bodies will sadly succumb to the elements, but other things are more durable; they don't decompose. They weren't found either though.

Jake's mother told the reporter, "There's a mystery here. Both were experienced. Two grown men can't simply disappear."

She was referring to six years prior to this, when a professor of mathematics at Oregon University, Dr Xu, went hiking near the spot where her son Jake had been. No sign of him has been seen either.

The search had covered one hundred miles of the forest using tracker dogs and heat seeking equipment. For a while they followed footprints that were thought to be his, but the trail suddenly stopped.

How can a trail suddenly stop and yet there be no explanation as to where he had gone from there?

Chapter Two: Hunting for Explanations. UFO and Alien Involvement?

In 2002, the strange story of what happened to Todd Sees began to circulate. Could it really be true what was being said?

Early in the morning on August 4th, Todd left his rural home in Northumberland, Pennsylvania to go up into the nearby mountain to do some deer scouting, prior to the season starting. As he left, he told his family he would be home by midday.

When he didn't return his concerned wife alerted authorities, knowing it was completely out of character for him not to return as he'd said he would.

By 2pm, a search party had been organized. The State police and a couple hundred local volunteers began to search for him. Quickly they discovered his four-wheeler at the top of the mountain, but search dogs could find no scent to go on.

The search carried on for two days, from top to bottom of the mountainous area.

On the second day a break came; something was seen in a thick brush area beside a pond, very close to the family home. The search party spent half an hour hacking at the brush to get to it. What they found was Todd Sees' body, virtually naked. He was wearing just his underwear. When he'd left two days before, he'd been fully dressed in outdoor clothing and boots.

His body was not bloated; it was emaciated. Immediately there were concerns. That would not be the usual condition to find a body in.

It got stranger. Though many locals claimed afterward there was nothing unusual about the incident, others, including Emmy award winning investigative journalist Linda Molten Howe, and Peter Davenport of the National UFO Reporting Centre, believed there was a lot more to the case. They pointed to the fact that the area had been previously searched, and yet the tracker dogs had not been able to pick up his scent at all. Why?

This led to speculation that his body could not have been there when the area was searched, but was perhaps placed there later.

His body was found in a thickly forested spot, so difficult to access that it led many to believe he could not have gone there voluntarily, by his own volition, if the searchers themselves had to hack their way into it to retrieve him.

But who or what had taken him in there if it was such a difficult area to get to?

Even odder, one of his missing boots was later found; high up in a tree a mile from where his vehicle was found, and no-where near his body. People wanted to know how the boot could have got up there.

There were claims that upon the discovery of his body, the FBI arrived, cordoning off the area and refusing to allow the family access to Todd.

It's implied by researchers including ex-detective Butch Witkowski, that Sees was an unfortunate victim of an alien abduction. Their claims are allegedly back up by reports of sightings by three local farmers of a large bright object just above the power lines, hovering in the area at the time of Sees disappearance.

The official cause of his death was ruled as a cocaine overdose. Those close to him state he was not a drug taker.

* * *

A case as strange as that of Todd Sees happened in the U.K. in 1980. Zygmunt Adamski disappeared from Todmorden in the rural county of Yorkshire on June 6, 1980 after leaving his house.

Five days later his body was located on the top of a coal pile in a coal mine.

The police attended the scene, where on examination they found burn marks on the man's shoulders and neck, and a strange green ointment covering the wounds. The ointment was never able to be scientifically identified.

His clothes were clean despite him having been missing for five days, although his jacket had been buttoned up incorrectly and his shirt was missing. There were no footprints in the coal.

The Mine Company's son was the last person in the area, but he'd been there before midday. He had seen no body on a coal pile. It appeared to have been put there after that time.

The pathologist ruled that his death had occurred between eleven and one pm of that day, but the burns on his body were determined to have occurred two days before his death.

He stated, "What led to his death couldn't be answered," but he ruled that the man had died of a heart attack due to shock or fright. His face had been contorted with fear.

The case was never solved any further than that, but oddly enough a few months after finding the man's body there, one of the policemen, Alan Godfrey, was on a night shift and claimed to have experienced an unnerving incident himself.

Searching for some missing cows, he claimed that he saw a strange large object in front of him in the road, hovering above the ground.

He tried to radio colleagues, but his radio went dead. Frightened, he remained in the car.

He was later to realise that over half an hour had passed that he couldn't account for, and he found that the soles of his boots were split wide open, looking to him as though he'd been dragged along the ground.

That same night other policemen independently called into headquarters with alarming reports of seeing bright lights descending into the valley, and a driver also called the police.

The cows were later discovered in a field which had been previously empty and the entrance gate to it was locked. The ground was muddy, but there were no prints from the cows. Like the man, it was as though they too had literally been dropped there.

The policeman himself was so disturbed by his experience that he underwent hypno-regression, in search of answers about what could have happened to him in the missing half an hour.

Under a state of hypnosis he began to describe being in a room with a black-robed, bearded man with a biblical appearance, accompanied by a huge black dog and other, smaller 'creatures' that were the size of five year olds and had robotic movements.

* * *

In 1992, *Napa Valley Register* interviewed young film maker Jake Polania regarding his plan to make a film about an incident that occurred in Flagstaff, Arizona. According to Polania, four young friends were on their return from a camping trip when somehow three of them, along with a farm hand, were found dead on a ranch. The fourth friend, along with the owner of the farm were missing.

The deaths were never solved. The fourth camper and the owner were never found. The bodies of the dead campers had strange marks on their necks and backs, but there was no blood at the scene. The local sheriffs spent two weeks searching for the missing men but found no clues.

* * *

Lecturer on paranormal and esoteric matters, Guy Tarade mentions a mysterious incident that most who heard about attributed it to a UFO abduction, though there were no reports of any witnesses to one being seen in the area at the time.

According to Miami police reports, in 1952 a Mr Tom Brook, his wife, and their 11 year-old son had been visiting friends thirty kilometres away from Miami, and had left just before midnight to drive back home.

Local law enforcement officers came across their empty car; the headlights ablaze and the doors open, just seven miles from their friend's home. Mrs. Brooke's handbag was found in the back seat, the money still in it.

The officers traced the family's footprints to a meadow at the edge of the roadside, but they abruptly stopped after a few dozen steps.

According to reports available, no trace of them was ever found.

Chapter Three: Invisible Assailants?

The oldest journal still in publication, The Scots Magazine, first issued in 1739, wrote of a very strange incident that occurred in 1761.

Five women were returning from collecting wood near Ventimiglia in northern Italy, when suddenly one of them cried out and dropped to the ground, dead. Her friends were terrified by what they saw.

Her clothes and even her shoes were apparently torn into shreds and scattered all around her. Her wounds were horrific; her skull was visible, her intestines hanging out, and most of her internal organs ruptured. Her femur had been torn from its socket and the flesh of her hip and thigh torn off.

The account was recorded in the French Academy of Sciences by Dr M. Morand. He wrote that there was no blood at the scene, nor any sign of her missing flesh.

***

Researchers John Mitchell and Robert Rickard wrote of an account from the famous explorer James Alan Rennie and his friend, who were in the remote wilderness of northern Canada in 1924. According to them, as they made their way across a frozen lake they encountered something that chilled them to the very core.

Tracks were appearing in front of them, coming toward them yet no creature was making them; there was nothing there except the recurring tracks coming closer. Then suddenly, something impacted against Rennie, then ventured on at great speed, its tracks still being made as the invisible entity made its way across the lake.

The explorer recorded in his published journal, "There was no animal, no sign of any life at all to account for them."

***

A few decades ago in the field of Ufology and Cryptozoology there began a growing field of thought that pointed to the possibility of invisible 'intelligences' on a grand scale.

Known as 'Atmospheric beings,' they're a theory of what one would think impossible. Sky-bound entities that roam the skies in silence, visible only by the use of infra-red but always there.

They remain one of the most fascinating of mysteries that fall somewhere within the Cryptozoology and Ufology fields, with a leaning toward the esoteric too. Their origins unknown and their intentions possibly sinister.

We don't know what they are, but they are there none the less, and these things appear to be alive. Organic creatures of some sort.

Large, voracious, invisible to the naked eye; these undetectable predators could take people without seeing them coming.

This is what Navy veteran Trevor Constable believed, dedicating twenty years to studying them. The idea that these morphic beasts he could capture with the use of infra-red cameras, that dwelt within the atmosphere of the earth, were monsters that only increased their density while in search of food; their food source being humans.

He blamed the accounts of livestock disappearances, mutilations, and indeed human mutilation cases, on these soaring predatory entities, along with the constant stream of people going missing every year.

In the 1950's he captured up to 100 images on film while out in places such as the Yucca Valley and the Mojave Desert; some showed dark objects, others showed shadowed dense beings looking like living cells. Others took the form of UFO's. All were framed by the landscape, enabling their size to be scaled in comparison to natural features. They were frighteningly big.

For the first time they were being captured by infrared, but for years reports have surfaced of strange creatures inhabiting the skies above us. Atmospheric beasts, or atmospheric life-forms, with bodies that are able to adjust their density from the almost immaterial and invisible to a more solid form; actual life-forms with an intelligence. Morphing, shape-shifting, and attacking.

He wasn't the only one to capture their images. According to Rense magazine, photographer Michael White was filming the night sky when he noticed an odd-looking dark cloud which remained stationary and did not move at all for at least thirty minutes, before then suddenly disappearing.

It wasn't until he later developed the images he'd photographed that he saw there was some kind of entity there; a mysterious object that looked like it had been *rippling*. Though to the naked eye it appeared solid, in the pictures there were shadows of light and fibrous looking shapes.

They roam the skies in silence; invisible, but always there. Shimmering predators that shift in density as they swoop down to attack.

Prior to both of these investigators, the late Ivan Sanderson was a proponent of the theory.

If this sounds too fantastical to believe, perhaps it should be noted that in 1949, the US Air force made a revealing official statement that, "the possible existence of some sort of strange 'ET' animals has been considered, as many of the 'objects' (seen in the Sky) act more like animals than anything else."

Then came some startling news. In 2013, The Telegraph Newspaper had the headline 'Aliens exist and have been found living high up in the sky.' University of Sheffield scientists had found organisms living up in the atmosphere. This they said could possibly be the first real proof that life had come from space to earth.

The article points out that this is not the first time organisms have been found; the skies are thought to be full of life.

"Our conclusion is," they said, "life is arriving to Earth from space...life is not restricted to this planet."

Chapter Four:
Malevolent Spirits? The Djinn, Fairies

"There is something taking these people; something terrible and evil," says Alan Lamers on Dreamlands talk show.

Alan Lamers is a telecoms designer who specialises in creating radio communication systems in remote areas. Contracted to work on the remote Indonesian island of Sulawesi, he found himself in the midst of some very disturbing recurring incidents. He describes in fascinating details these events.

It began he says when he was going to a small village and was told not to wear any coloured clothing; only black or white. Asking why, he was told that people who wore bright coloured clothing could disappear. Though puzzled, he politely complied, more out of cultural respect than any belief in what they were saying, and on arriving at the village destination he saw all of the locals dressed only in black.

As a group, Alan went with several of them into the jungle wilderness. One of his colleagues had not complied with the request and had on a pair of bright coloured socks. When they returned from the jungle that night, his friend started to become violently sick with a very high fever. His body was covered in mysterious scratches. He had not seen anything attacking him. The villagers commented that he was lucky he had not been "taken."

Lamers went on to hear some of the local stories. He spoke to a girl who told him that her cousin and four friends had gone into the jungle for a hike. After a week they had not returned and at great cost she hired a private search party. She went with them, spending a month searching for her cousin and friends.

Finally, they found her cousin; he was severely traumatised however and had no memory of what had happened to him. He was so distressed by whatever had happened to him while missing, that he could not talk for two months. The girl said she believed he had encountered the Djinn. As for his friends; they were never found.

Says Lamers, after interviewing many more locals about their stories, "There is something taking these people. Something terrible and evil. It is one of the strangest and most dangerous places I have ever come across. The locals claimed it is evil spirits, or djinn, snatching away any man who ventured disrespectfully into their terrain."

He finally managed to talk to the boy who'd disappeared and was told by him that he'd been taken by 'little people or creatures,' with black eyes and enormous gaping, grinning mouths. He kept seeing them, but his companions could not. Then they took him to a place filled with animals somewhat like horses or deer.

Although little is known about them in Western countries, The Qur'an refers to the Djinn many times. In Islamic belief they are thought to be made of a smoke-like yet physical form, and are able to interfere with humans, often to the effect of causing them great harm.

They are mostly thought to be unable to be seen by humans, and are believed to have the power to move at great speed. They have the ability to appear in our world in any form, though often they will look demonic when they fully materialise.

Their domains are naturally remote areas, desert, and mountains. They are thought to be elementals, who can take the form of storms and great winds, and many scholars believe that because of their malevolent nature, they take great pleasure in abducting humans in this guise.

Editor of the *Flying Saucer Review,* Gordon Creighton, expressed the opinion that these elemental beings known to the Islamic world as djinn, could be the culprits in many of the mysterious disappearances of people.

These Arabic beliefs in djinn spirits are aligned to the ancient Celtic beliefs in Fairies. If the idea of Fairies seems a little outlandish, French scientist Jacques Vallees spoke of the parallels that exist between Fairy 'kidnappings' and alleged alien abductions; ranging from seeing strange lights, missing time, and hypnotic mind control.

Fantasy writer Kevin L. O'Brien has significantly researched Celtic and 'Faerie Lore.' 'Faeries' he describes are beings that live communally in the hills, rocks, mountains, or underground.

They use the power of 'glamour;' a power of illusion where they can make people see whatever they wish them to see. They can mislead people in the wilderness by changing the appearance of landmarks, or disguising treacherous ground to make it appear that it's safe to cross.

Faeries have the ability to Shape-shift and transform themselves into any form they choose, similar to the Native American tradition of the Skinwalker.

Sometimes they snatch humans and carry them away, either to be taken forever, or disposed of when finished with. Every seven years the Faeries must make a sacrifice to the devil and give him one of their own, and many old tales describe human captives being given to the devil so that no Faeries will be lost.

Professor DL Ashliman, retired from the University of Petersburg, wrote a paper entitled 'Abducted by Aliens,' in which he quotes an extraordinary story from John Rhys' book, Celtic Folklore. A man in the Isle of Man, (situated between Ireland and England) many years ago suddenly disappeared from his family. He was gone for four years, when one day he suddenly reappeared. He couldn't explain how he had returned, but he told his brothers he'd been living with the fairies.

Obviously skeptical and full of ridicule, the brothers didn't believe him; until he explained that 'the other world' where he had been with the fairies was not far away from them and he'd been able to see what his brothers had been doing every day, though they couldn't see him.

To prove it, he described how the brothers had been collecting wood one afternoon when they'd been so scared by a loud cracking sound in a bush near them that they'd all run back home terrified. His brothers remembered that day well, and knew there was no other way their brother could have known about it. They took his story then as proof.

Perhaps the first study of Fairies was conducted in the 1600's by a Scottish Vicar, Dr Robert Kirk, who compiled accounts of sightings. He believed they were composed of ethereal bodies like clouds, and in a realm somewhere between humans and angels.

Sometimes just their voices could be heard. They could move around in the air and sweep down to snatch things or people away. Other times they materialised like miniature people.

In 1678, a small book was distributed in England containing the story told by a Dr Moore who claimed that as a young child in Ireland he had been snatched away by the Fairies on more than one occasion. He was relating those events to friends one evening in a remote countryside Pub when they witnessed him get violently attacked by something invisible to their eyes and dragged from the Pub.

They quickly went to the local 'Witch' who said he was being held in the woods. She told them that as long as he did not eat anything offered to him by his captors, he would probably return soon unscathed.

He did return, dehydrated and hungry, having found himself alone in the middle of the woods.

In 'Drolls Traditions,' Robert Hunt's book of true stories from Cornwall, England, 1865, he documents a tale one woman gave him. A young boy was out picking flowers in the fields near a wood one evening. He started hearing the most beautiful music coming out of the woods and he walked toward the woods to find out where it was coming from. It seemed to be coming from inside the woods and as he entered it seemed as though the music was in front of him but moving away from him at the same time, almost luring him further to it.

He knew he shouldn't be going further into the woods but the music sounded so beautiful to his ears that he couldn't help but follow it.

Soon he found himself deep inside the woods, and the trees and bushes were thick around him but something invisible was clearing a path for him to walk through, and it seemed almost like night had fallen now, and there were incredibly bright stars filling the sky.

He reached a lake and the music stopped. Feeling tired after his long walk he lay down and fell quickly asleep.

When the search party finally found him several days later, he told his parents that a beautiful woman had taken him into a palace made of gold and crystals of every colour of the rainbow. He had been missing for much longer than one night.

The woman telling the story said she believed it, as did many in a region where witchcraft and paganism have long since existed. She felt that he must have been taken to fairyland after being entranced by them.

In the 1930's The Dublin Press in Ireland had reports of boys sighting groups of fairies and trying to chasing them but being unable to catch them as they teasingly jumped through hedges and trees, all the while appearing as glistening and glowing figures, unscathed by the elements they passed through. At moments they appeared to have faces like those of men; hairy and rugged yet they had no ears.

It's said that Iceland is a nation that takes the belief in Faeries so seriously still that to this day they adhere to the principle of not building or disturbing places where they know fairies could dwell, such as boulders and rocky areas. They construct around them, rather than disturb their natural habitat, in respect for them.

***

Zimbabwe's Mount Inyangani is another mysterious region known for its number of unusual disappearances. *Bulawayo 24* news station on January 12th 2014, reported the search for missing man 31 year old tourist Zayd Dada, who'd been missing then for over a week.

Media and internet discussions began revolving around the mythos of the Mountain, of its belief by many as being 'sacred.' People were talking about the mountain that *FATE* Magazine once investigated for its disturbing reputation. The magazine had unearthed the local custom of offering sacrifices in blood to the mountain, in the hope that it would lead to the return of those who had been 'taken.'

Known disappearances there have included two children of a former Government Minister, and a few years later, a young boy Robert Ackhurst. No trace was ever found of any of them, despite extensive searching.

The Magazine however also uncovered several other incidents. Another Government Minister had once become lost there while hiking with two friends. He told of finding themselves wandering without direction in a strange state of disorientation without the normal sensations of thirst or hunger, and most intriguingly of all, as the search party looked for them, the trio spotted them and continually shouted out to them and waved to them but though they could clearly see the search party, the rescuers could not see them.

Another Official of the Government also went missing while walking there. Speaking to a District Assistant, the reporter heard that this man reappeared two days later, in good health but completely unable to recall where he had been or what he had done in the time he was missing.

Mutwa, a Zulu Shaman, has also told many of what happened to him while in the hillsides looking for herbs. Suddenly it became cold despite the heat of the day and he was shrouded by bright blue smog that engulfed him. The next thing he knew, he was prostrate on a slab inside a mountainside tunnel, paralysed and unable to escape while grey skinny creatures with long limbs held him captive, his throat burning from sulphuric stench.

Now in 2014 this latest 'victim,' Dada, had been hiking with his wife and two others when they'd stopped for a rest. He continued on aways with the intention of returning to them shortly; but that was the last time he was seen.

Many thorough searches were carried out over the next few days but no sign of him was found.

It was at this stage that traditional tribal healers gathered on the mountain, holding a ritual with the intention of appeasing the spirits of the mountain.

The District Administrator, speaking to the local newspaper was reported as saying, "Mysterious events continue happening."

He said there were many known examples of people who had disappeared there, to be found months or even years later, yet with no ability to describe what happened to them.

In Zayd's case a facebook page was set up appealing for any information, and on one post, a member of the public from the area writes,

"You should consult a witch doctor, I encourage you to; that's the only way you will find him. I'm a Christian but, they are the ones who you need...'

A Parks spokesperson told reporters at Coastweek news "People are dealing with a situation of the spiritual realm."

Chapter Five:
Shadow People?

Travel writer Logan Hawkes talks of having encountered shadowy entities in the Big Bend National Park. He describes how, a few years ago as he was travelling through it with a friend, they stopped at the hot springs to relax in the water for a while and enjoy the peaceful beauty of the area as it grew to darkness around them.

Finally it became pitch dark and they stared up at the sky counting the stars. Suddenly they could see what looked like silhouetted shadows of a group of people, standing on a ledge away up the river. He and his friend expected the group might approach them and became a little anxious. They waited with trepidation, knowing no-one else was around for miles.

Finally, after not seeing them move and hearing no sounds of talking coming from them, they shone the flashlight over at them to see them more clearly.

"Except there were no figures in the light; then turning the light off the faint silhouette outlines re-appeared."

Unnerved after repeating the exercise a couple more times and seeing the same response, they didn't hang around and quickly climbed out of the water, keen to get their clothes back on and get out of there.

"To this day we cannot say who or what they were. But I can confidently tell you they were not living beings."

Texas isn't the only State where these elusive and hard to define 'shadow beings' have been seen. In the Santa Lucia Mountains along the central coast of California, it was known that the Native Americans told of 'Dark Watchers'; shadowed figures who would appear on ledges as dusk fell into night. Human-like ghost figures, always dark shadows, standing silhouetted against the landscape.

Who they are, and what they want no-one knows, but many have seen them. Usually it seems they disappear without coming any closer. Many have speculated about them, and others have told of their encounter in forums on the internet.

'Weird California,' has a collection of compelling and highly mysterious contributions from witnesses who have written in to tell of their sightings;

L Brennan of Ramona, wrote: "While flying my aircraft I glanced toward the Range and saw what looked to be seven very large dark figures standing there."

"We saw a very large dark figure," says another, "standing at the edge of the mountain, staring off into the distance; it was over 10 ft tall. It seemed to have a cape, with broad shoulders... extremely weird; I travel that road daily. This was around September 2010."

In a slightly different account, G Garner says, "We see them here; they're almost like horses on their hind legs in the dusk."

***

Then, just as mysteriously, a lady from Tennessee recently called the Mutual UFO Network, not knowing who else to call and needing to urgently talk about what had just happened to her that morning.

It was around 6am and she was standing on the deck of her house drinking an early morning coffee, enjoying the warm and quiet beginning to her day, when suddenly she saw something that defied explanation.

The deck of her house was at an elevation of twelve feet from the ground below. When she turned around to go back into the house, she stopped dead. She could not fail to see the huge black shadow; the shape of a man but standing higher than the deck.

It was leaning against it. It was the shape of a man yet it appeared to have no face. She was frozen to the spot, unable to move.

Suddenly it turned its 'head' toward her. Then she watched as very slowly it peeled itself off the rail. It ran its fingers slowly along the side of the rail as though it was coming in her direction. Then it started floating away.

It had legs but it wasn't touching the ground as it walked. It moved its legs like a man would.

Then as it got some distance away, it turned back around in her direction again. She felt very sure that it was communicating the message to her that though it had left her unharmed; it was more than capable of hurting her if it chose to do so...

In Missouri too there's been sightings in a place that's called 'Zombie Road,' near the Mahoning River not too far from Ohio. A photo exists of what appears to show a group of Shadow People, standing along a tree line above a small lake.

It was taken in March 2005 by paranormal investigator Tom Halstead prior to his death. There are no reflections of their bodies in the water below.

It seems from accounts of those who have reportedly seen them, that 'The Watchers' are less sinister than the 'Shadow people.' While the Watchers do not seem to interfere with humans, unless those who have encountered them up close are no longer around to speak for what happened, it would seem that they prefer to be left alone. Shadow people however, according to medium Toiny Braden, "Are evil and full of malicious intent; those are the ones you never want to see. I've felt such intense levels of malice," she says, of the ones she's seen around her when assisting clients they've been terrorising.

***

In Kent, England, 1963, four young men said they saw a bright light descend from the sky as they took a walk through the woods one night. The glowing light then proceeded to follow them, stalking behind them, much to their confusion and horror.

One of the boys, John Flaxton, said the orb, hovering at a height just taller than them followed stealthily behind them. After some time, it moved behind some trees and they hoped it was leaving them, but instead as they watched, a horrifying black 'apparition' appeared, a jet black figure the height of a man but with no face. It looked as though it had wings, but they fled as fast as they could in sheer terror before it could get them.

One of his companions, Mervyn later described it as having webbed feet but no head.

The local Reverend, told the Press,

"Several youths have told me of strange things they've seen. All of them were very frightened and they've definitely seen 'something.'

***

Located northeast of Colorado Springs lies The Black Forest; a heavily wooded area amidst which is a home on a five acre plot that in the late 1990's had everyone, from the local Sheriffs, to Hopi shaman and even a Congressman believing that something sinisterly supernatural was there.

Steve and Beth Lee moved in to the home with their two sons. Strange things soon started happening. Numerous dark shadows and orbs of light would appear. There was often a strange chemical smell, and each of the family members would suffer regularly from burning eyes and throats.

In an effort to try to understand what was going on, thinking it must be people doing it, Mr Lee installed a high-tech security system to try to capture them. As soon as he'd installed it, the motion sensors would go off many times during the day and night, causing the alarms to ring out; and yet each time they could find no persons on their property.

Police responding to their numerous calls could find no sign of any intruders.

The children talked of seeing 'Shadow people.'

Startlingly, when the Lees replayed their security films they would see unexplained floating orbs, outlines of human forms, and even images of faces.

A local Hopi shaman came, and on investigation claimed that the property was located on a vortex that opened up to another dimension, allowing beings from that dimension to enter ours. Psychic detectives and paranormal investigators arrived to carry out their own investigations, all of whom appeared to capture the same troubling images, including translucent faces and dark human-like forms.

It seemed that no matter what different photographic tools were used; the images always appeared, ruling out any kind of trickery or malfunction of equipment.

In a bizarre twist to the story however, Mr Lee claimed that the phenomenon captured at his forest home was in fact not paranormal, but was the culmination of him being targeted by "Agencies of the US Government," harassing him using electromagnetic technologies.

Mr Lees felt this was because, in his belief, their home was close to a Government facility where 'mind control,' and other such experiments were being secretly carried out, heavily guarded from the outside by a military presence.

It wasn't only Shadow people that he was claiming to see.

"Outside I saw men in snow-camouflage. I got my rifle and started walking toward them."

They shouted a warning to him.

"I got within a few feet of them and they disappeared; just vanished. There were no tracks."

Another time, something even more bizarre occurred. Accompanied by friends, they all watched through infra-red binoculars as a team of men disappeared into a neighbour's doghouse!

He claimed there were at least a dozen of them, and putting down their binoculars they ran toward the men shouting out at them, yet the men appeared not to hear them.

He speculated afterward, "Did we actually see it or was it a hologram? If someone had told me this I would have said they're nuts, but the best thing to do in a War is to make them (the enemy) see things; after that they wouldn't put up a fight."

He feels that the images of soldiers, ghosts, and the shadow people his family and friends have seen are all being created by some kind of technological experimentation.

He hears disembodied voices threatening to kill him and his children. In his house; in his car.

"This isn't supernatural; someone is spending a lot of time and money trying to make it look like it is."

Mystery dizziness, nausea and fever have repeatedly hit them and those living nearby too. He claims hospital tests could find no answers.

Was he experiencing some kind of paranoid breakdown, was a demon trying to control him, or was it really even more sinister, as he suggests?

Another person, a man called Russell Elliot has also come forward to state that he's experienced strange events near his own home in the Black Forest, only a few minutes away from the Lees house. Mr Elliot too began capturing recordings of odd incidents, including strange lights around his home, to the extent of even posting YouTube videos of what he claims to be an alien being. His claims are as yet unsubstantiated.

Perhaps there really is something going on at the Lees property however. Mind Control through Holographic projections? Voice to skull microwaves making him hear voices?

Psychotronic weapons being developed to invisibly lock onto a victim and attack them subliminally? Bio-electromagnetic weapons; sending lasers, beams, or sound waves that work in stealth at the speed of light;

able to disarm, attack, and even capable of killing a person? Directed energy weapons?

Do they all really exist? Can they interfere with a person's state of mind; sending threats or self-destructive thoughts, or even causing much worse?

***

Others say the Archons are behind many of these types of manifestations of voices and apparitions.

'Deceivers,' who can mimic and take on forms in response to human belief systems.

Our interactions with shadow figures, spirits, extraterrestrials, ancient aliens, Djinn, humanoids and crypto's, are all said to involve these mysterious Archons.

The theory goes that Reptilians, Bigfoot, and all 'Paranormal' entities, are merely avatars that are manifested in the 'matrix' by a control system.

The suggestion is that whether alien, demonic, or Fey, they are all different forms of manifestation brought into being by a control system; a universal intelligence in control of us all.

Who; or what that 'pattern maker' is, and for what purpose it is operating the control system, no-one seems to be able to define or prove.

The belief is however, that it's malign and malevolent, and intent on creating fear and causing terror and destruction.

From the evidence of reported sightings and encounters, that would appear to be the case.

Ancient Gnostic texts say the Archons are inorganic beings that emerged in the world before Earth was formed and before humans came into creation. They envy the human form because they cannot take that form, and with this envy they come into our realm intent on causing havoc and harm, seeking to hurt us. They inhabit their own realm but manage to temporarily enter ours, taking these disparate forms to interfere with us.

The difficulty with this thesis is it's a 'catch all;' it implies that every strange sighting or 'paranormal' encounter exists only as some kind of holographic form, and that they are all one and the same in origin.

It's hard to imagine anyone who has encountered one of these many different and very sinister entities saying that they are the same 'indefinable' thing however. Witnesses would most certainly say that they were all too different and frighteningly real.

The ancient Mystery Schools of thought felt these intruders are strong enough to negatively influence us, have the ability to affect and play with our minds; they can disturb our sanity through devious means such as telepathy and suggestion.

As well as appearing in physical form as grotesque and frightening figures, in the form of Demons, Reptiles, or other disfigured and partly formed monsters, it's also thought they can attack invisibly to disorient us, confuse us, mislead and misdirect us. They can even send self-destructive notions into our minds. Telling a person to do something that will lead to injury and even fatality. Telling a person they want to cause injury or death to themselves.

Are they behind the demise or disappearance of so many?

Chapter Six: Spirit Helpers?

While it's believed 'spirits' or shadow people are usually malevolent, there are also accounts of mysterious 'spirit beings' helping stranded travellers.

On 1st June 1933, Frank Smythe was alone on Mount Everest. One by one, the rest of his team had turned back, too exhausted to continue, and the Expedition was left with just him to try to conquer the world's highest peak. He was up an altitude of over 26,000 ft; where the level of oxygen in the air is almost insufficient to keep a human being alive.

Smythe described being absolutely overwhelmed with exhaustion and a desperate hopelessness. He had only 1,000 feet left to the top, yet he was so weak. Standing for a few moments, he said, "on the very boundaries of life and death," he reached for a piece of cake in his pocket, to try to give him the last tiny ounce of strength he needed.

"I turned round with one half in my hand to offer it to my companion."

But he was completely alone. During that last desperate struggle against the elements, he had thought that he was being accompanied by someone. Though initially too embarrassed to talk openly about the experience for fear of ridicule, he did document it in his official reports.

He wrote: 'All the time that I was alone, I had a feeling that I was being accompanied. The feeling was so strong.'

Psychologist Peter Suedfeld and writer John Geiger, term this quite common experience in remote and risky environments 'a sensed presence experience'; a kind of subconscious coping mechanism in extreme environments.

They say the 'presences' themselves can vary in their appearance, identity, and their behaviour. They can include what appear to be angelic visitations, ghosts, or 'someone' seen or heard.

***

In Newsweek Magazine, December, 1993, a tragic story was covered about a young woman Chantel Lakey, and her fiancé Dale, who wanted to show her the view from a trail as they travelled along the Pacific highway 101. It was an area of dense forest with steep cliffs overhanging the coast.

They managed to climb to the top of the trail quite easily, but it was as they started to descend that they ran into trouble. Dale had seen an animal trail and thought it would be possible to descend it, however as they headed down they soon realised they had taken a very precarious path, as it virtually turned into a cliff of loose shale and rock.

It began to rain and the path became even more treacherous. It wasn't possible now to head back up and they had no option but to continue. Dale walked in front, turning around every few steps to help Chantel. As he turned around again, his foot slipped and without warning he fell to his death.

Chantel froze in shock and terror. Clutching onto the loose rock, she was unable to move.

She says "I had no particular faith in the being that others call God, but I think desperation draws out of us deep feelings we never knew we had."

She cried out to God, and describes that all of a sudden "it was as though the gateway between Heaven and Earth had opened up, and I saw Angels all around me, like a wall of protection, holding me, closing in around me."

She clung on and yet the next thing she remembers is looking up and seeing the cliff above her. "Somehow I'd managed to descend."

When the rescue team later went to retrieve her fiancé's body, they could not go down the cliff path that Chantel had descended, declaring the route impossible even with their experience and equipment.

***

Bill Burt, who's been a national reporter in the UK for decades, is someone for whom angel stories have figured heavily but purely incidentally in some of the News events he's gone to cover.

Mr Burt describes one odd incident when he went to cover a story about two schoolboys missing on a climbing trip in the mountains in Scotland. By the time he arrived the schoolboys had fortunately already been found; however, when he interviewed them they told him of how a woman in a white dress had approached them high up on the mountain and beckoned them to follow her. The lost boys didn't stop to think about it, they simply followed her and she led them straight toward the search party that was out looking for them.

When Burt later spoke to the leader of the search party, repeating the story the boys had told him, the leader stated that neither him nor anyone else in the search party had seen a woman with the boys.

Chapter Seven:
Mysterious Cases of Children Going Missing

A short news item in the July 2nd 1964 issue of the New York Times reported on the strange case of a three year old girl.

'A search party of 400 men found today a 3 year-old girl who'd been missing from her home for 17 hours. She was dishevelled, but otherwise in good condition.'

The child, Monica Mei, daughter of Armando Mei a well-known New York restaurant owner, had wandered away at some point from the family's summer home on Paradise Island in Orange County. Ernest Wippenger, a Middletown school crossing guard, had found the child huddled among rocks on top of Paradise Mountain, at an elevation of 1,606 feet.

Douglas Kinnear, Orange County Fire Coordinator, said the child had presumably walked across a footbridge connecting the 14 acre Nevesink River Island to the mainland, and then scaled the mountain.

The party of volunteers searching the thickly wooded area had included Police, Firemen and bloodhounds to try to pick up her scent. They had searched through the night and had already passed through the area where she was eventually found alive.

The 1,606 ft Mt Paradise is located in the most remote section of the A.T. in New Jersey. It has to be asked how the child managed to climb the mountain, and why she had done so, as well as why the trackers were unable to find her scent from the area she went missing?

A similar but much more tragic incident occurred back in the winter of 1890, when Ottie Powell was four years old. He was at school in rural Amherst County, Virginia, when his school mistress asked the children to go out to the woods around the school house to collect some timber for the classroom stove.

As all the children returned back indoors it was soon realised that Ottie was not among them. Immediately the school mistress sent the other children to their homes nearby to collect their parents and begin a search for the missing boy. The school was within the George Washington National Forest, on the Appalachian Trail, by Bluff Mountain, and surrounded by thick woodland.

Hundreds of neighbours and friends began a desperate search, spreading out in circles from the school, but they could find no trace of Ottie. Snow started falling heavily and an ice storm started, and it became impossible to continue searching the mountain for him. By evening, they had to stop.

Over the next few days and weeks, hundreds of volunteers continued searching the area, but to no avail.

Seven months later, on April 3, 1892, seven miles away on the top of the mountain, hunters heard their dog barking, and followed its trail up a steep path that led to the top of the mountain. There they found the remains of the little boy.

Everyone in the area, and those reading the newspaper accounts nationally, were baffled as to how and why the young boy had managed to climb his way over rocks, through hedges, and up cliffs to this lofty peak at the altitude of 3,350 feet, barefoot.

Local garden blogger Jeanne Grunert wrote recently of her hike up the mountain, commenting that it felt like walking up flights of stairs for two hours without stopping. On reaching the top she noticed the memorial there to the child. She says, 'his body was found on this spot – How had a four year old child wandered up a mountain that we had found so difficult to climb?'

***

The May 27, 1922 edition of the New York Times covered the bizarre story of a young girl in a small Brittany village who went missing.

"A baffling mystery is exciting the inhabitants of the small Brittany village of Goas Al Ludu, in the Brest district, (France). Early in April a little girl, Pauline Picard, disappeared from her parent's farm, all searches proving fruitless. However, as her parents had virtually given up all hope of ever finding their daughter, it was reported from the far away town of Cherbourg, that a small girl had been found there, whose age and appearance corresponded very similarly to that of the missing Pauline.

Her parents hurried to Cherbourg and said with much relief that the child was theirs. Strangely, however, it was reported that the child did not seem to recognise her parents and remained mute when addressed in the Breton dialect she had grown up speaking.

Taken home, the child was recognised by neighbours, and as such the terrible incident was concluded as reaching a happy ending.

However, the newspaper continues the story, 'Yesterday a startling discovery was made which makes the whole affair more mysterious than ever.'

A farmer crossing a field about a mile away discovered the horribly mutilated body of a small girl, entirely naked and decapitated. Close by, carefully folded, lay her clothes. The farmer returned with the Police and several villagers, including the Picard's, who instantly recognised the clothes as those worn by Pauline the day she disappeared. The body could not be identified. If the body was that of Pauline, who was the child the parents were already claiming was Pauline?

So thorough was the search carried out at the time of the little girl's disappearance, says the newspaper, that the body would have been discovered had it been lying all along where it was found. 'Everything now points to the theory that it was placed there, together with the neatly folded clothes,' it states.

The prolific Fortean writer of the time, Charles Fort wrote about the case too. 'It could not long have been lying, so conspicuous, but unseen. The body placed in a conspicuous position, as if planning to have it found? It seems that the clothes, also conspicuous, had not been lying there for several weeks, subject to the disturbing effects of rains and wind. They were "neatly folded."

***

The UK Spectator Magazine issue of May 3rd 1902, detailed what they called 'a strange story,' regarding a young boy William Llewellyn, 'who three weeks ago unaccountably disappeared in the street of a Welsh town, and whose body was discovered on the summit of a Glamorganshire hill on Saturday last.'

It is reported that the boy disappeared from a shop he was in with his mother.

'Every possible effort was made to find him, but it was not until more than a fortnight had passed that his dead body was found,' unintentionally by fox hounds.

The coroner said there was no evidence of a crime.

The magazine asks, trying to understand the unusual circumstances, 'Is there any plausible theory?'

It writes; 'Here are the facts. All hills, roads, fields were thoroughly examined. The child's boots are stated not to have been dirty. The child was five; the spot where he was found is some 1,850 feet. His boots were *not dirty*. His body was found ten miles away from where he was last seen. If he walked at all, he probably walked more miles. Could a child of that age do that?'

'Is it not remarkable that the body was found on the summit of the highest, most inaccessible hill in the area? Why? The instinct of a person lost is to go down, not up. He knows that the homes are in the valleys, not on summits. It is one of the strangest things that has come to light for some years.'

'Do we solve it by saying it was just an instance of 'superhuman' endurance, and total failure in a power of reasoning?' they ask.

His coat was placed beside him. He had no injuries apart from abrasions to his hands. It was ruled that he had been dead for a number of days, but not as long as the amount of time he had been missing for.

The newspaper also makes mention of the possibility that someone took him there to the highest spot, placing him there to die. It's interesting perhaps to recollect the Inca's tradition of ritual sacrifices on the summits of mountains. The mummified bodies of three children were found on the top of the Volcan Llullaillaco Mountain in the Andes, in 1999.

It was found upon DNA analysis of their preserved hair, that they were heavily drugged with maze alcohol and cocoa in the months prior to their sacrifice; it's presumed in order to make them more compliant and calm when it came to the time for them to be sacrificed.

Dr Andrew Wilson at the University of Bedfordshire, who carried out the analysis, calls it 'chilling.'

In the area where the mummies were found, there are thought to exist up to fifty sacrifice sites alone.

***

In October 1917, a young boy from Hampden went missing from his backyard near a place dubbed, 'The Forest of the Dead.'

Native Americans believed it was a cursed place of evil spirits, and it seems that the area has gained an unsettling reputation for mysterious disappearances.

Horror writer Joseph Rubas spent some time researching the history of this area of the Berkshire Mountains, in New England.

According to Rubas, when the boy disappeared the local Army Commander volunteered three hundred of his men to search for him. They found no tracks of where the boy had gone; no sign of him.

Eventually, a sheriff's deputy discovered the young boy, miles from his home asleep in a thicket.

The writer claims that from his research, during the search several of the soldiers searching for the boy themselves disappeared in the mountain, never to be seen again. The strange incident raises questions not only of how the young boy had traveller so far on his own, but also of the soldiers' inexplicable disappearances.

***

In the Pennsylvanian Allegheny Mountains two young boys went missing back in 1856. Nearly two hundred people rapidly began searching for them through the dense hill tops and ravines. They could find no trace of the boys, but for ten days they wouldn't give up. Everyone got involved, closing their businesses and stopping work to help in the search, knowing the unforgiving wildness of the area they were lost in.

Many stayed out at night, lighting fires on various spots across the mountain, hoping to draw the children toward one of them. While many searchers took a new route on the mountain each day, others would travel back over the ground they had already covered, guessing that the children could have come back to that part of the mountain in their wandering.

As the days went by without a trace of them, speculation and rumour began amongst the community; they were killed by a wild beast, they'd been kidnapped, their parents had murdered them.

Then, a farmer named Jacob Dibert who lived a few miles away began to have recurring nightmares. Several nights in a row, he dreamt that he was with the search party when he became separated from them, and discovered the boys.

Unfamiliar with the forest area himself, though he thought himself crazy, he described to his wife the detailed scene in his dreams and asked her if she knew of an area like it in the mountains. She replied that there was such an area.

Upon telling his brother-in-law about the dream too, his brother-in-law thought it impossible; for the boys to have got to the location in Jacob's dreams, they would have to have gone approximately six miles from their home and crossed a wide fast running creek, and climbed high. The two boys, George and Joseph Cox were only aged five and seven; he thought it impossible.

However, perplexed by such unaccustomed and disturbing nightmares, Jacob felt he had to investigate, and so his brother-in-law led him to the area he described. They reached a hollow, saw a deer he had described dead just like in his dreams, crossed over the creek and hiked up a steep ravine on the opposite side, where they saw the shoe of one of the boys he had also described from his nightmares. Shortly after, they found the boys bodies in the exact position he had described.

Spookily accurate, his nightmares had told him where to find the children, though tragically they had died of exposure by then.

Several aspects of this case are disturbing; not only the fact that the man seemingly had cognitive dreams telling him how to find them, but also that the boys had ended up where they did.

What on earth had made them cross a creek and climb upwards into the mountains, knowing they were going far from home?

Chapter Eight:
Snatched by Something Under the Ground?

Ufologist Scott Corrales refers to the densely forested National Forest in Puerto Rico as somewhere "that has a dark side which involves human disappearances."

A huge number of people have vanished from El Yunque forest, without any explanation for their disappearances. Park authorities tend to explain that they are caused simply by natural geography, such as sinkholes and yet, as the investigator points out, many of the disappearances have happened in parts of the forests where these natural landscapes features are not part of the terrain, and are indeed far from the site of the existence of these dangerous sinkholes or the possibility of quicksand.

He quotes as an example a report by native investigator Hermes Rivera, who published details of an incident in the late 1970's which told the tragic story of a group of children who had all disappeared inside the forest on a school trip there. The police even turned to a psychic, whose statement about their fate was chilling. He said they were no longer in this physical dimension.

The children were never found. The teacher in charge of the group, unable to cope with the sadness and feeling responsible for them, ended up killing himself because they had never been found.

Even armed soldiers, he discovered, have seemingly disappeared. In March 1976, two Marines stationed at a nearby naval base vanished inside the national park.

The area itself is rife with speculation as many locals report seeing strange lights coming from the mountain of El Yunque; reports of UFO sightings, alien craft and even sightings of humanoid beings suddenly appearing on the trails in front of hikers. Others say there is unusual military activity going on in the area.

American Navy Officer Jorge Martin, in the journal UFO Evidence reports that in 1993 during a trip to the mountain, without being aware of it, two visitors, N. Berríos and J.Ruiz, took a number of photographs that when looked at later, appeared to show a humanoid-like being standing near a rock close by.

When questioned about what he believed it was, J. Ruiz said in his opinion, "That's not from here; and people have for so long been saying that strange things are happening; I'd say that *they're* here; we're not alone. That is a fact."

The editor relates another case involving multiple witnesses. 'It was in February 1991, about 3am, just next to the Forestry Service hut. Police Officer Torres had been with his wife and a group of friends when in astonishment they saw close-by, two extraordinarily odd 'beings' walking down the road.

Jose Martin makes the statement that there are bases inside the mountains in which he and many other navy personnel have seen UFO's enter somehow, through the mountain itself. He told researcher Timothy Good of his claim that a large secret subterranean alien base was there, going deep under the sea, and built by an alien race.

"It is a base that appears to be extraterrestrial. We have been watching the situation for years - and we know that they are down there," he says.

***

'Alien-hunters,' like John Rhodes, believe there are many of these underground bases hidden in Mountains in the States and in other countries including England, and that a greatly advanced race who come from the 'Draco Star System,' want to take over the human race; Others say they already have, with mind control.

There have been thousands of reports over the years of ordinary people claiming to have been abducted by Reptilian beings, and 'abduction investigator' John Carpenter states he has worked with over one hundred 'victims.'

He says these entities are reported as looking virtually the same by everyone he talks to; as standing at least seven feet tall, with lizard scales all over their bodies. Their faces, he says, are described as a cross between that of a human and a snake. Their eyes are almond shaped, with vertical slits, and their mouths have no lips."

They are said to be highly evolved super-intelligent creatures, extremely strong, with muscular bodies and powerful arms. Perhaps most disturbingly it's said that they can shape-shift and impose holograms onto their faces to give them a human appearance. Contactees have said that they drain the victim of all energy so that they are helpless to resist.

***

In the 1940's, a peculiar story emerged. A man called Richard Shaver began to tell an extraordinary if not completely outlandish tale, starting with how during his job at a factory, he began to hear other people's thoughts. As if that wasn't enough, what he said next was mind-blowing.

He claimed that the "voices" he heard were coming from below the ground, where warring alien species were battling each other. These entities he called 'The Dero' and 'The Tero' races; which he claimed, with their advanced technology were capable of transmitting electronically-enhanced telepathic brain waves.

He said he'd been taken to the underground place, led there by a holographic image of a being, through a hidden entrance. The 'Teros' were friendly, but he said the enemy 'Deros' were planting thoughts in his head to make him sound ridiculous, so that no-one would believe what he said about the existence of these underground bases and to prevent the public from taking him seriously, because they feared their bases were soon going to become public knowledge.

According to Shaver, the 'Deros' kidnapped people from above ground by the hundreds and took them below, to use them for meat.

He said this species were capable of causing accidents, disasters and illnesses to people, and that they already exerted incredible power over the unsuspecting general public, who did not know they were being systematically mind-controlled remotely.

The editor of the magazine Amazing Stories, who covered his story, claimed that while in the presence of Shaver he heard several different voices emanate from Shaver as he talked aloud, and that chillingly, the voices were discussing the murder of a woman in one of the underground bases.

It all sounded like a mix of paranoia and a bad science fiction plot, and of course many declared him a loony; however, hundreds of subsequently people wrote in to the magazine in response to the details

Shaver gave, claiming that they too had had experiences with an underground world. Were they all insane?

***

In the early '60's, the story of Thomas Castello came out. He alleged that he worked as a security officer at a top secret underground facility in New Mexico. His job was to ensure the security of surveillance equipment there; but he soon found himself taking secret photos of the base, appalled at the activities going on there.

Located several miles underground, experiments were being carried out on human abductees by lizard-like reptilian creatures, he said, who controlled their victims using telepathy and mind manipulation techniques.

Castello said he had seen horrifying genetic monsters in the Laboratories, and that any humans who did not survive the experiments were fed to these Reptilians.

He also claimed that the Native Americans in the area understood that the base existed and spoke of the "underground 'life-forms', such as Bigfoot, that were spotted outside near the base.

Fearing for his life, he went on the run and disappeared; meanwhile his family he left behind, also mysteriously 'disappeared.'

***

Another character, a man by the name of Billie Woodard, once in the US Air Force, claimed that as a young boy he was abducted while walking home one day and taken through a vortex opening down into the earth.

The beings down there used Vortexes that they created, to act as exit points from their Hollow Earth bases, he said, enabling themselves and creatures such as the Sasquatch to come through.

He's been speaking out about his experiences for years, and claims that though the Government try to silence him, he is 'protected,' and impossible to harm. Many proponents believe his thesis and stories.

***

Writer K. Kizziar claims to have been abducted by Reptilians inhabiting an underground base in the Superstition Mountains of Arizona.

According to Kizziar, these beings dressed in dark robes use humans as their slaves inside the base as well as above ground; mind controlled to do their bidding. They kidnap their victims and take them below to their bases.

While these stories sound impossible to believe, it's interesting to note that many interested in the phenomenon of disappearing people have identified similarities between the alleged existence of maps showing the location of these underground bases and areas where there have also been a high proportion of people vanishing too.

***

Another outlandish story of activities underground comes this time from researcher Radu Cinamar, who broke the news of a startling discovery in the Bucegi Mountains of Romania.

The Bucegi Mountains are reported to be extremely mysterious. Some have been prompted by a number of cases of missing persons to claim that the area of the stunningly beautiful Carpathians have an altogether other-worldly character to them.

People mysteriously disappear, either never to re-appear again or appear in some other place, unable to tell what happened to them. Elders there tell of people disappearing in 'fogs' or being 'thrown' into other places from where they were hiking, done so by an 'invisible force.'

Other hikers tell of a euphoric feeling that comes over them, of an almost hypnotised sensation, of not feeling any tiredness or exertion on climbing the Mountain, reminiscent of some of the accounts from Zimbabwe's Inyangani Mountain. Electronic devices often stop working.

Geologist Dimitri Stanica says he has felt 'something special' in the area in terms of its geo-magnetic energy properties, and indeed there are stories of miracle healings occurring there. Once a year a magical 'shadow pyramid' appears around a Sphinx shaped stone at the summit.

In 2003, it was claimed by the researcher Cinamar that US military satellites had discovered two artificial energy blocks in the Mountains. The satellites seemed to show the first one was blocking access to a tunnel, while the second was a dome shape inside the middle of the mountain.

It was said to closely match a similar energy structure discovered in Iraq and which conspirators such as academic researcher Dr Michael Salla claim was the real reason for the Iraq War; in order to enable the US to enter this structure and seize the discoveries of advanced technology inside.

The 'find' was initially reported on Antenna 1, the local television channel; after which on YouTube is a snippet of the news presenter receiving an anonymous telephone death threat and being told to maintain silence over the subject.

Opponents have claimed Antenna 1 is a sensationalist TV channel not to be taken seriously.

There were claims of the US & Romanian Governments rushing to quash the information, and interference from the Illuminati, all determined not to enable the controversial and highly secretive contents from being discovered by the world. It would change our current belief systems and they did not want that to happen.

Cinamar and Peter Moon wrote of the discovery and what was found inside the mountain; three US Special Forces military, on touching the energy barrier were reported to have died instantly, but using technology they somehow broke through the barrier.

Inside, through a tunnel that appeared mined, they came to a huge gallery that seemed of a synthetic nature yet was the colour of oil. Green and blue lights glowed, reflecting the energy shields inside.

It was here that they allegedly found a holographic Hall of Records, left there by an advanced civilization and detailing the 'true' origins of man and civilisation, along with the most advanced technology ever found, including capability for time travel, and far beyond the current known physics concepts.

It was claimed that a race of Giants had left these secrets; their skeletons left behind as evidence.

There were also three mysterious tunnels leading into the Inner Earth.

If true, this would seem not the only anomaly of the mountain range. A Romanian Professor, Constantine Badger, also claimed to have entered a tunnel in the mountains of Ceahlau, also in Romania, and discovered underground chambers there, several miles deep.

He claims that he was contacted by an 'intelligence' that led him to the tunnels and inside was enabled to jump space and time, going through the tunnels at a speed ordinarily unachievable by foot.

The editor of *FaraSecrete* Romanian journal also relates a strange occurrence that allegedly happened prior to the underground Buecgi discoveries. In 1980, two siblings who were both highly experienced climbers were scaling the mountain. A quarter of a way from the summit, something caught the eye of one of them. He observed unusual archaic lettering carved in the stone of a narrow ledge. Beside it was a gold coloured item that appeared to be a chain. As the man went toward it and touched it, he apparently vanished.

His brother climbed up to the ledge and could see no sign of his brother there. At first the police refused to believe his account, yet he showed several witnesses the object that looked to be embedded in the stone.

The editor claims that after that incident, the area was permanently closed for access and Government investigators began to study the unusual rock-face and its alleged powers.

Interestingly, long before the Bucegi tunnels discovery, Professor Ernst Muldashev wrote of the discovery of caves on Mount Kailash in Tibet where soldiers attempting to enter them were overpowered by a strange and powerful force that caused them extreme nausea and severe head pain, some even having heart attacks and dying.

Are there geometric anomolies which can cause the disappearance of people, or is there something ancient and far more powerful underneath the ground?

Is time travel technology somehow involved?

***

Olav Phillips is founder of the *Anomalies Network*, a database resource which he claims has more than 140,000 reported sightings of paranormal anomalies, including of the UFO type.

In a recent article, he wrote of his opinion in regard to the mysterious disappearances of people in remote forest and mountain regions, referring to them as possibly being part of 'Batch Consignments,' taken as slaves to other planets.

A fairly large workforce would be needed, he reasoned, the work would be tough, and the death rate high due to the danger of the work and the hostile environment. So, you would need a constant supply of new people being kidnapped to provide the labour force.

'Where do you get large numbers of people over a long term?' he asks. 'Every year hundreds of people go missing under mysterious circumstances. There are disappearances which actually defy conventional logic.'

His implication is that the people who do disappear mysteriously without trace in the forests and mountains are being taken.

While it is a possibility, and while some think the number of people disappearing in wilderness areas is far higher than has been recorded, one does have to disagree that the number is anywhere near high enough to provide a significant workforce, and while young children go missing in forests, so too do the elderly, and these would not be of great use as a hard-labour workforce.

Many more people go missing in urban areas though, and as he points out, in war-torn and highly unstable regions hundreds if not thousands will simply disappear, so perhaps it could be said that the reality of these examples do lend credence to the 'batch consignments' theory being a distinct possibility.

One perhaps surprising proponent of the belief in a base on Mars comes in the form of Laura Eisenhower, the great-granddaughter of former US President Dwight Eisenhower. Not long ago she went public with an extraordinary claim.

Speaking on many radio shows, Laura Eisenhower claimed she had been lured into a pact to Teleport to Mars by her then lover, who she later believed had deliberately targeted her. Eisenhower described that after meeting the man who she formed a relationship with he gradually told her that he was attached to a secret Mars colony project.

The reason for the secret Mars colony he told her, was apparently to provide a survival civilization for the human race, should the earth be destroyed by something such as HAARP, a giant magnetic pulse strike, or nuclear or bio weapons.

A situation which really occurred? It is indeed possible, although perhaps not so convincing is her further statement; 'For the Mars colony to have control, they wanted the Magdalene (blood).' She goes on to say that through the many psychic readings she has had, it has been confirmed to her that she has this bloodline.

While being abducted to be taken to other planets may or may not be happening, there are some compelling testimonies available on the web from those who believe the batch consignment theory applies to bases underground, below the rural wilderness areas.

Chapter Nine:
Military Involvement in Disappearances?

Mary Joyce is an avid researcher of underground bases and their alien connection, with particular interest in trying to discover new activity and current construction going on related to military involvement. Joyce says she's heard many witness reports about secret military activity, particularly in the Smoky Mountains National Park.

In early 2013, what she calls 'a credible ex-military witness' spoke with her about the activity. He spoke of sightings of 'Rangers' carrying machine guns, he spoke of loud boom sounds in the area. He said there were many others who've seen unusual things in the Park, including actual employees of the Park but claimed that they are afraid to talk about those things.

She spoke to a lady called Jane Spottedbird about her trip in 2013 to a landmark off the Blue Ridge Parkway in North Carolina. When she discovered the road leading to it was closed, she left her car and decided to walk up. What struck her as she walked along was that she couldn't hear the sounds of any birds nearby. It was eerily quiet.

What she did begin to hear however, were deep and resonating booms.

"They reminded me of the type of equipment that's used to pound pylons into the ground. I went to the overhang to look and see where some construction was maybe going on. The boom sound continued all the time I was there, and at one point was continuous. By then, it was hard for me to think clearly. Since then, I've discovered that others who've got too close to a secret facility have been caused the same distress. Perhaps some kind of electro-magnetic 'pulse' is being used?" she speculates.

***

Controversial scholar Alex Putney makes the claim that those who point the finger of blame at Bigfoot or other entities for causing the mysterious disappearances of people in forests and woodlands, are doing so as disinformation artists on behalf of the CIA; to divert attention from and to cover up these CIA/military led abductions, to prevent people from discovering the existence of military-industrial installations secretly running below the ground, full of people.

He goes further; "The existence of dozens of these secret underground military bases were clearly exposed, he says, by surviving Nazi commander Otto Skorzeny, lifelong comrade of Hitler. One such base was identified as a breeding ground for the Nazi elite below Glacier National Park."

Researcher and futurist Michael Lindemann has spoken of what he calls the new 'Noah's Ark,' underground, to describe what he believes the US government has in effect been building. 'Underground bases, all over the world; huge bases that would shock you; able to support tens of thousands; to 'save' an elite, the 'cream,' who will survive the apocalypse.'

A Dr Steven Greer claims he has collected up to two hundred top-secret military, intelligence and corporate witness testimonies to secret projects that detail a covert alien/government agenda.

Researcher Miles Johnston of *The Bases Project* has filmed hours of testimony from a man named Barry King, who claims to have been a security member at one of the secret underground Bases in England, where he says the purpose is Mind Control and other experimentation on human abductees. He claims there are bases at Peasemore, Berkshire, and Greenham Common, also Berkshire, approximately fifty miles from London.

He states that abducted children and adults were used for both mind control and genetic testing. The 'aliens' were not doing this he says; the people running the bases *created* these aliens and programmed them. They are generated life-forms he says. These aliens were then used to abduct people, he alleges.

King first started making these claims in the '90's and still to this day maintains it is not fantasy. However more commonly now he claims that it's not the aliens who are doing the abductions but rather 'MILAB's;' human 'black ops' snatching people and convincing them they have been abducted by aliens with the use of generated and holographic images.

Recently in the most outlandish turn of events, self-titled British 'Super Soldiers' going by the names of James Casbolt and Max Speirs have claimed that they were both taken into bases as children and held there for years while they were 'programmed' by mind control techniques. They claim it was not Alien-led, but instead led by terrestrial 'black ops' projects and done with explicit complicity of the Military, Government, and elite Secret Societies, both in the US and UK. Indeed their claims go very deep in terms of who was really involved.

Occult ritual is used and much of it involves the harnessing of ancient demonic power by the 'power elite' according to 'whistleblower' Casbolt.

Some of his claims include that through the use of advanced alien technology, these trained abductees are able to 'remote view' victims. Occult symbolism is used for added power. Called 'Project Mannequin' he claimed he and other child abductees were 'weaponized' to remotely cause heart attacks or death to 'targets.'

Their stories make for fascinating listening, but are they just conspiracy theories and delusional fantasy? Science-fiction? Or could any of it really be true?

***

Some involved in theorising what lies behind the cause of human disappearances believe it's possible that advanced technology is now being utilized in the snatching of people; technology honed by the skills of advanced scientific experimentation that has been furthered beyond anything we could imagine, making the abductions sleek, speedy, invisible, and impossible to stop.

Invisible drones capable of tracking and snatching someone, their presence undetectable through the use of cloaking technology, rendering them completely invisible.

A substantive amount of speculation has been made in terms of these scientific developments, and many believe it has been developed based on Tesla technology seized from him before his death.

Believers in this capability point to the number of patents on record that involve advanced 'weapons' systems developed for controlling people by the use of vibration, infrasound waves, nano and plasma technology.

Futurist Alfred Webre, a Yale educated attorney who has taught at Yale and worked at the Stanford Research Institute now runs the Exopolitics website and Radio Show.

He claims that DARPA (Defence Advanced Research Projects Agency) and the CIA are in possession of secret time travel technology, and says that thousands of innocent people have been used by them in their experiments, resulting in their deaths or disappearances.

He says they have had Tesla-based quantum access time travel technology for nearly fifty years and it has been 'weaponized' for uses such as control over humans, surveillance, and "psychotronics."

Physicist Dr Elizabeth Rauscher once studied the effects of electro-magnetic weapons on people.

"Images can be impressed onto the mind without visuals," she revealed as far back as the early 1980's.

In other words, people can be made to see things that are not really there.

Silent Sound waves sent by distance at very low frequency can induce fear, panic, or suicidal thoughts. Psychotronic weapons can allegedly cause illness or even death at a distance.

Silent and invisible tools of covert attack. Neuro-weapons, Mind-control weapons, Directed energy weapons. Electromagnetic weapons. Smaller, personalised versions of HAARP and Chemtrails. All of these allegedly able to negatively influence and attack a target from a distance.

Invisible, operating in stealth, disabling or killing, and leaving no trace.

"They operate at the speed of light," says Harlan Girard of the Institute of Science in Society, London.

Are there invisible drones capable of lifting a person and abducting them?

Can directed energy weapons simply vaporise someone?

It has to be said that this particular field of study is full of disinformation, conspiracy theories, hoaxes, and opposing beliefs; everything seemingly impossible to validate completely, yet all entirely possible, and there is evidence of it.

Chapter Ten:
The Work of Satanists?

The Jamison family; husband, wife and their six year old daughter headed out to the Latimer Mountains of Oklahoma looking for a new home to move to, on October 8th 2009.

After their family realised they had not returned an enormous search party was organised with hundreds of volunteers, troopers from the Oklahoma Highway Patrol and agents from the FBI.

The searchers combed the area on foot, on ATV's and on horses but they found nothing; even with the sixteen teams of tracking dogs that had been used.

Then a few days later their truck was discovered by hunters. It was locked and inside it the family's dog was close to death. Investigators discovered the family's cell phones and a very large amount of cash. There were no tracks however to lead them to where the family could have gone.

The 31-year-old Sheriff, a former U.S. Army Ranger, said his mind was consumed by questions and theories.

"Throughout this whole process I've found myself going back and forth as to what might have happened," Israel Beauchamp said. "I'm at my wit's end. I asked for all the help I could get. FBI agents; private investigators who contacted me."

If it had been straight forward foul play, surely the perpetrators would have stolen the money; there was over $30,000 in cash in the vehicle.

A man who lived a quarter mile from where the pickup was found was the last known person to see them. He too was questioned. He saw no-one else in the vicinity.

Many have wondered were they drug users? Was it a drug deal gone bad? Others have wondered were they in the process of turning state's evidence against drug dealers?

Was it simply a criminal case, or was something much deeper to this?

As people in the area speculated and tried to understand what had happened to the family, an edition of *The Oklahoman* headlined the story. The mother of Sherilyn Jamison was telling the Newspaper that her daughter "was on a cult's hit list."

According to Oklahoma's *Red Dirt News*, husband Bobby had allegedly been reading a "Satanic Bible" and had asked a Church Minister how he could obtain "special bullets" that would enable him to kill the demons that were terrorizing the family.

Security camera footage recorded at their home, installed by the family due to their concerns of the alleged spiritual attacks they were complaining of. It shows both adults walking around at times in a trance-like states and disorientation prior to their departure.

Approximately a month before the disappearance of the family, local Pastor Carol Daniels was found horrifically murdered in her Church nearby. The local D.A. Mr Burns said of the crime scene that it was "the most horrific he'd ever seen," but he wouldn't go into details as to why. Her mutilated body though was found behind the Church Altar in a crucifix pose, obviously suggesting a link to Satanic ritual.

Then in November 2013 bodies of two adults and a child were found by a deer hunter about four miles from their truck. It was believed to be the skeletal remnants of the family.

This was odd because the Jamison father could not walk more than a few metres without experiencing severe pain, and Cherylin had chronic pain in her neck and shoulder. Both were on disability, yet they were found on the opposite side of the low mountain area where they'd left their truck.

Their 'abduction' has echoes of eerily similar unexplained missing person's cases that have been documented over the last couple of centuries; the 'abduction' takes place in a remote wilderness area with dense or difficult terrain.

The 'abductors' one assumes, must have had the ability to not only control and transport these people from their truck through rugged terrain; they also left no other vehicle tracks, nor footprints, nor scent.

While the Jamison's fate may simply be a case of human intervention, *Reddirt news* make a point of the synchronicity that both the area where their bodies were found, and the site of the Church where the pastor was murdered fall on the 'Occult line of tragedy;' on the 33rd parallel north.

Occultists see the number 33 as containing the highest of sacred power. Occult scholars and conspiracists claim that the Illuminati and the 'power elite' have staged murders on or near the 33rd parallel north throughout history.

In Occult belief, sacrificial rites enacted at the 33rd parallel have far more power than any other geographical locations. 33 is the satanic number of completion, and holds the power of transmutation.

According to expert Occultists and conspiracists alike, including the late occult researcher John Downard, it's the 'kill number;' and the murders carried out are for a ritual called the 'Killing of the Kings' where the life-force is believed to be passed from the victim at the point of death to those carrying out the ritual.

They point to the grand events of the Hiroshima atom bomb, the JFK assassination, and the bombing of Babylon in the Iraq War, as all being planned along this sacred line.

Curiously, there was a similar case in 2013 in Eufaula, the Jamison's home town. Thirty year old Native American Tommy Eastep vanished on his return journey after spending a July 4th weekend trip there visiting his family. His truck was found abandoned on September 29th, in a rural area north of Holdenville; his keys, credit card and driver's license locked inside.

According to his older brother Clint, talking on blog talk radio, it was a good four miles off the main highway on a county road more like a cattle road. He says, "It was parked as deep as you could go. It probably stopped because there was overhanging tree and the truck couldn't go any further. There's a lake nearby, lots of small ponds around, and a large heavily-wooded area to the south and west.

Clint says, "He was a family man. He had kids. He wasn't in any type of turmoil, you know, that he walked off without his license, his debit card, his keys, his vehicle, and his belongings. He did not walk away."

Despite tracker dogs searching throughout the area his truck was found in, no trace of him has been found still. There is no suggestion here of occult intervention, although again his abandoned vehicle was found at a cross roads on the same symbolic degree of latitude.

Returning to the Jamison family, some sources including Discovery TV state that the tracker dogs *did* trace their scent, to a water tank near where their vehicle was found. This was an indication that their bodies had likely been placed inside the water tank, but when it was emptied they were not found.

Were they killed in the water? They were found almost three miles away with no tracks and both were partially disabled and unlikley to have walked that far voluntarily. Despite the search radius being extensive, they were not found during all the searches. Where had they been? Were they being kept somewhere? Were they kept in the water tower?

This theory of the Jamisons deaths perhaps ties-in with the ritual motive when looked at other similar cases. The most comprehensive investigator into remote disappearances, David Paulides of the Missing 411 series of books, which lists hundreds of inexplicable disappearances, has pointed out that many of the cases he's covered involve bodies being found in or near water. Then there's also the unusually large number of college males disovered dead in water across many US States, as documented by journalist Kristy Piehl, initially dubbed 'The Smiley Face Killers.'

Since the mid '90's, scores of college age men have been vanishing without trace to be found weeks or months laster in rivers or creeks in areas search parties have thoroughly searched several times before.

Often it looks as though their bodies were placed there to be found. Piehl first brought these strange disappearances and deaths to light when investigating one of the deaths of the missing men and after being contacted by two retired police detectives, Kevin Gannon and Anthony Duarte who'd discovered many more similar inexplicable deaths.

Listing just a couple of the cases here, Chris Jenkins was found four months after he disappeared one night in 2003. His death was first deemed an accidental fall into the river and subsequent drowning, even though he was on the college Swim Team at Minnesota University. His body was found encased in ice with his hands folded over his chest in a manner that was wholly inconsistent with drowning.

Jared Dion was discovered in a Wisconsin River in 2004, five days after he'd disappeared. The coroner ruled he had not been dead any longer than 72 hours; that left 2 days unaccounted for, which implied that he had been kept somewhere and placed in the water later.

Todd Geib was last seen in June 2005. When he was discovered in a remote bed of water his death was ruled as drowning, however when a new autopsy was carried out he was discovered to have been dead for only 2-5 days despite being missing for more than 3 weeks. Again, he had been somewhere else, alive, for approximately 2 weeks prior to his death. Where he was found had been thoroughly searched at least 3 times.

Chillingly Piehl has counted over 100 similar cases; all young men, all actively fit and often even on the Swim Team. Some will say they were drunk and fell in the water, but for anyone looking into the cases, it's hard to believe this is what really happened.

Professor Gilbertson at St Cloud University, talking about one of the cases, has stated that the victim's blood was completely drained from his body prior to him being found.

The two detectives think it's got to be more than one killer. Bodies have been found in different States at the same time.

Gannon says of one victim, "He was stalked, adbucted, held somewhere for an extended time, murdered and disposed of."

It's been reported that sometimes it looks like the victim's clothes have been removed and put back on them, their I.D.'s always left on them but any religious jewellery they were wearing has been taken.

Jerry Snyder, former DEA and now founder of not-for-profit group Find Me, has studied more than 200 cases across the Country.

"We think we've only scratched the surface; that's what's really scary to me," he says.

Is it a gang of serial killers? A syndicate of some kind? Why is religious jewellery taken and their bodies often posed in the water?

There are several theories being put forward by many interested in the cases, one of which points to the possibility of their deaths being ritual sacrifices, again thought to be based on the ancient alchemy ritual of 'Killing of the Kings,' where the victim's life-force energy is said to be passed to the occult murder(s) at the moment of death, supposedly giving them greater power.

In alchemy ritual a solid substance is said to be 'disolved' in water in a 'slow and silent operation.'

Could this really be what is happening? Is some kind of elite group conducting ancient rituals to further enhance their desire for power?

In La Crosse, a former Medical examiner has taken to unorthodox means in order to try to find out the truth. Now retired, Neil Sanders believes there is much more to these deaths than accidental drownings. So much so that he made the documentary 'The Hidden Truth,' enlisting film producer Scott Markus who had worked on the Dark Knight and other Hollywood blockbusters. Everyone worked for free on the film, believing it to be an important cause and a film that needed to be made. Sanders brought in a team of paranormal investigators to assist in creating the documentary; having seen the evidence of the drowning cases and finding no answers there he prepared to consider less conventional alternatives in order to try to solve the mystery.

"All angles had previously been investigated when looking into these cases; except for one, and that's the paranormal," he tells journalist Ken Luchterhand. "Paranormal just means other than normal." However, he does feel he was prompted to make the film by a couple of very unusual incidents. "I had a visit from my dad and he told me I needed to investigate the deaths, then just a few days later my brother came and told me to do the same thing; my brother died four years ago, my dad two years ago."

Sanders took their advice and brought Wisconsin Paranormal Investigators (WPI) on board. He wanted to know if they could find any supernatural reasons for the deaths. He also spoke to elders of the Ho-Chunk Native American tribe. While filming them talking about water spirits, all of the microphones failed. None of the audio could be captured. Then it happened again when they took a boat out onto the river one night. They were trying to capture EVP, but all of the full charged batteries went dead. They had to abandon and return the next night. This time they did manage to make recordings, although they didn't think they'd captured anything. However when they listened to the recording later that night, they said they could hear voices on it and screams. The completion of the documentary left the makers of it just as baffled as before. Nothing provided anything like a conclusive lead or answer.

Then another college boy drowned. In July 2014 another young man was found dead in the river. There were no signs of foul play. He'd disappeared after walking away from the Marina, telling friends there that he was walking home. He was found upstream; not downstream, which is perhaps a little unusual. He was a bartender and not one to drink while at work, and he was an altar boy at Church. Which leads on to one aspect of the chatter on internet blogs about this mystery, particularly in the La Cross area. The deaths have been hotly debated by many on crime, paranormal and conspiracy sites for years, and it's been pointed out that close to the area in which some of the boys died is St John's Abbeyville. A private investigator hired by one victim's family used tracker dogs that allegedly led them to the Abbey, where the scent then stopped.

It has to be noted here that one significant thing was reported to be missing from several bodies; any of those who wore them, were missing necklaces that had crosses or other religious icons on them. This Abbey has what can only be described as a shocking history, and a history that spills over to the present. On the Abbey's website is a public apology to all who have been abused by Priests there, and it lists eighteen names, including nine monks still living there, being described as 'under a supervised plan.'

Pat Marker, who says that he was abused while a student there, goes further. He claims there are over two hundred victims of abuse, and more than fifty monks involved, as well as men associated with the college but not actual monks.

This has led many interested in the deaths of the young men to look more deeply into a religious motive. The combination of missing religious jewellery, the tracker dogs tracing the scent of two of the boys to the college and the sexual abuse of boys at the college, creates a potent theory.

This theory is taken further in an astonishing twist by some people on the forums. In particular what intriguingly appears to be someone highly schooled in alchemy has spent a significant amount of time and effort looking into this mystery, with some compelling conclusions;

'The Killers are committing Human Sacrifice as part of an alchemical ritual; using the human body for occult development, and transmuting the matter of their body into ever purer forms of energy.'

In particular 'the writer' believes she has identified the specific ritual. 'It's called "the killing of the Little King," by drowning.'

With the author's expertise in ancient alchemy and her interest in this case, she has even discovered that Monks at the Abbey were posting on very specialized alchemy forums that she too was using.

'Here they discuss this drowning ritual; it's a representation of the dissolution of matter and identity, and the first stage of the 'Great ritual'; "the Purification," and the alchemist will (later) bathe in a tincture taken from the dead man.'

Is this what is really going on?

Adding to the water ritual theory is also the very odd case of Elisa Lam, whose death features a water tower; only in her case she was found dead in the water, unlike the Jamison family, who it can be suggested had been placed in the water and then removed.

This time the water tank was on the rooftop of a hotel. Partly captured on film is the shocking and mysterious death of Elisa Lam.

In June 2013, investigators ruled her death as 'accidental.' Several important questions however have failed to be answered. One of which is, why did she climb over fifteen feet up into a water tower on the roof of a hotel to get inside it? Another would be, what exactly was happening to her in the security footage of her in the hotel lift prior to her disappearance?

The twenty one year old Canadian student was staying at a cheap hotel in downtown Los Angeles while travelling on her own, taking some time out from college. She was found naked in the water tower, having been dead for two weeks. She was last seen on the CCTV camera in the lift, sometime before she ended up in the water tower. The parts in between are a mystery, but so too is what's happening to her in the lift.

Able to be watched on YouTube, the footage is difficult to comprehend and very eerie to watch. There is something very wrong going on.

She is seen entering the lift and pressing lots of the buttons quickly, then peeking out of the open door several times while she waits for the lift to close. It's almost as though she is fearful that someone is after her. Looking along the corridors, she waits as the lift door fail to close. Becoming increasingly distressed, she's seen making odd gestures with her hands, stepping out of the lift and hiding in the corridor, seeming to be terrified yet not fleeing the scene.

Is her imagination playing tricks with her? Is her killer there out of sight of the CCTV, but lurking within inches of her, waiting to abduct her? Is there something otherworldly about what is happening?

Some people studying the tape have implied there are strange shadows and movement seen inside the lift; shadowy movement, and even face-type forms appearing on the walls of the lift. Is this merely poor video quality and over-active imaginations, or was there something unidentifiable and supernatural manifesting in the lift with her?

At one point, she is seen waving her hands around in front of her, as though trying to feel for what is touching her and talking to her, that she cannot see. When she realises there is an intangible, invisible entity inside the lift with her, her horror grows and she becomes terrified, wrenching her hands together and bending her knees in fright, trying to maintain her grip on sanity when she does not understand what is happening to her.

Her behaviour is one of disorientation, fear, helplessness and shock. Some will say she was on drugs but none were found in her system. Others will say she was having a break-down but the tragic case has fascinated many and there are some incredible theories going around. Some strongly believe she was about to be attacked by something unseen.

Others feel her strange behaviour points to demonic possession and that she was clearly hearing voices. There's also the theory that she may have she died in an occult ritual; that she was used as a sacrifice, hinting at her name and the likeness to Aleister Crowley's poem 'Jephtha,' written when he was staying at the Cecil Hotel in London, the same name as the hotel in which she died.

They have pointed out that the poem has the line 'Be seen in some high lonely Tower.' In the poem, 'Jeptha' was a judge in the *Pseudo-Philo* works, (an ancient biblical text) who offered his daughter as a willing sacrifice. The girl is called Seila; an anagram of Elisa.

A coincidence perhaps? A conspiracy too far?

Others have speculated that she had been wanting to commit suicide. The hotel itself has an unsettling history of murder which may perhaps have left some kind of supernatural imprint on the building; its malevolent aura urging people on to commit acts of murder there. There are records of two serial killers having lived at the hotel. The hotel has also had an unusually high number of suicides.

However, there were far easier ways to do it. Was it even possible to get into the water tank of her own accord? There was no ladder there.

Is this all hysteria and speculation? Was she simply trying to get an old tempremental lift to move, by getting in and out of it and pressing all of the buttons, trying to see which one would get it moving?

But why does the security tape look like she's talking to someone who is not visible and reaching her hands out and grapsing the empty space in front of her as though trying to feel for something invisble that is right in front of her but that she cannot see. What is making her so distressed and confused?

Adding to the mystery is Dr Douglas James Cottrell, PhD. A highly regarded Canadian medical intuitive who claims he, like his predecessor Edgar Cayce, can access the Akashic Hall of Records. Through this he has given thousands of personal readings to people regarding their health problems, accessing their undiagnosed illnesses through a form of 'remote viewing.'

A former skeptic himself, it was when his child was born with a serious illness that he sought help with the diagnosis and through this journey met others like him who could help heal people. He undergoes deep meditative states to look into the past and the future, and is believed to be able to make accurate predictions and see what happened in past events. In one session available on YouTube, he relates what he 'sees' as having happened to Elisa Lam in the lift and up on the roof of the hotel.

He alleges that she was hearing voices in her head; but this was not from a psychotic breakdown, and it was not a demon. The voices were being 'beamed' into her head. They were calling her name, beckoning her; she was looking for the source of the voices and could not understand why she couldn't see the person or people around her when the voices were so close.

They were high pitched and uncomfortable, they were causing her distress, disorientation and fear. She was obeying the voices, going to where they were beckoning her so that she could find them. They led her to the water tower, says Dr Cottrell. They led her to her death and when she got to the roof he alleges, in his meditative trance state, there were pains in her head as though someone was pointing a laser beam at her head. Self-destructive thoughts were being given to her through the sound waves being sent through this 'laser' he claims.

Chillingly he says he can see a dark figure on the roof; cloaked in dark shiny clothing, a shadowed figure with its head covered by a balaclava or hood. He thinks it's a man but he also says it's possible it's a *discarnate* entity.

Others point to her online activity. Was a tweet allegedly sent from Elisa's twitter account really hers? There's the claim that from her twitter account, before her stay in the hotel, she tweeted a post about a Canadian company being given funding from the US for developing a 'quantum stealth' type of camouflage for soldiers that makes them invisible. The gear blends light around the wearer/ or an object, to create the illusion of invisibility. In that respect, a soldier, or anyone using it, can render themselves invisible to everyone else.

Has the development of cloaking technology created invisible predators that the unsuspecting person is powerless to see coming? Are people being silently snatched by something human but invisible?

These wild ideas and speculations could all be a range of conspiracy theories that have gone way too far, but perhaps not.

***

In Northern Ireland lies Ballyboley Forest, where mysterious stone formations and circular trenches are embedded in the ground, giving rise to beliefs that it's an ancient Druid site and a gateway to "the Otherworld," according to the Celtic tradition.

Although forest workers of the Park Service maintain the landscaped trails for visitors to use, there are other natural paths that never seem to need maintenance, that stay oddly clear of any foliage or branches, their paths always mysteriously remaining clear. It's said that the local people do not like to venture into the forest.

People who do enter it often return describing the eerie feeling that they were being watched. Tales abound of seeing shadowy figures standing amongst the trees, cloaked in brown robes, their heads covered. Ancient texts tell of mysterious disappearances of people who never returned from the forest.

In 2006, a man's body was found in the forest. The Police had issued an alert after he'd been reported missing since leaving his place of work two days prior to this.

The following day his car had been found at the edge of the Forest and the police had started to search inside it.

It was ruled that the man, Ian Black, from the nearby town, had died of natural causes.

One has to ask how it's possible to die of natural causes in two days in mild summer temperatures? It was not hot enough or cold enough to have succumbed to the elements.

In 1994, newspapers reported the strange incident of a couple who were walking through the forest when they suddenly heard screaming. Moments later a 'large dark shadow' appeared in front of them making them run off in terror.

In 1997 two men reportedly said they were walking through the forest when they heard a flapping sound that was very loud. They didn't know what it was so tried to ignore it and carried on walking.

Moments later they started hearing what sounded like a woman crying and moaning in pain or distress. Concerned for her state of health, they quickly tried to find her but could see no-one nearby.

What they did see however were trees smeared with blood all around them.

Running in fear, as they fled they both glanced behind them and to their horror both believed they could see a group of figures in dark cloaks standing where the trees were.

***

In Italy in 2006, it was announced that the police were to set up a 'Satanic Squad' to deal with the growing violence of Satanists.

It was to include not only policemen, but also priests that were expert in the realm of the occult. It came as a response to the rise in the number of horrific murders being carried out by Satanists. In one case, an occult group calling themselves 'The beasts of Satan,' had beaten and buried alive two of their own group deep in the forest.

***

In Russia in 2008, four teenagers went missing from their homes. For weeks, police searched for them, at a loss as to what could have happened to them.

Three months later, a gruesome discovery was made in the local woods. The remains of their bodies were found. They had been mutilated and burnt.

The police were able to identify one common link between them – they had all had telephone contact with a local boy by the name of Nikolai Ogolobyak prior to their disappearances.

Scientific and trial evidence later found that Nikolai, along with others, had carried out a sacrificial ritual of these young people. Each had precisely 666 wounds to their bodies, they had been scalped before being 'roasted' on the fire and some of their body parts eaten by the group, who proclaimed themselves Satanists.

The killers had marked the site in the woods with an upside-down cross.

Chapter Eleven:
More Mysterious Disappearances

Former Marine and Special Forces member, Robert Springfield, disappeared while hunting with his son in the Bighorn Mountains in Montana in 2004, in an area he grew up exploring.

Searchers combed the area for him, using a helicopter with infrared sensor, two dozen trained dogs, and over two hundred volunteers, but found no sign of him. Several thorough searches for him were undertaken. They came back again during the spring and again found nothing.

Then just over a year later, skeletal remains were found by hunters, along with the wallet and I.D. of Mr Springfield, oddly, say his family, in an area that was only fifty yards from where they had camped whilst looking for him in the search. The family are adamant that searchers had gone over the exact spot where his body was found. For this reason, they wondered, had he been killed and his body placed there later?

"If he was actually up there in that area, we would have smelled something," his wife said to Indian Country Today. "The animals would have been there."

His cause of death was ruled as 'undetermined.' His wallet was found with his remains. Inside were his ID and Social Security card. When they were given back to the family, there were no signs of any weathering or damage from rain to these items. This, the family believes, means they were not exposed to the elements for any period of time.

The disturbing implication here is that this would surely mean he was not in the outdoors the eleven months he was missing.

The family are understandably seeking explanations and some kind of justice and closure on this tragic and concerning case.

***

In Canada, there's a highway that has long since been renamed 'The Highway of Tears,' after decades of local females disappearing along the remote and rural route.

With its stunning views and its mountain backdrop, Canada's Highway 16 is an incredibly scenic 500 kilometre road. However, since the 1960's, and still continuing today, it is estimated that over forty women have gone missing or sadly been found dead parallel to the road, in the depths of the forests.

Some of the missing women were found to have been the victims of serial killer Bobby Fowler, possibly as many as nine women. As to the remaining large number of women missing, their fates are still unknown. The police do not believe he was responsible for any more, yet they also have no clues as to what might have happened to them.

In May, 2011, Madison Scott vanished near Vanderhoof along the highway. She had been at a party in a camping area and her tent and car were left remaining, but she had disappeared without trace, and she is still missing. A reporter with the Vanderhoof Omineca Express said, from talking with her family and friends, "She had her head screwed on. We don't think she just wandered off drunk and fell into the lake. It is completely out of character."

***

Then in June 1995 in Arizona again, Newspapers reported on the odd disappearance of trucker Devin Williams. It apparently left the local police authorities completely baffled, and the public coming up with theories which included alien abduction.

He was a long distance truck driver from Kansas. He'd left with his eighteen wheeler fully-loaded and headed out on his journey. Along the main freeway in the National forest area of Buck Springs, off Interstate 40, he'd inexplicably turned into a remote forest road and started driving up it. It was not a short-cut route to anywhere but the forest itself, and certainly not on his route.

His boss said afterward, "Why he would have driven into a rugged area like that, I don't know. No one can figure out what happened."

His truck eventually got stuck on the narrow dirt road. He disembarked and walked away from the truck. Hikers nearby were witness to his odd and erratic behaviour. They asked him why he drove the truck there. They said he pointed to the truck and said, "I didn't; they did it."

They told how he was barefoot, and seemed disoriented as he "talked to a tree."

That was the last time anyone saw him. He then vanished without trace.

There was no-one else in the truck.

He was a happily married family man by all accounts, who was regularly drug tested by his employer as part of the condition of employment. No-one could find any hint of a reason as to why he would want to just disappear, taking nothing with him.

Repeated searches were carried out for him with K9's, and yet they could find no trace of where he'd gone.

Investigators also had no idea who "they" were.

Two years later, his skull was found not far away. Many felt, because of his reference to "they," that he was referring to alien entities.

Or were there other 'voices' that had told him to do it? If so, where did those voices come from?

Whatever was responsible, they were invisible to everyone else.

***

In Olympic National Park, government employee Mr Gilman went hiking in June 2006. After he didn't return, Rangers and volunteers searched the area for ten days after finding his car parked at a popular hiking area.

The search by land, air and in the rivers turned up no sign of him. Dogs were called in, an airplane with an infrared that can detect body heat was used, and they were to spend more than thousands of hours looking for him; all without success.

Searchers have found no sign of him.

"It's a mystery...no clues," said one of the rangers.

Relatives remained hopeful because of Gilman's military background. He'd been a paratrooper and had worked in Iraq. People believed his survival skills would aid him.

Four days earlier, Stephen "Mike" Mason also took a walk into the woods and disappeared without a trace, in the same area. His wife had dropped him at the Forks Camp in the Forest. Again, all efforts to find the man were made.

Masons wife says she's sure of only one thing about the disappearance of her husband. "He didn't walk out of there," she said.

***

Thirty seven year old Jeanne Hesselschwerdt was vacationing with her long term boyfriend in Yosemite National Park in 1995 when they stopped their car at a popular parking point along Glacier Point road and got out to stretch their legs. They wandered through a wooded area and became separated.

After losing sight of her, her partner walked back to the spot he had last seen her at, and then back to the car, looking for her as he did so, but thinking she would be back at the car. When he didn't see her there he began to get concerned and on spotting a nearby Ranger, he asked for help to find her.

A search was launched within forty five minutes; which was to last for an entire week. Teams of bloodhounds were used, two helicopters, and hundreds of people spreading out to search far wider an area than they believed she could have covered in her disappearance, just in case.

An animal attack was ruled out by a park spokesman, saying there had been no fatalities or attacks reported in years. In the subsequent report by China Lake Mountain Rescue, who assisted, rangers called out to her during the initial search, and to each other, 'to establish that voice contact could be made over a large area.' In other words, as the searchers had called to her during the hours of her being missing, she would have been able to hear them and thereby respond.

She was not found.

Her boyfriend passed a lie detector test easily and was completely exonerated with no evidence of there being any foul play.

The police and searchers were completely mystified as to how she could have completely disappeared in so short a time, without a trace. They were unable to positively identify any prints as so many of the prints they found looked the same as the searchers own prints, wearing similar boots as the lost woman.

The missing woman's sister-in-law Janet called it, "the most baffling thing."

Three months later, two men who'd gone fishing spotted a body in a stream. It was positively identified as that of Jeanne. It was three miles from where she had been last seen.

Talking to the San Francisco Gate news, one of the men, a Mr Ulawski, who was a local resident near the park, said that the location she had gone to was 'inaccessible to almost everyone except mountain climbers.'

If that is the case, the questions have to be asked, how and why had she got there? It is very possible to get quickly lost, disoriented and start to panic within a few moments of realising you are lost in such wilderness; but why would you then attempt to orient the most difficult terrain around you rather than seek a trail and the road, knowing you had not climbed rocks to get to where you were?

How she got to her location remains to this day a baffling mystery.

***

In September 2008 searchers began looking through a part of mountain forest for a missing man in the Adirondacks mountain region.

Jeremy Quinn, 38, had been reported missing at about 8 p.m. The search began as night fell and continued the next day. Quinn was a volunteer firefighter and caretaker for several camps in the area. He had last been seen at 7am that morning, saying he planned to check on a seasonal home before reporting in to his work head office; but he never showed up there.

His truck was found near the camp the following evening.

"He was born and raised here; he is very familiar with the land," Forest Ranger Capt. John Streiff said.

Forest rangers, sheriffs, and fire-fighters were combing the woods. An intensive Type 3 search was instigated, involving walking in a close-knit grid where each searcher can see the next searcher's feet. The Teams of volunteers walked the ditches, and scoured the landscape for miles around the command centre. Canine units worked the ravines, but they were unable to pick up a trace, and searches found no evidence of his whereabouts.

Nine days later, another caretaker found his body at the bottom of a cliff, a mile from where his pickup truck was found, and outside of the original search area. Police said they do not know how or why he had got from the truck to the cliff.

They ruled out suicide and there was no evidence of alcohol involvement, or foul play, they said. There were no signs of any kind of struggle or scuffle at the scene. They determined that Quinn died of multiple injuries resulting from a fall.

Reporter George Earl covered the story for Adirondack daily news, describing the special public meeting held at the Town Hall. For many, the meeting seemed to create as many questions as it answered. The range of responses to the police explanation of what had happened included disbelief, bewilderment, and fear.

"It's puzzling to figure out how he got from where his truck was to where he was found," said his fellow volunteer fireman and rescue worker Ron Konowitz. "It's difficult to believe."

Residents asked why his body was found so far from his truck. "We have no idea what brought him to that area," the Sheriff in charge said.

"He said he was going to check on a camp for a minute and then ended up way there?" town resident Terry Gregory asked. "I just don't believe it. It's all just very strange."

Residents wanted to know why the dogs in the search were not able to track the man and why an extensive 150 person search had uncovered no footprints or any other evidence that he had walked to the cliff from his truck. There was no evidence at all indicating a path of travel between the two locations.

Friends, co-workers, along with the media, had too many unanswered questions; of how and why he came to be there. His truck, with the keys in it, a mile away; between the truck and his body lay a tangled forest and steep ravines. Why would he go through that?

Astonishingly, over three hundred people go missing or are injured each year in the Adirondacks alone. Though it is an incredibly rugged area and nature itself can be deadly, some of the cases of missing people are simply very strange to say the least.

In these last two cases, what would make both people go to the most inaccessible and dangerous parts of the area, with no reason at all to do so?

Both were not known by those close to them to have had any mental disorder, depression or other reasons to want to end their own lives, just like the earlier case of Devon Williams and yet, their behaviour seems out of the ordinary.

There are other very strange cases of incidents that also lack any reasonable explanation, yet those who have survived them have spoken of possible reasons.

For example, in Massachusetts is Freetown State Forest, and in the forest there is a ledge called The Assonet Ledge. It's said that there's an association with it being a place of sadness, of a feeling of being filled with dread on approaching it. Indeed, more than a dozen suicides have been recorded here; the visitor being overwhelmed with the sudden inexplicable need to jump off the ledge, to throw themselves over it into the deep quarry below, often in front of their companions.

The ledge consists of granite; the same stone as the foundation of a bridge in Overtoun, Scotland, where as many as fifty dogs have inexplicably jumped to their death from the bridge, in front of their owners, each time at the same spot.

Dr Sands, an animal psychologist was asked to go there to try to understand what was happening. He took a dog over the bridge and noticed that at a certain point, the point where all the other dogs had jumped, it tensed immediately. The only thing in view at this point is the granite of which the bridge is constructed. This has led some to wonder whether the granite is the real instigator of the phenomenon.

Granite is composed of quartz crystal. Crystal is a conductor used in computers, radios, and televisions for its conductive capabilities. It also has the amazing ability to store and hold memory.

Many in the paranormal investigative world believe the theory that quartz is a conductor for paranormal entities, enabling them to manifest more easily in this world through the quartz generator, and that paranormal energy is held in the quartz, never dispelling but remaining there afterward, never leaving.

It is true that spell casters traditionally use quartz crystals for spell casting, using the crystal to hold and intensify the power of their intent within it.

Another place which reputedly seems to lure people to their death is a natural pool in Babinda Boulders in Far North Queensland, Australia. It's called 'the devil's pool.' To the aboriginal people the pool is sacred, but it's a popular natural feature many wish to visit.

It's here that at least seventeen people, and many say more, have lost their lives in the pool. Some while swimming, but many others from the banks of the pool, with stories of people being mysteriously 'pulled in' by the water and ending up drowning in it.

There is also the case of teenager Andrew Green, who accompanied his father to an empty house in London that his father needed to inspect for his job as a housing officer. This was in 1944.

When Andrew reached the stairs inside that led up to a tower, he felt as though there were invisible hands on his back, pushing him up. On reaching the top of the stairs, he heard a deep voice in his head telling him the garden was only a few inches below him and that he wouldn't hurt himself if he jumped.

Andrew was only made aware of the deadly height of the drop when his dad suddenly grabbed hold of him and pulled him back from the edge.

Confused and disturbed by the incident, his father asked a friend of his who was a policeman to look into the history of the house, and to his shock it was discovered that there had been twenty suicides reported at that house, all of which involved the person throwing themselves off the tower where Andrew had been standing when he had heard the voice telling him to jump.

So perturbed by this experience Andrew went on to dedicate his life to studying the paranormal, strongly convinced he had been affected by a demon.

Through history there are a plethora of accounts of demonic attack, and the descriptions are remarkably the same. They toy with a person, get into their mind, and direct the most awful and destructive thoughts into their heads. They want to see the person destroy themselves and they aim to wear a person down until they are unable to defend themselves anymore. They are relentless, and will not stop. Their voice insistently telling a person to kill themselves.

Are all these accounts simply from those who are mentally ill? Or can demons attack even the most balanced of people?

***

Houston News in 2012 covered the baffling story of a trio of missing men in the Liberty County region; all their disappearances so far unsolved.

Speaking of the families, they said,

'The woods seem to have swallowed their fathers without leaving a trace.'

"How can people be swallowed and never seen again? This is crazy," said Kim, whose father Dennis was one of the three men to disappear months ago.

As she went around to local stores handing out pictures of her father made into fliers, the staff thought she'd already been there; it turned out instead that the fliers they'd already been given were for two other men already missing.

The men all disappeared within a few miles of each other. They were family men leading regular lives. Two of the men disappeared by the roadside after mysteriously abandoning their cars, leaving their keys inside the cars. Still the families and police have no clues.

Despite intensive searches by hundreds of people, infrared camera, taking dogs, and trained searchers, no trace of either of them has been uncovered, except for the coat of one of the men, Mark Rhineburger, found in a remote area several kilometres away. His daughter said that on the day her father abandoned his car, he had told staff at two garages that he was being chased.

Dennis Rogers vanished while taking his regular walk. His phone was traced by the nearest cell phone tower to miles inside a swamp. Footprints found which could have been his, went round in circles, but there was no sign of him.

Of the other man, Edwin Rogers, who also abandoned his car on the main road, no trace has been found and yet his family say he was unable to walk very far at all due to old injuries from military service.

Currently there are said to be forty missing person's cases in the two counties of Liberty and Montgomery alone.

Conclusion

Invisible, undetectable, and it leaves no trace. You can't see it coming and as much as you might try, you can't run from it.

The disappearances just keep continuing. There is no one answer; only some very disturbing possibilities.

This is a puzzle. An often deadly one. But perhaps some of the possible perpetrators have now been identified.

Or perhaps the mystery remains as one of the most enigmatic and perplexing of all time.

TAKEN IN THE WOODS

Something in the Woods is Still Taking People

Stephen Young

~~~

Copyright © 2015 by Stephen Young

All rights reserved

Table of Contents

Introduction 214

Chapter One: Revelations of deliberate manipulations in space/time, and the possible future world plans of the elite 215

Chapter Two: Alternate dimension, time-slips, and ley lines 235

Chapter Three: The abduction & disappearance of innocent people? Ley line manipulation for a sinister hidden purpose? 241

Chapter Four: Occult & illuminate abductions and missing people? 254

Chapter Five: 'Underground Beings demand Humans' 265

Chapter Six: 'The first step in occultism is the study of the Invisible Worlds.' 273

Chapter Seven: Covert weaponization targeting innocent citizens?? A documented case of ' mass harm' in a rural area. 309

Chapter Eight: Abduction, mutilation and murder in remote wilderness places 330

Chapter Nine: A baffling case of triggered killers? .. 339

Chapter Ten: Strange deaths & disappearances 357

Chapter Eleven: More Strange Deaths 371

Conclusion 388

Introduction

Recently I received an email that led to a series of interviews with a man called David.

Our correspondence began innocently enough in terms of a possible accidental temporary entry into an alternate dimension, but as the correspondence and meetings developed, what was staggering was that it soon became clear there was a lot more going on; things that could potentially shed light on some of the perplexities focussed on in this author's previous book '*Something in the Woods*,' and a lot of what's covered in this new book.

It's a story, alleged to be true, that runs the gamut and plethora of deliberate time/space manipulation, the use of weaponized technology, naturally occurring vortices through which come manifestations of threatening paranormal entities, missing people, the secret existence of an invisible cloaked world, alien threat from off-planet, imposition of agenda 21 and sinister purposes for land grabs, and the startling possible future world plans of the elite; all encapsulated in a tiny island of intrigue and mysterious secret operations.

Could any of these things really be happening? Could any of this really be true? Just what was going on in a tiny remote part of America?

Chapter One:
Revelations of deliberate manipulations in space/time, and the possible future world plans of the elite

The man in question lives and works on one of the San Juan Islands, an archipelago between the United States and Vancouver, Canada.

David's first correspondence reads as follows, and what starts out as a single, simple yet inexplicable incident, soon develops rapidly into an ever complex labyrinth of mysterious events and sequence of revelations.

'I was compelled to write you this note once I heard your Coast to Coast AM interview. My story is so similar that I felt you would want to hear it. Having never heard of your book, and having had to work a lot of this out on my own, I've come to a few conclusions that I would like to share with you.

This happened to me about a year and a half ago, and the disturbing effects lasted for several months and then subsided. Nothing I have ever experienced prepared me for what I went through a year and a half ago.

As odd as it sounds, my troubles began when I absent-mindedly walked around the outside of a large fairy ring of mushrooms on a small island in the Pacific NW. I was talking on my iPhone at the time, and wasn't aware of where my feet were going. My legs began to weaken, as if I'd run a great distance. I never step into, or cross a fairy ring. Being Celtic Indian I have a great deal of respect for the warnings from both sides of my ancestry about this. I really knew better, and that was what made it so weird.

My legs were so numb, they felt frozen. Strange, inexplicable things started happening almost immediately: sounds became muffled, as happens when sailing in a deep fog. I got dizzy, and confused. A feeling of imbalance, of no longer "being connected" started to overwhelm me. I returned to my home, and fell into the bed.

When I awoke a few hours later, I was bewildered, and didn't know where I was. Even though I was in my own home it seemed alien to me, like I no longer belonged there. Somehow I made it through the first day, went through the motions of life, then dropped off to sleep.

In the morning I still felt profoundly "off." But I had a life to live, and forced myself across the island to work with an old client.

Returning home mid-afternoon, I recalled that there was a new industrial park near town that I wanted to check out. I was at the end of my lease, and wanted to relocate my business. So I pulled into the industrial park, and was surprised to see what looked like a modest-sized smoked glass and steel, government office complex. It had just been erected. About a dozen workmen were on-site, and a couple of specialty electrician panel trucks were visible. I drove most of the way around the complex, then had to turn around. At this point I got out of the car, and approached a man that looked to be project foreman.

I spoke to him, asking if there were still suites available to rent. He replied that he didn't know anything about that, and that I wasn't supposed to be there, and should leave.

I didn't think much about this, got back in my car, and resolved to return later when the park was open for business.

I did return a couple of weeks later, pulled into the park, and experienced complete dislocation. The smoked glass and steel office complex I had visited just a few weeks earlier had vanished. In its place was a small building that housed a fitness center and a few other small businesses. It's hard to describe what happens to your mind when what you see doesn't add up with what you are sure is there. I was so bewildered.

So I told my friend 'Ian' about it. He'd been an investigative reporter. He went to where I had seen the complex with his daughter, and witnessed paramilitary soldiers on guard on either side of the access road. When he came around the bend, the soldiers had morphed into black plastic wrapped objects!

Several days later; still feeling dislocated, I walked by an empty, dark storefront that has housed Sea Shepard, the notorious defenders of the oceans. It was odd, because I had walked by the day before, and it was fully occupied. Later, I mentioned to a woman friend that Sea Shepard had pulled a midnight move. Her husband had been one of the original Sea Shepard captains so she knew all about the recent doings of the organization and was certain that they had not moved. That was strange... The next day I went by, and sure as hell, Sea Shepard was open for business, WTF?

So... a month goes by. I'm walking by the Sea Shepard storefront, looked over and saw that now it really was empty. One month after I had seen it just so.

A week later something terrible showed up on my property. It was after a feral cat, which had hunkered down in the grass. But I interfered allowing the cat to make it safely to the bushes. It shrieked at me so loud it turned my guts to water. It was very aggressive, and swooped me, red eyes in the flashlight.

I ran into my travel trailer and slammed the door. It landed on the roof so hard it rocked it. The thing did resemble an owl, but seemed at least two-to-three times the size of a Great Horned Owl (which I have seen at close range here on the island). And it roared! It didn't shriek like a bird of prey, it roared like a lion.

This owl thing came back a couple of weeks ago, and tore apart a feral cat while I stood about 20 feet away in the dark. I think that it was the same cat that I had rescued two weeks earlier, which is eerie if this thing had held a grudge. The owl-thing was concealed by the shrubs, but we carried on a spirited growling match, until I chickened out and went inside.

Conclusions:

1. I circled, and then crossed into a fairy ring when the mushrooms were the size of dinner plates. Big mistake.
2. I got dislocated in time and space. And this took about a month to wear off.
3. I apparently visited two alternate timelines, even snapping a picture of the abandoned Sea Shepard Storefront.
4. A dangerous, very large owl-like creature showed up next to my home, and within 50 feet of the ferry ring. It came after me, and acted in ways that defy explanation.
5. Our island has experienced an enormous level of development and investment from the Federal

government. Keep in mind that we are a tiny town of 2,228 people.

Our Port of Friday harbor is in the processed of being militarized and quietly rebuilt and fortified.

6. The ferry landing was militarized, with the latest hardware, including a DHS Xray mobile scanner.
7. Department of Homeland Security rented the largest office building in town, and began rebuilding it into a garrison, with bulletproof glass, thick metal walls, detention facilities, despite universal public outcry.
8. The local airport has undergone massive renovations. The third wave is about to begin with another 27 million dollar grant from the Feds.

Military hardware has been reported showing up on the island at night. A friend witnessed 14 black Light Armored Vehicles driving in convoy from the ferry landing in the direction of the airport, where massive hangers have been constructed, and more on they way.

Last year, San Juan County, my home, was declared to be a National Monument. We are just now beginning to understand what that means, as we are getting reports from other places that have been designated national monuments as part of a coordinated land grab.

Add to this an NSA listening post, two retired Secretary of States, over twenty two retired CIA agents, and increasing Drone spying and strobe photography at night.

And finally: 9. A friend of mine (former intel) had heard of a top secret program, using inter-dimensional field generators that can create an artificial "time well" where personnel, equipment, even whole building complexes can be concealed. Other buildings can co-exist in the same space, but in different vibrational densities. I think that I was able to perceive such a government operation operating on this island, after my perceptions were blown wide open by my fairy ring misadventure.'

That was the first correspondence received from David. What followed next was a series of meetings and interviews to discuss these many astonishing and highly mysterious claims of a secret government/military program utilizing inter-dimensional field generators to create artificial "time wells" that are capable of concealing activity, drone spying and strobes, land grabs and underground construction, mysterious choke-hold detentions facilities, vortexes and fairy rings, and manifestation of an array of bizarre and threatening entities.

Could any of this really be truly happening?

What follows next is a transcript of some of the interviews that followed.

Question. So do you think the Government building that you saw at the industrial park is still there? Veiled by the use of this 'inter-dimensional field generator?' The paramilitary soldiers there too, but 'invisible' to our eyes usually?

Answer. I believe that I entered another timeline, and saw what was really there. I also believe that inter-dimensional fabric can become thin in places, whether by design, by cycles or by shear coincidence.

I am certain that technology is being employed at this site that is far beyond what is commonly known. Homeland security had a contract to move their new facilities to this building park, got well into the negotiations and retrofitting, then abruptly pulled out in favor of the DHS Garrison in the town's financial heart.

A woman friend who attends aerobics classes at the fitness center there felt and heard what sounded and felt like underground detonations.

In addition, an electrical infrastructure was put in behind the complex that looks like it could power our entire town.

Question. I wonder why the military presence and facilities are there, including detention facilities? How big do you think they are?

Answer. The DHS/CBP Garrison has a potential expansion to 24,000 feet (which is the whole block, as most of the current building residents don't want to stay if, and when DHS opens the facility for business.)

They are open about the detention facilities, as this came up over and over in the grudgingly-held public meetings.

The problem is that new laws that went into effect on Jan. 1st, force residents riding the ferries to make reservations, something never done here in 50 years. This allows them to monitor visitors, identifying every driver coming on or off the island.

The Garrison is a meagre 100 feet from the ferry landing, making the perfect choke-point.

If you look at a map of the Pacific NW you will see our island group just 10-11 miles from Victoria BC. It is a strategic stronghold. Weapon emplacements at the South end of SJI could control access to the entire Puget Sound and SW Canada. It has been used as such during three historic conflicts.

In addition, we have become a Disneyland for the Elite, who have littered our islands with multimillion dollar trophy homes.

Many people with shiny new government identities are sent here to hide, heal, or learn how to be in civilized society again. I was employed helping to remediate and repatriate some of these broken people; returning black-ops soldiers, and super soldiers alike. But that is for an entirely different conversation.

As I mentioned in the first email, we host a lot of retired CIA and NSA employees here and two retired Secretaries of State as well.

There are about a million reasons that they would put in a garrison and control center here, especially in the face of actual conflict with China and Russia.

Question. Where would people be coming from for them to need detention facilities do you think?

Answer. Preventing the flow of people from our little island to Canada is surely one of the reasons. I believe the real reason is because the elite know that global war is on the horizon, and, like Russia and China, are making advanced preparations. This island is a strategic asset.

For 20 years I've had dreams about an invasion from China, using the San Juan Islands as the entry point. As the global conflict intensifies, I'm sure that the island population will be "relocated." I plan to be in a safer location.

Just before 9/11 our island was used as a staging point for operations. We had many mercenaries, dressed as tourists coming into the U.S. on tour boats. One long time intelligence asset retired here pointed them out to me, and said: "What do you think of those "tourists?" One look and I replied: 'They are wolves among the sheep.' He replied: "Exactly."

One of the retired Super Soldiers here; (now in a federal prison) went around the island a full year prior to 9/11 telling anyone who would listen exactly what would happen, how many would die, how and where. The FBI came through and arrested him.

This is why this island is so vital for them. It houses many former operatives, retired government officials, and now a garrison for the DHS/TSA/CBP.

Question. Yes, I've heard of other 'National Monuments' where boom sounds are heard below ground and witnesses have talked of feeling very ill suddenly, as though something is being used on them.

Answer. The National Monument land grab is just that. The Elite are digging underground bases under every city with high chances of survival, so it makes sense to do the same under their hidey-holes.

"They" recently installed light-based control systems that strobe for 4-5 miles from a transmitter at the FH airport. Many have reported feeling nauseous and confused as soon as it is turned on.

I live inside a virtual 'faraday cage,' and can block out most electro-spectrum. But if I come out when it is turned on, I feel ill immediately and retreat inside; so faraday cages block "it" whatever "it" is.

The writing is on the wall, and I plan to depart here, moving to much higher ground.

Question. What do you mean the strobe is being used for?

Answer. Not entirely sure yet. All I know is that the patterned strobing affects thought processes and makes one nauseated and confused. But when I enter my faraday cage, and block the light, the discomfort stops abruptly.

Whether these are side effects, or the main goal - as in the "less-lethal" weapons used on U.S. demonstrators since the WTO riots in Seattle.

Right now, outside my window, Blackhawk helicopters are doing touch-and-go training missions at the airport. I live about 100 feet from the end of the airport runway.

This will go on for hours now

Question. I have to say the sound of helicopters flying overhead in the video (supplied to me) makes for an unnerving feeling and must cause a lot of disturbance to any tranquility there.

Answer. Many here are making plans to relocate temporarily to mainland, near CA border as this situation intensifies.

Question. With reference to 'Super-soldiers' and being aware of at least two possible self-titled 'super soldiers' here in the UK, in the interaction you had with them, do they think they really exist? And what/who are they exactly? What is their purpose?

Answer. Super Soldiers are very real. I knew one that won a bet jumping off of a 10 story building in Las Vegas on a dare. He lived on our island for two years. He was seized and imprisoned in New Mexico after predicting 9/11 in great detail in the late 1990's, and telling anyone who would listen. There are many on the island that remember him well. We had countless conversations over those two years. He worked at the Retreat Center doing odd jobs, etc., and he was very candid about his past (those parts he could remember).

Super Soldiers are the object of the new arms race between USA, China and Russia, and are living weapons that can be pre-programmed, or operated remotely like a drone robot. They look like ordinary (athletic) people, so they can blend in.

Recent models are unhampered by human "weaknesses" such as: pity, compassion, empathy, etc.

There have been a number of steadily improving versions of super soldiers. I worked with earlier models who had survived until retirement age (very rare). These guys were enhanced humans: Celtic Indian hybrids.

One SS I will call Jim was the last surviving member of his team of 36. He was Scottish and Native American, and had a very colorful career that put him at many pivotal historic events. I have a photo of him disguised as a news reporter as part of the CIA security squad at the RFK assassination at the Ambassador Hotel in LA.

The current generations of SS are clones of their very best soldiers; these are modified and genetically enhanced in many ways, physically, with electronic prostheses's and upgrades. Most possess DNA from non-human animals for enhanced night vision, etc.

I was hired by the DHS/DVR to work within my area of expertise in the repatriation of several Super Soldiers back into society, in a limited sense. These guys would always be under observation, with in-house "handlers" to keep them out of trouble.

Having worked with three professionally, I also know one other personally: He has broken through his programming, which rarely happens to these tortured souls, and is candid about his training and experiences.

Question. In your opinion what is the correlation between these 'Super-soldiers' and the UFO/inter-dimensional activities. Is any of it linked to one another?

Answer. These SS's are Earth's first-and-last line of defense from off-world, temporal or inter-dimensional threats.

They man the Space Navy, guard and defend against hostile Alien actions against human colonies and bases. The Space fleet had 139 Triangles, and Five interplanetary destroyers in 1998.

Question. The creature you describe, it sounds almost a Mothman-type thing and I've seen historic accounts of these from England to Germany. Do you know what its body looks like?

Answer. About the Owl-Thing. I am lucky that I have only seen its eyes. Bright red at night from the flashlight. What I will never forget was how far apart those eyes were. I'm guessing 8-10 inches apart. The thing had to be huge. Its head was larger than mine. A Great Horned Owls head is maybe the size of a cantaloupe, this was the size of a basketball. I did not go out of my way to get a look at it. And I hope that it never returns. Besides, our neighborhood is completely out of stray cats. Why don't I try to capture a photo? If you could feel the danger that emanates from this thing, you would know why-it is survival instinct and self-preservation.

We are also one of the hottest UFO hotspots on the planet, according to MUFON, who comes here regularly.

Question. Do you think it is biological or inter-dimensional? With intelligence too, as you say almost like it held a grudge?

Answer. There was a powerful feeling of rage and malevolence, but that somehow it had to hold itself back from attacking me. Don't know why. It could have decided that I wasn't just meat.

It was smart, and it used its voice like a weapon, and could project terror directly into your mind, like the Sasquatch does when provoked.

The aggressive Owl attacks have escalated. I'm now convinced (after the Monster Quest experiments here) that the perpetrator's a hybrid Barred/Great Horned Owl. It's becoming evident that these hybrid Owls are highly aggressive, dangerous and territorial to humans.

Question. The fairy circle is worrying, and the effects must have been horrible. I wonder where that power comes from?

Answer. These are naturally occurring vortices. We have many here in the San Juan Islands, as our archipelago is actually atop one of the oldest mountain ranges on earth; according to *Geology of the San Juan Islands* by Ned Brown, professor at Western Washington University Geology Department.

One of the biggest ones is under a Tibetan Stupa; a spiritual monument designed to concentrate spiritual energies, and to contain malevolent entities. It is in a Tibetan Buddhist Retreat Center, owned by Tibetan Royals. That is also another story, as the laws of physics were optional there.

Ferry rings are dangerous, but only if they are atop a naturally occurring vortex, and the stars and planets are aligned right.

There is a fairy ring about ten miles from here that is terrifying, sort of a cosmic bus station for inter-d travelers. Not the kind of place you want to hang out at during a full moon, when the shrooms are blooming.

I saw an impossibly thin white stick creature from a 2 meters away distance. It saw me, froze, then turned sideways, thinner and thinner until it disappeared.

Another time a large invisible malevolent entity blocked my path, and I had to walk around it, knowing it could rip me to ribbons. When I closed my car door and drove off, I was the luckiest man alive.

Question. It's interesting to hear about the invisible and white entities; I have accounts of these and there are some detailing white, translucent, and also black ones.

Did you sense the invisible one or could you see any of it? Where do you think this has originated from? Do you have any insight as to how these entities are manifesting, in other words are they a naturally occurring phenomenon or do you think there is any relation to the Gov/Military and even Super-soldier involvement in the timing of these manifesting**?**

Answer. The white stick man is well known to local Native Americans. I was very lucky to see one up close. The malevolent entity I had to walk around was completely invisible, and very large. My clairvoyance picked it up, and my survival instinct told me to ignore it, don't react, and just walk around it. It worked.

The energy signature of this entity was not demonic (I have had experience with these awful trans-dimensionals and this wasn't a demon.) The energy was more Draco reptilian. It was calculated rage and bloodlust, not the depravity and madness of demonic manifestation.

Both of these entities appeared from the same Inter-dimensional doorway, a large ferry ring about 7 miles from town. It sits on top of a very active vortex. The white stick man was as shocked to see me, as I was to see it.

Question. About 'the laws of physics are optional.' In what ways did this manifest?

Answer. Tibetan Masters discovered long ago that we are all trapped in an illusory matrix. They found that the endless cycle of birth death and rebirth is a trap designed to confuse us into believing that we are mortal, when we are in fact immortal 5th dimensionals who were intentionally trapped here by the reincarnation cycle, to be used as a resource by the powers that be.

Through lifelong practice and meditation, Tibetan masters explored the width and breadth of existence, and learned how to manipulate time, space and matter with their minds and spirits. To them it is "normal." Many of these practices come down to us through Extraterrestrial Lineages. Like the Red Dragon and White Dragon families, descended from Sky People, and have retained the wisdom and connection to their pasts. They have extraordinary abilities.'

The above account from David raises so many questions, not just simply could this all really be happening? But could it be coming to a town near us?

Some of his claims are so startling, so shocking, and point to an alarming range of possibilities that could affect us all. They raise so many possibilities that simply call out to be looked into more deeply in other geographical areas too.

From future world plans of the elite, land grabs and underground bases, sinister population control, mysterious military operations and weaponized technology, to the existence and manipulation of dimensions and vortexes.

Taking just one of the above and looking closer, do altered states of dimensions really exist? Can a person simply 'step' into another time frame or an alternate universe, parallel to ours, temporarily?

Chapter Two:
Alternate dimension, time-slips, and ley lines

An earlier account comes from the research of Allen J Hynek who received a report back in the late '60's of a strange experience that happened to a miner in a remote part of Northern Canada, in the Coppermine Mountains.

Two miners had gone prospecting. They usually separated and searched different spots. They'd been there for approximately two months when one day the first miner returned to their tent before the other, and while waiting for his friend decided to talk a short walk to the edge of a small cliff nearby.

He immediately noticed a kind of fog engulfing the small cliff. Curious, he quickly descended it and found a gouge just a few feet wide but large enough to get into. He felt a little nervous but decided to go inside and investigate, as to him it looked like the area had been mined previously and could certainly contain some of the minerals he was hunting for.

Immediately he noticed strange looking stones he didn't recognise despite his vast mining experience.

'Two steps inside in the mist, and my vision was limited, but I saw a grassy field. The more I walked toward it, the higher the grass got. I continued and the grass was three foot tall, now four foot. My vision widened and far off to the right was an oasis with trees growing in a circle. At this point I decided to retreat. I can't remember the sky; grey colored? My mind went completely blank apart from a small piece fighting a takeover of my brain, and I warned myself not to walk in the grass. Then I was on my hands and knees getting out of there.'

He never told anyone what happened to him, for many years. When he thought about it afterward, as he often did, he could not shake the impression that he'd somehow gone into another dimension of reality.

He wondered about the strange stones he'd seen in the gorge and subsequently he contacted the SETI Institute, as well as Dr Hynek, in search of some kind of explanation, though none was easy to come by.

***

Michael Graeme of the Rivendale Review has written about several incidents of apparent altered dimensions or time slips.

'In the 70's while touring the Lake District, Cumbria, I heard a story about some hill walkers who'd spent the night at a nearby Inn yet who were later told they couldn't have possibly done so; because the Inn was submerged by a reservoir since the last century.'

'Then a story about the two women who'd set out to walk a few familiar miles one night to a nearby village, only to suddenly find themselves in an eerie, unfamiliar landscape.'

'It's hard to come up with a rational explanation,' he writes, 'especially when the experience is shared. I experienced a similar thing myself. I dismissed it as an aberration of the mind at the time, but the more I thought about it...'

'I was driving from Windermere to Coniston. To get there, you have to turn at a very obvious junction. But the junction wasn't there. The map told me there was a junction. I guessed I'd driven past it. I turned round and came back.'

'Still no junction...nothing, just hedgerows and fields beyond. I turned around and tried again. Still nothing.'

'Eventually I pulled over, confused and telling myself to pull myself together. But it was no good; that day, it did not exist. I had to get there by taking a detour.'

***

Situated off the South Coast of England lies the picturesque Isle of Wight, an island of just 25 miles by 13, home of rock festivals that once saw the likes of Jimmie Hendricks and Janis Joplin; birth place of ex-

SAS soldier Bear Grylls, and now the home of David Ike.

The Island has the reputation as being the most haunted island in the world, due it's said to the disproportionately high number of ley lines that criss cross its land. Where the lines cross and intersect, 'power points' are said to create an energy vortex.

Stories of ghost sightings, time slips, and alternate dimensions abound; with tales from locals of seeing highwaymen being led to hangman's hill, and 19th century smugglers and pirates seen scaling cliffs in front of startled late night fishermen.

Of people finding themselves on strange paths they've never seen before, despite having lived there all their lives.

Of the many stories, one such example is that told to local journalist Gay Baldwin by Michael and Noeline Sleat, who were staying on the Island for a holiday, on June 16th 1999.

It was a warm sunny day and the couple strolled down a country lane on their way to a park. They noticed a large Victorian house surrounded by long lawns where a group of children were playing with what looked like a football. They were standing in a ring and on the floor were a pile of school bags and some old fashioned hockey sticks.

"One of the lads was wearing antiquated breeches and a girl beside him was in an old-fashioned gymslip. Another child, a chubby little boy, caught my eye as he was wearing a bright yellow shirt," Nolene said. "We could hear noise coming form the children but we could not make out any words. Curiously, although the ball was being kicked it didn't appear to go anywhere. It was like watching a video constantly replaying."

"I have never experienced anything quite like it. As we walked on down the lane, we saw two men with a very old-fashioned car, but they didn't appear to hear us when we said, "Good morning."

We soon got to the Park and spent a couple of hours there. As we returned past the old house again we were surprised to see the children were still there. They hadn't moved at all. I said to my husband, "Look, how odd!" But just as he turned his head, they disappeared. It was like switching a television off."

"We were so startled by the experience we hurried away up the lane. We just wanted to get away from there. I don't know what we witnessed- whether it was a moment from the past or whether we actually slipped momentarily back in time. Whatever it was I don't ever want to do that again."

Significantly more sinister, this next story, told in her Baldwin's, "Ghost Island," relates the history of

Duver Church on the eastern side of the Island at St Helen's.

It was here that in the fourteenth century a monk by the name of Aymo defied excommunication and continued to conduct devil worship. Satanic rites were performed on the altar with a coven of black witches in attendance.

The Church was eventually left to fall into disrepair and as is happening in many parts of the Island due to erosion, it was gradually washed away into the sea.

In 1784 however, workmen from the mainland arrived to fortify what was still left of the church steeple. As they commenced work, the foreman of the group was startled when he came across an old man up in the tower. The foreman called his men to come and look, astonished that anyone would risk being up there. The old man appeared very angry at the intrusion however and cursed the workmen, telling them they would suffer the same fate as the previous laborors who had come to do the job.

The workmen thought it was just a silly joke, but when the time came for them to return back to the mainland, they set sail for Portsmouth and were never seen again.

Chapter Three:
The abduction & disappearance of innocent people? Ley line manipulation for a sinister hidden purpose?

Not only are ley lines thought to be the cause of ghost apparitions and other paranormal incidents, but resident of the Island David Ike claims that because of the concentration of these powerful energy ley-lines, the Island is home to a determined presence of occultists, who seek to use these lines for their own agenda.

The Satanists he says, manipulate this strong energy field into a greater form of density.

'While we see everything as *physical*, the *energy* construct is the place where everything originates; that's why the Elite spend so much effort manipulating this energy; because if you want to affect all the fish, you need to affect this *energy* sea in which we all live.'

'This repetition of ritual practice has over time left strong impressions. Occultists work to keep this energy grid suppressed at these critical intersections, by ritual.'

'Satanic rituals are performed on these lines. Islands are particularly powerful energetically, because they're surrounded by water which is itself an excellent collector of energy.'

Arrangements are made, he says, for negative buildings to be deliberately sited on these places of power, such as nuclear energy stations and prisons, as well as satanic lodges, in order to manipulate and 'negatively charge' these energy flows.

If this sounds a little over-dramatic, perhaps we should consider researcher David Gowan, said to be an authority on Ley Lines. He believes, 'The world's ley lines have been used by secret societies for thousands of years.'

He believes that they who harness this ancient power are now able to control humanity by manipulating this energy system to meet their own agendas. Cowan, now published by David Hatcher Childress, believes both white and black energy spirals emanate from the earth in certain places, with natural white energy spiraling upward, but black energy spirals the other way and is extremely harmful.

These can be naturally occurring, or deliberately blackened energy, made so by occultists.

Gowan claims to have helped heal people suffering illnesses ranging from fatigue syndrome, heart problems, MS, epilepsy and motor neurone disease, by identifying black energy spirals close to where they reside.

He cites cases of poltergeists and demonic possessions that he's investigated as being caused by entities manifesting through this black energy, able to enter our dimension.

His years of studying these ley line routes as natural sources of power which were once used as a tool for healing, has led him to discover that there has been a deliberate occult manipulation of them, turning them into blackened energy lines which are used instead for evil purposes by garnering and enhancing their power to serve a cabal of dark worshippers.

In his opinion, some of these ley lines have been man-made and set with deliberate intention on a certain path to negatively influence locations, including the ancient stones across the world.

He believes that as the ley lines travel, they pass through water and lakes and through 'crevices' or 'cavities' in the land. They can be 'captured' in these cavities and the energy harnessed there.

'Cavities' can be ancient stones or buildings; such as temples or churches. A constructed 'cavity' can pull the energy into it from the ley line, trapping it and enhancing it. From this can be made the black energy spirals.

Just as the natural 'white' energy of the ley lines are positive and healing, so the black man-made occult ones are negative and destructive to those who encounter them.

If energy grids of pure black energy were created and criss-cross a region, it's reasoned that negative actions and behaviors could be caused.

And so the theory goes that these negative energy grids have been put in place by the destructive elite who wish to subliminally control the population.

It's claimed that his book was immediately mysteriously withdrawn from publication on the day it was released. Believers in his work and conspiracy theorists alike have speculated, was this man getting too close to exposing the truth about the secret elite societies harnessing and manipulating the ancient occult powers of these energy fields?

Was his book instantly pulled by pressure from those who control the puppet strings, in order to keep this ancient occult knowledge to themselves? they asked.

Some even claim to have charted a straight ley line running from Stonehenge to Sandy Hook school and state that satanic sacrifice ritual was the motive of the massacre at Connecticut. One is Fernando Tognola, of 9/11 Truth.ch, who charted them on his site.

Explanations of the precise geographic charting and numeric calculations required to chart this oneself are difficult to understand for a layman, such as the Author of this book, but it makes for some compelling reading attempting to understand it.

Suffice it to say, there are many who are able to understand the intricacies of charting and make claim to its accuracy, and they cite it as proof that the secret sects who seek to control society through a demonic agenda are always carrying out such atrocities in attempts to harness and grow the power they feed through such rituals.

Interestingly, Veterans Today writer Preston James Ph.D has also expressed a feeling that the children were 'kidnapped for human satanic sacrifice.' He points to historic uncoverings of the Organisation known as 'The Finders,' and the 'Franklin Cover-up' as valid evidence of the possibility of such things really happening.

Is this taking a theory too far? And, surely if the children were indeed sacrificed, it's counter to the argument of many who feel that the alleged conspiracy was orchestrated as a false flag hoax.

Interestingly, Mark Patrick Gibbons has spent over twenty years researching ley lines, UFO's, and the paranormal; specifically looking in latter years at the correlation between reported UFO sightings and the location of ley lines.

'A lot of theses phenomena happen over areas that are saturated in ley lines. I thought it was just coincidence at first; then I collected and analysed the data. Over ninety five percent of my reports of activity and sightings had all occurred on these ley lines.'

'In control tests I used psychics also, without any knowledge of the location of these sights or the phenomenon and without telling them what I was looking for. They found the spots and even gave me detailed descriptions of the entities that witnesses had reported as having appeared at the ley line areas.'

'The abduction cases matched the ley lines. I mapped it out, and I believe now that there is a very strong possibility that this phenomenon is drawn to them like a magnet draws things to it.'

'Specifically I found that the abductions were taking place at the ley lines that had been blackened by the occultists. For example, in the Alan Godfrey case (referred to in this author's book 'Something in the Woods,' the policeman who experienced missing time and was abducted shortly after he'd found a man's body dropped onto a coal pile with strange burn marks, after the man had been reported missing.)

'Godfrey's abduction was on a blacked ley line according to witness accounts of villagers who'd lived there for many years attesting to local occult practices being routinely carried out there on the ley lines.'

'However, I also found that the opposite was the case in the lines that had not been interfered with. Here, there were cases of contactees having positive experiences and indeed many people who visit positive lines and ancient stone places often find relief from illnesses and medical conditions such as arthritis and chronic pain, due to the positive energy flowing from the lines into their bodies.'

'Likewise, others who have reported very negative feelings such as depression and sudden anger are later discovered to have been at deliberately blackened ley lines.'

Do ley lines give off negative energy? he asks rhetorically. Yes, he emphatically concludes, in places that have seen black magic ritual carried out at the ley lines.'

Incidentally, there are some who say that a powerful ley line runs through the Sierra Nevada, through Yosemite Park, and in Joshua Tree, and Mount Shasta; and in some spots along the line there are believed to be side-by-side 'windows' of vastly differing vibrational quality, each from a different dimensional time and energy flow.

There's said to be a ley line triangle with the corners being at Mount Scott by Crater Lake, at the top of Mount Shasta, and at Eight Dollar Mountain in Oregon all joining together.

Many of the lines intersect each other. The points at which they cross are often in the more uninhabited wilderness and mountain areas.

What does this imply? What could then happen at these spots?

As Tesla himself said, 'to find the secrets think in terms of energy, frequency and vibration.'

All matter is now known to be differing vibrational energy, whether animate or inanimate. It doesn't matter if we don't accept that the earth's floor is formed of these dynamic energy grids, but perhaps we should at least be aware of those do and are, as has been suggested, seeking to use them to their distinct advantage against us?

As David Cowan believes, 'Those who knew of the ancient secrets of the earth's natural energy systems are now able to control humanity by the manipulation of these natural features in the energy grid for their own sinister purposes.'

Highly controversial numerologist Ellis C Taylor is explicit in his belief that not only does satanic ritual of the elite take place on these energy lines of power, but that this is inextricably linked to the disappearance and deaths of missing children in the United Kingdom.

He claims to have identified 'patterns' in these 'abductions and murders' of children and teenagers over the last few decades which strongly tie in with both important occult dates, numerology, and ley lines.

The path of travel in these abduction and murder cases, he believes, are via ley lines which intersect ancient places of powerful black energy. His implication is that occult ritual sacrifice is being conducted to harness the black energy.

He ties the location of where they go missing and the location in which they are found to these lines and links them directly through lines that run through Satanic places of worship, ancient sites, and indeed even claims that these lines directly lead to places that clearly indicate exactly who is involved in these ritual murders.

His alleged findings are highly controversial however, and whether they are indeed plausible is another argument.

Could there really be anything in Taylor's pieced together pattern of ley energy, numerology, satanic ritual and the abductions and murders of young people?

David Icke is a believer of this pattern-linking, and will openly say that those who are secretly in control of us, the 'shape-shifting bloodline,' need this negative energy of fear and pain to feed off.

That they actively need the population to feel anxious, fearful, scared and terrified in order for them to thrive off this fear and feast on it to maintain their own forms.

In one of Ellis' abduction/murder cases, that of a young boy Daniel Nolan, he believes that the black energy line runs from the Isle of Wight, crossing the ancient Stonehenge, and the Severn Bridge; a notorious bridge for suicides.

As outlandish as it sounds, do these horrific murders serve to energise the grid? Are the mass negative emotions and fears of the people in the area, knowing an abduction has taken place and desperately searching for the missing, deliberately caused by an occult cabal to create greater swathes of negative emotion to feed the grid and hence the entities that feed off of that grid?

Both Ellis and Ike assert that they do. Icke claims that from evidence he's directly received by a number of people heavily entrenched in ritual and the occult, of people that have attended and participated in the ritual killings of children in these ceremonies, this is for the purpose of harnessing greater powers of darkness to enable their ruling bloodline to continue and thrive.

Pure craziness, or is there something to it?

The abduction/murder case that Ellis refers to above is that of Daniel Nolan. Over on the mainland, across the seven mile stretch of sea from the Isle of Wight, a teenage boy disappeared after night fishing with his friends. It was early January 2002.

They'd been fishing off the Hamble waterfront, near Southampton. Fourteen year old Daniel had fished many times before. His main hobbies were fishing, canoeing and swimming. He was a member of the Sea Scouts.

When he didn't come home in the early hours of the morning as he had promised, his mother began to get concerned and after half an hour she went out herself to look for him, knowing where he would be.

She found only his fishing equipment. She called the police and by 4.30 in the morning a search had begun for him. Specialist sniffer dogs could pick up no scent of him. Five teams of police divers and two army sonar units could also detect no trace of him.

He'd left his friends at close to midnight after they'd all finished fishing early and hung out up the street by the local shops. When they all decided to go home, he headed back to the waterfront to fetch his fishing gear and go home too.

Almost a year later, a lady was walking her dog in a scenic bay called Chapman's Pool near Swanage, in Dorset. An entirely different county and over forty miles away. She stumbled across a shocking sight. It was a human foot still in its shoe, washed up onto the beach.

After DNA forensic analysis found that it was part of Daniel's body, tidal experts were brought in to try to explain how the foot, still in the trainer and sock, had managed to travel 40 miles in the sea.

It was determined that his foot had come away as a natural process from his body, but speculation obviously grew that he could have been taken by someone in a vehicle or onto a boat. His parents at the time of his disappearance were so convinced he was still alive and being held somewhere that they put up a £50,000 reward, but it was never claimed.

The area in which this part of his body was discovered, though accessible to those local to the area with knowledge and experience of climbing down into the bay, is not an easy nor simple path to take. It can be accessed though, and it can also be accessed by simply dropping anchor further out of the bay.

Police at the time, after launching a massive ground, sea and air search, concluded that the boy had fallen in and been swept out to sea.

Though he was under legal drinking age, he had consumed alcohol that night; however, as has been said, he was a Sea Scout, an active and highly competent swimmer and a canoeist, and very familiar with the sea in that part where he grew up.

His Mother doesn't find the police explanation acceptable. Talking at the time of the tragedy she said, "This raises more questions than it answers. We must emphasize; this does not tell us the circumstances of his disappearance."

She spoke out on news programmes at the time, expressing concern that it could have been the result of foul play, calling it a 'strange and bizarre case.'

She simply doesn't believe that if he had fallen into the water, he could have been swept away so far.

"Anyone else who's fallen in the water in recent years there has always been able to be found."

Crucially, of the waterfront where he was fishing, she says, "It's in an enclosed sheltered waterway."

Chapter Four:
Occult & illuminate abductions and missing people?

Little five year old Victor Shoemaker ran off to play in the woods with his two older cousins. Only his two cousins returned. They were made to take lie detector tests in an effort to find out what had happened to their cousin. They both passed the tests.

No-one could understand what had happened; or where he could have gone to. The two older boys told investigators he'd been hungry and he'd wanted to go back and even though the two boys knew they shouldn't let him go back on his own, they didn't stop him when he started to walk back.

That was the last time they saw him they said when they later returned to their grandparents' home in Hampshire County near Kirby.

It was May 1st 1994 and the remote, rugged, forested mountainside soon became dubbed 'The forest that swallowed a little boy.'

Victor had spent many days out in the woods behind his grandparents' home. He loved the woods and knew the area well, and he'd previously run home once before to announce his cousin's hunting prowess after killing a rabbit.

His Mother said he was so comfortable out in the wilderness that he preferred to run around and climb trees barefoot, even in colder seasons.

Though the FBI soon became involved in the search, there was never any evidence of abduction. Criminal record checks were run on several of the family members but can up blank.

"Nothing makes sense," his Mother said, after searchers failed to find any sign of him. "We've been through the Mountain with a tooth comb and not a footprint, a hair; nothing, and it rained."

Over five hundred people had voluntarily gone to the mountains to help search for him, along with heat seeking helicopters that hovered over the more rugged parts of the mountain to find him if he'd fallen into a crevice. Divers went into the ponds.

Local hunter J. Pindell, who lived in one of the cabins on the mountain was quoted in local newspapers as saying, "There's something phoney here. If he was here in the woods they'd have found him."

Toward the end of the month, TV coverage prompted a National Guard search for the little boy, then four months later a Special Forces Reserves Unit came, and then a team of cadaver dogs.

Still nothing; only questions, mystery, and the odd hint of a clue here and there.

A K9 bloodhound seemed to pick up a scent of him at the exit of the woodland that led to the road, but it wasn't reliable enough to go on; hundreds of people had covered that piece of ground in the searches for him.

Then there was the strange formation found in the woods, of three small rocks placed in the shape of a triangle with a piece of wood in the middle of it and three lengths of wood on the sides of it. Ruled another dead end, it was dismissed, but is it worth mentioning that his disappearance was on May 1st?

The night before this is known as 'Beltane' in the Pagan calendar, or 'Walpurgis Night,' in the Druidic Calendar, but the day of his disappearance, May 1st, is also said by some believers, to be one of the 'Illuminati's' most 'sacred' of days, and on this day, human sacrifice is said to be the requirement. It's also considered the founding day of the Illuminati, established on May 1st 1776 in Bavaria.

Was the triangle formation a Thaumaturgic Triangle used in satanic summoning rituals? If so, it had no protective circle surrounding it, which for those who believe it's possible to summon demons with this ritual, would be highly dangerous to the practitioners; unless the wood placed around it was an attempt to create as close a circle as possible?

A Thaumaturgic Triangle is used in ritual demonic summoning, with the triangle said to be the domain in which the summoned entity or negative energy will manifest itself.

Satanists are said to mark out a triangle area with symbols or 'charged' items, which could be rocks or stones, and these 'symbols' placed at the three points of the triangle.

This may be, and possibly is wholly unrelated to the disappearance of the child; however, when looking further into the relevance of this day in supposed Occult and 'illuminati calendars,' proponents of the ritual importance of these days have pointed out that it is one of the days of human sacrifice, with a particular emphasis on the need for it to be child sacrifice.

Indeed the theory of 'special days' goes a lot further, outlining the importance of the time period from April 19th to May 1st; said to be a critical 13 day period where 13 is the number of regeneration and sacrifice is made to the 'Beast' or the 'Master.'

A time of blood sacrifice from ancient times, said to be in worship of the demon 'Baal.'

Wild yet horrifying claims have been made of children being bred for this purpose, or being abducted to be sacrificed by the secret society. Claims which reach the highest levels of political and religious groups. Figures vary between 50,000 to 80,000 young children disappearing each year in the United States.

Could it really be true that children, and adults are abducted for sacrificial satanic cults? Do they become victims of a powerful underground elite, operating from the highest levels of government down? Is this in any way plausible or just crazy and unfounded speculation?

James Rothstein, a retired NYPD detective wrote extensively of his investigations into human trafficking and child abduction pointing to elite paedophile rings; shadowy groups concealed cloaked and hidden, held together by secret blood oaths.

In just one very complex case 12 year old Johnny Gosch was abducted while on his Newspaper delivery round in Des Moines in September 1982.

His Mother claimed an abduction 'ring' which was part of the earlier established MK-Ultra program, was behind it, even giving testimony in Court of what she believed to be a Nationwide Satanic ring.

Those who believe there is truth in the existence of satanic and occult ritual worship, also point to some important events in recent history as having occurred during this 13 day period, including April 19th Waco,

April 19th Oklahoma bombing, April 20th Virginia Tech massacre.

Then there is the high school student in Germany who killed 18 on April 27 2002, killing himself at exactly 13.oo hours, with '13' here allegedly flagging the illuminati power number, and conspiracists claiming that committing suicide to complete a mass killing is a hallmark of a mind controlled victim, as depicted in such books as Bill Cooper's *Behold A Pale Horse*.

Counter to this argument of course is that there are many other dates on the calendar, outside of this 13 day period, where mass murders and abductions have also taken place.

Going back now to the disappearance of 5 year old Victor, one local newspaper reported that a psychic by the name of Louis Gonot had contacted the Sherriff to say that he kept having visions of the boy being taken to a shack in the woods, and describing the natural features around the shack.

The Sherriff recognised that part of the woods exactly, despite the fact that the Psychic was resident in another State hundreds of miles away and had never been to the woods there.

The Sheriff however was also inclined to believe the psychic due to the fact that he had also once contacted a nearby Sheriff two years earlier and precisely described where a man's body lay in a creek in Marshall County. He was absolutely spot on and the man's body was found.

He described that in his vision of the little boy, a man with a beard and long hair was involved and that he had been stalking the boy in the woods.

His words were chilling, "There's only one vision I see every time. The little boy is in a hole in the ground. There's still energy there."

In other words, he was saying the boy was not dead, but being held there. "The police keep missing something."

The Sherriff went to the place described, and the shack was there, but the boy was not found. Given that Gonot said he had been in a shack and then in the ground, it would seem perhaps to imply he had been moved and taken somewhere else where he was held captive in the ground; and given his accuracy in finding the other man, perhaps his vision in this case was sadly correct.

Could serial abductors; experts in concealment and evasion, fit and elusive, and with a strong motive, exist and flourish in wilderness areas?

Perhaps the following true story is a good illustration.

In the 1930's, the bone-freezing winters and untamed wilds of the NW Territories of Canada were one of the most inhospitable places on earth. No heating, no modern comforts, and exposure in this terrain for anything other than a short time would have been clearly suicidal. But none of this deterred Albert Johnson; a man of infamy who led the Mounties on a ferocious hunt after shooting several of them.

Moving alone to the Territories he took up residence in a bare log cabin and set traps to survive off the land. Hunting for both food and fur, he eked out a lonely but presumably chosen existence.

The only people for miles around him were the local Inuit's, but he was interfering with their traps, on which their livelihood depended too, and they asked the police to reason with him.

The closest Mounties, almost one hundred miles away, arrived in the -50 degree cold. He refused to open the Cabin door. When they kicked it down, he shot one of them. He'd drilled holes in his cabin and from inside he shot at them.

Out-gunned by the trapper's firepower, not expecting him to be as heavily armed and on the offensive, they withdrew, but returned later with a larger posse of ten men, a pack of dogs, explosives and lots of rifles.

On their arrival the trapper held them in a gunfight for more than 12 hours until the Mounties threw a stick of dynamite into the cabin in an attempt to smoke him out, but as they entered to arrest him he surprised them by firing at them from a foxhole he'd dug in the floor of the cabin.

What followed next was astonishing and unbelievable yet it really happened. In what seemed utterly impossible, this man led the police on a 7 week manhunt across the snow covered wilderness which saw him climb a 7000 foot peak with no climbing gear, only to disappear once more. He was canny beyond belief. At one stage he crossed a frozen river using the tracks of a caribou in order to conceal his own footprints.

By the end of the chase, having been pursued for more than fifty days by police, army, Indian trackers, dogs and airplanes, he was finally cornered and shot, but only after he'd covered nearly 90 miles in the last 72 hours.

He never uttered a word in any of his encounters with the police. He was almost like a ghost in his ability to elude and evade until the finally confrontation when he eventually ran out of escape routes.

How did he survive and escape for weeks, amid blizzards and white-outs with no provisions except ammunition; climbing mountains and covering ground faster than the dogs? Somehow he managed to...

Could the psychic who said he'd had visions of a man stalking and snatching little Victor in the woods have been right? The story shows just how possible it is for a man with extraordinary guile, strength and intention to exist as a shadowy elusive figure in the unforgiving wilderness, living off the land and outsmarting fellow humans by the score.

Could a man stalk, snatch, abduct, escape and elude at will? With the right determination and motivation, it would seem so...

In one final reference to occult connections mentioned in the Shoemaker case, many researchers including Endtimelect.com blog, run by a supposed '4th generation escapee of the illuminati, speculate that in the well known case of the missing baby girl Lisa Irwin, she was abducted from her Kansas home in 2011 for the purpose of sacrifice, with her first birthday falling on 11.11.11.

This particular person however goes even further in making the astonishing claim that the child was smuggled out of the country and put onto a boat organised by a Trust run by the 'Luciferian Knights of Malta,' claiming that the Trust itself traces underwater Ley lines for the 'illuminati Satanists,' again another reference to the Ley lines connection.

Again, could any of this really be true? The same person also claims that 'DARPA' technology enabled the door to the house to be opened to allow the abductor in.

Crazy and preposterous? Quite possibly, however the connection to Malta is an interesting one for it leads to the apparent belief that in Malta, 'Underground beings demand Humans,' at least, they do according to researcher and archaeologist Graham Stuart.

Chapter Five:
'Underground Beings demand Humans'

Malta has long been an island of great strategic importance, and was a stronghold of the British Navy during WW2.

'Mythological creatures *exist*,' says Stuart, 'and Governments have long known. They are fed humans. When ancient priests who worshipped Baal came to the Island, they practised the offering of humans to their God of the underworld, who they believed lived under the Island.'

What is indeed true is that in 1902 labourers digging a Well accidently discovered a series of excavations which descended down into multi-level catacombs.

The Hypogeum of Hal Saflienti as it then became known, had long subterranean passages that were said to travel underground for many miles. When it was first discovered it was said that human skeletons numbering at least 7,000 were found inside.

C. Lois Jessop, a Secretary at the British Embassy, reported an incident regarding the caves to Borderland Science Journal. On a trip there to explore them, very curious and much against the advice of the official guide with her, she ventured into the small and less accessible burial chambers in the lowest strata of the caves.

As she entered on her hands and knees with a candle to light the way, she climbed through the small entry point and emerged through a passage into an enormous cave where she stood on the edge of its ledge looking down at what looked to her like a bottomless pit.

Opposite her at a slightly lower level, she noticed a ledge like the one she was standing on that looked to her as though it led to a tunnel. As she was observing it she claims that one after the other, a group of very large creatures started to appear on the ledge.

'Twenty persons of giant stature walked along the ledge. Their height about twenty feet, I judged. Long white hair that fell like a cowl. Their heads oval and elongated. They walked slowly with long strides. Then stopped, turned and simultaneously raised their heads. They beckoned me. Terror rooted me to the spot.'

As she fled in panic back through the tiny gap and back to find the guide, she said her panic did not seem to shock him; indeed it was almost as though the look he gave her was entirely knowing.

"I knew he had seen what I had seen at one time."

His look also held caution; as though warning her not to speak of what had happened, and for many years she didn't.

Prior to this experience she says, a group of school children had gone to the caves on a tour with their teachers. They too had come into this 'burial chamber,' but as the last child had entered, the walls behind them had caved in and the children and teacher were never found. 'The walls just happened to cave in, trapping the children?' she mused, knowing that when she had been in there with the giant humanoids, a terrific wind had blown across at her as the group of creatures had raised their arms at her and her candle had been snuffed out.

She didn't think the walls collapsing were a natural accident. She knew what had happened to her, and could only wonder how she had been lucky enough to escape.

The editor of the journal, Crab Riley, found her story hard to believe, especially because she could not provide evidence of the children disappearing, and he was inclined to dismiss it as fantasy until he researched archives, where mention of the disappearances was indeed found in National Geographic Magazine.

'Teachers and school children descended and did not return. Search parties and excavations found no trace. After weeks, they were given up as dead,' it said.

The article, by archaeologist William Griffith, also made mention of the skeletons found when the caves were first discovered too, although the number was far higher than had been realised by most.

'There were human bones to account for thirty thousand people. It was a "restaurant" I rather think, for Atlantean descendants.'

Could underground races of carnivorous species really dwell in the deep substrata below ground, coming up momentarily to snatch and feed off humans?

Interestingly, in some excellent research, Dustin Naef says there are over 700 caves and tunnels in Lava Beds National Park alone, and over 150 in the Marble Mountain area near Mount Shasta, with over thirty miles of tunnels mapped so far.

And in another part of the country, in the El Malpais National Park, underground disappearances are a common possibility.

It was here that James Chatman's daughter suggested they go to El Malpais 'Badlands' National Monument for a short walk to the Big Tubes attraction to celebrate his birthday. Leaving the car in the parking lot, a team of archaeologists saw them set out on the mile long trail toward it.

It was June 2002. The attraction comprised nearly twenty miles of tunnels and larval tubes, but they only intended taking a look; they weren't wearing hiking boots and had no backpacks. It was just supposed to be a gentle stroll along the path to the Monument.

They were reported missing shortly afterward. A rapid search and air rescue was instigated with sniffer dogs, helicopters and over 200 people. The search party covered over 35 miles looking for them. The dogs thoroughly combed the area.

No trace of them could be found; that is until 8 years later when their skeletal remains, tattered clothes, I.D and bank cards were discovered.

The family and authorities simply could not understand what had happened to them on that an innocuous one mile walk, and they particularly couldn't understand how they had got to where they'd been found; over four miles away across the lava flows where their bones lay scattered.

Where they'd been found required extensive travel over rough and precarious larva troughs. Spokesman for the park Leslie said at the time of the search, "If they were on the surface, they'd have been found."

Helicopters had flown repeatedly over the area where they were later found. Yet air searches, dogs, and people had seen no trace of them.

"Crossing lava is not 'a walk;' it's rough, and a mile can take an hour. We're perplexed," she admitted.

Helicopters had repeatedly flown over the lava. How had they not been seen? If they weren't on the surface where were they? Had they been underground?

"Spelunkers searched the caves," she said. "We don't know how they got to where they were."

Were they in the caves at some point? If so, why would they go further away from safety when they resurfaced? Were they taken into the caves, into the labyrinths were eyesight is handicapped by the murky darkness beneath.

Was something human at play here or something far less easy to define?

Since then, 5 more people have disappeared in the same place.

Interestingly, in Socorro County SSAR reports, the organisation also lists other inexplicable disappearances in New Mexico wilderness areas, including in 2001,

'Subject walked away from camp during the night. Presumed to be out of the area. Remains found by hikers in 2012.'

'March 2012, Male runner from Wilderness Lodge Hot springs didn't return from run. After 4 day search involving 16 teams and 5 aircraft, subject found deceased.'

And the SAR Council of New Mexico relates a strange July 2009 case where they searched for an elk hunter in Pecos National Forest. Over 12 teams with dogs searched for the man reported missing by his friends.

His vehicle was at the Camp with all his clothes and gear inside apart from his gun and hunting bow. Dogs tracked him along a trail and back to the vehicle, but no where else. Eventually the mission was terminated without finding him.

What had managed to overpower an experienced hunter with a gun?

Where did these, and the many other reported missing people disappear to before they were discovered dead or not found at all?

***

Going back to the Malta caves, Riley, the editor of *Borderland Science*, took things further in the 1900's by using the experience of testimonies from others both in regular positions in life and those more involved in esoteric and auric study, to become convinced in a theory that;

"There may exist many races in the interior of the earth, of different densities dependent on their plane of vibration. I believe some of these underground races can shift between 3rd and 4th dimensions so that sometimes they are visible to human sight and *invisible* at other times."

Riley's conclusion also came from studying among others the works of Max Heindel's *The Rosicrucian Cosmo-Conception*, in which Heindel writes,

'The first step in Occultism is the study of the *Invisible* Worlds; non-existent and incomprehensible, because we lack the sight to perceive them. The mysterious force which causes phenomena remains invisible to us, but if with methods our higher senses are awakened, we are able to behold the Worlds hidden.'

'The reality of these higher Worlds and the objects in them appear as 'mirages' or even less substantial, yet in truth they are much more real and more indestructible than the objects in the 'physical' world.'

Do these include the invisible entity that confronted David's in his encounter earlier in the San Juan Islands? And other people's accounts, such as Suzie's, who contacted me recently?

Chapter Six:
'The first step in occultism is the study of the Invisible Worlds.'

Here follows the correspondence from Suzie, received a few weeks ago;

'I saw what you are going to be discussing on the show on Coast to Coast tonight and I felt you might be interested in reading about what I witnessed a few years ago. I wrote to Dave Schrader to ask him to pass this info to you. I am writing you to ask you to take a look at my own personal report. It scares me to this day and I feel it's important to get the word out about this. I do not know if those entities are still there to this day, but I hope people can be alerted to the fact that these things are out there.

My sister moved to a different town since then and I have not been back to New Hampshire. I wish someone would go check it out because these things are totally invisible and who knows where they are, or where they went. Anything that was that intelligent and in tree tops needs to be investigated in my opinion. I try not to think about it too much because it could freak me out. I hope this report helps people stay safe. Something is out there for real and we can't see it with our eyes at all!'

This is Suzie's account; she was staying at her Sister's home in a wooded subdivision of Hampstead. It was spring 2003 and it had been rainy the last few days. Often late at night, Suzie would go out onto the front deck to smoke. She described that each night, as she sat on the deck after midnight, she would hear large sticks breaking in the forest. It happened every night.

Being a seasoned camper and having been brought up by Scout leaders, she didn't think anything of it at first, but she did notice that she never heard any rustling of leaves, but she brushed it off as being some kind of animal.

But night after night the sounds continued, and she could also hear the sounds of scraping on the tree bark and of something dropping out of the trees. She would look into the forest for any kind of movement but couldn't see anything there. The porch and driveway were well lit by the flood lights. She used a flashlight to beam light into the trees. But she couldn't see anything at all moving.

Then the sounds started to move closer. The longer she stayed out on the porch the closer the sounds started to come.

In the daylight she checked the trees for any marks and looked for animal tracks. She sent her nephew out into the woods to jump on sticks to measure the sound she was hearing at night. He could only break smaller sticks but Suzie could break the large ones by jumping on them. This implied that whatever was doing it was larger than an 11 year old boy; yet Suzie didn't know of any animals that large whose habitat was in this area.

Not only that, but at night they were coming closer to the house. Getting her nephew to move around in the woods, she was able to estimate that the distance the sounds were coming from had to be no more than 20 or so feet away from her.

And, she knew there were more than just one of 'them,' because at night the sounds would come from the front of the house and from behind at the same time. They were coming from two directions simultaneously.

Yet they were not visible to human sight, and they weren't showing up on any photographs she'd taken, but even inside the house now Suzie began to feel like she was being watched.

On the laptop at night, sitting by the curtainless window, she felt like she was being observed. The dogs were picking up on something too, because from their basement crates they would start howling.

Then one night Suzie was outside on the porch again when she heard them coming. Again the floodlights were lit up and she could see the panorama of trees clearly, but she could see nothing there and there was no rustling; only sticks breaking, and they were coming closer.

About eight feet away from her, some plants stood in pots on the lower part of the deck, and she watched as the plants moved to one side and then sprung back into place, as though something had brushed past them, except nothing was there that she could see and there were no other sounds like footsteps, or the sound of steeping on grit.

The night had no wind or breeze, but the flowers had been pushed aside a significant distance.

Whatever it was, it had come up the stairs toward her.

In absolute shock, her head running through what she'd just seen happen, she turned and ran inside, locking the door hurriedly.

Shortly after that incident, she was sitting by the window on the computer again when the eerie feeling of being watched returned. As she looked at the living room wall she thought she could see shadows above it on the ceiling, as though someone had just walked past, but everyone was in bed. She thought it had to be her imagination playing tricks and she decided to take a shower and relax.

The bathroom was situated across from the basement, which was closed.

When she finished her shower and came out of the bathroom, the basement door was open. As she went upstairs she saw her nephew's bedroom light on but he was fast asleep in bed.

She believes it's possible that whatever it was outside had somehow got into the house.

How did they get in? She's not sure; "Through the walls, the basement door?"

But she wants to know what they are, and why they are interested in humans?

She says, "I'm a person who's been through a lot and has seen and experienced a lot in life; I don't scare as easily as others which is why I stood there so long and why I went back night after night to listen and see if I could see them. There was no movement whatsoever visually, and it was reasonably well lit. No-one in my sister's house was up late and outside so they had never experienced this before and they tried to make all kinds of excuses for it, like it was the trees popping from the cold weather or small animals. I wish I had had equipment to record it."

"I was only about 4-5 feet from the door the whole time. I wish I'd been able to get my brother-in-law to stand out there with me. He's a total non-believer in anything unexplained. Too science based. All things are explainable to him. Oh and a tiny aside, I tried to flip my cigarette in their direction but it didn't fly right and I lost that opportunity and fled. I wanted to see if it would bounce off of whatever was there."

"Were they just watching? testing? hunting? Or abducting?"

"On the grass there's no sticks; they're silent. How many other homes did they go into?"

"There were no other sounds and no communication of any kind. Not even telepathically. These things are either inter-dimensional entities, or cloaked, or perhaps out of our visual range of ability to see. We need to learn about them as fast as we can so we're not caught with our pants down. I had no other way to get my story out back when it happened. Calling into shows is hit or miss and paranormal forums only reach a small portion of society. I know they are still out there, I just know it."

"It would be different entirely if I were not well versed in camping, forest sounds. I easily can rule out a lot because of my background. All animals of the forest rustle dry brush and leaves on the forest floor even a little bit when they are trying to be quiet. I am a seasoned camper who was raised by scout leaders camping a lot in my life. I know the forest sounds and the animal behavior."

"A lot of people initially accused me of making up a scary story; they didn't believe it was real. Then they made every forest animal the source of the sounds as if I don't know about regular animal sounds. Of course a few said it was Bigfoot because they believe he can go invisible. I know beyond any shadow of a doubt this was no Bigfoot. Bigfoot breaks trees and beats on things. He walks heavy and rustles the foliage and dry leaves on the forest floor. This was quiet creeping and no rustling at all. I know a coyote howl from a wolf, and the sounds that fox and raccoon make."

"Through further discussion on a paranormal website a few things came to light. One person suggested the sound wasn't actual breaking sticks but a sound they make. Who's to say? One person interpreted the situation that the entities were testing me to see what I'd do. This comment/thought made my hair stand up straight and I have long hair! This put a twist on it that had not occurred to me before. Prior to that I thought the entity accidentally brushed the flower as it passed closely by it. If it were done intentionally to observe me, that involves high intelligence and that really means we are up against something ...frikin' scary as hell."

"This will haunt me the rest of my life. I hate that. I feel that way out of pure fear. Terror in fact. I know in my gut this is going on everywhere and has not been discovered yet. I can add this too, they were up in the trees for a reason. To me, they hunt at night. They go in the trees to watch like hunters in a tree stand. This means hunting/observing in my opinion. Question is, are they documenting or planning dinner?"

"I really haven't been the same since. I never feel okay in the woods anymore even in the day light, though I have not had many chances to get out in the woods in recent years. Hell, I don't feel safe in my own yard especially at night. We all need to track these things because they pose a threat in my opinion."

"This was nothing normal at all. These things were sneaking up on me, synchronisticaly. They had obviously communicated to each other in some way to be so perfectly in sync. That's what really scared me bad. It showed high level of intelligence. Question is, were they sneaking up to observe me, or to stalk me? Was I prey or to be captured, or just observed? THAT is what made me run inside and lock the door."

***

An interesting account on godlike productions forum is very similar to the account Suzie sent to me. This person's account is in response to a fellow reader on there who also had an experience with *something invisible.*

'In Colorado here seen something similar a few years back; only this one settled into a cottonwood tree next to my house. There was nothing there to be seen but it was active. All day it broke branches, snapping them from the tree and throwing or dropping them down, regular.'

'A friend came over and I told him and we sat outside looking. There were no animal sounds; deathly silent, not even insects. No wind. Every couple of minute's branches snapped, forming a pile on the ground.'

'Bolstered by my friend I walked the sixty feet to the tree, but staying about thirty feet from it. I could see nothing, then a branch about fifteen feet long got thrown in my direction! I backed off quick and said a prayer. It stopped immediately?!'

'About a year later I learnt by chance about a man and his wife walking by a creek who became aware of something moving through the tree tops, breaking off branches as it went along - they said they saw a 'shimmering' aka Predator-which I didn't.'

'Another very weird thing; we have people occasionally go missing here, in the mountains. One man went missing several years ago. They found his skeleton with his backpack. The Skeleton was intact, but the skull was missing.'

It's interesting to note that he claims in his case, it stopped after he said a prayer. Very similar to the plethora of accounts of people who say they've had encounters with demonic and reptilian entities, and have found that by praying aloud it has forced them to leave. Though not successful in every case, in the majority of cases it does seem to work. Does this give some kind of clue as to the origins of these invisible beings?

The person above was relating the account to another person who'd posted the following account below, and was asking for suggestions to help him understand what it was that he'd seen when out walking his dog one day by the woods.

'First off, I don't do drugs, drink, and as far as I know I'm sane. I don't believe in aliens. I have a college degree. Yesterday I was walking my dog; I'm in the country and the woods are all along that road. Just off the path I saw something that disturbed me; the only way to describe it is it was Predator-like.'

'My dog didn't notice it apparently. We were shaded under the cover of the trees, with no broken streaks of light. It was a clear sky anyway so it wasn't the sun and it wasn't shadows of leaves. I investigated all of the possibilities.'

'It was off the ground by about a foot and it was shadow-like. As though holographic in nature.'

'It was running into the woods. At first I thought it was like a sort of enormous snake but I realised there was no solid form. It really looked like a scene out of the film, although I haven't seen it for a few years, where you see the feet moving like a holograph, as though superimposed over the plants and leaves.'

'It was the strangest thing I have ever seen. I saw the plants moving where it went. There were no sounds of wildlife but I noticed that after it ran the sounds began to come back.'

'One thing is a lot of things are found dead on this road. There's always road kill.'

'What did I see? Was it an illusion I just couldn't figure out? Did I see a different dimension?'

***

Then a lady maintaining anonymity forwarded an account of her experience to the *Phantom universe UK blogspot*.

'It happened early in the morning around 7 am in April 2010. My husband and I were travelling from Breckenridge, in Summit County, Colorado to Abeline. My husband was driving and I was just looking around when in the road ahead of us my eyes locked onto something.'

'We were coming up to a small incline in the road. It was visibly very clear. I saw something run across the road on the top of the rise in front of us, from left to right. There was something visible there above the road by a few inches. It looked like small feet and part of legs, moving fast over the road in a trot. I couldn't see above mid level except for a rippled sky behind the thing about the size of a person's body. It reminded me of the Predator effect in the movie.'

'As we passed the spot, there was nothing there. I looked on both sides of the road, down into the ditches but there was no animal, no nothing. Nothing further into the trees, although I got this feeling that something was watching us.'

'I told my husband after I saw it cross but he didn't notice it. For the rest of the way I kept looking, to see if it was my eyes playing tricks. What was it I saw? The light? A cloaked entity? Heat waves? But the morning was cool and it had been a cool evening. The heat hadn't risen yet. The sun was barely up.'

'The only thing I have is that as it crossed the road I felt a presence. It still gives me chills.'

***

Sharon Lee runs the Bigfoot field reporter blog. While not necessarily believing in the possibility of 'invisible' creatures herself, she received a report from a woman who described a puzzling incident at Salt Fork State Park in May 2008.

'I'm still mystified by this. Something crossed the trail in front of me. It was very big but what I couldn't see was the shape of it, just a glimmer, and a transparent outline, yet it seemed upright. It was about twenty yards away from me.'

'For years I was too uneasy to tell anyone, I didn't have the words to describe it, but was it a Bigfoot in a non-physical sense? There's no other way to describe it, but it still puzzles me. Then I heard a radio talk show and a caller who was a Marine related the same exact thing happened and he compared it to the Predator film, where the alien-type creature is seen first only as a shimmering outline. It's exactly what I saw and still to this day I'm terrified by it.'

She even thinks that whatever it was could still be following her somehow.

'Recently a collection of twigs and leaves was left on my deck chair within the space of a couple of hours; this isn't the first time it's happened.'

Sharon herself had a different but still very strange experience while out for a jog with her husband one summer at Hogback ridge in Boulder, Colorado.

They'd already looped the trail once and he'd left her behind, being a faster runner, when she needed to use the rest room near the parking area.

On leaving the rest room she caught sight of her husband out of the corner of her eye go past the side of their parked car and duck down behind it, about eighty feet away.

She presumed he was planning on playing a trick on her and was going to jump out on her to scare her.

She jogged toward the car to tell him it was too late; she'd already seen him, but when she arrived at the car there was no-one there.

'I looked all round the car and in the trees behind. No-one there! It was at this point that my husband arrived from the *other side* of the parking lot running out of the woods. I had to assume then it was just me seeing things...?'

Then there is this very strange account from MUFON.

'I was hunting in Wilson, N. Carolina. November 2009, around 6 am. A burst of wind hit me, but it was strange; this wind was blowing in a circular fashion and it was making a humming sound; a bit like an high powered electric motor.'

'I would've thought it was a natural thing had it not been for the humming. It had to be blowing 40 mph, but in a circular pattern. I know this because I could see the tops of the trees bending in a circular pattern. This noise stayed over my head for approximately two minutes before moving. As it moved away, I watched the trees blowing in a circular pattern.'

'My feelings at the time was one of terror. I was armed with a rifle and gun but I was terrified. Something flew over my head that I could not see. Of that, I'm certain of it.'

Then consider this account from the Muskegon Chronicle of May 21 1998 in Minastee National Forest, when school children and their accompanying teachers were witness to a large silent object, described as shaped like a 'protozoa or omeba,' which appeared to float slowly over the tree-line above them.

The body of the object was described as being 'like shimmering gossamer,' and 'almost transparent or insubstantial' yet it also seemed to be illuminated by lights.

With the exception of lights, this last account is reminiscent of Navy Veteran Trevor Constable's twenty year study of 'Atmospheric Beings;' his theory of Sky-bound entities that roam the skies in silence, visible only by the use of infra-red but always there.

Organic creatures of some sort. Large, voracious, but invisible to the naked eye; these undetectable predators could take people without seeing them coming.

His theory was that these morphic beasts he captured with the use of infra-red cameras were monsters that only increased their density and became more visible while in search of food; their food source being humans. Shimmering predators that shift in density as they swoop down to attack.

He blamed the accounts of livestock mutilations and disappearances, human mutilation cases, and the constant stream of people going missing every year on these soaring predatory entities.

In the 1950's he captured images on film in the Yucca Valley and the Mojave Desert; shadowed dense beings that appeared to look like living cells. Others took the form of UFO's. All were framed by the landscape, enabling their size to be scaled in comparison to natural features. They were huge.

For years reports had surfaced of strange creatures inhabiting the skies above us. He now believed he'd captured images of them in infra-red. In the Journal of Borderland Research he wrote,

'Objects would be in the films but as a 'stirring' that followed the lines of their structure. This was a puzzle until we came in contact with George DeLaWarr's work, a radionics pioneer who'd discovered that everything living has an 'etheric' axis.'

'Etheric energy transfer could be captured on the film, just like photographs that capture the auric energy field of humans.'

Constable believed he'd captured the 'churning turbulence' of auric energy, as the objects changed form and shape. 'Pathe film technicians, who handled millions of feet of movie film footage, said they'd never seen anything like this before.'

His conclusion; 'We now know that creatures and crafts exist in a range of forms beyond human sight; that this life is invisible to human sight.'

'Some forms not fully materialized indicate that they have perhaps emerged from an even more remote range fifth state of density.'

Then more recently in the Oxford Countryside of England between 2010 and 2011, Nik Hayes decided to adopt a different approach.

'For the filming where I captured them I used an infrared full spectrum converted 330 canon digital camera with a nanometer ultraviolet pass filter to film ultraviolet, set in movie mode. I've taken out the 'hot mirror' and used a piece of clear quartz in its place, which opens up the whole spectrum of infrared, ultraviolent and 'invisible.' Then used various filters to filter out the infrared and normal light and leave just the 'invisible.'

Shown with the footage slowed down to a speed of $1/8^{th}$ due to the extreme speed at which these things are flying, they were filmed in daylight hours, and swarms of these entities can be seen above the tree line and several of them swoop down below the tree line, heading toward the ground. They can be seen on YouTube Quest for the Invisible QFTI.

'What I've found is that with non-infrared they don't register at all on the footage. They do however appear to look like solid creatures; and they are all around us all the time.'

Eminent Physicist at Stanford University, Dr William Tiller has previously stated, "We see only a fraction of the electro-magnetic spectrum; perhaps we similarly perceive only a small fraction of a greater reality spectrum."

Professor Fred Wolf, in his groundbreaking book of 1985 stated, "As fantastic as it sounds, Quantum Physics posits that there exists with this world another world, side by side."

Nobel Laureate for Physics, Professor Brian D Josephson refers to the discovery of subatomic particles in physics; energy that 'behaves in a way that is seemingly paranormal; that moves faster than the light, and passes effortlessly through matter like 'ghosts.'

Lynne McTaggart in her findings in 'The Field; The Quest for the secret force of the Universe,' discovered that significant numbers of scientists were coming together to establish scientific proof of an 'Energy Field,' that everything in the universe was interconnected by waves, spread out through time and space that tied everything to each other.

The basic most fundamental laws of physics state that energy cannot be destroyed; it is infinite. It cannot be destroyed, but it can be converted to different form.

'Quantum physicists discovered that matter was completely indivisible. The Universe could now only be understood as a dynamic web of interconnectedness. Indeed, time and space themselves appeared now to be just arbitrary constructions.'

'There now appeared to be scientific validation for a model of consciousness that was not limited to the body but was an ethereal presence- an idea which had largely been the domain of religion, mysticism and new age spiritualism.'

A group of scientists, including two astrophysicists have been conducting experiments and solving complex equations that they believe even furnish irrefutable proof of human survival of bodily death.

Michael Roll, who heads *The Campaign for Philosophical Freedom*, is the spokesman for the group. R. D Pearson, one of Roll's colleagues, a former University lecturer whose specialty is thermodynamics and fluid mechanics, has written a book called *Intelligence behind the Universe,* in which put simply, he claims it contains mathematical proof to explain the cosmic force that drives the phenomenon of continuing life.

Pearson et al see post-mortem survival humans as just part of a multi-dimensional sub-atomic matrix, on which all 'forms' of life exits.

In this model, physical materialisations are but the temporary merging of different frequencies, from two separate levels of the unifying 'grid.'

Are these above accounts, findings, and statements validation of the possibility that a very real 'invisible' realm exists very closely to our own and it is from here that entities or unfamiliar creatures can emerge, just as we ourselves will one day enter another 'state' and dimension?

Has the likelihood of invisible entities and creatures existing become an ever more real possibility? Cloaked veiled and hardly visible, yet appearing temporarily through changes of vibration and density.

Many will say that ancient esoteric knowledge has known this for millennia.

Is it through these realms that angels and spirit helpers are said to emerge from?

Phil Bolsta is a writer on spiritual topics, and on his blog he relates a story told to him by his friend, the clairvoyant Christopher Barbour, who, with his gift, is said to assist police in helping to solve murders.

One day Christopher decided to go for a long walk in a forest close to his home in Northern Arizona. After walking for nearly an hour deep in his thoughts, he realised he'd veered off the path and was walking through a thicket of tress and shrubs.

He says, "As I kept walking I heard a woman calling my name. The voice was female and she shouted my name as someone who knew me well would.'

'It stopped me on the spot and I looked around at where the voice seemed to be coming from, and I saw a woman there, who disappeared after just a few seconds. She had long hair and was wearing a gown.'

'In front of me was low shrubs and as I looked I realised that if I had taken another step, I'd have fallen down onto some jagged rocks far below.'

***

A famous true story goes back to the time of the Korean War in 1950 when Michael, a young US Marine, sent a letter back home to his Mother describing an astounding incident.

The Navy Chaplain of the Marine's unit, Father Walter Muldy later corroborated the story, describing it as exactly how the Marine had told him, and the Father later read the letter to a gathering of five hundred Marines at the Naval Base in San Diego.

The young Marine wrote, 'Dear Mom, you will find it hard to believe but I have got to tell somebody. Remember you told me to say a prayer to St Michael every day?'

He then goes on to describe in great detail what happened that fateful day. He and his patrol had been sent out to scout for enemy soldiers in the dense jungle terrain when he suddenly realised there was a huge Marine walking alongside him.

He started to talk with him, expressing that he found it strange that he did not know this Marine when he knew everyone in his Unit. The man told him his name was Michael, to which the young Marine expressed in surprise, "But that's my name too!"

"I know," said the stranger, and started to recite "Michael, Michael of the morning," – the first line of the prayer the younger Marine said every day.

The weather was bad; it was freezing cold, and soon it had started to snow. Oddly Michael realised that he couldn't see any breath coming from the stranger, but ominously, he heard the stranger say to him, "There's going to be trouble ahead."

Suddenly the snow cleared and they were face to face with enemy soldiers. Michael dove for cover, shouting at the stranger to get down too, but the big Marine just stood there, stock still. Bullets were flying at them.

Michael jumped up to pull the man down to the ground and it was then that a bullet hit him. In the letter, he writes of remembering being held by the stranger, his big strong arms holding him, before the stranger stood back up.

"There was a terrible splendour on his face, and he seemed to grow, the splendour intense around him like wings. In his hand he held a sword."

Later, recovering in the hospital, his Sergeant came to visit him. "How did you kill all those soldiers?" he asked Michael.

Completely confused by the Sergeants question, Michael asked him to explain what he was talking about. "Their bodies were strewn around you, each one killed by a single sword stroke."

***

In the realm of strange invisible and sudden manifestations, there also appears another phenomenon that at times is completely baffling.

As mentioned in this author's previous book 'Encounters with the Unknown,' the highland mountain ranges in Scotland are wild and magnificent places, but witnesses have claimed that their terrain can hold a dark side that has terrified many, and quite possibly led to the deaths of others.

Ben MacDhui is the highest peak in the Cairngorms. Many mountaineers are certain that this region harbours a malign entity called Fear Liath Mor. Translated this means 'The Big Grey Man.' Grey in colour, huge, and fearsome for all those who encounter it. Legend tells of it stalking anyone who trespasses into its territory. But is it just a legend?

When Professor Norman Collie spoke at the AGM of the Cairngorm Climbing Club in 1925, he reported an unnerving incident that had happened to him.

It was back in 1891 he told them, that after conquering the summit he was in the process of descending through heavy mist and fog when,

"Suddenly I began to hear noises in the loose rock behind me. Every few steps I took, I would hear a crunch behind me, then another, as if someone was walking behind me, but they were taking very heavy steps, many times the length of my own."

He continued on descending, trying to tell himself he was just imagining it, but the loud crunches behind him continued too.

He started to become more and more unnerved, out in the wilderness on his own, with something very big coming fast behind him, and it wasn't long before he found himself seized by terror and running blindly down the mountainside amidst the fog until he reached the forest at the bottom and ran into the covering of the trees.

Stopping to look behind him, he was unable to catch sight of the monster through the fog, but he knew he was being stalked by some huge menacing creature, and he ran on, exhausted but desperate to get to safety.

He told the climbers at the meeting that he had vowed he would never return there alone again, so convinced was he that there had been something deeply disturbing tracking him. Though unable to catch any real sight of it, he never forgot the sound of the crunching behind him as the huge creature stalked him.

After hearing of the Professor's experience, other mountaineers at the meeting began to admit that they too had experienced some very strange things while on the mountain.

They told of rapidly developing sensations of uncontrollable fear, panic and terror, yet with no logical reason causing these sensations. Some even exclaimed that they had felt irresistibly drawn toward a dangerous crevice or cliff as though in a trance, and coming perilously close to going over the edge before somehow being able to snap out of it.

Murmurs and rumours grew, speculating on how many climbers might have been chased to certain death by an entity or some malevolent force.

Following his telling of this story at the meeting, he received a letter from a doctor, who told of his own frightening experience on the same mountain.

The doctor and his brother were on the deserted mountain near the summit, when they suddenly saw a giant figure coming toward them. Terrified, they fled that instant, never having seen anything like it before and terribly aware of how small and alone they were out on that mountain.

One does have to wonder how many climbers did not see it coming and were not lucky enough to have been able to flee?

Wendy Wood, heavily involved in the founding of the Scottish National Party, has been described as one of the most rational people anyone could meet. However, she was gripped by a blind panic when walking through the Lairg Ghru Pass.

She was hiking there alone when she suddenly heard a voice. Thinking it might have been a fallen climber, she went to see if she could help, but she could find no-one around. She later described the voice as being extremely loud and close, and sounding like it was spoken in the Gaelic dialect.

Looking all around her she tried to see who it was that had spoken to her but no-one was there.

Spooked by the incident she hurried to get away from the area, but she became overwhelmed by the feeling that she was being followed by someone, or something, with an enormous stride. She could hear footsteps following behind her as she went.

At first she tried to reason with herself that the footsteps were just echoes of her own footsteps, thinking the mountainous setting could cause echoing to occur, but then she realised to her horror that the footsteps sounded wholly different to her own steps, and she could not stop the terror as she fled as fast as she could.

Then in February 2015, climber Chris Sleight, a producer of BBC Scotland's Outdoors Show spoke about a remarkable incident that had occurred just a few days ago, when he was climbing the peak of Ben Nevis, the highest mountain in Scotland, with a close friend.

'When I climb I listen, hard; there's so many clues that will tell you what's going right, or wrong. Sounds that comfort, like the thud of a pick in good ice; the clip snapping shut holding the rope that will hold you if you fell.

There are sounds that warn, and there are sounds you never want to hear. So when I heard a blood-curdling scream, I feared the absolute worst. Terrible sounds.

It started out almost indistinct, muffled, but quickly came sharp, visceral, piercing. I was hearing someone who'd just watched a loved one fall to their death. There was so much loss and pain in the sound. I wanted to be off the mountain, but I was hanging vertical off a wall. I froze. It sent my blood running cold and brought home consequences. But there was no where to retreat.'

He and his friend had no choice but to continue upward; the safest route. As they continued their climb and managed a safe descent, they both wondered why there was not more noise, more activity going on.

What they expected to see was a rescue party, voices searching for the body and the screaming friend or partner. They knew something terrible had happened; a fatality, a climber had fallen to their death. But there was no noise, no activity.

As they emerged from the misted mountain top they did their own search of the area but found no people. At the base of the mountain they talked with other climbers. They'd heard the piercing wailing too. One had even abseiled to investigate where he thought it was coming from but had found no-one there.

Even more strangely, none of the climbers there could find any evidence of an accident having taken place and when they contacted the police, no accident reports had been made in the last few hours and no-one had been reported missing.

He and his friend carried on trying to investigate over the remaining hours and yet no news came and no evidence showed up.

The Mountain Rescue Team came and searched yet they yielded no sign of anyone either and eventually stopped looking.

"We don't know who it was screaming, and we don't know what happened that day. We probably never will."

It was the only conclusion he could make...

A very human sounding but wholly unearthly scream could send the most prepared but unsuspecting climber falling, loosing their grip, or making a terrible fatal mistake from the sudden shock of it, causing them to flounder and fall, or unnerve someone so badly that they stumble, get disoriented and loose their bearings, get lost and wander into treacherous unforgiving territory. How many times could this have happened out alone in the wilderness?

***

Hiker and blogger SS Jrem of *Misguidedghost* writes about a youthful encounter in the abandoned grounds of the West Mountain Sanatorium, Pennsylvania, on "What remains the scariest night of my life."

Set atop West Mountain in what was once an old mining community, he decided to venture there and explore.

'A few friends and I took a trip to the Sanatorium. We'd never been there before. We never imagined what would follow..As a friend was dropping us off there for the night, another car was there. As we walked inside past the gate it seemed to be watching us. In the dark we couldn't see inside it, so had no idea why they would be watching us. Slightly uneasy we got off the main path and ducked behind a wall. The car drove toward the asylum.'

'Now I was unsettled. We wanted to go in the buildings but the car had gone up there. The car returned and went slowly past us, as if it was looking for us. We decided we should get out of there, so we decided to stay off the road and go back down the hill through the woods.'

'As we slowly made our way down in the darkness, we could clearly hear behind us the sound of crunching footsteps; we were now being followed on foot'.

'We continued down through the trees, but got low when they seemed to be coming closer. We were all crouched down as our friend who'd dropped us there called. I was pleading with him in a hushed voice to get back there and come get us.'

'The crunching came closer. I noticed that there wasn't any laughing or any talking among them. How could they maintain cold precision I wondered? And I was starting believing something really sinister was going on. And then it happened. As we hid there the most horrifying, inhuman, blood-curdling scream. It was *real;* it was *in-human*. It echoed off into the night.'

'Unable to even think straight, whatever it was that was happening to us was real and we all took off down the dark hill and out onto the road; we were sprinting. I couldn't remember a time I had been gripped by fear such as this.'

'But by the time our group was back together again, we seemed to be past the worst of the ordeal. That's how it happened; no embellishment. I think it was just guys wanting to mess with people; but there's still that small chance something supernatural was going on up there. That horrifying, blood-curdling scream was *inhuman.*'

***

Fifteen years ago Anna Evans took to posting in internet forums that dealt with paranormal topics in an attempt to find anyone else who'd had a similar experience to hers, in an effort to understand just what had happened to her back when she was fifteen.

She was staying with her family; Mom, Dad, younger brother and two younger sisters in a cottage they owned in an isolated and deserted valley close to the West Coast of Donegal in Ireland.

It was summer and as the family finished lunch Ana took herself out to the front door step to stand in the sunshine. The cottage was remote and there were no neighbours for miles. The nearest property was a twenty minute walk up a small trail but the owner had died and now it lay empty. The cottage had no electricity or telephone lines.

'At the time it happened, it was a calm warm afternoon. I was enjoying the rare sunshine. Suddenly I became aware of a sound. It sounded like voices calling my name, in unison. There were several of them, and it was like low whispers as a collective, continuous.

I listened to it for a few minutes, attempting to gauge it for fear of making a fool of myself, then I called my Mom and asked her if she could hear anything.

She said she could; she said it was voices calling my name. The whole family could hear it, including my father who's a Professor and Doctor and highly sceptical, but none of us could find the source.

It could be heard at the same unwavering level outside and in every part of the house in every room. We even stood and looked up the chimney in an attempt to put it down to wind but there was no wind.

In desperation to explain it I walked 500 yards up the hill by, where I could still hear it.

Persistent, incessant whispering; my brother was petrified and got under his bed clothes with his hands covering his ears.

But after about half an hour we became numb to it and eventually the voices were no longer present. I have never again experienced anything like it again, and an explanation to it continues to allude me. No explanations offered to me over the years are sufficed. There was no-one within miles of us. There are limited birds. There was no machinery. The area itself is barren mountain and valley.'

How many more people might have experienced the same phenomenon? Out alone, the sound of voices calling your name, luring and enticing you to find them, to follow them in the wilderness, to a destination unknown?

***

A really odd incident is described by NUFORC (the National UFO reporting centre, run by Peter Davenport) of 'a public employee holding down a job with responsibilities for over twenty years,' who says that he was out deer hunting in Illinois in mid afternoon November of 2014.

He was perched in his stand when all of a sudden something that 'looked like a ball of shiny motor oil,' appeared from above him approximately four feet away and hovered there.'

'It was a ball. At first I thought it was an insect. I stared at it for a few seconds, realizing it was not an insect. I'm used to seeing insects and moths when hunting but it'd been below freezing for several days and you don't see insects in that weather.'

This 'ball' hovered there in front of me at eye level moving up and down but not getting closer. I grabbed hold of the seat stand and reached out with my other hand to try to grab the ball. It dropped to level with my feet and began hovering again.'

'I sat down and it rose to eye level and above. It went slowly up and down about 1 foot in front of me and then hovered at eye level. I didn't see this out the corner of my eye; I looked at it close and clear the entire time. Before I could reach out again it curved away from me and as it blended with the leaves on the ground I lost sight it.'

'I couldn't understand what I'd just seen and I tried explaining it away in my mind. With the wind blowing toward me it stayed the same distance there the entire time, hovering without gravity. It just looked like a ball of shiny motor oil.'

'It had no wings, legs, propellers and it was *not* a stick or a leaf. I'm used to seeing insects and moths when hunting but it had been below freezing for several days and you don't see insects in this weather.'

'I was very concerned by this and still am. It troubles me as I cannot think of a logical explanation for this...'

Was it simply a biological entity of some unknown kind? Had it come from an alien craft somewhere nearby? Or was it some kind of drone? A form of surveillance or monitoring mechanism?

If so, what was its purpose? And why had it been sent to observe this man, out in the wilderness?

Chapter Seven:
Covert weaponization targeting innocent citizens?? A documented case of 'mass harm' in a rural area.

The theory that ever more sophisticated drones of all types exist and are used, as well as other advanced technological 'monitoring' equipment or 'weaponised technology' is proposed by many.

Is 'technology' being used on us and against us, without our knowledge or consent? If so, for what purpose? Are their purposes sinister?

Thinking back to David's initial email to me about the 'strobe lights' being used on his Island, and the deleterious psychological and physical effects on him and his friends there, including his need to have gone so far as to turn his home into a 'faraday cage' makes for concern and questioning as to how far the agenda has come in the use of technology against citizens and the real agenda behind it.

One striking case that has been raised by some observers as a clear example of the most sinister possibilities of how technology can be used against the masses now follows. Whether this is really what happened in the following pages, only the reader can decide...

Teenager Jenna Jones was found hanging from a tree in woods named locally as 'the Snake Pit' by a man walking his dog. The horrified man in his sixties said of the terrible discovery,

"I was shaken to the core; it was so shocking to find this young girl. Why are young people doing this? I can't understand it at all. What's going on round here?"

One of her best friends Dan said to reporters who came to cover the story, "I can't get my head round it; she was completely fine when I was talking to her yesterday."

Lisa, the Mother of the dead girl's best friend added, "I saw her only last night and she didn't have a care in the world; she was always laughing and giggling. That's who she was. I can't understand what's going on round here."

'Here' is a rural post-industrial area of Wales called Bridgend, a small town surrounded by woods and moorland and approximately an hour's drive from the Brecon Beacons National Park.

Only a few months prior to this young girl's suicide, her teenage cousin Zac had also hung himself.

It was 2008, and this girl at Snake Pit Woods was now the 17th suicide of teenagers in the same small area. It began with 18 year old Dale, who hung himself in 2007. His friend Dai hung himself the next month.

Two days before the funeral, another friend hung himself from in the woods.

Dai's step-father spoke to *The Times* Newspaper, describing how inexplicable to him it was. His step-son was a naturally friendly boy, liked by everyone, with a lively nature and plans in place to train as a painter. "Why did he do it? We'll take that question with us to the grave."

After an evening hanging around the local streets with his mates, he'd set off to walk home and it was during that walk that something seemed to happen, something that caused his decision to kill himself.

Sixty days later, 21 year old Leigh got up from his laptop, went out, and hung himself. Then a boy called Liam was found hanging in the woods one day after Boxing Day. By the start of 2012, 79 young people had hung themselves.

'Happy-go-lucky' Sean Rees hung himself from a tree on a hill; followed by 26 year old Neil, also found hanging in the woods. Kelly was found hanged hours after her cousin Nathan was declared dead by hanging. Natasha and Angie followed suit. Then Carwyn was found hanging from a tree in the woods. Followed by Anthony, then Elaine.

The list of names just seemed to grow and grow; every time suicide by hanging.

Justin's mother cannot understand what drove her son to do the same thing. He walked out the front door and was found hung in the woods.

"It can never be explained," she told reporters, "he'd looked me in the eye and told me he would never do that. Then one evening we had a silly argument, he stormed upstairs, came back later and threw a cord at me.

"It snapped," he said, showing her that he'd just tried to hang himself. At this point he called himself an ambulance and at hospital was assessed by the mental health nurse. Bizarrely, he was then sent home; despite telling her he "had voices in his head telling him to do bad things."

Shortly after his return home, despite his girlfriend being with him in his room, he left the house again taking a belt with him. The family and police quickly searched the woods for him but they were too late; by the time they found him he was dead.

"To this day I have no idea why," said his mother.

Even a young woman, Michelle, who didn't live in the area, suddenly hung herself on a visit there to see her boyfriend.

There were others who were not successful in their attempts. Fifteen year old Leah has no recollection of having tried to hang herself, though others close to her know only too well that she had tried.

What was highly unusual about all of these suicides was that not only was this only happening in so large a number in a relatively small rural area, they were also only occurring in a specific age range, and again highly unusually, missing from practically all of these suicides was any kind of suicide note. They just didn't leave any.

There was never any evidence of foul play however, and no implications at all to suggest these were murders. The evidence was very clear that they were suicides. And they were all carried out in exactly the same way, using the exactly same method.

The Guardian Newspaper consulted with a Dr Johansson of Umea University, whose specialist field is the study of teenage suicide.

"It's the largest cluster of teen suicides of modern times," he said. This was a unique occurrence; previously nothing on this scale had ever been heard of.

The area itself is one of high unemployment; it's not in a city and job prospects are not good for teenagers or adults, so the result is higher poverty, less advancement, low motivation and a lower standard of living.

This however is a very common problem to a lot of areas in both Wales and the United Kingdom, particularly in areas where coal mines and other industrial industries have declined. But young people hanging themselves had not become an epidemic in any other rural or post-industrial areas apart from this one.

The first theory developed by the Media was that this was some kind of interlinked suicide pact, a sort of domino-chain effect from 'emotional contagion,' where each friend, so upset from the death of their friend, followed the previous one to death; but although they almost all occurred within a 15 miles radius, not all of the victims knew each other.

One of the girls whose attempt was unsuccessful told a Vanity Fair journalist, "I never knew the others, but my head kept telling me to do it because everything would be ok."

While the local authorities and the police at first dismissed any connection between the suicides, they then went on to state that there was a strong link to social networking sites, given that all of the young people had access to these sites; and yet there was no evidence of any kind of collusion or encouragement toward each other, no taunting or egging each other on to kill themselves.

The Coroner also followed the theory of the internet playing a major role, yet the police didn't find any clues online. There was no internet 'death pact.'

Suicides among young people have become more common in school aged children where there has been evidence of online bullying, but none was found in these cases, and never before had such a cluster of cases been found.

The media, particularly the tabloids then came under attack by the local authorities and police, accusing them of sensationalist reporting, and there were those in the local area who felt that by covering the growing numbers of teen suicides, it could somehow be normalising the procedure, if not blatantly encouraging people to kill themselves by having each case on the front cover of their newspapers every day.

It's even suggested that there was a resulting Media Ban imposed on reporting the cases, but that's where the more sinister theories come in later.

The only thing that was becoming more clear was that everyone, from those who lived locally to nationwide, were becoming more and more concerned and perplexed by the seemingly inexplicable and unceasing outbreak of suicides.

People wondered why they were all using the same method, when research suggests it's not the most common method particularly for young women to use.

Some of the victims were discovered during their Inquests to have been taking anti-depressant medication; in nine of the inquests, there is made mention of the fact that they were taking them.

Some were also found to have traces of drugs such as Marijuana, but Coroner verdicts in these cases stated that the amounts in their system were not of a high enough level to have given them suicidal ideation.

Independent of the Coroners, a Dr David Healey, Psychiatrist, came out and stated, "The link here isn't the Internet. Drugs like anti-depressants and anti-anxiety can trigger suicide."

Being an expert in this field, he's surely right about the suicidal side-effects of these meds, however of the millions around the world currently taking them, the resulting suicides are no-where near as high as that of the cluster in the rural Wales town, and probably aren't all by hanging. And again, only some of the suicide victims were taking them.

What he also added however, is startling. 'The hangings continue unabated; and the true figure may be in the 90's.'

He wrote this in 2013, so in fact it's probably even higher than that now, and perhaps there really is a Media blackout, because the cases are not being reported like they were before, and according to Dr Healey, Coroners do not legally have to rule deaths as suicide unless there is very clear evidence that they are.

Of course it can be stated that a body hanging is clearly a suicide; but coroners can rule these cases as 'misadventure' 'accidental,' or leave them 'Open.' They rely in their ruling on clear evidence, he says, such as a suicide note, which we know in the Bridgend cases have not often existed. The possibility then is that recurring suicides could now be being ruled as otherwise.

Now in 2015, despite everyone thinking they suddenly seemed to stop a couple of years ago, "as though a switch was turned off," which in itself is high strangeness, one such critic of the lack of 'true' figures is investigative journalist Derek Gough.

'There's been 134, but the official figure is 79.' He said this in February 2014. 'There's a media blackout.'

He calls it a place 'Wrapped in secrets.'

Some have not stopped speculating as to what these secrets are either, and there are a number of theories as to what was and could still be happening to cause these suicides.

Is there something far more sinister going on then we could ever imagine?

Fringe groups from the outset began to speculate that there was something far more malevolent happening. People were asking, was *something driving* these young people on to kill themselves; urging them on, telling them to do it?

Were they somehow being influenced, other than by just by hearing about other young people's suicides? Were they hearing *something else* other than the local chatter about the deaths?

Was something literally getting inside their heads?

Perhaps we should look more closely at what some of the survivors have said. What did one of the girls mean when she told *Vanity Fair magazine,* after her unsuccessful suicide attempt,

"My head kept telling me to do it because everything would be ok."

And Justin, who was deemed fit enough to be discharged from hospital as having no mental illness despite having just tried to kill himself and telling the nursing staff that he had voices in his head telling him to do 'bad things.'

They both claimed they were hearing voices telling them to kill themselves, yet neither had any previous history of schizophrenia which would be the only mental illness that would induce voices in their heads, and is not usually a sudden onset.

And why did Leah, who also attempted to hang herself, say she had no memory of it afterward? Why could she not remember? Had something temporarily happened to her to cause the episode?

If it wasn't mental illness causing it, then where were these voices coming from? Indeed, one could even speculate that the sudden increase in young people there seeking sudden help from psychiatrists and being put on medication to control their newly manifested symptoms of anxiety and severe depression, could possibly have been because of what they were hearing in their heads.

So where were these voices coming from?

Why did one of the deceased, who lived in another part of the country, then go on to kill herself while on a visit there to see her boyfriend? Was *something* happening in the geographical area to cause these voices?

And again, because so few left suicide notes to show preparation of what they were intending to do, was it almost as though something inside of them suddenly snapped?

Or worse, was it as some were beginning to think, more likely that they were somehow targeted and triggered to kill themselves?

The *Daily Express Newspaper* featured the claims of a Dr Roger Coghill who said he'd discovered that all the young people lived far closer than normal to a telecommunication mast. He claimed there was strong circumstantial evidence that the masts could have triggered a depression in them.

The newer masts are now of higher power, it's said, in order to enable more data to be passed through them from phones and laptops.

But surely there were other areas in the U.K. where this was also the case? In much more built-up cities for example, and award winning science writer Ben Goldacre refutes Coghill's claims, stating that his data is highly flawed. Telecomms companies also adamantly denied the claims.

Many people still believe however that proximity to Masts can cause them illness, and only time will tell with this, but mass youth suicides? There was no proof.

Others then pointed to TETRA as the possible cause; the Police and Government Agencies' new two-way radio communication system, with some police officers said to be reporting that it was making them sick due to its microwave pulsed frequency radiation.

The implication here was not just that it was being used however, but that perhaps its frequency was in some way being manipulated and directed at the young people. Not by the police, but through subversive use of the TETRA towers.

Are these simply wildly far-fetched claims and wholly off-base? Quite possibly. However, Dr G. Hyland of Warwick University, UK, an expert in Physics and Biology, has said,

"With low frequency pulsing, behaviour and mood can be influenced- from depression to rage, depending on the frequency modulation used," and perhaps most crucially he says, "It's actually possible to inter-cranially induce sound and words."

He was saying that words could be sent to someone's head. They would hear words and sentences inside their heads that were not their own, and which no one else could hear.

But again, this TETRA system is in use everywhere. Why manipulate it in this one area? Why would they wish to do so?

There had to be more to this, something far more specific, but speculation grew in the minds of conspiracy theorists that either these TETRA towers or telecommunication Masts were being used in a nefarious way by 'government agencies' as a way of transmitting microwaves into the heads of this specific targeted group of young adults as some kind of twisted experiment in covert mind control and remote influencing.

Is there any possibility this could be in any way likely? Certainly far less harmful, but perhaps useful to serve as an example of technology that has been developed, is the introduction of the Mosquito device, which has been used on UK Streets. Serving as a form of remote influencing, to influence and control behaviour, this has been used as an anti-social behaviour sonic deterrent, designed to 'repel' troublemaking youths from an area.

The device emits a nasty sound-wave that only young people can hear. Generally it can only be heard by those under the age of 25. When installed in a rural town, Swindon in Wiltshire, the results were said to be effective, with a decline in criminal damage and vandalism and fewer aggressive altercations in the area in which the sound was targeted.

Some have said that a Mosquito device was installed in Bridgend, but according to Council planning records of April 2008, though the idea was indeed discussed for a small underpass near a new housing estate, the council and police both advised against installation on the grounds of potential infringement of human rights.

Were the Masts being used?

Alleged former MI5 Agent physicist Barrie Trower claims he has first hand knowledge of the sinister use of scalar waves; microwaves in Wi-Fi and Masts. He claims that intelligence agencies have misused microwaves to negatively influence people, from triggering heart attacks to taking control of a person's mind by reading their thoughts, and changing their thoughts.

They can remotely control someone without the person ever knowing it, and people can be programmed to kill, or kill themselves he claims.

'It is easy to make people hear voices in their skulls. This is not mental illness,' he says, 'it's technology.'

His claim is that 'thousands of innocent people,' have been used as guinea pigs, and he believes the testing of psychotronic weapons has been extensively carried out.

Then there's Tim Rifat PhD, whose work is the study of mind control technology, and who quotes Dr Ross Adey of 'Project Pandora,' whose behaviour modification experiments, he says, used ELF on the exact frequency as the current systems such as TETRA use, and that Adey's experiments 'caused frenzied emotional imbalance.'

As cited by several books on the topic, the USAF Scientific Board published a report back in 1996 stating that, from its studying of how the brain can be manipulated,

'It's possible to create speech in the human body, for the possibility of covert suggestion.'

Dr John Hall is renowned as a specialist in this field and has himself explained how subversive agencies can even directly access laptops and computers to remotely target the emotions of those using them.

"Nothing is too far-fetched now," he says.

He cites Michael Persinger, expert in behavioural neuroscience, as having once said he could himself quite confidently control every brain on the planet.

Dr Hall says that when someone suddenly starts hearing a voice in their head, telling them to do something to themselves, it can also be done by 'audio spotlight;'

'A hand held device zoning in to focus only on you, so that no-one else around you can hear it even though they are walking right beside you;' - in a street, in a wilderness area; anywhere...

Was there really some kind of human experimentation going on here in this small rural town?

Using the technology on a specifically narrow target group to see if it were possible to cause self destruction en-masse but only in a certain type of demographic?

Was this some kind of sick test run? Or just overwrought imagination?

Then came more claims, and this time they became even wilder and in the form of someone else who claims they were an insider at M16. James Casbolt, also known as Michael Prince, who says that from an early age he was kept 'underground,' first in Canada and then taken to England where he worked as, amongst other things, an assassin for the Government having been trained to kill people by remote influencing as well as physical means.

Of Bridgend, he wrote on conspiracy sites,

'I could be killed for this; but what's going on here is Black Ops are in the area searching for 'something.'

That 'something,' he claims was an escaped Reptilian Shape-shifter that absconded from a nearby underground base below the Brecon Beacons.

Calling it a 'Chimera,' he claims it came for these young people, and,

'Engaged with them, talking with them and telepathically hypnotising them, then finally remote viewing them and feeding off their energy as they committed their terrible acts of self destruction.'

'Being near to one creates such intense feelings of depression and suicide, as it lives to feed off the fear it generates in a person,' he says.

'Reptilian Chimeras; shape-shifters who walk among us and appears as men, many embedded in the population, and many more under military bases. A race 'progressed' into technology without emotional development; their mind is totally malevolent,' or so he claims.

These hangings he says, are remote killings performed by these modified entities.

He goes even further, 'Increasing amounts of children have gone missing in England and America. I've been told that up to a million children have been given to the Grays.'

It has to be noted that this man in now on remand awaiting trial for an unrelated matter that if found guilty could see him sentenced to over ten years. Is he a fantasist? It's highly possible and extraordinary claims require extraordinary evidence, or at the very least, some form of proof and here is where the difficulty lies; the tangible physical evidence is not there. But he's not the first to have come out with claims as outlandish as this and he won't be the last.

But what's most interesting here is that for those who've been following his interviews over the years, many feel there are times where he seems to have been triggered himself; as though he's an entirely different person, with an altered personality in the more recent interviews than he is older ones, and some even claim that his physiology seems changed or altered.

Again, who really knows if he himself is some kind of genetically modified creation as he claims, a mind controlled victim, a disinformation artist, or just a complete fantasist.

Regardless, it doesn't detract from more founded studies of the use of 'weaponized' frequencies and microwaves, and the more credible proponents such as Dr John Hall et al.

In seeking to explain the suicide cluster, perhaps it's also worth mentioning that very nearby is an atmospheric place called Candleston Castle, which sits amid dunes and marshland.

A 14th Century ruin, it features heavily as a location in Kenneth Grant's books. Grant was a writer of the occult and a ceremonial magician who was once the personal secretary to Aleister Crowley. He was founder of the Thelemite Organization and on Crowley's death, he was appointed head of the OTO; Ordo Templi Orientis.

There is evidence at the ruins of occult ritual's having taken place and Grant was an accomplished practitioner. Was some malevolent entity released from Candleston Castle?

Grant does not reveal this in his books, though we know for example that one time with Crowley at his summer cottage, after a ritual summoning, they both believe they managed to evoke Pan, the great elemental spirit.

"We saw Pan the satyr, an almost human countenance wreathed in foliage amid brilliant light. A haze hung over the ground."

Did he release something else that had been evoked and summoned at the ruins near Bridgend? Or was it subsequent occult practitioners, who followed in his footsteps to carry out rituals and demonic summoning at the castle?

Were the ritual texts of O.T.O. being taken too literally, leading to occult ritual workings being carried out there to release powerful negative entities to deliver 'child sacrifices,' as mentioned in the texts of Aleister Crowley?

Whichever is the real reason, and perhaps it is just the product of a deprived area, for people like Derek Gough, that answer is far from satisfactory; he maintains the number of suicides is far higher and is still growing.

As a journalist who prior to this was involved in investigating the alleged military/government involvement in cases of alien human mutilation at the Brecon Beacon National Park, 50 miles away from Bridgend, he's used to dealing with strange and dark things few would believe could really happen. As described next...

Chapter Eight:
Abduction, mutilation and murder in remote wilderness places

After numerous reports of possible UFO sightings in the remote Brecon Beacons National Park in the late 1990's, Gough claims he was contacted by a 'military man' who said he was part of a "response team for Find and Secure;" a secret Black Ops group, under American led NATO command.

As a Special Forces soldier, he claimed he was part of a team that would be dispatched to areas to search for human remains, and to undertake "clean-up" operations; sealing and securing an area and ensuring the remains of people were removed by scientists, and removing any UFO evidence that remained.

The human remains were, he said, what was left behind after they'd been mutilated while alive and killed by alien entities. The man showed him some photographs that he'd managed to take. Were they real? It was far harder to fake them in the '90's.

Gough described the content of the photos to British investigator and documentary maker Richard D. Hall, of RichPlanet TV. One set of pictures allegedly contained the bodies of two young people, a boy and girl in their late teens. The boy's skin had literally been peeled from his body; both victims had missing eyes, teeth and lips.

The girl's breasts had been removed as well as both of their genitals. All of their hair was gone.

The horror is audible in Gough's voice as he describes what he looked at. But the man had more pictures, of other bodies in the same conditions, found again at the National Park.

Gough claimed he took the photos straight to the police, afraid for his own safety, thinking this could be the work of the Special Forces man he'd just met with. Had he done this, not the supposed "aliens?"

The police said they were going to arrest the man, Gough says. Then the investigating officer went on leave, and later after several attempts by Gough to find out what was going on, he said the police told him that the man had confessed it was all a joke. Gough knew it wasn't. The photos he saw were too real.

The man then dropped all contact with Gough when he found out that he'd shown the police the photos and secretly recorded him. Gough says he then started to receive anonymous telephone threats. But they weren't coming from the mystery man.

Worried for his own safety, Gough ceased any further research after that, but it seems he still takes a keen interest in the possibility of black ops incidents.

It was Richard D Hall more recently who followed up on this alleged incident of human mutilations in the

National Park, claiming to have successfully tracked down the 'military man' who'd first revealed the story to Gough.

In his new documentary, Hall says of the alleged Special Forces man, "He knew exactly what I was talking about. Everything I was putting to him, there was no look of "What is he talking about?" - he knew."

But the man was hesitant to be seen talking to him at his home, understandably. He certainly didn't want to be recorded. But he did agree to meet and in those meetings he did describe his involvement in a black ops unit that he said he had volunteered for but had no idea it would ever involve human mutilation.

However, once he was 'in' there wasn't an option to leave, he said. He emphasised he did not want to be identified for fear of death himself and for his family. Now some 16 years later, he says he suffers from radiation illnesses, and claims that most of his old team are already dead from tumors and skin cancer.

He told Hall that he witnessed alien craft, and entities emerging from them. He said they looked nothing like how we imagine, "with big eyes, like in 'ET' films; it looked like a devil, and they would rip you apart," he said. "There are no friendly aliens."

He said that he would sometimes get a glance inside a craft and he implied that there were human body parts inside.

He refused to talk about the mutilations in detail. "You wouldn't want to see it," he told Hall.

When asked how long he thought it had been going on, he replied, "Since before we've been here."

Hall compared what the man told him with the original notes Gough had taken 16 years earlier; notes which this man did not have a copy of. The information he gave to Hall matched the information he had given before.

He confirmed there had been between 30-40 human mutilations during his time in the black ops group.

He also maintained that it is still going on, all over the world and he said they always target remote, out of the way locations.

The man maintained that he travelled as part of this group all over the world to crash sites. This is certainly possible, but one could question here why a team from the U.K. would travel to Australia or Russia, both of which he claimed to have gone to on clean up missions? Obviously if this really did go on, it was the sort of thing that needed to be kept under wraps from the general population, but surely there must have been closer 'clean-up teams?' There couldn't have just been one. Particularly when these would have been time-critical missions, to ensure the mutilated bodies were not discovered by innocent hikers passing by? But were they counting on the remote locations buying them time to get there, thinking the chances of discovery by hikers or walkers stumbling across them were slim?

Why did he not give greater detail? Is there any way this unidentified man's claims could possibly be true?

Well, prior to this, Tony Dodd, (now deceased) a former policeman in the North Yorkshire area, spoke to David Cayton, a prominent animal mutilation researcher, about other cases of strange deaths that had happened in the late 1980's.

In Dalby forest on the North Yorkshire Moors, a series of mutilated bodies were allegedly found. There were said to be seven separate incidents. In each case, all of their hair had been removed, as had many of their body parts; all the classic signs of human mutilations that mirrored the animal mutilation cases.

When word started to get out, the story was allegedly spun into one that was absurd. The newspapers started reporting that tailor's mannequins were being found in the fields. Seven different times? And, what of the hearse and unmarked car, spotted leaving the scene? asked Tony Dodd in the lectures he gave afterward about the 'cover-up.' And in one case, he said, hikers had even discovered one of the bodies.

Then in another case in the Brecon Beacons, it was claimed that a family of four were found lying by the side of their car. Their injuries identical to all the others.

Of course, without the evidence for ourselves, it's very hard to know, but it does make for uncomfortable possibilities...

***

Unrelated to these cases but in the same area, on August 4th 1900, a miner from Rhondda Cynon Taf, a county in Wales, decided to take his five year old son to visit his grandparents who lived on a farm in the Brecon Becons National Park.

They reached the nearby town in the early evening still with hours left of daylight and from there set out on a walk of just under 5 miles to reach the farmhouse that lay deep in the valley.

As 8pm came they reached a military camp where they bought drinks and biscuits at the army canteen.

As they ate them and rested for a while before finishing the last short lap of their walk, the grandfather arrived there with his 13 year old nephew, Will, the little boy's cousin.

On greeting them, his grandfather told Will to go back to the farmhouse to announce the imminent arrival of his son and grandson.

As he left, little Tom said he wanted to go with Will and ran to catch him up. His father was relaxed about letting him go the remaining short distance, it still being daylight and not far to go.

To get to the farmhouse the two boys had to go over two small wooden bridges, one of which had no handrail.

As they got about halfway to the farmhouse, Tom started to cry and said he wanted to go back to his Dad.

The two boys separated, with Will carrying on to the farmhouse, which he quickly reached, giving the family the message and turning straight back to re-join his grandfather at the army base within 15 minutes.

Tom however was not there. He had not come back. His Father and grandfather immediately started searching for him and within only a few minutes they'd asked the army men to help them, which they did.

There was no sign of him anywhere between the short distance of the camp and the farmhouse, but with light fading fast they carried on searching in the dark until it was halted at midnight.

At 3am it began again however, with the police there now and members of the public who'd learned of his disappearance.

The search continued for weeks. Every day search parties of volunteers, police, soldiers and farmers searched every inch of the area. Bracken was hacked away and the woodland almost ransacked in an attempt to find the little boy. They climbed to the top of the mountain and covered every spot all the way down.

Speculation grew that he must have been kidnapped by local gypsies as there was no trace of him, and the police searched every caravan, but found no clues.

National Newspaper's offered monetary rewards for information on the boy's whereabouts, but there were no leads to go on.

Then, a Mrs Hamers, wife of a gardener who resided several miles away at Castle Madoc, kept having dreams about the little boy. She perhaps could have dismissed just one dream but they kept recurring each night and she found herself confiding in her husband and persuading him to borrow a pony carriage and take her to the mountain, even though she had never been there before.

As they hiked to the top of the ridge where Mrs Hamers said they must go, they walked over a piece of open ground and suddenly her husband who was a few paces ahead of her recoiled in horror as he saw the remains of the little boy directly in his path.

Later, the coroner ruled the cause of death as exposure, but neither he nor anyone else was able to come up with an explanation as to how this boy of just five years old had managed, after a very long day of travelling already, to reach the spot at which they found him.

It was a climb of several miles over difficult and rough terrain, and in the dark. And why had no-one seen him? His Father and all the other searchers had been up this high many times looking for him but never seen him.

After his burial his parents kept the little suit he'd been wearing that day and the whistle he wore around his neck. Some wondered, why didn't he use the whistle that night to call for help? Was he just too young to think about that, or had something stopped him?

Chapter Nine:
A baffling case of triggered killers?

Recalling the earlier interviews with David regarding the possible existence of super soldiers on San Juan Islands and his employment repatriating them, and the comments made about self-professed super-soldier James Casbolt seeming to have become a different personality and physiology over time, there follows now an extraordinary true account of a startling event that was captured live on camera, which may or may not shed some light on this phenomenon. Again, it is for the reader to decide.

In 2008 an astonishing incident was captured live on CCTV, and by a BBC film crew who happened to be filming a documentary about the British motorway police.

Two women are observed on the live screens at the M6 Motorway traffic control room in a rural part of Northern England near Stoke on Trent. They are walking along the central reservation of the motorway. The control room dispatches highway patrol officers to the scene immediately to stop the women. It's completely illegal and a highly dangerous and illogical place to be walking.

As the patrol car approaches them, back at the control room the live feed shows both women climbing over the short barriers of the central reservation and running straight into the path of the fast flowing traffic on the motorway.

One of them is hit by a car in the fast lane. Inexplicably, despite having just been hit head on by the car, she immediately gets straight back up and continues on to the other side of the road. She is seen to be oblivious to any pain.

Immediately the control room call the motorway police to go to the scene. The BBC film crew go in the car with the two police officers, filming their arrival within moments and expecting to find the woman who was hit by the speeding car very seriously injured and needing urgent medical treatment.

As they pull up and get out of the police car, the women suddenly seem to notice the police and become highly agitated. As the police approach them and start to question them on the roadside, the BBC cameras capture the astonishing moment one of the women side-steps the police and runs straight into the oncoming traffic, again, followed quickly after by her sister, who does exactly the same thing.

One of them is hit by a car and sent flying over its roof; the other is hit head-on by a lorry. This highly disturbing scene is captured by the cameras.

The police immediately call for an ambulance, stating to the emergency services over the walkie-talkie that it's probably going to be two fatalities; they were both hit at full impact by the speeding vehicles.

The woman hit by the car, at a speed of at least 60mph, is lying unconscious in the middle of the traffic lane. The woman hit by the lorry has broken bones visibly sticking out of her legs.

As the police minister to her, she's heard saying, "I know you are not real."

Then she starts becoming aggressive, and though her legs are busted, she becomes increasingly violent.

"I can't understand it," says attending police officer Paul Finlayson, "for a person to survive being hit by a lorry is very very rare. Seeing her thrown violently, seeing her run over by the wheels; no human was going to survive that."

"What I couldn't understand is that I've got a person who is smashed from the waist down but from the waist up is extremely aggressive, spitting, shouting, screaming. You start to wonder what's going on here...it was very very strange," says PC Cope at the scene.

Then, still on camera, the woman hit by the car suddenly regains consciousness, seems to be in no pain at all, stands up, and punches a policewoman in the face knocking her to the floor.

The policewoman is visibly credulous afterward. Being filmed she's saying, "I can't understand what's going on, I saw the car hit her; it threw her in the air like a doll."

The woman runs and climbs over the central reservations barrier and again runs into the oncoming traffic on the other side of the motorway. This time she's not run over, but is trying to flee into the woods that run parallel to the road. She seems to have no injuries at all.

It takes six police as well as concerned members of the public who've got out of their cars to help to restrain her, and she's threatening violence to them all.

"Her strength was phenomenal; she's got incredible strength. It's *inexplicable*. Both of them appeared to demonstrate such intense focus. They just wanted to fight us. Why were they on the motorway? Why did they want to fight us? Why were they trying to commit suicide?" The policeman is simply stunned by their behaviour.

But both of them appeared to be absolutely terrified of the police, irrationally so as the police were simply trying to calm them down and kept telling them they were there to help them.

Their responses included screaming the most bizarre things, "You are not the police," "What country do they come from?" "You are not real," "You cannot protect us", and one sister was screaming to the other one, "They want our body parts!"

Both women are eventually restrained and subdued and taken to hospital, but the woman hit by the car is released quickly and taken to the police station where she is charged with trespass and assaulting a police officer.

What no-one there could understand however was why she seemed not to be physically injured in any way. She'd been thrown over the roof of a speeding car, and yet she was physically fine.

They also remarked how strange it was that she didn't once ask at all about the health of her sister, who'd been rushed to hospital. In fact, her entire demeanour had suddenly changed to one of friendliness and almost flirtatiousness.

It has been suggested she was given tranquilising medication at the hospital, but interestingly the police found no evidence in her medical records of any sign of mental illness; nor did they find any drugs in her system. Some observers of the film footage have speculated that they must have taken some kind of strong drug such as PCP or 'Bath Salts,' but again nothing was found in their system, and neither of these drugs are common drugs to take in the U.K. Others have said they must have been on Steroids, but no traces of any mind-altering or mood changing drugs were found in either of their systems.

The women turned out to be identical twins of Swedish nationality, who allegedly between them had only one passport. It transpired that the women had been refused re-admittance to a coach after it had stopped for a refreshment break at the nearby service station. After the coach driver had seen them acting 'very suspiciously,' he informed a manager at the service station.

The manager observed them and felt they were carrying their bags very close to them and conferring with each other and in her words, she thought it looked almost as though they were plotting something. She became concerned there could be a bomb in their bags. She called the police and the police came. They couldn't find anything of concern however and let the women go.

It was then that the women set off onto the motorway on foot.

Fast forward to the police station and as the woman is being charged for assault, she's still being filmed.

One of the policeman with her at the station says on camera,

"She behaved as though nothing had ever happened, or as though she had no recollection of what had transpired. You can honestly say that person; that screaming banshee of a woman is not the person that we picked up from the hospital. She's not exhibited any aggression. I was quite happy that she could be conveyed without being handcuffed." Which seems a remarkable diagnosis, but he continues,

"It was the little things that bothered her, like what she looks like and what she's going to wear; she's not asked about her sister once and that surprised me from start to finish dealing with her; it's as if her sister doesn't exist anymore. I don't think she knew anything that had gone on; she either didn't care or she didn't remember."

"She was almost jolly, even flirtatious. With her it clearly worked to be pleasant with her, to flirt with her," the custody Sergeant noted, which is a bizarre thing for a policeman to say, but it seems she had somehow almost charmed him.

As she's being charged with the assault on camera, she's heard remarking that in her native country, "We say an accident rarely comes alone; usually at least one more follows."

Why would she make this statement? Well, in hindsight, it seems that she was possibly sending a message about what her next intentions were, but no-one took any notice of the comment.

When the story hit all the national newspapers shortly after the next set of events transpired, no-one could understand how it was that she was not only physically unharmed and seemed impervious to pain, but that she was then released from police custody after a only few hours. She'd endangered her own life several times as well as the lives of others. Was she mentally fit to be out in general population?

What followed next was another highly mysterious chain of events. Released the next day, she found her way into the small rural town and was next seen by two men in the early summer evening standing in the middle of the road as they walked along it.

They'd just left their 'local;' the Pub they frequently went to in the evenings for beer and a chat.

As the men left the Pub and entered the street, they couldn't fail to notice her standing in the middle of the road, and she called over to them, telling them how nice the dog was that they had with them. They strolled over to her so she could make a fuss of the dog and they got into a conversation, and she explained that she was looking for her sister who was in hospital and also for a Bed and Breakfast hotel where she could stay the night.

One of the men, Glenn Hollinshead, pointed out to her that the small village she was in didn't really have any Bed and Breakfasts in it, but suggested she go back with them to his house and he would make them all a bite to eat and then help her find her sister and a place to stay.

"We'd often sit in the pub and talk about his days in the Royal Air force and other chat," his friend Pete recalled. "As we started to walk home, you couldn't miss her, she stuck out with the big coat she was wearing and carrying all her possessions in a big transparent bag. She seemed a bit lost, unfocussed. Part of me was thinking something's not right here. Why has she got all her possessions with her?"

"Glenn was being a Good Samaritan; he was just trying to help her. Her personality opened up as we walked and she was really friendly. At the house we were having beers and I asked her what happened to her sister and she went cold and changed. In the quiet moments between conversations she was getting paranoid and getting up and looking through the curtains out onto the street."

"She got her cigarettes out and offered them to us and we took one each but just as we were about to light them she snatched them back and said we couldn't have them because they might be poisoned. I thought, is she hiding from someone? Glenn was more relaxed about the whole thing though."

And in fact, because he thought she was perhaps just a bit introverted, he let her spend the night there at his house.

The following day, she stabbed him to death. He managed to make it out of the front door and tell his neighbour she had stabbed him but tragically he died shortly after. She fled the scene immediately.

British Army soldier Josh Grattage, driving in a street near-by saw a woman walking along the pavement, smashing a hammer into her own head. "I was seeing lots of blood on her head. I felt a sickening feeling," he later told reporters.

He slammed on his brakes and rushed to stop her hitting herself, only for her to pull part of a brick out of her pocket and hit him over the head with it, momentarily stunning him, and she ran away. It was of course the same woman who'd just killed the man.

She was finally spotted again and chased by the police on foot as she headed toward a bridge. Without hesitating, she jumped straight off it and fractured her skull and her ankles.

Sabina Erikson was jailed for the killing in 2010. She was released on parole in 2011.

Now the UK penal system is a lot more lenient than that of the United States, but it still seems an incredibly light sentence. Additionally, due to the very evident display of propensity to self-harm, it's absolutely astounding that she wasn't sentenced to a Mental Institution instead of Prison.

Two psychiatrists deemed her to have experienced a sudden but brief and temporary outburst of madness.

"The mental illness resolved itself quickly," said one of the judges, in explanation. "It had a sudden onset and resolved rapidly."

If that was indeed the case, how do they know it would not resurface again in the future?

Many watching the films on YouTube showing the strange case have said afterward that as drugs have been ruled out, it was indeed caused by mental illness. There is no evidence of this in their medical records however, and this has led to a couple of interesting conclusions.

One is that their seeming inability to feel pain and their demonstration of strength implies they could have been under the control of a demon; both of them becoming possessed and driven to cause mayhem and death, including serious harm to themselves.

Many victims of demonic possession are driven on by a voice telling them insistently to kill themselves. Is this why they repeatedly threw themselves in front of speeding cars, and why Sabina was hitting her own head with a hammer?

However, both of them possessed at the same time? So suddenly and explosively? Is that really plausible?

Others have said they act as though they were being compelled somehow, as though receiving thoughts or instructions to make them kill themselves; sending them instructions to self-destruct.

They point to it being the reason as to why one of them was hitting herself over the head with the hammer, trying to rid herself of the insistent voices inside her head.

Others have explained that their behaviour is very self-evident of having been triggered. Of these theorists is veteran investigator Miles Johnston of the Bases Project, who makes his opinion very clear.

"Their behaviour was "Self-Terminate. Do not get captured."

They were seen to be terrified of the police on the film footage, and yet they had no criminal record or any known reason to be running from them.

They did indeed tell the police who were trying to calm them down on the Motorway, "You cannot protect us."

They were scared, and running. But from what or whom?

"They have been underground," says Johnston, and points to their shouting,

"They will take our Organs."

Having spent over two decades interviewing witnesses of secret Military/Government Underground Bases, Johnston and his followers believe there is a lot more to this story than has been covered. They believe the women were part of a growing number of MILAB's, Military Abductees taken to underground bases and kept there for experimentation.

These particular women, they suggest, could have been genetically experimented on; their DNA altered and their bodies 'modified and enhanced,' with the use of advanced alien technology but done at the hands of human collaborators.

The purpose? To create programmed assassins who feel no pain, are as such 'rechargeable,' and ultimately are disposable after no longer of use.

When in disposable phase, it is then that the thoughts of 'Self-Terminate' are 'triggered' in them.

Is this at all plausible? There has been a new breed of whistleblowers of late, who purport to be victims of underground mind programming and mind control, through the use of deprivation and abuse techniques to split the mind by trauma into any number of split personalities. Used in Projects like Monarch or Mannequin.

Perhaps there is some evidence here, from the apparent ability of Sabina to go from suicidal self-destruct mode on the motorway, to flirtatious charmer in the police station where she seemingly captivated the policemen; then from her paranoia at the man's house the night before to her sudden murderous outburst the next day, followed by further suicide attempts.

This sounds like mental illness, and the psychiatric professionals stated it was an exceptionally rare case in which it came and went very suddenly. So rare in fact, that it could be said to have never really been heard of before, and this has left some people scratching their heads.

Miles Johnston and his many witnesses who say that mind control is very real and is happening, point to her switching from one fractured personality to another as evidence of her programming and due to obeying her controllers wishes that she self-terminate.

It's even more sinister than that however, because the theory behind this programming is that these MILAB's kept underground are programmed to kill on command for their controllers. And there could be any number of them, programmed as assassins and ready to go active.

Impervious to pain they go into battle without flinching; devoid of conscience they attack on triggered command.

It is true that they did seem strangely disconnected from each other, and completely unconcerned for each others well-being.

But quite what the objective of their 'shadow controllers' would have been, if we believe this theory, is very unclear. What purpose did their attacks serve? They seemed completely random.

Were these two sisters quite simply going into meltdown? Yet they seemed afraid of being captured, of going back to have their 'organs taken' again. Is this a real clue as to who or what they really were? Why would they say such a strange comment otherwise?

Johnston's current investigative work is now focussed on a military base where, in what would seem too grotesque to really be true, it has been alleged by witnesses that the woods nearby were used to hunt and kill children for 'sport.'

He feels that the killing of the man who gave Sabina a place to stay for the night goes deeper; that because he was of the same military branch as bases like that one, it may be the key to why she killed him; in his opinion, though the victim had nothing at all to do with these allegations, the idea proposed by Johnston is that she went on the offensive when she discovered he had been a military man and that triggered her traumatic memories of having been abducted and held by such men in a mind control base where experiments and trauma took place.

The biggest problem here with the idea that these women were abducted, held, mind controlled and genetically enhanced, is that the other sister did have to spend three months in hospital due to her injuries; hence surely they clearly cannot be super-human? That doesn't mean they couldn't have been mind-controlled however, if such a thing really does happen.

But what was their 'mission?'

Taking things further, Johnston and many others say this was a planned event by their 'controllers,' as a demonstration of their power 'in plain sight.'

This is kind of the same line of thinking that occult researchers would say is done by MK Ultra type operatives, like the 'lone gunman' theory of alleged staged 'false flag events;' their purpose being to send a direct but subliminal mocking message of their power.

Some who have watched the TV documentaries where the women are hit by the vehicles have said it was all a set-up, that it was completely staged, they were never 'hit;' that if you watch closely enough, (on YouTube) you will see that the cameras pan away at the critical moments. That you never actually see the impacts. That if they had been real accidents, they would both be dead. That it was a 'psy-ops,' and add to this the comments from the women saying to the police, "You're not real," sending some kind of subliminal control message to the masses.

It's a line of thinking I find particularly hard to follow, but others perhaps will find it easier.

Then there is a journalist called David McCann, who's spent a lot of time looking into the case and he believes the sister did not even carry out the murder; that other people did, who entered the house and took advantage of her mental illness and used it as a front to commit the murder and blame it on her. Unfortunately, there's no real logic to his argument.

Curiously however, in posts all over the internet he says that 'disinfo' agents are trying to discredit his theory that she did not commit the murder, and claims that her and her sister were drug smugglers and that they were also mentally ill.

Strangely, he also states that he himself used to write 'under numerous names' speaking out about the existence of super soldiers and publishing the information all over the internet, but that his conclusions now have changed as a result of looking into this case and that these women had nothing to do with supposed super soldiers.

In this respect it would seem that he's trying very hard to steer everyone away from the idea of it being anything to do with MILAB's and super soldiers and trying to explain it as a drug deal, mental illness and a set-up murder all at the same time. Which is incredibly strange to say the least.

Why is he speaking out so strongly in opposition of the possibility of super soldiers and mind programming, and coming up with a completely different theory having once been a proponent of spilling the beans on these super soldiers existing?

The question here then is, is he being leaned on to say this? Or does he just genuinely believe the finger has been pointed in the wrong direction in this case?

What is unarguable here is that it's a highly strange and perplexing chain of events, resulting in a particularly short prison sentence, and what is extremely odd is the lack of mainstream media follow up on the case.

Chapter Ten:
Strange deaths & disappearances.

Very different, but another highly strange and ongoing situation is happening now, both Stateside and in the UK.

In February 2015 the distraught parents of a young man went to the newspapers to speak out about their distress, caused by having to endure listening to their son screaming down the phone to them one night in the last moments of his life.

Holding their phone to another phone which was connected to the emergency services operator, they were begging for help to find where there son was and what was going on.

Their son's last moments of life were heard by the emergency dispatcher but not recorded, contrary to standard operating procedure, due to the recoding equipment not working.

The officer later resigned over the matter, upset that it had added to the parents distress. The parents do not feel that the subsequent disappearance of their son was investigated to the extent to which they would have found acceptable.

The police say they are still trying to piece together what might have happened to him, his body having been discovered dead in the Ship Canal three weeks later.

The 21 year old student and volunteer Civic Centre worker had been on a night out with friends. He was last seen at a music event at a racetrack in Manchester city centre.

In the early hours of the next morning, his parents were concerned that he had not come home and called him.

His Mother told reporters, "We rang him and when he answered he was incoherent. I could barely make out what he was saying. There was no noise in the background and it struck me that he was on his own. Minutes into the call he started screaming. He was howling and yelling. It was horrific."

While she called the police, her husband took over the phone. He was still screaming.

"It was a howl. I raised my voice at him to try to get him to snap out of it, but I couldn't get through to him. Then suddenly there was silence. There was a total silence, and it was so eerie."

The problem was that they couldn't really do anything because they couldn't find out from him where he was; they couldn't go to his aid.

That phone call was the last anyone heard from him. He was found dead three weeks later in the Canal.

It was later suggested that David had been asked to leave the music event, where all alcohol had been free, for being inebriated. Indeed the coroner then wrote to the event organisers, admonishing them for simply evicting someone from an event which they were responsible for, rather then ensuring a duty of care was provided to someone if they became drunk.

When the police tracked his mobile phone records later, it was determined that he'd been a couple of miles outside of the City centre, no-where near the canals.

At the inquest, the police dispatcher who took the call from the parents described her own trauma from the night's events.

"I took a very distressing 999 call. He was in a distressed state but his parents couldn't hear anything other than his screaming. I stayed on with them for well over an hour, trying to provide assistance for them and him. The incident haunts me still and with each and every new death I see in the news I am more and more convinced that these are not accidents; these are murders."

The death was classified as accidental drowning. His parents clearly disagree with this verdict. They know only too well that he was terrified of something so horrifying he could not even articulate it to them. Whatever he saw was so chilling he could not find the words.

His mother, a former Head Teacher, spoke out, "It is not a case of 'young man drinks too much, falls in canal.' Someone is responsible for his death and the version of events that have been given are simply not adding up, and the case leaves many more questions than answers. He could have been attacked, he could have had his drink spiked; anything.."

In a case across the pond that bears some similarities, Student Daniel Zamlen was reported as a missing person on April 5th 2009. He'd been at a party but his friends who were at the party said that he had left on his own to meet up with another friend at Minnesota University.

They say he was talking with them on his cell phone and was near the Mississippi River Boulevard and St Clair Avenue. Quickly bloodhounds, a helicopter and searchers covered the area where he had been walking, but found no trace of him.

In what is one of the most disturbing phone calls, reminiscent of the call received by the parents in Manchester, his friend Anna says she was talking to him when he began to become distressed. By then she says she had left the party and got in her car to go and find him.

'It took a really bad turn,' she told newspapers at the time, "Where are you?" she asked him.

"Oh, my gosh, Help!" – "This was the last thing I heard," she says. "His voice became distant as he said those words, as though he was moving away his phone, and then the line went dead."

She called him back but it just remained unanswered she claims.

It has to be said, his parents have spoken out about the accuracy of statements made by his friends, particularly disputing the content of his last known call.

Disturbingly it was reported that there's significant evidence the drinks at the party had been spiked.

Back in Manchester England again, in June 2012, Chris Brahmy had been to a rock concert on the outskirts of Manchester with a group of friends and after it finished he decided to go into the City Centre to retrieve a new pair of trainers he'd hidden earlier in a car park rather than carry then at the concert all night.

CCTV this time captures (again on YouTube) over ten minutes of his journey, from retrieving the trainers in a shopping bag to carrying them through street after street in the city centre.

He can clearly be watched walking in a perfectly capable and coherent manner through the streets from around 1.45am until the last CCTV camera films him walking through a passage.

He is not stumbling or wandering around without co-ordination. In other words, he does not appear at all inebriated or under the influence of drugs.

Ten days later, his body is found in the Canal. What the police still do not know is how he ended up in the canal, which at the spot where he was thought to have entered the water, is a high railing that would have required climbing.

"While CCTV follows his movements, we still cannot say how or why he died," the police said.

The spot in which he died was not covered by CCTV. The police also made it clear they had no evidence leading it to be considered suspicious, despite the fact that the coroner found him to have a fractured cheekbone, bruising and cuts to his face.

There were traces of alcohol in his body, and indeed the drug MDMA. Clearly, one could argue the drug caused him to climb up the fence, and jump over it into the canal, although it does beg the question how he managed to find his shoes and walk so capably through the city centre without any signs of being influenced and made incapable by a drug?

Interestingly, the forensic pathologist Ms Carter stated that because the injuries he had sustained had no bruising, they would have happened *after* his death not prior to his death.

In other words, this ruling would imply that he died or was killed without these injuries, then suffered the injuries afterwards. He didn't experience the injuries as a result of throwing himself in the water in a desire to commit suicide. And if the injuries occurred after death, he didn't not inflict them himself.

Professor Gary Jackson, head of Psychology at the University of Birmingham, England has officially joined the growing number of people who are perturbed, alarmed, and feel there is something more sinister at play than accidental drowning after more than 65 men in the last five years have been found dead in the canals and ponds of the Northern City of Manchester.

Talking to the broadsheet *The Telegraph*, he says, "The number is far higher than one would expect and from the data I just don't believe these were suicides; canals are not a popular site for suicide, and people rarely choose this for their method; but they make for ideal grounds for predators. Many of the reports from the coroners are inconclusive."

Professor Jackson, having accessed freedom of information reports regarding many of the deaths, has come to a grim conclusion. He doesn't believe they were accidents.

Pointedly he adds, "If you're trying to commit suicide by drowning, it's very hard to do in a canal- unless you can weigh yourself down with something heavy."

Some of the deaths it seems have clearly indicated that something else might be going on other than an innocent accidental fall into the canals.

He also points to the very clear victimology - they were all young males. He says there is a clear connection between the cases from the fact that the in at least 48 of the cases, the bodies were so badly decomposed as to be impossible to identify. This links them together connectively in his opinion.

If these victims were being randomly pushed in by someone vindictive, they would not all be successful attempts. At some point, one of the victims would fight, struggle, and not drown. People would soon hear about it. No-one has come forward to say this has happened to them, although doubtless the dark and dimly lit canals are excellent places for drug deals, and muggings.

If they were all cases of criminal attempts and 'success' by psychopathic muggers, why is it not happening in Cambridge, another University town with canals, or Universities by the sea, of which there are many, such as Bournemouth or Brighton?

Not only that, but with Newspaper reports carrying images of police teams being able to walk through some stretches of the canals because the water is not even knee deep, it does beg the question how could they all so easily drown in shallow water?

The canals of Manchester run through parts of the city centre, mainly the old industrial parts but also quite close to very busy nightclubs and bars. Manchester is both a thriving University town and has a popular Gay Village, and every night, bars are packed with drinkers.

Many will inevitably on occasion drink too much, some will as a result have accidents, however the canals are not obvious routes to take. They are not renovated scenic canals; rather they are dimly lit, strewn with litter and damp.

They aren't a short cut to anywhere and they aren't a route home. They're not somewhere anyone would go for a pleasant walk.

Yet some of the deaths have clearly indicated that something else might be going on other than an innocent accidental fall into the canals.

Is this the work of a serial killer, or is it more likely that it's the work of some kind of organised gang, reminiscent of the accusation levelled against whoever is causing the deaths of the college men across America, as determined by Professor of Criminology and gang stalking expert Professor Gilbertson?

That is his opinion, based on thorough scrutiny of the individual cases, the identical victim type, and what he believes is their abduction, confinement and subsequent death by drowning.

One link that also stands out is that very often the young men who go missing have been kicked out of clubs and bars and left to wander the streets often without the means of getting home.

This is either a case of grand negligence of care in the case of doormen, or is there something more sinister going on in terms of collusion and cooperation with the as yet unknown and unidentified gang allegedly stalking and abducting these men?

In some cases afterward it has been found that although they were kicked out, there was no evidence of them causing a disturbance or fight, or even being that drunk.

Take the case of Shane Montgomerry, a student at West Chester who was escorted out of a Bar in Manayunk, PA, after accidentally tripping into the dj deck.

His body was found 13 days later in a part of the river close to the bar where search divers had thoroughly and repeatedly searched. The implication here then being that he was not in the river for all of the time that he had been missing. Unusually in this case, the FBI quickly became involved in the investigation searching for him.

It has since been reported that subsequently the bar involved stated that there was no disturbance inside the bar.

Is this all mere speculation when it could be drink and drugs and inevitable accidents?

One researcher however takes a very different angle to these strange deaths, in an unusual twist, attempting to tie it in to a very alternative explanation.

Half a century ago, office cubicles were architecturally designed to assist administrative personnel in being able to work in a busy environment with less distraction from colleagues repeatedly passing by their desk. The cubicles were used for the purpose of enabling the worker to have their peripheral vision blocked.

In the modern office, this design has largely given way to a more open plan style of desks and seating arrangements, with repetitive detectable movement occurring in the workers peripheral vision from all angles of the busy office.

This applies also to college libraries, dorms, and indeed the modern home where laptops are commonly used on couches or tables in busy family homes where there is constant movement around the user.

One researcher claims this has led to a phenomenon he terms 'Subliminal Distraction Theory,' and startlingly he ties it into cases of missing people in wilderness areas, the college drowning deaths, and even allegedly 'false flag' mass shootings by individual perpetrators.

He claims on *VisionsandPsychosis.net,* that the phenomenon harks back to our cave man instinct when we were wired to become alert to the presence of predators circling us. In those days, we would immediately respond to the detected threat. Now, in a world where we are bombarded by constant interruptions in our field of vision, we see these 'threats' and register them in our brain but our mind overrides them as non-threatening and not requiring a fight or flight response, as would have been warranted in earlier civilisation.

We learn to ignore these threats; we know that they are not real 'threats.' A co-worker walking by our desk at work, seen out of the corner of our eye, we know is not a threat to our safety. A family member passing by us from behind and coming into our peripheral vision, we know is not a real threat.

However, in his research he believes that this constant blocking of these potential 'threats' can in some fashion cause the brain to go into a kind of meltdown and trigger a form of psychotic breakdown, and a mental break or fugue occurs, causing the sufferer symptoms of sudden paranoia, extreme anxiety, confusion, muddled thinking, fear and panic, which can then manifest in the form of bizarre behaviour such as suddenly leaving the place they are in, rapidly removing all of their clothing, jumping off buildings, or ending up dead by entering water and drowning.

The idea is that after numerous and continual repression by our brain of our natural 'startle response' to these sudden and threatening stimuli, without warning, a new sudden 'threat' could trigger this instantaneous meltdown, where perhaps the 'flight' mechanism goes into overdrive.

The problem with his thesis is the lack of academic research available to back it up. Is it plausible? It's very hard to determine without rigorous scientific evidence.

However, in his belief, the theory applies to the many disappeared or found dead in unexplained circumstances in wilderness areas and in many drowning cases, as well as the lone gunman rampages that others would say are false flag Manchurian candidates.

The difficulty with this particular theory is the lack of rigorous scientific data to support the phenomenon. However, perhaps there is something in it. He lists examples such as the case of the missing engineering student Aju Iroga who vanished in the woods near Lake Superior, and Chris Jenkins, 21-year-old University of Minnesota student, who disappeared after being kicked out of a downtown Minneapolis bar and whose body was found in a posed position in the river, months after his disappearance, both described in this author's 'Something in the Woods.'

In that latter case however, the death of Jenkins also has possible occult ritualistic and alchemic indicators.

Chapter Eleven:
More Strange Deaths

Here are a couple more stories that just seem to baffle the mind, and where no answers come easy.

It was March 2006, and an Ohio med student was having drinks with friends to celebrate spring break. During the evening he called his girlfriend to tell her he was looking forward to the trip they were going to take in a couple of day's time.

In the bar he was seen on the security camera at the top of the elevator, but then he moves out of shot. That was the last time he was seen. An emergency exit was covered by camera; he was not picked up on that either.

The only other route would have been to walk through an area of new construction, although tracker dogs did not detect his scent on searching that area. He has still not been found.

Brian Shaffer seemed almost to have vanished from inside a bar. Despite there being 3 surveillance cameras, capturing people entering and leaving the bar, he was not seen leaving.

Observers have suggested, 'Something else took him right in that bar.'

***

The haunted dormitory is a well known ghost story among soldiers young and old in Singapore, S.E. Asia. It seems to have been passed down from generation to generation of new recruits, at least in one particular army training base, but its origins lay in a true story.

It started in the early '80's, after a new batch of soldiers was out on a routine 16K training march one day. It seems that one of the recruits began to feel unwell about half way through the march, and telling the Sergeant, he was ordered to stop and rest and the attending medics would see to him shortly. The rest of the group continued on their run amid the thick jungle forestation.

When the tired army recruits returned to base later, having completed their gruelling run fully laden down by heavy backpacks, it wasn't until the middle of the evening that the Officers realised the sick young recruit was no-where to be seen, and they were one rifle short in the munitions locker.

Due to what turned out to be a mix-up in communication, it seemed the medics had not received the message that there was a sick recruit left behind along the trail awaiting assistance.

A search party was immediately launched with all the soldiers and even senior officers going back into the forest to search for him. They retraced the route of the march and when they came to the spot where he had told of feeling sick they expected to find him still there, but he was no-where to be seen.

The search continued long into the night but the darkness was hampering the effect of their search in such a heavily dense forest.

It wasn't until the next morning that he was found. The soldiers visibly shrank from the horrific sight that greeted them.

He was splayed out on the ground. His internal organs had been taken out of his body and placed beside him. A knife was plunged into his stomach, with the handle embedded in his stomach and the blade sticking upward out of him.

All the items from his backpack were neatly laid out on the ground.

He was carried back to the base as the terrified soldiers tried to determine *who or what* had killed him in such a way.

No soldiers had been reported as AWOL or missing from duty throughout the base, and all records showed where they were during this time.

It was after this horrific death of the young recruit that the dormitory in which he'd been staying began to be affected.

Numerous accounts began to be reported of the bed of the dead soldier suddenly starting to shake violently in the night, waking and terrifying any new occupant in it.

Some even reported that they were physically thrown from the bed during the night. Often a new recruit assigned to the bunk would wake up in the morning to find deep red scratch marks running down his body.

A Priest had to be called in to try to dispel the spirit that was causing so much fright to the soldiers, and taking a firm stance to prevent further rumor and speculation, and to mollify the recruits, the army prevented any one else sleeping in the bunk afterward by barricading it off from access.

Who or what had killed the soldier, no-one ever determined, but soldiers over the years afterwards would always make sure they stuck closely together whenever they went training in the forest.

***

Netty, also known as Norah Fornario, spent much of her early life living in the affluent London suburb of Kew in the early 1900's.

From a young age she'd shown a keen interest in the rising field of spiritualism and the possibility of communing with the dead. It's speculated that this could have arisen from the loss of her Mother.

Those who knew her said she had an extraordinary intelligence, and as a young adult, she wrote reviews and articles for *The Occult Review*. She preferred solitude, and rarely socialised except for attending Spiritualist meetings and Psychic gatherings.

She joined the Alpha and Omega Temple. This had been established as an offshoot of the infamous Hermetic Order of the Golden Dawn, and was established by ritual magician Samuel Liddell Mathers after he was thrown out of the Golden Dawn.

Mathers was a prominent occult scholar who had led a revivalist movement of the esoteric and occult in the late 1800's. He had held office in the Rosicrucian's before founding The Golden Dawn, where he created ritual occult workings by studying the ancient Egyptian magick systems and Dr John Dee's Enochian magic to create a potent array of rituals.

Sir Arthur Conan Doyle was one of the many prominent members there, as was Aleister Crowley, who was initiated into the Order at the age of 23, shortly after leaving Cambridge University, and a battle of ego and power ensued between the pair.

Fighting for control of the Order, it's said that the pair engaged in a fierce battle of spiritual warfare, with Mathers summoning a vampire-type entity to attack his foe, while the other retaliated by summoning and unleashing an army of demons.

Both ended up being expelled from the Order and Mathers then founded his own order, The Alpha and Omega Temple. Thirty years after this, Netty came along and joined them.

Raised by her grandparents, as an adult Netty soon found herself turning to spiritualism to meet her need for esoteric knowledge, and was a regular attendee and developed friendships in that circle.

It was during this period however that her interest turned almost to obsession, and she decided in her late twenties to set off for an extended and possibly permanent stay on the tiny and remote island of Iona, in the Hebrides, off the West coast of Scotland.

Legendary English Diarist of the time, Dr Samuel Johnson, on describing his visit to the Island wrote of the strange magnetic yet seemingly inanimate and abstract yet highly powerful 'energy' that could be felt on the Island and the effect it had on him.

In the 7th Century, the abbot of the island, a monk named Adomnán, wrote in his journals about the Saint Columba, who legend had it could control the weather on the Island and keep away dragons and serpents. Descriptions of his encounters with these beings as well as angelic visitations are mentioned.

Renown for its tranquillity and peacefulness, at the time houses there had no electricity or running water and no phone lines. It seemed she had gone there in search of this kind of peace, but also in order to focus on what had grown into a fixation; her need to commune with spirits and the dead, through any means.

From accounts of those who knew her, she was said to have been experimenting with crossing the bridge between the living and the dead by means of astral travel.

She found lodgings with a family there, but it was later reported by them that she spent almost all of her time in her own bedroom, or out at night on the moors. It seemed that she grew to spending almost all of her nights out roaming alone, returning in the early mornings to write in a journal in her room.

No-one really knew what it was she did at night when she went out, but her behaviour was disturbing to the family, especially when they witnessed that her jewellery and her nails had turned black, and her initially healthy skin seemed to have become increasingly pallid.

It was almost as though at times she was in a complete trance, the family later said, for she would look at them with a far-away look through glazed eyes, not really focussed at all on where she was or what they were saying to her.

Then one day she became suddenly terribly distressed. Frantically she told the Mother of the family that she needed to leave the Island immediately. She would give no reason, and the family knew she had received no telegram or letter indicating that there was any kind of emergency at her Grandparents in London.

But with her continued insistence and desperation increasing, the Mother helped her pack up her belongings to be taken down to the Harbour.

However, because it was a Sunday and a day of rest in those days, no ferries operated on a Sunday and she would not be able to get off the Island until the following day.

She had no choice but to remain in her room. She spent the rest of the day quietly there, until evening came when she hurriedly came out of it and told the family she no longer needed to leave.

With what they later described as a resigned countenance, she spoke as though her decision had been made after having accepted some kind of inevitability, as though there was no way to change things now.

The next day the Mother of the family realised she had not heard or seen Netty for an entire day, which was unusual because her habit was to go out at night but spend the day in her room in the house.

A little puzzled, the Mother knocked on her door several times and after several attempts to rouse Netty she opened the door to find it empty but with all of her belongings still there. Curiously, in her fireplace lay the burnt embers of what looked like a manuscript. Her bed appeared not to have been slept in.

Concerned now after her recent distress and subsequent absence, the family immediately set out across the moors of the tiny Island to look for her, but though they searched for hours they found no sign of her out in the wilderness.

The next morning they left the island to collect and bring back a policeman to help them search. The policeman and many volunteers from the island set out searching for her again across the moors, and late in evening the son of the family she lodged with stumbled across a shocking discovery. Led by the barking of a dog, he was taken to a spot where he found her dead body.

She was lying naked except for a long black robe with occult sigils on the lapel. Her body lay over a large cross-shape that appeared to have been carved into the grass.

In her left hand was a long knife which had to be pried out of her death grip. On her face was an expression of absolute terror. On her body were deep and fierce scratch marks. The cross beneath her was thought to have been carved by her perhaps as some form of attempt to defend herself from psychic attack, or perhaps as some kind of ritual she'd been carrying out

Her toes were cut and bruised, which seemed to indicate that she had been running at speed over rocks and rough ground, quite possibly in flight from something that was chasing her.

However, what is extremely odd is that the soles of her feet and her heels were in no way injured or damaged. How had she travelled over rough, broken and sometimes perilous terrain without any marks to the soles of her feet?

Also what was puzzling to them was that her body had remained undiscovered for two days, despite the island being tiny and thorough searches having been conducted. She seemed to have been missing from sight for two days.

Her cause of death was ruled as heart failure from exposure, though most believed from the expression of her death mask that it was heart failure from sheer terror.

Dion Fortune was one the woman's closest friends. She declared her belief on hearing the news, that Moina Mathers, the wife of their leader of the Alpha sect, had killed Netty, even though Moina was dead; she declared it was done by means of psychic attack.

Whatever the case, it appeared that she had spent the last few hours of her life in a desperate fight with something not of this world. She appeared to have quite literally been frightened to death, and for her the supernatural powers of occult black magic had become a deadly reality.

Had overwhelmingly powerful dark forces been sent to attack and kill her? Or had she inadvertently dabbled a step too far into the occult and naively unleashed demonic forces that ended her life and dragged her to hell itself?

Perhaps it's also worth pointing out that more than four known mistresses of Aleister Crowley all killed themselves in succession; and the obvious thought has to be, were they driven to it by forces unleashed during ritual occult summoning? Or were they killed by some form of astral attack, however outlandish that sounds.

Looking back to her life in London, it turns out that not only was she heavily entrenched in occult practice, she was also obsessed by the writings of Fiona MacLeod, or rather the writer William Sharp, a Scottish poet and novelist who also wrote under the pen-name of Fiona MacLeod.

At one point Netty had gone to see an Opera based on MacLeod's writing more than twenty times, and wrote a subsequent review of the production.

The Opera was a tale of Faery folk and magic, in which the Fey are cast as a breed of strong immortals that humans are in fear yet awe of, because of their ability to interfere with and manipulate people.

But Netty had an unwavering fascination with them. She writes of 'Students of mysticism who are able to understand the great truths behind the gossamer curtain of the Fey.'

However she also makes mention of the appearance of the demonic in the Opera, 'Symbolising dark atavism,' and crucially she points out,

'The reaction of these 'lower principles' to the stimulus of super consciousness often produces disastrous results.'

In other words, demonic forces may react strongly to anyone opening up their consciousness to the hidden realms, and implying here that she did seem well aware of the dangers of dabbling in the unseen world and of the possibility of being confronted with the malign forces that dwelt in it.

However, it seems this failed to stop her in her quest. Continuing in her review she quotes the lines of a character from the original version of McLeod's/Sharp's work,

"There is no dream save the dream of death," and interprets this as making explicit that "death itself is only a dream; the ultimate reality lies in the other world where all of life is one."

She remonstrates that these lines should not have been left out of the Opera, and clearly this is a crucial clue as to where she herself may have wished to go; to where she believes is life beyond death, where a life continues after bodily death.

Then there is a story written by Sharp/MacLeod, in his 'Herbridean Legends,' in which he tells the story of having lived on the Island of Iona when growing up.

One day he went to visit his friend Elsie, who he hadn't seen for a few days. When he got to her house her Mother was there but his friend wasn't and he asked her where his friend was. Her mother told him cryptically that she had been gone for a few days now.

Sharp wondered how he could not have known this, as the place was so tiny everyone knew everybody's business. The girl's mother continued, telling him that her daughter had believed she was communicating with the long dead spirits of the monks who had lived once on the Island.

She said that her daughter had felt that they were attacking her and that she must go to the only place on the Island where she would be safe, a place where they would not be able to follow her; the Fairy mound.

She went on to tell him of how long ago when the Monks had their commune on the Island, "They burnt a woman. She wasn't a woman but they thought she was. She was a faery. A 'Sheen.' And it's ill to any that bring harm to them."

She said that though the spirits of the Monks was still strong, the Fey were stronger, and the Monks were not able to enter the Fairy land; a particular spot on the Island along a path to a fairy mound, and this was where her daughter had gone to seek refuge.

It was said that this was the spot where Netta was found.

Dion Fortune, her close friend, offered intriguing possibilities too.

"I knew her well and at one time we did work together but before her death we went our separate ways. She was too interested in contact with the Green Ray Elementals and I became very nervous. I wouldn't work with her. I don't object to reasonable risk but it appeared she was going in too deep, and trouble would come. Whether she was killed by psychic attack, stayed out on the astral plane too long, or whether she strayed into an elemental kingdom who shall know? The facts however cannot be questioned.'

The Green Ray elementals derive from the Seven Rays in esoteric philosophies such as Gnosticism and Theosophy; the 'Rays' being types of light matter comprised of waves and energy that were thought to have created the Universe.

The Green Ray is believed to be on a substrata of the etheric planes at a higher level than those of the lower astral planes where the darker deities of Akkad and Babylon dwell (as in the Babylon workings of Crowley and Jack Parsons)

The Green Ray is thought to be the plane in which the Fairies and other benevolent nature spirits dwell. If Netty was trying to access entry into this plane, these wavelengths of energy in which the fairies are said to live; did she somehow access the lower planes by mistake?

Or did the Fey turn against her for some reason? Scholars versed in the way of the Fairies would point out here that Fairies are nature spirits whose loyalties lie with nature not humans; they do not have human emotion nor any empathy toward the human species.

According to the Scottish Newspaper, *The Caledonian Mercury*, Pre-Raphaelite artist of the time, John Duncan would paint there and he often spoke of hearing fairy music coming to him from the distance while he worked, and spoke of his many encounters with fairy entities there.

Head of the Order, Mathers himself claimed to be able to summon the demon Beelzebub, but he had given very strict and ominous warnings to his fellow members of the Order that unless the magical circle of protection was created with complete and pristine accuracy, the magician would be killed instantly or would self-destruct as a result of perilously imprecise summoning during these treacherous ritual workings.

Adding even further to the compelling story is the accounts from Island witnesses of having seen a mysterious hooded cloaked figure with Netta shortly before her disappearance. The island was once the domain of ancient druids. Was this hooded figure a terrestrial being or something from more ancient times?

Talking to the *Scotsman Newspaper,* investigator Ron Halliday, who spent much time on the Island of Iona trying to understand what had happened, expressed the idea that Netta had somehow 'levitated' as the only logical explanation to how she had no injuries or marks on the soles of her bare feet and only injuries to the edges of her toes, despite having traversed over rough terrain during the two days she was missing.

Then there were the reports from Islanders of seeing strange glowing blue lights at the time of her disappearance....

Conclusion

As perhaps this last case illustrates, just as one answer seems to present itself through the fog of confusion, other possibilities clamor for attention, to puzzle the mind even more and raise only further questions in the search for explanations into the Unknown....

And perhaps that is where the attraction lies, to always be searching for answers in a never ending quest of intrigue and mystery....

Predators in the Woods

Stephen Young

Copyright © 2014 Stephen Young

All rights reserved

Table of Contents

Introduction 391
Chapter One: The Predator Effect 392
Chapter Two: The Stick Men 405
Chapter Three: Shifters 410
Chapter Four: Something on two legs. 415
Chapter Five: Anomalous Beings 428
Chapter Six: Things with Wings. 444
Chapter Seven: A New Sentient Intelligence 455

Introduction

The woods can be tranquil and enchanting, yet there are moments when everything goes quiet and time seems to stop, and the hairs on the back of your neck start to stand up, and you could swear there's something out there in the trees, just watching you.

Suddenly everything goes quiet and that's when the fear sets in as a strange buzzing seems to fill your ears, and your eyes are searching everywhere for a hidden predator.

A powerful, menacing and sinister force is nearby and you can sense the imminent danger.

Then it shows itself. And that's when the panic sets in....

Chapter One:
The Predator Effect

Russ Chastain, a hunting aficionado who writes on the subject of hunting for about.com, recalls an event that twenty six years later still gives him shivers when he talks about it.

He'd gone hunting with his Father. They were in separate trees, laying in wait for passing deer as the quiet afternoon turned to evening.

"All of a sudden I heard some noises; something was moving nearby. I looked in that direction but all I could see was a bush moving that had been disturbed.

Somehow 'something' had got past me without being seen.

Then suddenly the quiet was filled with a blood-curdling shriek; it was the most primal cries I'd ever heard. It seemed human, animal, *and spirit*; and completely evil. Every hair on my body rose.

Then it came again. My heart froze, but it was hard to pin it down; it was ethereal. I tried to shrink to invisible. I held my gun tight thinking how effective was it going to be against something from hell? This was freaky, and guns don't kill demons.

I got out of the tree and ran.

What was even more freaky; my Dad had not heard it!"

To this day, he has no idea what it was....

~~~

Other witnesses claim to have encountered something that has been likened to the alien in the 'Predator' movies; able to evade and elude and attack through the use of artificial cloaking, that masks its body and renders it almost invisible.

Doctor of Physics Bruce Maccabee, an expert on optics, sounds and lasers at Naval Surface Warfare Centre, and a researcher into ufo's, orbs and other unexplained anomalies describes a case of a 'Predator in the Forest,' on his site.

A lady called Jan had set up a hunting stand in her native Ohio at the start of the hunting season. Sitting in the stand about fifteen feet up between the trees in a forested area, she patiently waited.

As she sat there, she passed the time texting friends and taking photos with her phone.

Suddenly the woods went silent. She noticed that there was no noise at all around her; the birds had stopped, there was no rustling in the foliage. Just dead silence. It made her feel suddenly anxious and she was so unnerved by it that she sent a text saying

"Something is wrong here. The woods just went dead silent...It's odd."

She thought it was possible a panther or coyote was approaching. As her eyes roamed the area, she suddenly noticed a strange visual effect that seemed to be moving across her field of vision, about twenty feet away. It looked like a mirage in a desert; but it was not hot there.

She removed her glasses and rubbed her eyes, wondering if something in her eyes was causing it. But when she put her glasses back on it was still there.

It travelled from left to right in front of her, above the ground, and then eventually disappeared from sight. When it did, gradually the animal sounds of the forest returned.

She later described it as 'like the invisible creature in *Predator*.'

Shortly after this, her nephew was at his High School not far away with other students. Several of them there reported seeing strange bright moving lights in the sky as it got dark. They were on their sports field, and the lights were directly above them, changing colour from white to amber, then they disappeared.

"Airplanes don't just disappear," he said, adding, "Every now and then I felt I could see something out of the corner of my eye, but it was probably my imagination."

Or was it?

~~~

Michael Ian Black, of '*The black files,*' (michaelinablackwix) claims to have captured images of chameleon-like reptilian creatures in the Clapham Woods in Sussex, England.

An area rife with rumours of decades-long occult worship, the pictures if genuine clearly show reptilian-like entities blended with the trees on which they sit. Up to six feet in length, with arms and legs and in the form of what looks like a preying mantis.

"They have the ability to blend no matter where they are; they are masters of disguise, making them almost impossible to spot."

They were not seen while taking the photos, but afterward upon looking more closely at the captured images.

He claims one of the pictures shows a black shape that does not fit with the surrounding greenery. "This one has been caught before it has had time to merge with its surrounding. You can't normally see them with the naked eye."

He goes on to make an astonishing claim; "I believe this is the reason why they can abduct with ease. I believe a race of reptiles is using our forests. Clapham woods, like Rendelsham Forest has had quite a lot of UFO sightings over the years."

He ponders, "balls of light" are seen in groups coming and going from woods. Are they related?

Reptiles can change their colour to match any surroundings. They could be in your house and you would not be able to see them..."

~~~

It gets weirder....

Mary Margaret Zimmer of the Mutual UFO Network in Florida writes about a CCTV camera capturing a peculiar set of images.

In 2005, she received footage sent to her from Kelantan, Malaysia. It had been captured from a private CCTV camera installed on top a tall apartment building.

The film showed a mysterious black mass of no definite clear shape, just a dark mass; but it was moving. It was approximately four by three feet, and it was crawling fast over roof tops. It scaled walls, and moved with speed, faster than any animal. Oddly, while the building walls and roof tops were clearly focused, the entity itself was blurry and any features could not be clearly seen, as though it were masking its true form.

~~~

An anonymous contributor writes on a forum, 'My husband told me he saw something when he was in the woods the other day. He described it as being almost twenty feet with big broad shoulders, incredibly long arms, and a 'long' head. At first it was jet black. He said that it was walking in a peculiar way; that it was like it made long exaggerated strides. Then he said it became a brownish shimmering colour. He said it resembled the effects of the things in the Predator movie, but that it disappeared within thirty seconds.'

Spanish Paranormal Radio Show Mira Lo Oculto (See the Unseen) reported on an odd incident experienced by a couple in January 2005, near Getafe; half an hour's drive south of Madrid in Spain.

The man and his girlfriend were in their car and were parked along a quiet and isolated road. Suddenly the man observed a strange shadowy shape moving near the car. His girlfriend then saw the shadowed figure. They said that it seemed to be moving and that it was in one spot one moment and then instantaneously it would appear in a different spot. At one point it came right up to the car and seemed to be peering in, though no face was visible.

After it moved away again, the shocked and frightened man found the courage to get out of the car and walk around, perplexed by who or what it could be, but on hearing shuffling noises in the grass by the car he lost his nerve and ran back into the car. The noise was coming from different directions at the same time.

He started the car engine and put it into reverse, keen to get away from the eerie place. The shadowy thing was still in sight, moving at great speed from one place to another, and they could see it was the average height of a man, yet it moved so fast.

Despite the headlights lighting the area in front of the car, the figure did not look any clearer and they could still not see its true form.

The man drove backwards and on reaching the end of the road, began to drive away fast, both of them too scared to remain any longer.

When they arrived home, they parked up and as they were leaving the car, the man noticed that across the windshield, among the mist from the cold night air, were two hand prints, clearly visible.

~~~

In the autumn of 2000, twenty five year old paramedic Mariusz was cycling home with his friend after spending the evening at another friend's house.

They were cycling through the forested region of Koniewo in northern Poland. They'd done it many times, and this night, though it was close to midnight, the moon was full and it lit up their route.

They were passing through the valley when they suddenly heard the most awful screaming.

"Terrible sounds were coming out of the forest. I couldn't compare them to anything I've heard before."

Loud rumbling, moaning sounds followed; fading, them coming louder again.

Then something caught his eye.

"Suddenly, a flying figure appeared at the rim of the forest, flying in our direction. My heart fell into my mouth. We stopped, perfectly still, in shock. Its face was grey. The entire figure was grey, but like a shadow. It had long hair. It seemed to have feet."

He was frozen in shock, but his friend managed to flee.

Unable to move, Mariusz watched the figure, "in sheer terror," until eventually he found the ability to move again and cycled as fast as he could away from the figure, back in the direction of his friend's house, in desperate fear that the figure was following him.

When he reached his friend's house, he insisted he could not cycle back home and his friend's mother drove both him and his friend home.

"Still today when I talk about it I feel uneasy," he tells *Truth Behind The Scenes*.

~~~

Husband and wife, Neil and Sally Pike were keen UFO watchers. They often went out to the hills in Warminster, Wiltshire, to see if they could spot any flying objects in the skies above them.

One winter night in 1971, Mrs Pike was at the top of a hill keeping watch while her husband was at a location a short distance away from her, also keeping a look-out.

The area at the time had been having all kinds of strange reports about unknown phenomenon, and the media was often reporting about peculiarities in the area, including local journalist Arthur Shuttelwood.

As the night drew on, she was getting ready to call an end to the evenings uneventful hours, when she suddenly started to feel very nervous for no reason. Then she caught something out of the corner of her eye. Turning her head toward it she saw the clear outline of a figure coming toward her. The moon lit up the figure and she could see that it had the shape of a man, at least seven feet tall, but his arms were almost of an equal length and hung loosely at its sides. It seemed to have no neck; his head seemed to rise straight from the shoulders, with no neck....

Meanwhile, her husband was over near an old deserted military post. As he glanced at the nearby path leading up to the post, he suddenly saw three figures of giant height. Startled, he shone his torch toward them, and in that moment the figures seemed to disintegrate into thin air; only to re-appear instantaneously in another spot close by him. Alone and confronted by these giant beings, he fled in absolute panic and terror.

~~~

A witness reported an inexplicable incident to Mufon (Mutual UFO Network) in January 2014.

He was driving along the Interstate 5 near the Padden Parkway overpass in Vancover, WA, at approximately two forty five am, when a translucent entity over seven feet in height crossed the road.

Slamming on his brakes hard, it seemingly appeared in the middle of the road out of no-where.

"It was there in front of me and it was staring straight at me. It was hovering. All I could feel was fear."

The witness then describes it in more detail. "It was about seven feet high, with long lanky limbs, a human form with a smooth head yet translucent and reflecting everything around it. It had flaps of skin attached to the head."

Then it started to move.

"It took off running, but not like any human or any animal. It ran with its whole body bending and contorting repeatedly, extremely fast."

~~~

A couple of years ago, the Taiwan UFO society was sent a very strange image that had been captured by policeman Chen Yung.

While hiking with friends at Jiaming Lake in the central mountains in Tailung, he had taken some pictures.

After returning home, he was looking through the photographs he'd taken when he saw something very strange. In one of the pictures was what looked like a half-human, half-mantis type creature, just visible on the skyline.

Unsure about what it could possibly be, he sent it to the UFO society; the only place he could think might be able to help explain it.

They spent twelve months analysing the picture using forensic specialists but none of them to date have been able to discredit it as a fake; nor can they say exactly what it is either.

It's big, almost transparent, and appears to have webbed hands. While they all agree it's a very unusual looking creature, and not entirely human, they don't know what it is, where it comes from, or why it is here.

~~~

"I made some 'Whoop' sounds while fishing, just joking around. Then something intimidating came crashing through the trees, breaking branches as it came," says Scott Carpenter.

"That began my fascination with bigfoot, and studying the existence of it, particularly in the National Parks."

He believes he's had another encounter; only this time it was much closer and he claims the creature was 'in stealth mode.'

"It was squatted down. I could make out just its eyes and body shape. It was dark green; it was reflecting the foliage surrounding it."

He didn't see this at the time; he discovered it when watching back the video he'd recorded as he'd walked through the woods.

"After walking past it, it turns back to black; that's when it comes out of the stealth mode."

He posts his images online at the bf-field-journal. He says he's scrupulous at ensuring the camera is clear of smudges and debris.

Could this really be the case? It's hard to make out the images clearly, but is it equipped with these talents and if so *how* does it do it?

It's certainly true that there's hundreds of reports of sightings of bigfoot that seem to vanish right in front of witnesses' eyes; to disappear into thin air in front of them, with no idea as to where it could have gone or how it has managed to disappear without any obvious hiding place.

Chapter Two: The Stick Men

In the Supernatural and Crypto-zoological worlds of the strange, it's unusual to find new entities. Ghosts, demons, and creatures of the night that come to life straight from our very nightmares, or beasts we once thought purely mythical, reappearing once more; but recently, there does seem to have been an emergence of a new, or perhaps never reported entity.

The spirit seekers blog believes that something new has begun to make an appearance; black 'stick men,' like children draw, but very real.

Incredibly tall and thin jet black stick figures with no faces. Their heads are just a black mass with no facial features. Their walk is a "lolloping" gait.

Their appearances have started to be described on the web in just the last couple of years. They move silently, smoothly, eerily. Are they real? Are they really new? And why would they show up now? Or, wonders the blog, have they always been here but are choosing to show themselves now?

If so, what do they want with us?

Kathy Casey says: 'In May 2013, I was coming out of my studio behind my house when I saw movement. It was dark; the only lights were from my porch but they weren't enough to cast a shadow. I saw a very tall, solid shadow, with no features. It was very thin, about thirteen feet tall, moving fast. It had an elongated head and its arms were very long and thin. It was solid. It was taking large steps. I could see no facial features; but this was not a shadow; it was upright, moving fast. It felt like it was old and alien. I'm not easily frightened ...but now I think twice

before going outside at night...'

Rob Bobson describes what happened to him; 'My parents sent me to a farming school in South Africa. Every weekend by myself, I would hunt and fish. I loved it. Then one day, a day I will never forget, I went down to the river to swim with friends.

Clouds came as we began the long walk back. About half way, we all said that we felt as if we were being watched, but we looked around and nothing was there, so we carried on. But then we got the feeling again, and we stood there for about a minute or so looking around the forest, and just as we were about to carry on walking, a tall, featureless black creature crossed the path about twenty metres away from us.

It was like nothing I had ever seen before; the way it walked, it was like it was gliding, extremely fast. None of us moved or spoke; then fear set in and we ran all the way back.

The next day we spoke about what we'd seen, and we all agreed we'd seen the same thing...'

Cody thinks he saw one; 'Me and a friend were on a dirt road in the mountains in Idaho, stopping at a gas station, when my friend said, "What the ...?' then... "Oh, never mind."

I got out the car to go to the pump and a loud noise scared me and I saw the trees shake. I jumped back in the car and took off!

I saw it move quickly toward the car. I told my friend what I thought I'd just seen, and he said he'd said he's seen the same thing near the pump when we pulled up but it had run off. He'd thought it was his eyes playing tricks. The weird thing was it killed the car stereo, and my cell phone battery.'

~~~

On Pararesearchers.org of Ontario, Andy contributes his extraordinary encounter which happened in London.

'Early on a weekday morning when I was a student, my friend and I were walking back to my house from another friend's house where we'd spent the night revising. No alcohol or drugs or alcohol had been involved. We were very tired and didn't talk as we entered my street.

Dawn was breaking and I saw a man coming towards us in the distance.

"See that man? He isn't a man, is he?" I asked my friend.

She replied, "No."

Did I just say that?"

"You did. He isn't."

The figure had changed. It was all black, like a silhouette and now it was very very thin and had very long arms.

It was taking lolloping dancing steps. It didn't have a face.

We freaked. We ran.

I rushed through the front door and we ran inside.

The front door was glass. It pressed up against the glass. We couldn't breathe.

It stayed for what felt like an eternity, before suddenly disappearing. One second it wasn't gone.

It was definitely not of the world we know.

This was not imagined; it was real and we both felt great fear. We also felt it was like it had changed form as though its 'glamour' had gone; its innate ability to become invisible, and it was angry.

I never want to see it again, whatever dimensions it came from...

Chapter Three:
Shifters

Stories of a creature known as an Aswang are especially common in Malaysia and the Philipines, where it seems to specifically target the vulnerable; the elderly, infants, and the sick.

Stories abound of them attacking people, kidnapping people, and even robbing graves to eat the dead bodies. They have been described as appearing like a vampire, a witch, or a range of terrifying mythical-like beasts. It seems that they can shape-shift at will; they can appear in the form of a beast or as a human. It's believed they are cannibals of both the living and the dead.

Xiao Qian writes on True Pinoy ghost stories, "My grandfather was suffering due to age, and we were just waiting for his last days. Those last few days were the most terrifying and hair raising of my life. My family were all awake attending to my grandfather, bathing him and feeding him and so on.

Suddenly a smell like a rotting cadaver came. It gave us a feeling of panic. Then came a strange sound; like a huge bird. It was so loud, and it was screeching. Then something landed on the roof. Its shadow could be seen on the neighbour's house. The sound it made petrified us; it was scratching on the roof and it sounded like metal being torn apart.

Our servant boy went outside to look and started screaming, "There's a big black thing; its eyes are bloodshot red!"

The family huddled together in fear until finally the thing departed, moving on to terrorise another family before it would choose its next victim.

~~~

Micha F. Lindemans, of Encyclopedia Mythica says, "I have had a real experience of this monster.

At the time, I was a boy. We lived in a small village surrounded by trees.

That night I couldn't sleep as the neighbour's dogs kept howling and I opened the window to look outside. The moon was very bright and I saw the dogs. Then I saw something else, something dark floating horizontally in front of my neighbour's window. It looked like a person floating. I was very scared and I quickly closed my window and covered myself with my pillow.

The next day I talked to my neighbour. I asked him if anything happened last night. He said he and his sisters and brothers were trying to guard their Mom because there was an Aswang."

It's said that the Aswang can enter a person's body; and when they have done this, they use that person to inflict terror and great harm on their enemies. Most usual are the female Aswang, who in their own form will appear to witnesses as unsightly with dirty long mated hair, evil blood-shot eyes, long sharp nails, and a long black tongue. Like the traditional witch, she allegedly has the power of flight, and she may then transform into a huge bird to hunt her prey.

~~~

According to author and occultist Jimmy Lee Shreeve, one instance of a shape-shifting entity was even a matter of a murder trial in South Africa in 1987.

Zane Metshiavha was suddenly woken in the night by strange scratching noises at his front door. He went to the door and called out, asking who was there. When he got no response he became scared and to protect himself he went and fetched an axe. More confident now that he had something to protect himself with, he opened the front door and went outside. To his horror he saw what looked to be large bat hanging from the rafters of his roof. He struck it with the axe, making it fall to the ground and then he fled in blind panic.

He went to his neighbours for reinforcement and having roused several of them he returned to his yard with them. These witnesses later described seeing the creature dragging itself across the yard toward a fence. Zane struck it again and again until it lay still. The group of people watching him approached it to look at it more closely.

Each of the witnesses described it in a different way when they spoke in court. Some of them described it as looking like a mule, others said it was definitely a winged creature; but all of them stated that the creature's form was changing shape before their eyes. They watched it changing. All the testimonies stated that began o form into the body of a child, and then into a fully formed man.

After it died from the injuries sustained from the axe, it was identified as that of an elderly man, Jim Nephalama, who was reputed to be a wizard.

The villagers said he would often tell people that he had "the power to do whatever he wished with them." He would boast that no-one had as much power as he, and he warned his enemies that his battled were not fought in the day time but at night. He was feared by all who encountered him.

When the case went to the Supreme Court, the judge ruled that Zane should have recognised that the creature was a man. He was found guilty of behaving in an irresponsible and violent manner and sentenced to ten years in prison for culpable homicide.

On appeal, and further witness testimony, the sentence was later reduced to four years.

~~~

David writes 'I was on my way to my job in Freeport, Illinois. It was about 10:30pm and I was on State Road doing 60 MPH when I saw it running alongside my car. It was keeping pace with my car. It looked at me several times.

It was half the size of my car. It had black fur that was hard to focus on, like it was almost shifting. I felt it was pursuing me. It had red eyes. At some point it turned and disappeared.

I do not know why I saw it, but there were other supernatural events occurring in my life at the time, so I assume it was linked somehow. I'm glad that I was in a car and not on foot; I can't imagine what would have happened otherwise.

Chapter Four:
Something on two legs.

By January 2013, the population of a Reservation in Oregon had been putting up with night after night of screeching and screaming sounds coming out of the surrounding swamps and brush.

Cries, screams, and high pitched screeching would sometimes be followed by roaring; and the combination was enough to chill everyone on the Umatilla reservation to the core.

Colleen Chance lives there and works as a housing assistant. She took to recording the sounds on her Iphone, as she was so disturbed by them.

"It's spooky and I don't know what it is," she says.

According to reporter Richard Cockle of the Oregonian, she's not the only one concerned and disturbed by the nocturnal disturbances that wrecks the nerves.

The housing authority has received many worried phone calls reporting the screaming and enquiring as to what on earth is causing it. Some say their dogs are too scared to venture out any more at night.

Fellow housing authority worker, Mr Luke, told Cockle, "Many here are woods people. They're familiar with animals and they're not prone to taking fright."

Witness Silva Minthorn says, "It's not the same sound as foxes; it's not even close."

Her Mother believes there's more than one of them; she's heard screams coming from two different places at once, as though whatever they are, they are communicating with each other; and maybe planning something....

~~~

A woman contacted the Gulf Coast Bigfoot Research organisation to describe an incident that happened to her in Connecticut.

"I was riding my horse along a rail road that opens into a meadow. There's a stream there and I stopped to let my horse drink. I had a very strange feeling I was being watched and the hair on the back of my neck went up. My horse was looking at a hill and was very anxious.

A smell came. It was foul. Then something started down the hill after us. It sounded like an elephant charging and its screams were so loud it hurt. I could hear branches being snapped. The horse bolted but I managed to stay on. It kept pace with us on the other side of a stone wall. I was beyond terrified.

I finally started to breathe again after we got back on the road, but my horse never recovered and it died a month later.

~~~

The Toronto Sun reported on the day Helen Paphasay and her Mom got the fright of their lives. As they were driving to a blueberry site to go picking, just off the Grassy Narrows First Nation reserve, they were suddenly confronted by an unnerving sight.

"I seen a tall black thing walking toward us," she recalls. "I know it wasn't an animal because it was walking upright, walking like we walk; human-like. It wasn't an animal. It looked about 8 feet tall; black as night."

Her mother saw it too and she sat rubbing her eyes in sheer disbelief at first; then fear took over them both and they drove away from it fast.

When they reached home they told the rest of their family, who were so intrigued by their story that they insisted they go back with them to try to see it too.

With strength in numbers, they all went back to the same spot. What they discovered there was highly strange; they found footprints in the woods. The footprints, nearly 16 inches long, showed the outline of not five but six toes.

Similar to this Mother and daughter account, CBC News carried an eyewitness report from 2012 where two friends had also gone berry picking, in Nunavik, Quebec.

As they gathered the berries amongst the trees, they thought they spotted another person close-by also picking berries. They saw her long dark hair. Then they realised the hair carried on past the 'person's' head; it covered their entire body.

As they watched in horror, they saw 'it' start to walk upright with incredibly long strides, then sometimes crawl along. It was coming their way.

"It wasn't a human," says Maggie Cruikshank, "we weren't sure what it was at first, but it was really tall and it kept coming toward us, and then we could tell it definitely wasn't human."

She estimated it was between 10-15 feet tall, and that's definitely not human. They were too frightened of what it might do to them to let it get any closer, and they ran to their ATV and raced away in terror.

They went straight back home to warn everyone of what was roaming out there.

Footprints later discovered in the area where it had been, were over 40 centimetres long; that's nearly 16 inches. The average length of a man's foot is 27 centimetres; that's just over 10 inches.

~~~

On March 4, 2014 on Vancouver Island in British Columbia, a Marine officer had a shocking sighting. Luke Swan, a young First Nations man says he was on routine patrol at White Port beach, when standing on the shore line he suddenly saw a large dark figure perched on a near-by rock. Then it stood up.

"The first thing in my mind was to get off that beach," he laughs, telling CTV News. "I pushed off as fast as I could and got into the deep water. Something really big was standing there. It was huge. It was eight to nine feet tall. It had broad shoulders.

When I saw it scared me. It was no bear. Probably a lot of people want to see it, but in the end it might scare them too and I don't wish that on anybody. It's definitely out there," he says, not able to define what 'it' is, but definitely not keen to encounter it again.

After telling his father what had happened, his father and friends went to the spot where Luke had seen the creature and attempted to track it.

They came across footprints that were sixteen inches long and eight inches wide. They spotted bark pulled off a cedar tree at a height of over nine feet.

Though they didn't see the creature itself again, Luke has no doubts he saw it.

~~~

In Chatham, Massachusetts, the police were called by Michael Patrick and his mother in 2011, after enduring night after night of screeching and screaming noises. Then they came across an unusually large footprint in their back garden.

"My neighbour's dog won't leave its owners side at all now. It had gone outside to investigate the other night, after they had heard the screams too and been disturbed."

The police department told the State Journal Newspaper that an officer had seen the footprint and it was over eighteen inches long. It had claw marks.

The footprint was found beneath an apple tree, and apples had been taken from the highest branches. Local investigator Stan Courtney says that a headless rabbit found beside the house could well have been left by the creature as an offering or 'gift.' He says this is often the habit of these large beasts.

"Its head had been pulled off; not cut or bitten, but actually pulled off."

Whatever did it, it was strong.

~~~

Sightings are coming again in Gideon, Oklahoma, according to residents there. The sounds of thudding footsteps coming, the ground shaking beneath them.

Cheryl Mast knows it wasn't her imagination when something loud thudded against her trailer in the night.

With the nearest neighbours several miles away, her and her boyfriend and their friend in the trailer next door are pretty isolated.

"My dog was crying and something had broken the door of the pen. I think it threw the dog. My friend is certain something shook his trailer. Her whole trailer has been shaken. It went on for several minutes. It's happened before," she tells Taklequah news.

"We are scared to death," she says. "There's that feeling it's watching you. With so many incidents it makes me think we're getting close to a confrontation."

~~~

Does a creature known only as 'the hidebehind' really exist? Allegedly a fearsome creature that preys upon unwitting hunters and hikers who wander into the woods, it was certainly credited as the cause of the disappearances of some of the early loggers who worked in rural regions.

When they never came back to camp at the end of a hard day, it was said they had been taken by the hidebehind.

Its success is said to lie in its inherent ability to become unseen; hiding behind trees when stalking unsuspecting victims and snatches them away in the blink of an eye.

The hidebehind are not the only ones who play this game. Could it be true that a cannibalistic humanoid lurks in the beautiful wilds of New Zealand? According to Maori legends, the fearsome Maero are a race who live in the woods and mountains.

They are masters at snatching people in the wilderness. They steal people away and then fight them to their death. Wild, hairy and exceptionally ruthless, these Maero leave no one alive. Once dead, they feast on the bodies.

The Maero, also sometimes called Mohoao, have hair that's long and unkempt, all over their bodies, and long cruel fingers. One story tells of a man called Tukoio who was once captured by a Maero. He fought with the savage creature and managed to overcome him. He chopped off the beast's head and decided to carry it back to his village to show off his trophy, but as he began to walk along with it, to his horror, it began to talk to him. He threw it to the ground in shock and fled.

Later, fortified by some villagers accompanying him, he returned to where he'd dropped the head. It was gone.

The Maero had reassembled its head onto its body and back to life to terrorise and kill and eat more villagers.

In the 1800's, New Zealand's Governor, Sir George Grey, said he had been told about this 'creature' by the islanders,

"They say they're like a man but covered with hair, with long claws; strong and active, and they say they are afraid of them."

It was indeed reported that a headless partly eaten body of a gold miner was found in 1882, followed by the dead body of a woman just a short distance away, who had been dragged from her shack in the night. Her neck had been snapped....

~~~

Does a ghoulish man-eating monster really exist? Taller and larger than a human, with fangs and a grotesque face, such a creature has been spoken of by generations of Native Americans, and translated to mean, "An evil spirit who devours men."

Called the Wendingo, it was believed to be a terrifyingly real entity by First Nations tribes. When 17th century missionaries and explorer came, they at first ridiculed the accounts of such a creature existing; until they themselves began to experience their own threatening and horrifying encounters.

They described coming across a strange and terrifying beast they could only describe as 'the devil himself,' or 'a werewolf,' because of its fangs and glowing eyes.

~~~

Floods devastated many rural areas in the southern parts of England in the winter of 2013. Farm land and homes remained flooded for weeks on end.

It was during this time that a twenty five year old student, who would not reveal his name for fear of worldwide ridicule, spoke to Cryptozoology News.

What he told them was far from ordinary. He said he had been on a train heading back to London, after having been to visit his parents. He'd dozed off occasionally during the lengthy journey, but when he opened his eyes, he claims he saw something completely inexplicable.

"When I woke up, I looked through the window and saw a man about nine feet tall running through the wet fields; at least, I thought it was a man...until it got closer to the train. We were moving very slowly because of the water.

It wasn't a man. It had horns and ears like a wolf. It had hair all over its body. I don't know what it was... I thought I was still dreaming, but other passengers also saw it."

~~~

Mark Miner claims he has collected more than twenty first hand modern day accounts of what were possible werewolf sightings in Oregon State. He claims these are fully verified accounts. He's keen to stress this, obviously used to sceptical reactions.

One of those accounts is his own.

"One night my fiancé and I were lying down on a deck in Montieth Park, Albany, just looking at the stars when we suddenly heard something jump in the water. We got up and looked over and something black was swimming, approximately over 7 feet long and was covered in hair. It grabbed hold of a sleeping duck and started biting into it; we could hear the crunching of its bones. We were extremely frightened as it climbed up onto the bank, but I wanted to see this 'thing' closer so I jangled my keys to attract it. It let out a growl like a dog does when you approach its food bowl when it's eating; but times that by a thousand. It was deep, guttural; its tone was the deepest anger, and it made my blood go cold. We both thought we were going to die."

"We ran and I caught a glimpse of it as I ran. It was huge and it was the wildest, most evil thing I've ever seen."

Was it a werewolf? A wolfman? One of the scariest legends in Cajun folklore is that of the Loup-garou, or rougarou. Described as a beast with the head of a wolf and the body of a man, it's thought to be an original werewolf; a shape shifting human that can transform into a wolf at will. Its natural habitat in wolf form is the thick bayou where the swamps and forestation keep it camouflaged and hidden and where unsuspecting hunters can inadvertently fall prey to its hunger and mindless slaughter of them.

~~~

Sightings have been made over the years of a horrifying half-human, half-goat creature.

Referred to as 'the goatman,' the most well-known sightings were in Maryland. J Nathan Couch has studied reports in his native Washington, and details one account received by a lady called Mindy Rosete. She hoped he could help explain to her what she and her daughter had seen.

"It was about 9.30pm, and we were driving on Highway K. The creature was about four foot, grey/brown, hairless, running on its back legs. The car just missed it. I really want to know what it was. It was not our imagination."

Brian Vike also saw what he thinks was a goatman. Now director of HBCC UFO research organisation, he was once a security policeman at Fairchild Air force Base in Washington, responsible for guarding the nuclear storage area there.

Late one night on patrol with another policeman, he saw someone running toward the vehicle they were sitting in, just beside the storage building. He reported it immediately and fellow officers raced to investigate, flooding the area with lights. They searched the area for two hours but found no-one. They joked that he had seen the Goat-man; many of them had seen it before him.

Another night he saw it climbing a security fence.

"I swear it turned and looked right at us," he claims. "It was a running joke with us; but those who've seen it, they know better. It scared the hell out of me."

He and his co-workers had no doubt about what it was...

Chapter Five:
Anomalous Beings

Heather told of her confusing and frightening encounter on Unexplained Mysteries, which happened while trekking with a friend and their horses in the boreal forests of Northern Saskatchewan, Canada.

As the sun started to set on day one of their trek, they looked for a good place to set up camp.

'We set up the tent and realised my hat was gone; couldn't find it. Going back along the trail I found it about a hundred feet away. As I picked it up, it really stank. Anyway, we went to bed, and saddled up the next morning.

That night we set up another camp. At 3am I needed the bathroom. Just before I went into the trees, the same smell was back. I was nervous now, because whatever was making it must have followed us. I was scared it could have been a cougar and I grabbed my rifle. A shadow moved slowly behind a tree about fifty feet away.

I hummed, thinking I might hear it move so that I could figure out what it was. It echoed my humming; perfectly, gutturally. My heart started pounding; only a person could do that. The smell came back, so strong I began to heave as I made it back to the tent. My friend shouted out and started pointing the flash light, and leaves scrunched and the thing started to run; what we saw, it was dark; I might be wrong, but it looked like a man but it had an animal's head... I know what I saw.

The thing was the height of a man, but its legs looked like they were broken and thin. It was covered with hair. It looked distinctly human, its body was human, its arms were human, but it had a goat-shaped face... and it had horns.

What the hell did I see? My friend insists it must be supernatural. I have no way to explain it and I haven't slept well in days...'

As to the origin of this 'thing,' there are many theories. Some say Goatmen were created by the Nephilim; the fallen angels who procreated with women, resultingly creating a hybrid race of strange creatures; however, since its appearance is incredibly similar to that of the demonic entity Baphomet, once worshipped by the Knights Templar, and now a significant figure in Satanic worship, it's creation could well be the work of dark alchemy and sorcery.

Given that they disappear without trace, and no bodies are ever found, perhaps it's more likely they are indeed inter-dimensional entities that have been summoned from hell itself. Demonic creations that begin as mere shadows, weaker in strength until they fed off the energy of human's, taking sustenance from them to gain strength and vitality, until able to fully develop into their hideous monster-like forms.

Now fully equipped, they move at lightning speed and can disappear in an instant, never to be caught or trapped, playing with human fear as though a game to them.

~~~

Margaret Zimmer of Florida MUFON describes the report she received from a man in Pennsylvania. The man, along with his brother and his son, were on a fishing trip at a reservoir.

They'd made a fire to give them some lighting, as well as having a large flashlight with them. With the fire glowing behind them, they sat along the dock waiting for the fish to come.

The son was playing with the torch, flashing it behind him when caught between two trees about thirty feet away, he saw something absolutely terrifying. It was approximately eight feet tall, according to the adults present, and its arms were almost as long as its body. It was hunched over. They could not see its face. But it was definitely not a human being. Almost like an albino, it was white, and when it moved, it walked "as though its knees were on backwards..."

~~~

Author Graham J McEwan collected the very strange account of a Mr John Farrell and his girlfriend Margaret Johnson.

On a warm night in 1966, they were driving on a quiet road in the rural county of Louth, Ireland. Suddenly, in front of them on the road was a creature blocking their path. At first it looked like a horse, but its face was that of a man's. Its appearance was not only extremely odd, but the menace that excuded from its eyes was terrifying. In palpable horror they both met its gaze as it loomed nearer, where it remained blocking them from going further and preventing them from escaping it.

"It had horrible eyes, they were bulging. We both screamed we were so frightened. We were completely paralyzed. It was a horse's body but the face was hairy and leering and huge."

It was so big that it covered the stretch of the road entirely in front of them, before thankfully vanishing into thin air after a few minutes of silent terror. "It just *vanished*...John turned the car around and drove to my house. He drove straight through the front gate he was so frightened. We woke up my Father and told him. We weren't drunk; we didn't drink, and both of us couldn't have imagined it."

Her Father spoke to the Press some time later, saying, "They were still terrified when they arrived home. They must have seen something awful. My daughter was ill for days afterwards, and both of their stories tallied."

~~~

Writer Elliot O'Donnell was collecting scary ghost stories for his 1954 publication 'Dangerous Ghosts.'

One night after he'd finished giving a talk in Northern England, a Mr James McKaye came up to him to tell him about his own frightening true story.

The man said he had recently gone to view a house, wishing to move himself and his family closer to his place of work.

As he was going up the stairs, he thought he could hear footsteps behind him. He turned around quickly but no-one was there. He thought how strange it was, but decided to put it down to the acoustics in an unfamiliar place.

Upstairs he went into the first bedroom. The footsteps followed him. That's when he started to get truly frightened; it was the middle of the day and it was bright inside the house. How could there possibly be a ghost in the room with him, he wondered. But then he saw the shadow on the wall, and it was not his.

It was not the shadow of anything he'd ever seen before. Petrified, he ran from the room and out of the house itself.

Strangely despite this, or perhaps because of it, McKaye could not stop thinking about the house. He dreamt of it, always as a mystery which he was about to be given the answer to only to suddenly wake from the dream.

In a most bizarre decision, he applied to rent it. It was available at a remarkably low rent, which at the time he didn't think anything of; he just desperately wanted to live there.

He moved his family in immediately and all was quiet for the first few weeks until one morning when he was working in his study, and the maid came in asking him to quickly hurry to the nursery upstairs where the children were playing.

"The children are playing with something like a dog, but it's not a dog. I don't know what it is," she cried.

In the nursery he saw the thing; it was a blurry outline of a form that seemed shaped like a great dog, but on seeing him it rushed from the room.

That night he was in his study after the family had all gone to bed. He was ready to call it a night and go to bed himself and as he rose to turn off the light his hand was suddenly gripped by something cold and clammy that didn't seem to have fingers. He screamed in fright and just then he heard a tremendous crash from upstairs. Rushing up the stairs he ran into his wife's bedroom to find her talking in her sleep to something that was crouched on the floor; a black figure that looked like the shadow he had seen on his first visit to the house.

It was a hideous combination of wolf and monster and human, and it emanated sheer evil, but it vanished in front of his eyes.

Within the next few hours, the family left the home, never to return there. Though McKaye did his best to find out the history of the house, he never did get to the bottom of what the creature was or why it had appeared. He did however discover that the rent was low for a reason; no-one ever stayed there long.

~~~

The infamous Hellfire Club, though founded in England in 1735, also had an isolated meeting place in old rural house at the top of Montpellier Hill, South West of Dublin. Built over an ancient sacred druid Caern, it was the scene for much debauchery and allegedly occult worship by the members of the Hellfire Club.

Reputed activities included the burning alive of black cats in black magic rituals, the murder of a dwarf, and the killing of a woman. The skeleton of the dwarf was discovered many years later under the floor along with the statue of a demon, and it was given a consecrated burial. Perhaps not surprisingly after this, there have since been many unsettling accounts of supernatural incidents and reported sightings of both black cats and huge black dogs.

Frequently visitors to the now derelict club claim to feel an ever-present sense of dread and fear when they are there; almost as if some ancient power has been harnessed and trapped within the walls of the building.

Here's just a couple of many reports from those who have ventured onto the site, from Irish site *Blather.net*;

"I was there today with my friend. I'm very sceptical about these kinds of things; however as we started going up the stairs I suddenly felt really ill. It was very strange; it just came on suddenly... and I began to think that there really is something not right about the place, and I really couldn't wait to get out of there. I felt very uncomfortable the whole time I was in there."

Domhnall O'Huigin writes, 'As a young teenager I was there with three other friends. To this day I remember the feeling that there was death in the ground, almost like an odour. That's the only way I can explain it: like someone or something had died there and there was still a sense of it all these years later that. You could ignore it but if there was a lull in conversation it returned to the forefront of your mind and felt oppressive.

I then went there years later with my kids, but I got exactly the same feeling; all I know is it was imperative to get my kids out of there. Make of that what you will. For the record, I am relatively credulous but do not think I am psychic or similar. I do not know what this was...'

Ciara says, "For years my parents and me would go up there to walk our dogs. But the last time I went up there would be the last time; for a reason.....

It was the early '90's, I was about 13, and me, my mum, dad and our dog went for a walk up there. My dad was doing something fixing the car after we parked, and me and mum went on ahead with our dog. It was no different feeling to any other time I was there. It was early afternoon, sunny, me and mum were chatting and the dog was a bit ahead of us."

"Suddenly she stopped, which made us stop. Her hackles went right up, and we looked forward and encountered this big black dog. Its eyes were black. It was snarling at us and showing its teeth. We froze not knowing what to do.... Mum told me to go back and get dad. I turned very carefully and as I looked back at my mum I saw it was gone."

"I can't ever explain it. It had literally vanished. We ran back to my dad and tried explaining it to him, but he just thought we were being hysterical women.

I've never been up there since; I don't think I could again. When I speak about it, it gives me serious chills."

At the bottom of the hill stands Killakee House. In the '60's a Mrs Brien bought it and turned it into tea rooms. However, the Irish Independent newspaper reported that something was very wrong there.

Spending the first few nights there alone, Mrs O'Brien experienced some terrifying things. In the middle of the night she was woken by the sounds of her dogs howling so weirdly, "that it was as if they were frightened out of their skins."

She herself had also been terrified by strange noises, and in the mornings she would find destruction throughout the house, yet no evidence of anyone breaking in.

Workers who'd been contracted by her to carry out the renovations before opening for customers, refused to lodge in the house after witnessing unnerving incidents including a door that would not stay closed despite it being locked with a heavy bolt. One night a worker watched in horror as the door began opening and through it came a large black cat as big as a large dog. It glared menacingly at him.

Then an artist, Tom McAssy, was contracted to design paintings in the house. He was painting in the hallway when he allegedly saw a similar enormous black cat with red eyes. Oddly, he claims that the cat then spoke to him, saying, "You cannot see me." Then a hunched three foot tall man appeared through the door. As the painter started to back away from the apparitions, he watched in disbelief as the man himself shifted into a cat too.

As though to capture the strange experience, the artist then went on to paint a portrait of the cat with a human face.

If true, it would seem that perhaps brought about by occult ritual magic, there was still shape-shifting going on in the area all these years later.

With repeated nightly disturbances, the owner had no choice but to call in an exorcist. It's said that the manifestations then desisted; though reports still come from visitors to the area that it's a place where the atmosphere is filled with uncertainty, apprehension and unease. The house is now a private residence, and information about any current disturbances is not public knowledge. The Hellfire club lies in ruin, but sightings are still reported and many visitors vow never to return to the Hill.

~~~

Just around the corner from the Old Bailey Criminal Law Courts in central London, was a prison that housed people accused and convicted of serious offences, and it was here that condemned prisoners were hung in front of huge crowds of people who flocked there to watch.

Since the 16th century there has been a legend of a mysterious large black dog appearing there. Witnesses said they saw it accompanying prisoners to the scaffolds before they were hung, only for it disappear before their eyes. Others claimed they saw it climbing walls and walking along rooftops.

Prison conditions were appalling; with vermin, bitterly cold conditions, overcrowding and very little food. A highwayman imprisoned there called Hutton wrote about the black dog while he was awaiting execution. His account describes how whispered tales were told about a group of inmates who were so starving that they ganged up on a new prisoner and killed him, then ate his body.

What the gang of prisoners didn't know however, was that this new inmate was a highly educated scholar who had been schooled in the art of black magic.

It was soon after his murder that the sightings of the black dog began; its appearance taunting and terrorising those who had killed him.

To this day, sightings are still reported, though the prison is no longer used.

~~~

Occult British scholar Richard Cavendish recorded the strange case of a Mrs & Mrs Smith who in 1940 were sitting together in their front room, when the wife said to her husband, "It will come over the hill when it comes; it will come over the hill when it comes."

Afterward, she had no idea what she had said, or why she had said it; despite her husband telling her, in shock and confusion, that she had said it.

She did however become very scared of being in the house after it got dark.

She did not repeat what she had said again, but about two months later she woke in the middle of the night and told her husband that the thing from over the hill was nearly upon them.

Then they heard the downstairs door opening and heavy steps coming up the stairs. As they grabbed hold of each other in terror, their bedroom door swung open and a hideous thing came through the door.

It was bloated and naked with discoloured blotchy skin. It had an odd shaped head, a thick neck, and feet that were webbed.

"It was the essence of evil. Never have I experienced anything so terrible. I have never been able to find out what it was. I hope I will never experience it again," said Mrs Smith.

It crossed the floor in front of them, went to the bedroom window and went through it somehow, vanishing without attacking them, but neither of them ever really recovered from the shock of what it was, or what it wanted with them.

~~~

Wallasea Island is a truly bleak marshlands in Essex, England. In the 1970's English writer Eric Maple, in his book *Realm of Ghosts,* describes a disturbing incident of a beast-like creature that appeared in a barn on the Island.

The barn was situated on land owned by a house that had been known as 'the Devil's House,' since as far back as the 1600's.

A labourer was reported to have been at work in the barn when he heard his name called several times. After this he says that he was overcome with an overpowering, obsessive desire to kill himself, and unable to stop himself, he hurriedly grabbed hold of some rope, tied it around his neck and walked toward the ladder to scale it and secure the other end around a beam, all the while hearing a voice telling him, "Do it, do it."

Suddenly, he was confronted by the sight of a monkey-like creature staring at him with wild red eyes, which scared him so much that he ran at full speed from the barn.

Locals believed the creepy experience had been due to the rumoured satanic worship that had been going on in the house, many years before.

~~~

In September 2013, 120 elk were found dead in New Mexico. All were scattered near each other. Close-by was a newly formed crop circle. Had it been an infectious disease, it would have killed gradually them, not all at once.

In an area rife with mysterious cattle mutilations, many are wondering if something unknown came out from the crop circle and attacked the animals.

Curiously, a 1647 picture made by a method called woodcutting, called 'The Mowing Devil,' clearly depicts a demon-like creature creating a crop circle. According to the legend that inspired the picture, the circle appeared in the crop 'so neatly done that no living Man could do the like.'

Had crop circles really been appearing way back then? And how many sightings had there been of demonic creatures emerging from them?

Chapter Six:
Things with Wings.

Caretaker Mr Marielli who lives in Oakland Creek, California, claimed he saw a very odd and terrifying sight one night back in October 1975.

He didn't speak out about it then; he was sure people would think him crazy if he did.

He recalls that as he took out the garbage that dark evening, something above him caught his eye.

"It was like some fearsome gargoyle, on the edge of the roof of the house."

It was staring down at him.

"It was very broad; much bigger than a man. It was monstrous. I was always afraid to tell anyone though; but it was like the devil himself."

What he didn't know at the time however, was that he wasn't the only one to encounter such a monstrous thing. Winged, gargoyle-like monsters were being seen in trees and on roof-tops throughout the area. They had massive wings, and seemed to glide silently without needing to flap their wings.

Unknown magazine, published from 1997 to early 2001, interviewed a group of youths about their strange encounter in an Illinois park. One of the boys, Ron Bogaski, told of how he and several other of his friends came face-to-face with a gargoyle.

The night it took place was in 1981, in a park on a late summer's night. They were sitting beside an old mausoleum inside the park, when suddenly they noticed an incredible sight. Sitting on the top of the gothic structure was a creature, estimated to be possibly ten feet in height, with dark leather-like skin covering it. Its body was 'very muscular with thick arms. It had enormous wings and horns on its head.'

All four of the teenagers could smell the stench of decay coming from it, along with an overpowering smell of sulphur. They watched in awe and horror as it unfurled its wings and flew up into the night sky.

~~~

Respected researcher Stan Gordon reports on the alleged sighting of a dragon-like creature seen flying in Pennsylvania, in 2012.

In a rural part of town, a man was out walking his dog at close to midnight. He heard a 'woosh,' and looked up at the night sky. Flying over him was a large thing approximately fifty feet above that looked like a mythical creature; "It looked like a dragon," the shocked man reported.

It flew over a light and the man was able to catch a better look at it. He described its body as being over twenty feet in length and with a wingspan almost as wide. It didn't have scales, but rather had a shiny, almost reflecting skin. It was coloured reddish-brown. He could see arms that were muscular and legs that were thick. Both its mouth and its eyes appeared to be glowing. The noise coming from it was deep and throaty.

~~~

On unexplained mysteries forum, a lady in her sixties now relates the experience she had as a teenager.

"In 1963, I was 15, and my younger sister and I lived in Colma, California. My Mom used to send us berry picking in a wild area nearby. That day, as we started collecting the berries, I looked down the hill next to us and saw a large dark object lying there.

I was curious and climbed down to it. There was this huge dead dragon-thing. It was about 8 feet long with huge wings and claws. It was stiff. It had long sharp teeth... It was grotesque. I screamed and my sister came running. We both ran home screaming.

Over the years I have found stories that say they are mythical; but I know what I saw and it was a real gargoyle. My sister and I both saw it."

Recent Gargoyles have been reported since 2010 in Puerto Rico, according to investigator Reinaldo Rios and the Guanica police.

Incredibly similar eyewitness reports describe demonic looking entities of reptilian appearance, at least 6 feet in length, with leathery wings and skin, and red or yellow eyes full of intensity and menace.

~~~

A few days before, and directly after the 9/11 terror attacks in New York, witnesses and images show a huge winged entity flying from the twin towers. It seemed that Mothman had re-appeared at a scene of devastation, as it had allegedly done before; showing up at the Chernobyl nuclear disaster, and indeed at Fukashima.

Eminent researcher Colin Andrews posted a reported sighting by English businessman David Haith, who had written to him to tell him of what he had seen in 2011; prior to the Fukashima disaster.

"I was in Japan for business and staying with a friend who was teaching there. After dinner, he said he needed to see a weather project the students had created, near a power site."

"As we walked toward the small weather project, we heard a sound like a bus's brakes in need of service then a scream that made the hairs on the back of my neck stand."

"A young couple nearby were staring at the power plant, and a figure was silhouetted there on top of one of the buildings. To say that this creature was large was an understatement."

"Suddenly it unfurled a huge set of black wings and took flight, circling several times, its attention fixed on a building below; that I was to later find out were the nuclear reactors."

"Then it came toward us. It had two large eyes, glowing blood red. It was looking straight at us, but it flew toward the town.

We went straight home. My friend was shaking as he bolted the door shut; he couldn't believe what we saw. Finally he convinced himself it had just been an optical illusion; until he saw the News and the Nuclear disaster was reported."

~~~

There are other reports of a Mothman creature being seen at an area of swine flu outbreak. Engineer Fransisco Torres told *Inexplictica* investigators that people had been seeing a tall creature, over nine feet tall, with huge wings and red eyes in La Junta, Mexico.

One witness, a young student at the North Region University, who asked them for confidentiality, claims that the strange entity even chased him.

He said that he was driving home after class one evening when he saw something in the road ahead of him. It looked like a man, hunched over and wrapped in something. Then suddenly it stood, and taking two steps it opened a huge pair of wings and flew toward the young man's car.

It kept apace with the car as the student tried to drive faster to escape it until after several minutes of sheer panic, the enormous 'bird like' thing flew away.

~~~

In September 1978, workers arriving for their shift at a coal mine in Freiburg, Germany, saw a tall man standing in the opening of the mine, wearing a trench coat.

As several of the coalmen approached him to see he wanted, they were suddenly stunned to see a cape-like cloak unfurling around the man. Then they began to feel the most terrible horror as they realised it was no man standing there.

As the 'cloak' unwrapped they realised it was a pair of huge wings, uncovering the body that was not human.

The scream it then emitted chilled their blood and hurt their ears.

Reports were that it sounded like fifty people screaming all at once; others said it was more like a train screeching on tracks as though the brakes had been applied in emergency.

Recoiling in utter fear and horror as it stood motionless in front of them, the miners retreated from it. They remained some distance away from it for a long time, until it disappeared inside the mine entrance.

Very reluctant to enter inside, the miners continued to stay out of the mine, until suddenly they were all thrown to the ground by a huge explosion coming from inside the shaft.

When the mine inspectors arrived to investigate the damage the explosion had caused inside, they were adamant that had the miners been inside at the time of the explosion, they would all have been killed.

Speculation rose that the creature, though terrifying in its appearance had come to warn them and to prevent them from going to their death. Others felt the creature had somehow purposely caused the explosion.

~~~

Esoteric Philosopher of the 1920's Geoffrey Hodson, claims to have experienced a terrifying visitation that he believed was a 'nature spirit'

Going on to write a book about Fairies, he was to describe this experience in detail in it.

He was hiking alone in the picturesque Lake District of Cumbria, when suddenly in front of him appeared, "a huge crimson bat-type thing about twelve feet high with burning eyes. It was not human but like a bat with outstretched wings, and a human face. As soon as it felt itself observed, it shifted into its shape, with its piercing eyes upon me."

Then it disappeared, only to return again, this time in a smaller form, he claims.

~~~

In March 2005, numerous residents of Santa Fe in Argentina called the police with perturbing reports of seeing a baffling character who became called, "The crazy roof man."

All independent witnesses said the same thing; that he was some sort of cat-man, who performed the most athletic of maneuvers in front of them, leaping from roof-top to roof-top with astounding super-human agility.

Each report put him at over seven feet tall, clothed in black, and with some kind of cape and stick. Some said it was as though he was a comic book hero come to life, with legs so long he could jump across streets with a single bound and scale walls with ease.

One woman claimed that after the silhouetted figure pointed at her, his eyes red and his gaze intense, she lost all ability to move. Perhaps the shock paralysed her, though she hinted at something more powerful than that. Others claimed the figure would simply de-materialise in front of their eyes.

Dora Ruiz claimed to have seen it prancing on the rooftops. No features of his face could be determined other than glowing red eyes. One resident exclaimed that he had fired numerous shots at the figure with his gun, only to see it completely unaffected by the direct hits. In fact, it howled back at the man and continued to jump around on the roof tops, as though taunting him.

The police were alerted but they could not catch it. He leaves no trace, other than scratches along the walls from his long fingernails.

Though sightings eventually ceased, whatever it was it was never apprehended....

~~~

Barry Chamish, a leading UFO researcher in Israel, reported on the bizarre case in 1997 of a young girl, Suha Anam, who had to be rescued by neighbours in the Dir AL Awasan district when an 'alien' creature tried to snatch her from her second floor balcony. The case was reported to the police and apparently the incident was recorded in their reports.

She was standing alone on the balcony at the back of her apartment when 'an alien' suddenly appeared out of no-where and began tugging her by the arm, trying to pull her with him. Screaming in hysteria, her neighbours heard the commotion and came quickly to her aid.

Telling the police about it, one neighbour said she heard the screams and the sounds of what she thought were like a helicopter. When she looked out of her window to see what was happening, she says she saw whirling in the air and an ash-like substance filling the air.

The girl was treated in hospital for scratches and shock.

Then, that same week, two other people say they witnessed 'aliens.' Schoolboy Muhand, 16, said that he was walking his usual route home when he saw an odd looking man in the road; but it wasn't a man, he said, "the skin was the colour of a frog. It had only three fingers on its hands." With its hands the boy said it came toward him trying to scratch at his face.

In terror the boy watched as it then screamed something indecipherable at him and suddenly flew into the air.

Before this incident, another man came forward to say that he had seen something in the sky that had 'the figure of a man with arms and legs.'

Police took all of the accounts seriously and even went so far as to set up some kind of ambushes to try to trap the entities before they could cause serious harm; but they did not catch it....

Chapter Seven:
A New Sentient Intelligence

A highly unusual, sinister and sentient entity seems to have been discovered in the last thirty years. Something that appears to have its own intelligence.

Put simply, it's a black substance, called by those who have studied it 'black goo,' for want of a better term.

It's an oil-like substance that some conspiracy theorists believe was the real reason England went into the Falklands War in 1982. David Griffin of Exopolitics UK claims that there was a hidden reason for War. It was not a war over territory but instead was driven by the need to seize this powerful biomorphic substance.

It's thought to be some type of sentient being. It exists not just as a physical fluid, but also as an intelligent morphogenic energy that has consciousness. It is multi-dimensional.

This living intelligent organism hibernates in temperatures below freezing, but if it is exposed to warmer temperatures, it becomes active. It can then attach to anything; including animals and people.

Some believe the goo comes from an Alien base in the area. It was allegedly seized by the British during the War with Argentina and exported to English laboratories to be studied in the hope of weaponizing it. It is not definitively known whether that was achieved or not.

Its purpose is said to be for use in 'the end times,' and conspiracy theorists such as Broadcaster Miles Johnston of 'The Bases' you tube channel has been interviewing people who say that 'factions' of the Government/Military are creating hybrid beings by injecting them with the black substance, altering their DNA.

U S Veterans Today senior editor Gordon Duff, a global intelligence specialist has written about this black substance too, with a different explanation from his sources.

'The Nano-substance had been activated by a device from an off-planet location. It has become sentient and aggressive. It has shown itself capable of disarming fleets and killing people.

He says the Military, *so far*, have been able to protect us, through their use of 'technologies', but the Chinese are in league with a "group" that are able control this substance. Intelligence agencies believe that the Chinese are acting to try to 'control' us for an off world civilization that they have a 'relationship' with.'

He says that China has spread a rumour that it has an ethnic bio-weapon capable of killing all 'non-Mongolian' people, and has asked other Countries to ally with it.

As though to silence doubters, he then points out that 'America has had diplomatic relations with an 'off world' civilization for at least fifty years, and anyone who lives in denial of these factors are as crazy as the 9/11 deniers.'

Witnesses Miles Johnston has interviewed say it was discarded by the British military as unpredictable.

The rumours are rife.

If any of it is true, then more than one Military Industrial complex may have it. It's alive, it has its own intelligence, and it may soon develop its own agenda....

It will either be used for nefarious means against parts of the world population, or it will break free on its own, and if it does, no-one knows what devastation to human life it will cause.....

~~~

HUNTED IN THE WOODS

Sometimes predators are animal or human

....and sometimes they are not.

Stephen Young

Copyright © 2015 by Steph Young.

All rights reserved.

Table of Contents

Introduction 460

Chapter 1: The Chitauli, Hunting humans, and Body drops 464

Chapter 2: Magickal Working, Art, and Ancient Races 505

Chapter 3: Caves, Caverns, and Screams. 536

Chapter 4: Silence & Blood-curdling Screams in the woods. 555

Chapter 5: Non-humans in the woods 568

Chapter 6: A case like Dyatlov 582

Chapter 7: Hunted by Humans? 596

Chapter 8: Taken, Held, and Drowned 611

Chapter 9: Shape-Shifters & Missing Time 667

Conclusion 674

Introduction

The mysterious disappearances of people, both adults and children, have taken place around the world since antiquity, leaving no tracks, trails, or any possible evidence as to what might have happened to them, and so often, the missing are never found; or, they are returned in a very different condition to when they disappeared..

Thoughts, ideas, and theories about each individual case of 'the disappeared,' and the causes of each of these disappearances are often well documented and discussed ad infintum, and yet overwhelmingly, what they lack in each case are accurate conclusions and definitive proof about what really happened to the missing, and often this is never discovered, despite the comprehensive and exhaustive involvement of law enforcement agencies, the military, expert searchers and trackers, and hundreds of volunteers.

Other cases seem to slip by with far less attention and investigation, and yet they display the same mysterious and often inexplicable characteristics of a person anomalously disappearing.

What really lies behind these many mysterious disappearances? What is the real reason for the ones who are returned either dead, or returned but changed, never to be the same again?

This book deals with some documented cases, many previously unknown, and takes a deep look into what are some of the most compelling, perplexing, and disturbing cases of strange and unexplained disappearances of people across the world. Some of the evidence uncovered is both surprising and shocking. Some of the possible causes are both terrifying and horrific. Some of the possible answers are ones that we probably don't want to believe....because that would change the entire way we view our world and force us to reconsider who the predators really are.

In a famous interview with John Keel in 1973, called 'The Great UFO Wave,' by Glenn Wayne and David Graham, Keel made some interesting comments,

"On the ground, and air, there are things happening that they don't want us to know about. What they are trying to hide may be frightening, even incomprehensible, but it does seem they are using us."

He then makes a very shocking statement. "It may be more than rumor that young people are being 'collected' from colleges after the memories of their families and friends have been altered so that they will not remember the existence of their children. As farfetched as this sounds, there may be more truth to it than to some of the other theories kicked around."

Unbelievable as it may sound, he is saying explicitly that he believes college kids are being permanently abducted and not returned. Not only that, but he says their families are being tampered with too.

"We are being used in some fashion,' he says, just as his predecessor Charles Fort once said, "We are being fished," and, Keel continues, "intelligences" don't want us to discover how they are using us... so, all this other stuff is camouflage."

This 'other stuff' he refers to, is the manifestation of strange and anomalous sightings of entities which appear to defy both categorisation and explanation.

"(We) have been misled for years by deliberately misleading manifestations and chimeras, (which) range from complex hallucinations, to elaborate transmogrifications."

Both Keel and Charles Fort then, sincerely believed that there were people going missing...who never came back, or came back changed, and diversion tactics are put in place to conceal this.

As wild as this sounds, some of the cases that follow appear not only to sound just as unbelievable and far-fetched; but equally, they also appear to back-up what both men believed, and horrifically, they're cases that really happened.

Sometimes predators are human or animal....and sometimes they are not.

This book deals with the stuff of nightmares. It revolves around allegations of the most horrific kind, involving missing children, non-human predators, patsies, and assassinations. Could any of it really be true? Here is a presentation of the twists and turns of a stream of allegations and supposed revelations to horrify anyone reading it.

Chapter 1:
The Chitauli, Hunting humans, and Body drops

Credo Mutwa is an internationally known Zulu shaman and healer. He gave a startling interview to Rick Martin of the Spectrum Newspaper back in 1999. What he said, is a terrifying revelation, if it could possibly be true.

"Over 1,000 children disappear in South Africa every month. The Newspapers say it is organised child prostitution, but I don't think so. These children are not street children; they are school children who stand out in class, because they are good at subjects."

"When shamans in Zaire talk of 'the Lords who control Earth,' they are the Chitauli's, although there are 24 other alien races we know of. The field Chitauli's eyes glow red. They are tall with large heads. They walk gracefully. Some have horns around their heads; these are the warriors. The royals have no horns. They have a claw which is very sharp and straight, which they use to punch into the human nose in order to drink human brains in their ritual."

"If they are sick, a young girl is kidnapped by the servants and taken to the underground. There the girl is bound and forced to lie next to the sick one for weeks, being fed and cared for, but kept tied. Once the sick one is well, the girl is given a chance to escape, *a chance which it isn't*, for when the girl escapes she is chased over a long distance underground by flying creatures made of metal, and captured when she reaches the peak of fear and exhaustion."

"Then she is taken to an altar and sacrificed, and her blood drunk. The victim must not be sacrificed until she is very frightened. This chasing was practiced by Zulu cannibals; their descendants will tell you that the flesh of the human being who was made to run to try and escape and has been very frightened, tastes better than the flesh of a person who was simply killed."

"Here, and it is still ongoing, five white girls disappeared. Each one was a highly talented child, either developing in spiritual ability, or a leader in school subjects. It was a big story in the News and people came to me and persuaded me to try and find these children. Then my phone started ringing and with very angry voices, I was told to stop helping. 'They' told me that if I didn't stop, my children would be murdered. Sure enough, my youngest was brutally stabbed, and so I stopped."

"After the disappearance of the children, the police arrested a reverend called Reverend Van Rooyen and his girlfriend. Before he appeared in court, a very strange thing happened. They were shot in their vehicle. After they were shot, their vehicle managed to come to a stop; something a moving truck would never do."

"They had been murdered. Why do I say that? Because he had a gunshot wound in his right temple, and yet, all who knew him said he was left-handed man. So, who murdered them? It is one of the ugliest mysteries."

It should be pointed out here that the Newspapers of the time have a different version; they say that the man's girlfriend lured the children away, the children were spotted in the man's company, and that it was the Reverend who sexually assaulted then murdered them. Their bodies however have never been found to confirm this belief, though the police didn't doubt he was their suspect. Credo's belief however is that they were not the right suspects; that the suspects were not even human.

"I can't help but wonder if the Chitauli are in the U.S. because of the large number of underground bases. The number of missing children in the U.S. alone is so astronomically high that the slave trade does not answer the question."

At the time of giving this interview, Credo said that he was visited by three people who told him to stop talking or his wife would die.

Could this really be what happened? Is there really a blood-drinking reptilian race of beings, who take pleasure in hunting humans? While many will say his account is pure fable, thousands around the world believe what he says and he is highly respected for his nature and conservation work and recognised as one of the most distinguished healers internationally.

A few years ago, another man came out with claims just as horrific. Investigative conspiracy researcher Dave Starbuck, now in his 70's, has been producing DVD's of highly controversial conspiracy related topics for decades in the U.K. (his website is revelationaudiovisual.com)

In 2006, he interviewed a man called Dean Warwick. Dean claimed he was a civil engineer who worked on bridge and tunnel projects for the US government in the mid '60's. He described himself as a "whistleblower." He was also an 'alternative energy' pioneer and claimed to be "an insider within US intelligence." He also claimed to be ex-British intelligence.

Originally from New Zealand, he said his Grandfather worked in the justice department and was a high level Mason. Warwick said his grandfather was also a world renown expert in 'Chinese detection.' In Chinese, 'detection' means the inspection of an 'object' which can't be observed; and in Warwick's case, he meant the detection of 'people,' picked out and stalked without them knowing it; in other words, putting a tail on someone.

Warwick says that when his Grandfather was on his deathbed, "he told me something as he was dying; he said that later on in life I would learn something which he couldn't divulge to me. I was 15 at the time. He said it was something that would practically destroy me, and I'm quite convinced that I do know now what it is that he was talking about, and it is truly horrifying."

"It is not being made public; I have yet to see, read or hear anywhere of evidence of that which I have learned, and I have many confirming reports from police around the U.K. and from Church groups that I was mixed with in the U.S. before coming to the U.K."

"I was drafted into the New Zealand Army, and topped every course in the officers training while preparing for Vietnam. I was taught how to bring down the Twin Towers using nothing but infrasound; we were made to study the experts; the Russians, the Americans, and the British in the late '50's. When I was in the military, there were these joint manoeuvres in the late 50's by these Superpowers, bringing down tower blocks using nothing but sound waves. Later, I became a civil and structural engineer."

"Now back to what I mentioned earlier; it's to do with the killing of the children. We have got a release from the US department of statistics in which it's said that every year, there will be 150,000 children disappear and never be heard of again. A similar report said in Central and S. America there will be 350,000. That's .5% of the population of N. America; and .5 % of Southern and Central America. Exactly the same figure; that can't be a coincidence. Then one day I've got a suit walks into my office and we get talking and he says he has a meeting at the department for social security, work and pensions.

So I tell him, "Have a look at something; I think you'll be interested," and as he looks at the reports I say, "We don't have anything like that in the U.K."

He replies, "I will tell you who I am; I'm head of that department, I've been there more than 3 decades. There's 20 to 25,000 children a year disappearing in the UK."

Warwick continues, "*The Mothers of the Disappeared* group says that each year in the UK, 120,000 children disappear, and 20% will never be found again. That's the same figure this man walked in and told me. So what's happening to these kids?" he asks rhetorically; and here is where it gets truly horrific, if it's at all possible that it could really be true.

He says, "I have it from an officer in the police in a southern police force; each week they find up to 7 or 8 children in the New Forest that have been slit around their necks and down their shoulders; their skin has been peeled off their backs and their flesh has been eaten while they are alive."

He continues, "And this brings me to the Jessica & Holly case."

(Here he is referring to the murders of Jessica Chapman and Holly Wells. In August of 2002, the two young best friends, aged just ten years old, and probably best remembered for the photo taken of them wearing their Manchester United football T-shirts, went missing after going out to buy some sweets after dinner.

When they didn't return home, their families tried to reach them on Jessica's mobile phone but they couldn't get her to pick up. Holly didn't have a phone. By midnight, the police were out searching for them in the small Cambridgeshire village of Soham. Volunteers joined them and they searched all night, the next day, and for the entire week.

During that week, many witnesses came forward to say they had seen the two children that evening when they had gone to buy the sweets, and one of these witnesses was a Senior School caretaker, Ian Huntley, who lived with the girls' Primary School teacher, Maxine Carr. He said that he had seen the two children that evening when they had walked by his house.

When the police talked to him about the children, they found his behaviour unusually 'emotional' and it aroused their suspicions when he kept asking them lots of questions. As the days passed by, he seemed to be maintaining a high visibility in the search process and with the visiting media too, and subsequently, a few days later, they returned to his house and searched it, but found nothing there that would indicate he had anything to do with the children disappearing.

In the second search of the School where he worked however, they found the half-burnt football T-shirts the girls had been wearing, and he was arrested for their murders. It was 13 days after the girls went missing that their charred bodies were found in a ditch in the woods near the US Air Force base Lakenheath, in Suffolk, discovered by a man who kept pheasants in the area. It was a thirty minute drive away from the village they lived in.

Forensic evidence of fibres matching the girls' clothes was found in the suspect's car and house, as well as his hairs on their T-shirts and fibres from his clothes.

He was sent to trial and found guilty of double murder and sentenced to life in prison.

Shockingly however, according to Warwick, "Anybody who believes that Ian Huntley had anything to do with it needs their head examined."

His interviewer, Dave Starbuck concurs. "I agree; I did a presentation about it and the response was so tremendous, including from two Solicitors and a Barrister," he says.

Why would these two avid researchers make such a claim? Well, it appears that it has to do with what Warwick said earlier, about the claims he makes about bodies being found in the New Forest, and about how he believes the two children in this case really died. As wild and outrageous as it sounds, Warwick, (now deceased, and this I will come to later) insists that the murderer Huntley was a 'patsy,' to cover up the real cause of these children's deaths. It has to be said that his belief, which he says has been corroborated, makes for very insensitive reading when it concerns the real deaths of these two children, and for the parents of the two children, it seems wrong for Warwick to makes such allegations when it would be highly distressing to them.

However, in his words, he says, "What we have is he was there (in the woods where the girls were found) because they found seeds in his trousers from the plants there. (But) He could have got them from anywhere *or*, they could have been planted."

In other words, what he means is that for the Crown Prosecution, the existence of the seeds gave them clear evidence that the man was there and dumped the bodies there because of the seeds found in his trousers; what Warwick is suggesting however, is that they could have been planted on him to enable his prosecution, by deliberately placing him at the scene, when in fact Warwick clearly believes he wasn't at the scene and the evidence was tampered with.

He continues, "So, he takes their bodies to the woods, takes off their clothes, and pours petrol on their bodies. No! You would leave the clothes on to soak up the petrol and make the fire burn better. Then, he takes the clothes back to his school, finds a bin and puts the clothes inside of it, and pours some petrol on them and sets them on fire. Nonsense!"

Again, what he is saying is, why would he burn the bodies in a remote part of the woods miles away, to try to hide them and destroy the evidence, but then take their clothes to his place of work to burn, thereby risking a far higher chance of the remains of the clothes being found where he works and obviously certainly implicating himself; which he did when they were then found by the police. Also, how were hairs found on the T-shirts yet the T-shirts had been burnt?

And now here come the chilling parts alleged;

Warwick says, "We have the lady who tried to get a newspaper to print her story. Whether it's true or not I don't know but she says she walked her dog in that wood *every day* for two weeks before their bodies were found. She said that the military police were there then and they were blocking off the path."

His interviewer Starbuck adds, "Correct; I heard that from another source."

Warwick continues, "We have the jogger interviewed outside the court as the trial was ongoing. He said that *for three nights* he had been running in those woods and he had heard girls screaming. My information comes from high level US intelligence. Those girls bodies were treated with a set of talons and they were raped. Now whether this was part of a cult or it is a part of a 'transmutation' of a presence is open to argument."

This sounds utterly horrifying, but utterly insane. Surely this is crazy? Isn't it very bad taste to even suggest that these girls suffered an even more horrific fate than at the hands of a child predator of human origin? What he is saying is that they were attacked and killed by 'entities' with talons, as with the other cases, and "their skin peeled off and their flesh eaten while they are alive," and the 'murderer' used as a 'patsy,' to cover it up.

However, if we look closer at the murderer, he would appear to be the perfect candidate to commit these killings. He would appear to completely fit the perfect profile of a human predator. It seems that he was known to the police for a while before he was arrested for these murders. He'd been investigated in 1995 for having relations with an underage girl. He was arrested for house burglary that year too but the charges were ordered to lie on file rather than convict him. Why was that? He is accused again of having underage sex. Then the following year another 15 year old alleges he is having relations with her, but her family decide not to take further action.

The following month the police and social service investigate him for allegations he is having sex with a 13 year old. The girl refuses to co-operate. A month later he is arrested when a woman says he raped her after they shared a taxi home from a nightclub. The police say there is insufficient evidence. A month later he is arrested for rape of a woman walking home alone from a nightclub. The crown prosecution decide the CCTV footage is insufficient and there is insufficient evidence to charge him. Two months later, a 12 year old girl alleges he sexually assaulted her. Again, the police decide there is not enough evidence, despite her detailed testimony. In February 1999, a 17 year old girl tells the police that he raped her. He says it was consensual. The police drop the case.

Of course, those who believe Warwick's version that it was not a human who did this but entities with talons, will say that these arrests and charges against Huntley make him the perfect candidate to choose as a patsy. He fits the perfect profile of a serial sexual predator, whose behaviour has then escalated to murder. He couldn't really be a better candidate for the prosecution to get their hands on.

While the idea that he was a patsy sounds completely outlandish when aligned with the claims Warwick makes of 'reptilian' entities skinning children alive; it does arouse suspicion because he was never convicted of any of his offences, and it has to be asked why a man accused by multiple girls and young women of very serious assaults was never, in all of those cases, even once taken to trial and convicted of them. This would certainly add fuel to Warwick's belief that Huntley was the perfect patsy to be used; it was almost as though he was 'allowed' to get off with these charges as part of a pre-planned cover-up of the 'reptilian' child killings; that, or he was 'selected' as the perfect candidate from the criminal database.

On the other hand, a more sensible explanation probably lies in the fact that its really not uncommon for Social Services to fail vulnerable children who complain of assault; there are cases repeatedly in the News where the 'system' has failed to safeguard them, and its also common for the police and crown prosecution to fail victims of sexual assault. It also seems that in this case, there was also a failure too of liaison between different organisations and departments, and there was also the fact that when he applied for the role of caretaker at the school, he used a different surname. This meant that his robbery charge did not flag up.

Of course, none of his sexual assaults showed up either because the police and crown prosecution service said there was 'insufficient evidence' in every case. The headmaster of the school had no idea of the real background of Huntley, and different jurisdictions and departments seemed to fail to notice that he was repeatedly flagging up as a perpetrator of serious assaults. With the repeated complaints against him, and lack of any convictions, it certainly adds fuel to the conspiracy theory that he actually didn't do it. However, the alternative explanation is far too crazy and horrifying to believe, surely?

Another argument against Warwick's case of the 'skinning alive' non-human predators, is that of the Australian investigative journalist & conspiracy theorist Joe Viallis (now deceased) who also put forwards the theory that Ian Huntley was a patsy, but for an entirely different reason. He says that just metres away (although it was more like half a mile) from where the bodies of the girls were found is LakenHeath US Air Force base. Viallis' reason for Huntley being the patsy in this case was, he alleges, to cover up the real perpetrator of the murders of the girls, because, he believes, he was a US military man and it was done for diplomatic reasons to ensure the Air Force base kept a sterling reputation and could maintaine its good relationship with the people of the UK, however closer inspection in this shows that there is no obvious proof, but it does perhaps add to the belief of some people that Huntley was set up. While there are those who believe he was, the overwhelming majority of the public however simply do not believe he is innocent.

Another controversial researcher, David Dixon however, claims that a man and a woman had been seen before the children disappeared, staring at them intensely from a car, as though following them, and that a woman had tried to abduct a child nearby recently from a school. There are reams of information carried out by independent researchers who have looked into the myriad of discrepancies in this case, however, it's not the intention of this book to go off topic and look into that, and he certainly appears to have been a monster.

Returning instead to Warwick's revelations about the Huntley case and how it ties in with non-human predators, he doesn't stop there. His theory and alleged evidence gets even wilder. He refers to the Bible. In particular, he says, "A piece which recurs many, many times; 'And they ate the flesh of children in those days.' There is a reason it says that. A client of mine is a scientist high up in British government research. In the Bible and much of what Zecharia Sitchin has written, is the story of how the Nephilim or Anunnaki ate the menstrual fluid of woman because from it, they derived the ability to read the mind of a person."

Surely this is unbelievable? He then goes on to explain that when these giants came down to earth and mated with human women, the women often died in childbirth, leaving them without women from which to 'eat' the ingredients he mentioned. As a replacement of this, (and while not addressing why they didn't just abduct more women) he then argues that instead they switched to something else, "The Nephilim or Anunnaki discovered that if a terrorized human child's flesh was eaten; and this I have (corroborated) from this scientific base, but I won't say where in the U.K; if that flesh is eaten, it's full of serotonin and adrenaline and it gives them these similar ingredients, which allows them to read minds."

"There are so many references to it in the Bible; it doesn't say they ate the bones, it doesn't say they ate the skin of children; it says 'ate the flesh' and that means that they had been skinned."

"I have this confirmed by police. And, the guillotines, as quoted in Revelations, are appearing. Thousands brought into military bases. What for? How are you going to 'reduce the population by 6 billion?! Okay we can play games with the weather, we can cause floods. An English doctor and his family were walking in a Canadian forest near the American border and came to a disused rail yard with box cars and inside of them were shackles with a guillotine. Just consider that we are shackled and are left pointed at the guillotine and left waiting to be put into it until the next day; You're going to be terrified!" So here we get the adrenalin running!"

"The majority of people will say this is nonsense," he rightly says, but he points out that he believes it's because it's too big a thing for most people to even contemplate. Or, is it indeed nonsense and just the product of a wild imagination and too much reading? His claims are outlandish in the extreme, but then, even a cursory look on YouTube and you will find these alleged box cars and the stacks of empty coffins lined up in various parts of the US.

Has this man drunk too much conspiracy fuel? Or cobbled together a sci-fi story and is putting it around as some kind of factual existence? Of course, having no named sources does not help his argument at all. The New Forest is not a vast dense forest like a National Park in the US. Is it at all within the realms of possibility that something so extreme as the killing, skinning and eating of 7 to 8 children a week by the Anunnaki could be happening without people knowing? It sounds the most preposterous thing to suggest, and why would a policeman who is on the verge of suicide from witnessing the remains of the children not come forward and speak out against such things? His source, "this police officer, tells me that one of his colleagues is the one who has to inspect the bodies, and each time he is nearly suicidal from what he finds."

If this is the case, why doesn't he, or any of the other alleged witnesses or sources this man claims to have speak out too? On the other hand, what does happen to all the missing children he refers to from the official statistics? And, there's also the allegations that this man himself suffered a very drastic consequence as a result of speaking out.

The idea that he was onto something has grown somewhat in conspiracy circles, because of his rather sudden and possibly strange death, which occurred shortly after he came out with these allegations in the above interview. His supporters say he was killed. It happened, it's alleged, at a UFO conference in 2006, in Blackpool, England. He was giving a presentation there and was the last guest to go on stage. He had told his supporters and friends before the conference that he was going to blow the whistle on some highly controversial topics; missing children, ET's, NSA, the 9/11 attacks, and apparently he was even going to name 'the anti-christ.'

Just minutes into his talk however, he collapsed in front of the audience. He died there and then. The general consensus among his supporters is that he was hit by an ELF weapon. On the other hand, he was not a young man and could just as easily have had a genuine heart attack. One source quotes him as having heart problems but refusing to go to the Doctor, and laying a concrete path shortly before the conference, which perhaps might have extenuated his existing medical condition if that is what he did.

While some who attended the conference make claims of having seen a smartly dressed man leave the audience moments after the speaker collapsed, go down the stairs and exit the building merrily whistling, and making a telephone call on his mobile phone in which he was laughing heartily, having just seen the man collapse, Warwick's wife however told the New Zealand Newspaper's that she was satisfied her husband died of natural causes.

Whichever the case, we will probably never know; however, the things he came out with are certainly disturbing.

Another mysterious case comes from the 1970's, however in this case; it appears to be the unfortunate product of an over-active imagination and some embellishment. Or does it?

In 2008, 'The Watcher,' began posting on the Project Avalon forum. He appears to go by the name of Paul Grant, also nee Barry King. He says that the well known writer Andrew Collins wrote of the events in his life in a special report in 1978, but this has not been confirmed.

Part of his story revolves around an intriguing and highly sinister case, and appears to be backed up by now declassified letters sent to the Ministry of Defence. However, the real scenario will later turn out to be most likely wholly different.

Paul writes, "In 1970, my research centred on reports of sightings of lights and craft entering the King George reservoir, (in Waltham Forest, Enfield, England.) In March of 1970, two young children went missing in the area, and searches included the reservoir."

"Three months later, their bodies were found in a copse there. Great mystery surrounds their deaths. A press blackout ensued. The families were told not to speak with anyone. Strangely, the official word was that, even though summer, they died from exposure."

"I went to the scene myself and it did look very strange. The Police were in plain clothes, and the stranger part; the army were there too. The public were standing nearby, held back by police. No one knew what was going on. The Army were carrying spades and sacks. They removed the soil. Years later the grass still hardly grew there. The official version was that the children died of exposure, in summer, even though they were less than 500 metres from a street and houses."

"I trod on toes trying to get hold of information. A few months later, over several nights, two people were sitting in a car looking toward my house. Then saw my first run-in with MIB's; these were black-suited and of the NSA variety. The non-human ones came later."

Of the non-human MIB's he claims to have encountered, he says, "Most people will scoff; but many have come under their attention. They're menacing only if you show them fear; if you stand up to them and don't appear disturbed by their appearance, it's like a process kicks in as though they're not programmed for that response and they 'shut down.' If fear and stress is shown when under their attention, their pre-set programming of intimidation will continue."

His story about the missing children appears to be backed up by a 'persistent correspondent,' according to documents released by the Ministry of Defence, and now in Archives. Indicated on the files by the Ministry as 'closed,' yet according to the pen marks on the document it is labelled for "permanent retention."

The correspondence deals with a matter that according to the writer of the letters, is a very serious issue, and one that would certainly require attention in his opinion. It involves the account of the abduction and deaths of two children, caused allegedly, according to the UFO researcher, by aliens.

The researcher in question released a document called 'Age of Enigma,' from the West Country Unidentified Flying Object Research Association,' in March 2002.

In March 2011, the U.K. Department of Defence released UFO related correspondence it had received from members of the public, and the author of 'Age of Enigma,' had written to them concerning this case. The researcher from the UFO group (name redacted but presumably Paul Grant nee Barry King) says that he was an active researcher in this field after he had a sighting of his own, back in 1970. He subsequently joined the British UFO Research Association, or B.U.F.O.R.A.

The 'Age of Enigma; West Country Unidentified Flying Object Research Association report of March 2002, sent to the MOD reads, "'REDACTION ON ORIGINAL DOCUMENT"

'Myself and (Name redacted) left the pub in The Ridgeway, in Chingford, North London, at about 10.40 pm, Tuesday before Christmas, December 1970. When I reached home I decided to walk along the line of shops close by. There were some people still out by the fish n chip shop. I continued on, then stopped and looked towards the top of the bank of the King George V reservoir when I saw two white horizontal round objects attached to a cable ascending the reservoir at 200 yards distance. There was no noise emitting from it. Then it descended, then veered upwards at a speed, then down, the cable still attached to it.'

'I stood for a minute or so before running back to the fish shop and said, "Quick, you must see this. A U.F.O. has landed!" We all ran back. After a period of about 45 minutes, the two silent objects descended inside the retaining bank.'

'Looking back now, I think it was a form of scanner. For some time after I was wondering about it, what had happened, but it wasn't until 18 months later that there was the strange disappearance of two children. They lived nearby. They turned up dead in a clump of trees, northeast of the reservoir. Police had gone all over with tracker dogs. It's strange they should disappear then reappear next to trees which had been burned from above. The local press printed that they died from bum marks and that they died from over exposure.'

(The first point regarding burn marks, I have not been able to corroborate)

The report continues, 'Their bodies were not found close together, and one of the girl's shoes was missing. The other shoe she was wearing was clean. If you drop two stones from the air they will not land in the same place or spot. Their bodies were not found together.'

'UFO's have been known to leave burn marks, they have been known to kill animals. The sun could not have caused the burns, just as it's unlikely that the children die from exposure- in June. I strongly believe that they came into contact with aliens. I feel they died under duress at the time of a U.F.O. flap.'

'When they were found and we arrived there, there were crowds of people and the police were everywhere, and the Ministry of Defence.'

(However I have found that in fact they were found close together, if it's the same children, and it's highly likely they were the same. Additionally, some of their clothing had been taken from the scene, but most likely by an altogether different predator; a man by the name of Robert Jepson, a convicted child killer who, three decades later confessed that he had killed them, more of which later.)

The witness continues, 'May 11th, 1974 (two years later) myself and fellow BUFORA Investigator were driving by the area when we stopped and got out. We gazed over in the direction of the copse. We talked about that time. Looking around casually, I noticed what looked like a person standing by the trees on the ridge and called my friend's attention to it.'

'The ridge and tree line from our position is approx 400yds. We decided to have a closer look and reached into the car for our respective binoculars and then focussed on the figure, standing completely still, facing us. Through the 10x50 binoculars the figure was indeed perplexing. It was approximately average human height, and wore what could only be described as a black gown which reached from the neck down to the ground. It had long blonde/white hair but what disturbed me was that it had no facial features at all. My fellow investigator was just as agitated as I was at seeing this. Talking between ourselves as to what the hell was going on, he said, "Look to the left of the trees." I raised my binoculars and followed his pointing finger.'

'There stood an identical being. Swinging back towards the right, the first 'being' had gone, then left again, but that 'being' had gone too. Totally bewildered I lit a cigarette and leaned back on the car. My friend shouted "Look, along the hedgerows." These were about 200Yds away from us. Now this sounds funny, but was only funny looking back afterwards; at the time I was seriously concerned.

Along the hedgerows ran, at a pretty fast pace, a white roughly human shaped 'thing.' It had no features at all. This was joined by another nearby. These were simply aimlessly dashing about.'

'My friend said "****" and got back in the car hurriedly, saying, "Lets get out of here."

We drove away and stopped in a car-park a mile or so away and discussed what we had just seen. It was dark by now and we decided to drive back. We got out of the car and with our binoculars, stood at a fence, looking towards the area and scanning the copse. After a short time I noticed a small red light just above the trees, it was a slightly bigger red light through the lenses.'

'Early next day, Sunday 12th, my friend and I visited the then BUFORA NIC Ken Phillips, gave him our reports and detailed what we experienced. We talked of other witnesses, mentioning the two young girls and the man standing outside his house. Onto possible photographic evidence; even though the camera my friend used was an Instamatic 126 cartridge camera, not best type for night shots, there was a slim chance something might show up in print. We discussed possible inside sources for development of the film rather than risk a commercial company. I suggested Omar Fowler, a prominent Ufologist at that time in Surrey. The Film cartridge was sent to him by Ken with a covering letter explaining the event. We waited anxiously for results.'

'Tracing the two girls was impossible, we drew a blank with the man too, when we knocked on his front door and explained who we were and what we wanted he stood expressionless and said he was sitting watching TV all evening, said he never left the room.

When I told him I saw him outside his house watching the 'display' he emphatically denied it and told us to **** off and never come back!!'

'This was not looking good, we returned to Kens place and stated we drew a blank with other witnesses. He suggested any other possible evidence, traces maybe at the site. It was agreed we would return to the area and have a good look around. In the bright sunlit afternoon walking up towards the ridge we stopped at the copse and could not resist a quick peek inside, the place where 4 years earlier those two small bodies were recovered. At the ridge, by the trees I looked around and smiled, looking up at the end trees and I smiled more. Branches lay on the ground, branches were damaged on the trees too. I took many color photographs of this damage. Fully detailed reports were drawn up by myself and separately by my fellow investigator, and presented to BUFORA along with pictures. I also sent a similar detailed report with pictures to the Ministry of Defence and to CUFOS in the USA. (This report was later detailed in the CUFOS backed report by Ted Bloecher, 1976 "Physical Trace Cases".

'A week or two after sending the film to Omar we received bad news. Evidently the film had jammed in the cartridge, we had no photo evidence!!'

Interestingly, in an old Journal called 'The Voice,' from 1997, the same man explains being at a base for his job as a security officer, being tagged with a chip, and of being aware of programmed generated life-forms, as well as the development of A.I. capable of reading every person's thoughts and emotions. Possible? Recently, suggestions were made about the true reason behind Jade Helm being an A.I. program, by whistleblower 'DJ' on various podcasts including John B Wells 'Caravan to Midnight' episode 309. Interestingly, this UFO experiencer's claims were made many years before this.

While his account of the faceless entities and strange red light in the woods is perplexing and disturbing, the big problem with the account of the two missing and returned children is that 30 years later, a man in prison confessed to their murders. Already imprisoned for the murder of another child, Ronald Jebson confessed after three decades that he had done it.

Whille no names are given in the UFO experiencer's reports of the two children found dead, they were found in the same proximity as the bodies of 11 year old Susan Blatchford and her friend 12 year old Gary Hanlon, who were discovered in the copse in March 1970. The likelihood of it being a different pair of children is extremely small. The case became known as 'The Babes in the Woods,' and had remained unsolved for three decades until Jebson, already serving a life sentence for the 1974 murder of eight-year-old Rosemary Papper, confessed to the murders.

Certainly, the UFO researcher didn't know, when he wrote his account of the alleged mysterious goings-on in the copse that summer, that a human killer would later confess to the crime. So, was he mistaken in his first-hand account of a UFO sighting at the reservoir and the subsequent find of the two children with burn marks? Had he 'guessed' at the reason for the discovery of the dead children and presumed that they had been the victim of alien abduction? He stated at the time that the names of the children were not released and that the parents were forced to move away from the area and not talk to anyone about what had happened. Did he have inside sources? Or had he naievely manipulated the facts to suit his own agenda? Of course, it's perfectly possible that he did really see UFO activity at the reservoir and woods, and the strange creatures, and as a result of his UFO sighting, he believed that the two children had died of alien intervention.

According to the accounts of Newspapers at the time when the two bodies were found, the names of the two children were clearly stated, and the coroner's official report stated that the children were lying next to each other but the cause of death could not be given other than "unascertainable," due to the degree of decomposition that had taken place. They were found partially clothed, and the coroner speculated that some of the clothing had been 'removed by foxes.' To some of the police however, the coroner's statement defied the clear evidence that the children were victims of homicide, because of the circumstantial evidence found at the scene. For one, the girl's underclothes were missing. The unofficial view of most authorities however, was that the children had simply gotten lost and died of exposure. Neither Nipper Read, the legendary policeman who put away the infamous Kray Twins, nor the parents of the victims, believed this and were reported as firmly believing it was murder.

Of course, the one thing on the UFO investigator's side is that the police tracker dogs and cadaver dogs had been over that site repeatedly and found no scent. The children lived a quarter of a mile from the site. On the other hand, the killer could have placed them there at a later stage; although the bodies had badly decomposed and from the coroner's report it seems that the belief is they were at the site for some time.

There's also the very slight possibility that the UFO researcher is referring to two other children, as their names were redacted in the letter he sent to the Ministry of Defence. One other possible clue to back up the UFO investigator's belief of a non-human agenda perhaps inadvertently comes from the policeman Nipper Read, who would later say, "Many senior officials at Scotland Yard tried to dissuade me and were insistent that it was a just tragic accident that the children had become lost and died of exposure."

Like the UFO researcher, he also simply couldn't believe that two children could die of exposure in the summer months and within a quarter of a mile from their own homes, and so close to a street with houses on it nearby.

Why were 'many senior officials' so keen to press their opinion on the policeman trying to solve the case, trying to get him to drop the investigation and convince him that two children could die of exposure during a warm summer?

UFO researchers and conspiracy researchers would perhaps suggest that this could indicate that there really was some kind of cover-up from those in high places, because they did not want the public to learn of the visitation from malevolent alien entities.

Perhaps it could also be suggested, that as in the case of the other two murdered girls in the woods near to the Air Force base, this killer too was a convenient patsy?

Interestingly, it appears that there could be another altogether different reason why the police didn't want the case investigated and the killer caught. In another twist, in 2014, Don Hale of the Daily Star Newspaper wrote a story about the killer's prison cell-mate, which could reveal another possible explanation for what was quite possibly a cover-up, again, if at all credible. His cell-mate made the extraordinary claim that he had been deliberately placed near to the killer Jebson, in prison, for the specific purpose of trying to extract information from him about his involvement in a paedophile ring. The cell-mate went on to claim that the child killer had told him he had been a chauffeur employed to drive children to sick 'auctions' in mansions in the Surrey countryside, where high level people placed 'bids' for the children.

"Killer worked as chauffeur ferrying innocent youngsters to be abused at sick orgies by high-ranking officials, it was claimed." The article came out amid the on-going allegations and investigations into the child abuse scandal in the UK, involving 'the establishment,' but that has so far also failed to find any firm proof of it existing, although conspiracists will say that too has been covered up.

The likelihood is that both the murderer and his cell-mate were lying about this too; however if he was lying about this claim of being a chauffeur to child sex trafficking for 'the establishment,' then it serves useful if only to show that the murderer could potentially also have been lying about killing the two children.

Again, was it human or alien abduction and murder? That is for the reader to decide. These cases seem to lead from one twist and turn to the next, and almost always appear to go even further down the rabbit hole as they say, when looked into more deeply. Do they begin as naive beliefs and germinate into the wildest of speculations founded on nothing more than imagination and supposition? Or are there kernels of truth within?

Why is it, that when these stories are looked into, very often they lead to a very strange set of circumstances that appear to be revealed as the story goes deeper and deeper?

There's someone else who talks about the alleged abduction and murder of humans in woods and forests too. This time it's another 'whistleblower' called Corey Goode, who in his own words, describes himself as having been "identified as an intuitive empath with precognitive abilities," who subsequently "found himself recruited through a MILAB program at 6 years old." He says that he was trained within this program for a decade. Towards the end of his time he claims he was assigned to a "rotating Earth Delegate Seat in a "human-type" ET Super Federation Council."

Talking with David Wilcock, on Jimmy Church's Fade to Black radio show, (September 13, 2015, on YouTube) he made some astonishing and very disturbing comments and allegations of his own regarding the possibility of sinister things happening to people in woodland and forested areas.

He talked of "body drops" in "areas used by different ET groups." He said, "they drop the human bodies back from high altitude down onto the ground."

"A lot of them are in National Parks and other isolated areas. A lot of Park Rangers know about this. A lot of these are federal employees that are deferred to these areas. There are areas where different ET groups come in and abduct human beings. They do experiments that go wrong, or utilize different parts of human beings for different things, and the humans perish. They drop the bodies in dumping areas, like a serial killer would do, and these are areas that seem to be used by different groups but they're common areas spread out across the planet and a lot of the time these bodies are dropped form high altitude. The Federal agencies go in there and investigate it, keep it quiet, clean up the situation and then they do not inform the families that they found bodies, and they do not return the bodies back to the families."

Is there any possibility that this could be true? Different rogue groups of alien races snatching up humans, and then discarding them in the woods and forests once they are done with them? Certainly Corey Goode thinks so.

Referring back to the previous incident discussed, about the two children found dead in the woods by the reservoir, and what UFO researcher 'Barry' also claimed was of his subsequent encounters with 'MIB's,' as a result of his investigations; when he said,

"They're menacing only if you show them fear; if you stand up to them and don't appear disturbed by their appearance, it's like a process kicks in as though they're not programmed for that response and they 'shut down.' If fear and stress is shown when under their attention, their pre-set programming of intimidation will continue."

There's another highly controversial figure, a man called Dan Burisch, who some believe and many others don't, when he makes the claim "MIB's are J-Rods that 'wear the dead' and act as 'guards' of 'timelines,' to ensure that sensitive issues are not disclosed that could change our future history to any considerable degree. Their bodies belong to human cadavers."

Are there really 'Rogue Aliens' called J-Rods who transfer their 'intelligence' or 'consciousness' into dead human bodies to facilitate their mobility here on earth? His claims are terrifying, but of course, what it lacks is easy-to-verify evidence, as is so often the case. Dan Burisch claims to have encountered J-Rods at Area 51 and said this was what the Men in Black were. Could it be at all possible in any way? An alien race, abducting both children and adults, killing them, and wearing their skin as masks to hide inside?

One man claims a similar thing, only this time it concerns the Black Eyed Kids, or B.E.K's. On a variation of Burisch's theme, John Kettler of johnkettler .com, claims that B.E.K's also seek to get inside you; only this time, they are after your soul.

This man claims to have some inside info on the 'Black Eyed Kids.' According to him, he's a man who has a background of 'a lifelong study of military technology and black programs, covert operations and espionage.' He says his father was an engineer who worked on 'Top Secret' projects for the Air Force and CIA. He says that he himself then worked for Raytheon for a decade as a military analyst working with 'Spooks.'

He claims, on johnkettler.com, that from his insider sources, he knows who these mysterious, menacing and sinister black eyed kids are.

"The power of the dark is way beyond our simple understanding. Information recently received indicates a very real and potentially mortal threat to anyone who encounters them. Is this serious? - They eat souls and destroy that which makes us who we are. They are not human. Their appearance is merely a disguise to make them approachable. They are slaves of the Reptoids and the Cabal, and their task is to 'clean the planet up.' -It means, ridding the planet of us." Crucially, he describes humans as their "prospective dinners."

"What follows," he says, "is from 'sensitive sources;' because people are essentially absolutely dumbed-down about the realities within this sector of creation, we cannot ascertain what their possibilities might be. Because they need to be invited in, they are giving 'lip service' to the laws of the creational, where one must agree to be consumed. To the predator, being invited in means you agree to whatever comes next."

He continues, "An inquiry to the ET side" (implying this is from an ET source) "indicates that these (BEK's) are of an insect nature. They are here to get rid of humans. Although you can't see their true form, they are not human."

His 'source' continues, allegedly having come into contact with them.

"They wanted me to know who they were. They spoke in their childlike voices. I said, "I know you're not children." Then came a more masculine voice. They said they were soul eaters."

Then the source said he asked them to show him their true form.

"It was one of the most stupid things in my life. I will never forget it. It was a triangular form with the top point being the head. I could see sucking tubes. I don't dare to guess their true size."

The source came up with further details indicating that these sentient beings are apparently winged.

Kettler himself recounts an incident that he is aware of where the occupants of a rural house let in some of these black eyed entities. The result, he claims, was not good.

'They (the people) were 'incubused;' their souls were taken and a holographic imprint of their soul was merged with an incubus. It's hard to tell the difference between the clone and the original. These entities then, have a good cover. One of my contacts knows people who have been incubused. She could see a subtle but definite change in them."

In other words, he claims that the people were infested by entites that took over their souls and merged their personalities with their own. Those who knew them could tell they were 'changed' somehow, though they didn't know it was as a result of a visitation from the BEK's, but they knew the people were no longer the same.

"They were inhabited and possessed by the non-human entities who had knocked on their door. My contact could tell the difference in them by their lack of interest in certain matters; and a lack of responsiveness to matters that used to be important to them."

How utterly chilling. Or is this man's information again just another crazy sci-fi story? Many people have claimed to have had encounters with these entities but not given in to letting them in. There seem to be no accounts from those who have let them in. Is this because it's too late; they have been changed now and do not know it?

In June 2014, Cliff at Pararational blog received a highly detailed account of what happened to a 26 year old man called David, who works at a college in Michigan.

David writes, 'I'm an average man. I don't believe in the paranormal. I love to camp and hike and I was at Sleeping Bear Dunes just out of season in late August. At the Ranger station, I used the bathroom. Coming out of the stall, there are two kids standing there. I wash my hands and glance in the mirror, and see they are looking at me. My spine tingled with fear. They have completely black eyes. No whites in their eyes at all. I froze in fear. They looked around aged twelve. Fight or flight took over.

"Can you help us?" said one of the boys. Despite my fear, I wanted to help them. I stood thinking I wanted to; until finally my head said, "No," and I left.

I remember thinking that I was certain I was going to die as I turned my back to go; that they were going to rip me to shreds. I'm six foot! Anyway, I get the hell out of there; I can't bring myself to look back.

I drive to the camp-site parking lot, and then it's a forty minute walk to my camping spot. When I get there it's completely empty of campers. After building a fire, eventually I sleep.

As dawn came the next morning, I felt foolish for the fear I'd felt yesterday. A calm guy, I couldn't explain the intense dread I'd felt when I'd seen the kids.'

He spends the day hiking and driving into town for dinner. On his return, he heads out on the 40 minute walk back to the camp. A storm has come and it's dark now.

'As I walked, my dread grew. I walked and stopped every few metres to look round with my headlamp, but saw nothing; then I walked on and just knew someone was there, watching. Then, I turned around, and there they were, both motionless. I can't put my terror in words. The boy came toward me. My light flashed across his face; his grotesque eyes.

"Help us."

I couldn't breathe. The boy moved closer. The other boy was slowly circling me.

"We're lost. Take us with you."

My flight response hit as the boy reached for my hand. I recoiled. I ran. I don't look back. I don't know if they're behind me or not; all I know is that I must run faster.'

Back at the tent, he eventually manages to fall asleep.

'I thought it was a nightmare at first, when I heard the unmistakable voice.

"Help us."

I couldn't help it. I screamed.

"Please let us in."

"No," I screamed, again and again and again. Then I waited for death....'

Though he stayed awake all night, they didn't enter his tent; instead they stood menacingly outside of it.

'It's been almost two months since this happened, but I still remember it all like it was yesterday. I haven't gone camping since, and I don't know if I'll ever feel safe hiking again..."

Did this really happen? Only the man in question knows but the account is certainly a chilling one.

Chapter 2:
Magickal Working, Art, and Ancient Races

There is another man who also claims he has the answer to the origins of the B.E.K.'s. It's a fascinating version of a possibility and in my researching of it, it led to a story with a compelling mix of the occult, the esoteric, Art, and ancient races.

In November 2015, one of Amadeo Modigliani's paintings *Nu Couche*, or, *Reclining Nude*, distinctive for its beautiful shaping and those endless dark eyes, became the second most expensive painting ever sold, at a price of $170 million.

His *Bust of a Young Woman*, too, had those deep black eyes. His painting of Anna Zborowska was the same; the blackest of eyes. When he painted Jacques and his wife Berthe Lipchitz, again they were painted with jet black eyes; no sclera at all.

Why would he paint jet black eyes with no white in them? Why were their entire eyes black?

Italian painter Amadeo Modigliani, (1884-1920) would say, "When I know your soul I will paint your eyes," but one researcher makes an astonishing and outlandish claim that there is quite simply much more to this than that statement of intent.

The famous painter's Mother, Eugene Garsin, began keeping a diary in 1886, when the artist was just a small boy.

"We know very little about his life and work from 1886-7, and the problem of sources now becomes particularly acute." This quote comes from Jeanne Modigliani, from her own biography of her father, the famous Italian artist, and his life was indeed shrouded in elements of great mystery and intrigue, but in his mother's diary, according to one researcher, there are allegedly some very interesting clues that he believes may possibly reveal what really influenced the artist to paint those black eyes.

In the diary she writes, "Isaac (his grandfather) is getting too attached to Dedo (Amadeo), taking him everywhere. He is taking him to the temple but not our temple."

This is according to researcher Danti Sartori, who has kindly given me permission to include his extensive research into the diary in this book. Sartori explains that in the late 1990's, he spent several years tracking down the diary and exploring it, searching for something specific; something which would, in his mind, lead to a startling revelation on the origins of the phenomenon of Black Eyed Kids.

Quite possibly the temple that Amadeo's mother refers to is a Masonic lodge, as researcher Mr Sartori points out that Amadeo's grandfather was allegedly a Mason and his own father, Solomon Garson some say was possibly a 33rd degree Mason, and furthermore, Sartori alleges he was involved with the Illuminati. Of course, this is impossible to verify; however, it is true that in the Italian town where they lived, in Livorno, 18 of the Masonic lodges, that's half of the total number of the 34 lodges in Italy, were based in the town, so it was certainly an important centre of Masonic activity in Italy. Whether he really was involved in the illuminati however, is another matter and one that cannot be proven by Sartori unless evidence is furnished, despite his own confidence. This too applies to the Diary. What Sartori goes on to claim quite possibly may be entirely fallacious, but it certainly makes for compelling reading.

Sartori spent a significant amount of time in the Library Biblioteque d'Alcazar in Marseilles, in the South of France, where the diary of Euegene Garsin was said to be located. He had been translating it and reading it, interspersed with frequent and often long trips away during the second gulf war, as a member of the Italian Special Forces. When he managed to return to Marseille the last time, he discovered that the diary was gone from the Library.

He explains all in his videos on YouTube, AHK: app 59 – Black Rain.

"During the 1980's I spent a lot of time researching the life of Modigliani. Unfortunately where I was living at the time the resources were somewhat trivial. I knew there were several private collectors who had Modigliani's private writings. I contacted them asking if I could have a look at them but was refused. I also knew that there were 2 libraries in Paris and Livorno where he was born that had some of his writings. I contacted them again, again was refused."

"But my life has a way of taking me to the right places at generally the right time and so in the mid '90's because of work I found my self living in Marseille. And why is this important? Well Marseille happens to be where Eugene Garsin was born and raised- his mother. I tried to find out about her, then one night I went to a bar where I used to hang out under my apartments, which turned out to be owned and run by the local mob. Anyway, I got talking to an Irish guy (I'd been going to the bar now for six months) and chatting and I told him what I'd been trying to do or find and he said "Oh I heard something about that a while ago," "I said, ' Really?' He made a phone call and a local mob guy arrived and tells him his boss had some papers either related to Modigliani or his family in his possession and said he would talk to him about what I was looking for."

A few days later this Irish friend from the bar tells me the boss did not have the papers anymore; that he had given then to one of the local Libraries Biblioteque de Alacazar. (mafia philanthropy!)"

That was how he managed to get his hands on them, Sartori says, and that was where he spent most of his time. After having to go away once more for his army work however, when he returned again he found them gone from the Library. It turned out that the mafia boss had requested them back, but according to Sartori, he allowed him to go to his house where he kept them, to continue with his research.

It was what he says he found in the diaries that led him to make the most astonishing claims.

Inside the diary, he alleges, are the following entries,

'July 1889. "Amedee (his Uncle) and Isaac; I know they want Dedo (Modigliani) to be one of them. I know they want him to be the new face of the movement."

Sartori comments, "the illiuminati have always sought to recruit and promote those at the fore-front of art and music. They have always chosen/recruited artists; because it influences a whole generation."

His inference, from having studied the alleged diary, is that the men were actively looking to groom and place Modigliani at the prominence, to promote their hidden agenda to the masses.

If Sartori's findings are correct from the diary, it would seem that Modigliani's mother was against this and concerned enough by it that she planned to take him away. (Other historians will say that it was because the child was sickly and she took him away to recuperate.)

'August 1889. "Now I know that I must take Dedo out of here. Isaac is furious about it. He wants him close by more than ever."

'September 1889. "I must take Dedo out of Lisvorio – I must, I must. I don't want him to become them-no; not one of those soulless eyes. I've seen them, they are close. Closer. My son is going to paint them."

Who is Modigliani's mother talking about him painting? Who is *them*? Her father and brother? Or someone else? Paint who? Why does she describe them as having '*soulless eyes*?'

She does take her son away, first to Tuscany and then on to Florence.

In 1901, researcher Santori remarks that there was a UFO phenomenon occurring in Northern Italy, in Tuscany, called locally 'The Lights of Berberiro.'

In the diary, according to Sartori, the young painter's mother refers to them in a disturbing way,

"The lights of Berberiro seem to follow us everywhere we go." (In Tuscany)

Then, "We are in Florence now. So are the lights. What could they be? Plenty of people ask the same. Dedo seems amused by them."

If this is really true, why and how does this tie in with her son?

It gets worse; they seem to be a constant presence now;

'1901. "We are in Rome. Dedo is increasingly interested in the lights. Last night I found him walking around in the garden. I swear I heard him laughing."

'1901. "We are in Venice. I know what I'm seeing and I have seen them. I am not going mad. They are here. I am sure Dedo speaks to them at night."

'1901, "I sat outside Dedo's room all night. Just before sunrise I heard a voice, saying "paint us, paint us."

Amadeo was just a small boy at this time.

Who are they? Sartori says that around this time there were "many strange phenomenon" and "many 'alien abductions' taking place, mostly aimed at young boys and girls."

Toward the end of 1901, according to Sartori, the diary allegedly continues, in a fatalistic and ominous tone,

"I must return home. I know they are part of his life now. Maybe even more than myself. Those deep black eyes, dark like the night...and they are young, so young; Dedo's age, even younger."

Clearly then, from the diary that Santori claims to have uncovered, according to his supposed findings, not only was the boy's mother trying to get her young son away from the alleged Masonic-Illuminati influences of her Father and grandfather, in order to stop them from inducting him and using him as a public face of the organisation, but it seemed she and her son were being 'followed' by unidentified beings; children with 'deep black eyes, dark like the night;' beings that wanted him to paint them.

Given that many of his subsequent paintings were of those very distinctive and sometimes disquieting black-eyed people, the inference here is very obvious; that the entities who visited the boy when he was young, led to his life-long pursuit of depicting these black-eyed entities, these 'soul-eaters;' the black-eyed-kids in his portraitures.

Is there any way at all that Sartori's claims about the diary are really true? Besides it being a fantastical story, is there any grain of truth in it? Mysteriously, between the 1901-1903 period of his life we have 'the missing years,' where allegedly nothing is written in the diary. What happened to him during those two years?

As one art critic, Michael O'Sullivan in the Washington Post has written, "What is perhaps most unusual about his portraits is not the elongation of their features, but their eyes. His portraits are like masks, both in their reductive sameness and in the emptiness of their eyes. His gift lay not in the painting of eyes, but of souls."

But whose souls was he painting? Through Sartori's decades of research into the diary, he clearly feels that it was the souls of the black-eyed creatures who had stalked him, accompanied by the strange lights in the sky and the stories of missing children happening in the area at the same time. He also clearly feels that there is some link between these Black Eyed Beings and the Masonic-Illuminate desires of the artist's patriarchs.

The resarcher makes for a compelling case that the reason for Modigliani's black eyed portraitures is because he was made to paint them; he was made to depict the entities that appeared to him night after night as a boy, and Sartori believes they are tied in with the accounts of people going missing and the lights. On the other hand, we do not have the diary to verify this, and they could also just as easily have been manifestations of the occult and of demonic origin. Or, they could simply be the product of Sartori's wild imagination.

Looking more closely at Modigliani's childhood however, it was unorthodox to say the least. With his grandfather, Isaac, having both possibly a deep Masonic and Illuminati connection, the boy also came from a line of Jewish scholars with an in-depth knowledge of the ancient texts and the magickal practices within them. Then there was his aunt who was said to have been entrenched in 'mystical practice,' and another account from Modigliani's daughter, who cites the time the boy painted two skulls on a bookcase in the house when he was 12 years old. In his own words the boy described how the woman's skull was a symbol of "love in all its destructive power," and the man's, a patriarch with long divided beard was "the male succubus, which is what he too often is." The male succubus presumably being a demon. This is quite deep for a 12 year old, and perhaps a good reflection of the spiritual nature of his upbringing.

His own letters in later life perhaps also could be construed as containing hints,

"Dear friend,

I write to pour myself out to you and to affirm myself. I am the prey of great powers that surge forth and then disintegrate."

He could of course be referring simply to his artistic nature; or he could be referring to something more supernatural.

Like many artists, during his lifetime he was never wealthy and famous, though he was well-known in Paris. It was after his death that his paintings began to sell for astronomical sums of money. He knew mostly poverty when growing up, although his father was a money lender/banker, and according to Jeanne, his daughter, his mother would say during the times the bailiffs came to take away their possessions, that 'the Modigliani's used to be bankers to the Pope.'

Jeanne corrects this often uttered phrase by saying that in her opinion, it was more truthful that the family once loaned money to a cardinal associated with the Pope, but whatever the finer details, the family believed themselves far richer than their circumstances proved them to be.

Although, perhaps they were not so wrong about their position within the banking world. A distant cousin of Modigliani, Leah Modigliani in the late 1990's developed the term 'Modigliani-Modigliani measure', also known as 'M-squared;' which is a measure for 'risk adjusted performance' which seeks to adjust leverage artificially then measures the returns. She developed it while she was in charge of 11450 brokers at New York's Morgan Stanley. Clearly she was very well placed within the banking industry, although that could have had nothing to do with family connections.

The family were Sephardic Jews, and Jeanne says that the practice of passionate Talmudic learning and discussion was very much alive in the household she grew up in, with her paternal aunt, after Modigliani died and her own mother committed suicide the following day.

It was from Modigliani's great-grandfather on his Mother's side that the Rabbinic Judaism came from, as he had been a commentator on The Sacred Books and had founded a school for Talmudic studies. The Talmud normally alludes to the collection of writings that make up the Babylonian Talmud. Within these texts are sources of high Magick, although at the time written, the practise of Witchcraft was forbidden.

Especially in the Babylonian Talmud, a great number of the passages allude to magick, which, according to the 1906 Jewish Encyclopedia, by Joseph Jacobs and Ludwig Blau, "furnishes incontrovertible evidence" of Magick's wide-scale use.

Although forbidden to be practised, because it was so widely used, it was deemed necessary for those in positions of authority, such as members of the Judiciary, to have a knowledge of this Magick.

In fact, 'this ingrained belief in Magick infected even the scholars, who would sometimes counteract the black magic with white.' Furthermore, it says, 'They were even able to create food when they needed it. Some scholars were adepts in the black arts, and the Law did not deny its power. Many scholars consumed men with a glance, or reduced them to a heap of bones.'

The great-grandfather of Modigliani then, had an in-depth knowledge of magickal practices, as did perhaps his own son, Modigliani's grandfather, Isaac, with some biographers of Modigliani alluding to his grandfather's ready use of Magick and Spells. He was also described by many as a very cultured man who could command many different languages.

Isaac came to live with Modigliani when he was just a child, after Isaac suffered from what Jeanne describe as a mental breakdown following the failure of his banking business. It's hard to verify whether this is really so from other sources, but what is apparent is that Isaac and Modigliani became inseparable. Modigliani's own father was seldom there, usually away in Sardinia where his businesses were located.

The other version is that Isaac, Modigliani's grandfather, had gone to live with them after the death of first his wife, then their daughter, Clementine, who had lived with him. This is where perhaps things get interesting, though there is more than one path to take when it comes to attempting to get to the bottom of the biggest enigma surrounding Modigliani. It wasn't so much him; rather, it was the subject of his paintings. They were all of people. Invariably they all had long cone-shaped heads, and very often, the blackest eyes imaginable. Some had white sclera; but many others did not. Why was that? Why would he paint jet black eyes with no white at all? Why were their entire eyes black?

Almost all art commentators fall back on Modigliani's own statement, "When I know your soul I will paint your eyes."

His daughter, who was a babe-in-arms when her father died, mentions Clemintine, Modigliani's aunt and "her marvellous black eyes," as Jeanne describes them, and says that she was a woman who was "entrenched in a mystical religion."

Did she inspire Modigliani perhaps?

On the other hand, Jeanne also speculates that a close friend of the family, Leone Opler's daughter, who she says had a pale elongated face, could have been the muse for the great painter. "The girl cannot remember him ever painting her," however.

Modigliani's main patron when he became an artist was French Physician, Paul Alexandre. He wrote to his sister after the artist's death. "In his drawings there is purification of form. He reconstructed the human face in his own way by fitting them into primitive patterns," and there are no sinister implications in his mind as to where the inspiration came from, believing them to be 'from African masks.'

However, he does add, "Max Jacobs," described by many as 'the poet-alchemist' of the time, was someone who "stimulated Modigliani's taste for magick and the occult, which came out in the cabalistic signs that appear in a few of his drawings. Like Jacobs, Modigliani took a keen interest in the mystical connections between material and spiritual realms and mystical correspondences."

One of his drawings, 'Tete de profil,' belonged Paul Alexandre, and bore inscriptions next to it written by Modigliani.

The inscriptions are a poem, translated as; 'Just as the snake slithers out of its skin So you will deliver yourself from sin. Equilibrium by means of opposite extremes. Man considered from three aspects. Frustration!'

Is this the three Talmudic aspects? Or the Body, Soul, Spirit connection? Or the 3 stages of Freemasonry?

Alexandre's son, Noel, an ecclesiastical historian, says "We know very little about the place the occult sciences held in Modigliani's life. This drawing is rare for it captures unusual inscriptions on the right side of the sheet" and to him, it clearly "offers proof of his (Modigliani's) personal commitment to the esoteric."

He continues, "Paul Alexandre, who was never interested in the esoteric, was nevertheless struck by these mystical correspondences that his artist friend was searching for in alchemy. These brief lines are particularly precious to us, even if, in the absence of any other documentation, we are unable to understand their full meaning."

Of course, 'esoteric' does not necessarily mean anything sinister by its definition, but it does mean 'understandable only by an enlightened inner circle.'

Mystery seemed to enshroud Modigliani's life, and he appeared strongly attracted by the occult. 'I am the plaything of powerful forces that are born and die in me,' Modigliani once wrote.

Meryle Secrest, who wrote a biography of the artist, says, "Modigliani came from a family interested in the occult, and Beatrice Hastings (a lover of his) was into Theosophy, among other things. As for alchemy, he once worked alchemical symbols into a statement he appended to a drawing, so he was certainly familiar with the subject."

When selling the pencil sketch by Modigliani, of Conrad D Moricand, a previously unpublished artwork from one of his sketchbooks, the Lempertz Auction House wrote that the artist had been close to Moricand, "an astrologist and occultist," and had painted him several times.

Art historian and expert on Modigliani, Marc Restellini points out the 'motifs' he found in the artist's works that feature the occultist Conrad Moricand. 'An oil painting depicts Moricand, as do at least eight other drawings, and inscriptions and comments by Modigliani bear witness that the artist was obviously not averse to the occult and was interested in esotericism.'

In art, a 'motif' is an element of pattern in an image, or a symbol that is commonly used so that it becomes iconic.

Writer Leslie Camhi comments, about a series of sculpted busts he created, that they 'viscerally evoke its origins in occult practices that fascinated the artist, who is rumored to have embraced their strange geometries by candlelight.'

Not only then are there multiple sources who overtly make claim that there is evidence of the artist's fascination with the esoteric, occult, and magick, but there appears to be another researcher too who makes the claim, whether true or not, that "Modigliani, as with Dante Alighieri, was also Illuminati. Dante Allighieri was an initiate who wrote *The Divine Comedy* to perpetuate Illuminati secret codes," says Alex Ribiero.

He continues, "The 1925 book The Dante Esoteric, written by Rene Guenon, shows that these Illuminati codes are placed, since antiquity, into monuments, architecture, movies, music, literature and art. That's what Dante did with the Divine Comedy, starting with its structure; a poem in three parts, of Hell, Purgatory and Paradise, under the three Illuminati pillars, The Unholy, The Initiation and Enlightenment, with messages in the form of codes included in the stanzas of the poem. Modigliani, was initiated in the occult at 5 years of age by his grandfather Isaac Garsin as well as made literate in this by his grandfather, and his mother Eugenia Garsin, with The Divine Comedy."

"All the symbols found in the pictorial part of 'Velieri to Livorno' are skulls, snakes, horses, demons, fly, boat; all these symbols in the are Illuminati codes."

"Velieri to Livorno' is a painting that Robiero has been in the process of trying to have authenticated; a painting that he attributes to Modigliani, and presented to the 3nd Latin-American Symposium on Physical and Chemical Methods in Archaeology, Art and Cultural Heritage Conservation, in 2011. It is still awaiting attribution and may well turn out not to be by Modigliani.

"Like all Illuminati, particularly Dante Allighieri, Modigliani recorded Illuminati codes subliminally or disguised, without calling direct attention to them; hidden information. Like Leonardo Da Vinci," who he says, "was also Illuminati. Modigliani also wrote Letters and Numbers underneath the paintings."

So there is speculation and indeed possible clues that Modigliani was influenced by the occult and perhaps indeed even had ties to the illuminati. These observations of course however do not indicate a necessary proof of Sartori's research and the notes he claims are in the mother's diary, nor do they indicate that Sartori is correct in his alleged 'proof' that Modigliani was directly influenced supernaturally by BEK's, who he clearly believes are of extraterrestrial origin; but it does make for a compelling possibility if nothing else.

Interestingly, sculptor Jacques Lipchitz, who wrote of Modigliani after his death noted that his mistress, (who later threw herself off a balcony after his death) "was a strange girl, with a long oval face which seemed almost white rather than flesh color."

Was Modigliani simply influenced to paint the black eyes of his figures by those around him? It's clearly quite possible; but he had started painting the black eyes long before he met his mistress. Is there anything in Dante Sartori's theory that Modigliani was visited and influenced by visitations from BEK's and those strange lights in the sky? Without the diary it is very hard to say, but something influenced him to paint those unique black 'soulless eyes.'

As Sartori alleges, his mother writes,

"I know what I'm seeing and I have seen them. I am not going mad. They are here. I am sure Dedo speaks to them at night. I sat outside Dedo's room all night. Just before sunrise I heard a woman's voice, saying "paint us, paint us. I know they are part of his life now. Those deep black eyes, dark like the night...and they are young, so young, Dedo's age, even younger."

While perhaps the research of Sartori should be dismissed as mere fantasy and just a fascinating but impossible story, there is another interesting link that he highlighted with regards to possible missing children and child abductions at the time, and the influence of the occult and supernatural. As researcher Alex Robiero as well as Sartori also pointed out, the artist became a connoisseur and admirer of Dante Allighieri. At 13 years old, Modigliani could already recite the Divine Comedy from memory, which is no mean feat.

This is corroborated by a close friend of the artist, sculptor Jacques Lipchitz, who wrote,

"Now, I always associate him with poetry. Is it because it was the poet Max Jacob who introduced me to him? Or is it because when Max introduced us in Paris in 1913, Modigliani suddenly began to recite by heart the Divine Comedy at the top of his voice? More often than not he would recite by heart their verses."

Around the same time, there was another boy who could also do exactly what Modigliani could do. It wasn't just Modigliani who seemed to have the remarkable and exceptional talent for reciting by heart the verses of Dante's poems. There was another little boy who lived with his brother in the village of Ruvo di Puglia. At the same time that Modigliani was allegedly, according to one researcher, receiving visits from Black Eyed Children, two young boys, Alfred 7, and Paulo, 8, began to disappear in seemingly impossible ways. The affair involving the boys was a long one and it was documented and recorded by the no less than the physician to the then Pope Leo XIII, as well as later by Charles Fort, Lombroso Cesare, Lapponi Giuseppe, the Occult Review and and the 1906 Annals of Psychical Science.

It seemed that it began after the parents of the two boys unwisely allowed them to take part in a séance that they attended. A few days after this, Alfred began to have inexplicable bouts of extreme tiredness, during which it was said that he frightened his parents by speaking to them in languages they had never heard before, and in a voice which did not seem to belong to him. He spoke as though he was reciting verse, and it sounded as though he was speaking Latin, or Greek. Soon, he was reciting cantos from Dante's Divine Comedy, in Latin. He had never studied Dante's Divine Comedy, and he had never been taught Latin.

The family was so concerned about the changes in their son that having sought religious counsel, they sent him to a boarding school where he remained for the next two years. It hadn't just been the strange voice coming out of him at home; there had been numerous 'miracle' manifestations of food and other items which had appeared from out of no-where.

At the school, he disconcerted everyone. Any time anyone went to ask him a question, he would answer it even before the question came out of their mouths; and on a range of complex topics of which the boy was too young to have studied.

When he accompanied three of his school professors to another séance, they sat around the table with a triangle formed of paper to be used as a planchette for the Ouija board. They began the session and asked if anyone was there and they received the reply, 'Yes; but you must use a triangle made of wood.'

One of the participants replied that they had no wood, to which the small boy told the group that there was a wood triangle in the kitchen, that he said he had got from the carpenter's shop. They looked in the kitchen and found a perfectly constructed wooden triangle. The boy, as far as they knew, had never been to the house they were in, nor the carpenter's shop located in another village.

The little boy was returned to live with his family. What happened next was an increase in unexplained phenomena. There were strange and frightening noises inside the house, glasses were thrown by invisible hands, the furniture was shifted around without anyone touching it. While this all sounds ridiculous and a story based in folklore perhaps, it was in fact documented by among others, the chief Doctor to Pope Leo XIII. The ongoing saga was also documented in the national newspapers.

The local priest was called to help and he conducted an exorcism but in his presence, the furniture continued to be thrown around and glasses smashed against the walls. The table with the holy water was thrown across the room.

The priest left in helplessness and the phenomena continued unabated. The little boy continued to speak in a voice that did not belong to him, and in languages the family did not know. Then the voice told them that it had been sent from God to drive out the dark forces in the little boy. After this, sweets and chocolate began to be found around the house, yet the family had not purchased any of the candy. One night the little boy, after falling into a trance, told his parents "a terrible battle is taking place between Good and Evil."

The oddities didn't stop there; in fact, they got even more bizarre. One day the little boy was with his brother when they were found at a Convent in another town. It was 9.30 am. They had been at home at 9 a.m. The town was more than 30 miles away. It was an impossibility for them to have got there. There was no car to have taken them. A few days later, the family were having lunch around 12.30pm when the father realised they had no wine. He asked the older brother to fetch some and bring it to the table. After thirty minutes the boy had not returned and the father asked Alfred to go and look for him and bring him back. At 1 p.m. the two boys were found in a boat on the sea outside of the port of a neighboring village. The fisherman had suddenly found them on his boat and was shocked, and the little boys had started to cry. Confused and dumbfounded by their appearance, he took the boat back into the harbour and a coach and horses took them back to their home. They did not return until 3.30pm in the afternoon, the ride back being a considerable journey.

Their parents could not understand how they could both possibly have got on the boat, nor how they could have reached the port in the 30 minutes when it was further away than that. It seemed they were being instantaneously transported.

Franz Hartmann, a medical doctor but also a keen scholar of the occult, was one of the many who took an interest in their strange experiences. The boys had been thoroughly medically examined by doctors and scientist and no one could come up with anything that would explain how they seemed to be getting teleported. Hartmann wrote of the case, "They were taken away in some mysterious manner and found fifteen minutes after, in a place 55 miles away."

According to Aaron, researcher of esoterx. com, the doctors and the scientists tried to test for various medical explanations, such as "ambulatory automatism" or "muscular hyperesthesia" neither of which really offered anywhere near a reasonable explanation, and the newspapers who were covering the strange incidents interviewed eye witnesses of the events and felt it was "inspiegabile;" that is 'unexplainable.'

The theory most easily accepted by the scientists and religious experts of the day who looked into the matter, was that it had to be a case of 'ambulatory automatism;' that is, a form of nervous disease where the subject suffering from it is overtaken with an irresistible urge to run!

The Annals of Psychical Science wrote in 1906, that even allowing for the possibility that the two boys might have run flat out for a long distance, they felt the argument did not hold water when applied to the fact that the boys appeared to have run nearly ten miles in just under thirty minutes. They add also that the boys were seen by no witnesses along the route at all. Besides which, one time Bishop Bernandi Pasquale had locked the two boys in their room, sealing the door and windows, yet within a few minutes the boys had somehow disappeared from the room.

A well known criminologist Cesare Lombroso also studied the case, interviewing those who had seen either the boys before they went missing or where they turned up, and he too could find no distortion of events, nor any logical or reasonable explanation. The boys' experiences stopped suddenly when they hit puberty and never occurred again.

Calling to mind Modigliani's paintings with the black eyes and strange elgonated necks, English essayist in the 1800's, Maurice Henry Hewlett, wrote Lore of Posperine, which features a true account of the strangest of 'creatures' with an elongated neck, and the sinister results of it's appearance.

"The facts were as follows. A Mr Stephen Mortimer Beckwith, 28, clerk in the Wiltshire & Dorset Bank at Salisbury was living in Wishford. He was married with one child.

At approximately 10 pm on the 30th November, 1887, he was going home after spending the evening at a friend's house. It was a mild night, with rain and a wind was blowing. There was a quarter moon and it was not completely dark.

Accompanied by his dog, he was riding a bicycle. He stated that he had no difficulty seeing the road nor the stones on it nor the sheep in the hillside. He recalled quite clearly seeing an owl flying.

A mile or so along and his terrier dog ran through the hedge and ran barking up the hill. The man imagined he was after a hare and called him, but the dog took no notice and ran to a gorse bush then stopped, paw uplifted and watching it intensely.

The man watched him for some minutes, dismounting from his bicycle. He could see nothing up there himself but the dog was in a state of excitement. It was whimpering and trembling, and his master decided to take a look at what was causing this behaviour in his dog. The dog would not take his eyes off whatever was up there.

Now standing just behind the dog, the man looked but could see nothing there. He had no stick and imagining it could be a drunk man in there in need of help or a rabbit caught in a trap, he urged his dog inward, but the dog wouldn't move and eventually it began to howl.

It shook his owner, who because of the isolated location and a 'mysterious shroud of darkness,' wanted nothing more than to leave the spot, but he now couldn't get his dog to leave. Finally, he braved it and put his two hands inside the bush to try to feel for what was in there. It was during this fumbling that he suddenly saw a bright pair of eyes staring back at him, and a pale face.

He found his voice and asked who they were, what was wrong, why they were in there, but no answer came back. He tried to reassure them that he meant no harm to them.

There was no movement at all of the features of the face. It was a very small face, "about as big as a large wax doll's. It was longish and oval and very pale. I could see its neck and it was no thicker than my wrist. I would have said it was a girl had it not been for the size of her and her face. It was, in fact, neither fish, flesh, nor fowl. Strap my dog had known that from the beginning, and now I was of Strap's opinion myself."

In his mind he called her 'a foreigner;' for he had no other word for it. To him she was something he could not define. Her face was that of an older girl, a late teenager at least but her size was under three foot. She couldn't seem to understand what he said to her and said nothing back to him. Her clothing was odd too. It seemed almost like it was made of cobwebs.

It was all of this that made him suspect her of being 'something outside experience,' but this was just the beginning. Suddenly he heard footsteps and a torch coming up the hill toward him and it was the local policeman. The man told the policeman immediately that there seemed to be some kind of foul play at hand, because he had found this tiny girl and didn't know what else to say. The policeman followed the direction the man's head went in, as the man indicated the girl he now had in his arms, having pulled her out of the gorse, but the policeman couldn't appear to see anything in his arms. In fact, he made a joke and walked back down the hill.

Now the man really did know something was wrong. However, he didn't feel he could just leave her there in the rain and darkness and so he took her back home with him.

When he got home his wife was waiting anxiously at the front door looking out into the dark, worried that he was so late. When he began to explain what had happened, it became evident that just like the policeman, his wife also could not see the girl. In fact, she placed her hand on the handlebars of the bicycle where he had propped up the girl to ride home with her. His wife's arm went straight through the girl.

"It was as if my wife had drilled a hole clean through the middle of her back. Her hand went through the skin and bone and dress; how I do not know."

He could not bring himself to take this invisible creature into the house with them, so he put her in the dog's kennel.

"I blame myself for it, myself only," he was later to say.

He kept the small 'child' in the kennel for almost six months. She shared the kennel with his other dog. He fed her though she never ate any of it. She spent her time dancing and playing with the two dogs; then later she would play with his own child, a four year old girl. The little girl would never tell him that she was playing with the other strange girl, but it was evident they were playing together, though the four year old denied it. She too could see the strange girl, though his wife never did.

"We might have been spared if, on the night I brought her home, I had told my wife the whole truth. And yet, how could I? Is not that an absurdity? Yes, but the sequel was no absurdity."

In the Otautau Standard and Wallace County Chronicle, Volume V, Issue 231, 5 October 1909, his tale continues.

'Now I come to the tragic part of my story and wish I could leave it out, but beyond the full confession I have made to the police and the newspapers, I am to blame. On the 13th of May, she and my daughter disappeared."

The search party covered a radius of miles, searching every fold of the hills, every hedgerow. He told his wife, the Reverend, and the police about the strange girl he had been harbouring. He told the newspapers.

"In spite of my wife's absolute incredulity, and scorn, I repeated the tale to the Chief Inspector and details soon got into the local newspaper and the London journals."

Neither the Newspapers nor the police at the time accused him of any involvement in his daughter's disappearance; They believed his testimony.

"I don't doubt now that she was bewitching my daughter. She had been crowning her with a wreath of flowers she had made for her."

His daughter was never seen again.

Chapter 3:
Caves, Caverns, and Screams.

The Green Children of Wolfpit is a mystery that sounds like a fairytale and yet several texts from those times report it as being genuine.

It occurred during the reign of King Stephen in the 12th Century, outside of the village of Wolfpit, in the rural county of Suffolk, England. Farm workers were toiling in the fields during harvest one day when two small children were spotted emerging from a deep ravine that had been dug for the purpose of trapping wolves on the edge of the forest that lined the fields.

As the workers watched them getting closer, they were shocked and perplexed by their strange appearance, because their skin appeared to be green. Not only was their skin a glowing green hue but their clothes also did not appear to be the same as everyone else's.

They appeared strange and unfamiliar in both fashion and material. The children too looked just as perplexed and confused as the farm workers did. They looked all around them as though they didn't know where they were.

Not knowing what to do, some of the farm workers led them into the village. They had tried to talk to the two children, who both looked to be under the age of ten, although they did not look like normal children, because of their skin colour. When the farm workers had tried to ask them if they were ok, the children did not seem to understand what they were saying to them.

The children answered them, but they seemed to be speaking in a language the farm workers could not understand. It wasn't a different dialect or accent; it was an entirely strange language that they had never heard before.

In the village, the villagers too could not communicate with them and eventually they took the two children to the home of the Lord of the Manor. His servants brought food and water for them but the children refused to eat any of it.

This went on for several days, with the villagers growing concerned that they would end up starving to death and it was only when they took them some freshly harvested green beans that the children accepted them and ate them hungrily.

Sadly the two children seemed to be very depressed and unhappy in their new environment, and after a few months the boy died. The girl adjusted more easily to her new life to a certain extent, in that she managed to learn the language everyone around her spoke and was then able to at least communicate with people. Of course, everyone wanted to know where they had come from and now she could tell them.

She said that her and her brother had come from the land called 'Saint Martin,' where everyone lived in permanent twilight and everyone was as green as them. She couldn't say exactly where that land was but believed it was across a river. She said that they had been looking after their father's cows when some of the cows had gone into a cavern and the children had followed after them.

Inside the cavern she said that they heard the beautiful sound of bells ringing softly and the sound encouraged them to seek its source. They walked deeper into the dark cavern and arrived at an entrance that glowed so brightly it stunned them and they lay down.

She says they lay in a daze for a long time until they found themselves in the field with the farm workers. They had been trying to escape the cave and return home but had found themselves in a new land instead.

Two original texts from the 12th Century seem to verify the strange story. One is by a Monk, William of Newburgh, who wrote,

'It was as if they had been fashioned from summer leaves and soft meadow grass; their skin was green as was the strange hue of their eyes."

He goes on to note that their land, according to the little girl, saw no sunlight, and when they came to the bright sunlight at the exit of the cave, it overwhelmed and stunned them. They were struck terrified by it; they did not know what it was.

"I was overwhelmed by the weight of so many and such competent witnesses," he writes.

In the 1977 November issue of FATE magazine, another strange tale was told.

"Recent violent occurrences in Veracruz again have brought the Chanques into prominence.

Apparently, the story in question features a little boy who was abducted and held in a cave in a thick forest.

Senora Cirila Laguens, a shop owner, told the magazine,

"My 3 year old son Ramiro, he wandered from home. He was missing for six days. He was found by the Chaneques. Instead of telling us, because they are very timid, they told our neighbour's young son, that he could be found in a cave ten miles away."

"A search party went to the cave and found my son asleep inside. Although he'd been gone for several days, he was in perfect health and not hungry or thirsty or unhappy. He quickly told us that he had got lost near a river and five little men had found him. They had taken him and given him food and milk and then he had slept. When he woke he said he found himself in a cave. He said the little ones stayed with him and played with him."

Knowing that no-one will believe her son's story, the mother continues, "Of course, my son, not wishing to be told off for not staying near to home must have invented the tale, not wishing to be chastised; but it's not that simple. He is a little young to invent this. Moreover, the entire hillside where the cave is, right up to the mouth of the cave, is covered with extremely dense shrub that's five feet tall with spines and limbs. My son's rescuers had to cut their way into the cave to reach him.

They all suffered bruises and scratches; some even had puncture wounds on their arms and legs. My son, who was barefoot and bare-legged, was found without a single mark on him. It's also foolish to say that his friend had brought the food and drink to him for those days he was missing, not just because of the inaccessibility of the cave, but because it was an 18 mile round trip."

The editor adds, 'this is similar to the accounts of caverns east of Phoenix and south-western New Mexico where they have been seen by ranchers standing like sentinels on the ridges and have reportedly led children out of dangerous areas and fed them.'

Says FATE magazine, "This next account was given us by Senor R. Gutierrez. He told us that in the summer of 1970 he was walking with his little nephew Arto in the Forest, near Mixtequilla in Veracruz. Though his nephew was walking right by his side, he suddenly became aware that the boy was no longer there. As soon as he realised this, he immediately began to search the area around him, but could find no sign of him and no answers to his calls.'

'Making a return to the nearest village, after a lengthy search on his own, he gathered together a large search party and together they returned to the spot and carried out an extensive search, but they had no success in finding the little boy. As a result, the man was arrested for murder, but while he was awaiting the start of the trial, his nephew reappeared. It had been more than 30 days since he had vanished, but he appeared completely unharmed and looking as though he had been well looked after, fed, and kept clean. He simply walked back into his house to the shock of his parents. The boy was completely content and not in any distress at all.'

'Said his uncle, "When we asked him where he had been all this time he told us, 'I've been with the little men. They gave me honey and milk, and we played lots of games."

The murder charge was dropped and the authorities took no further investigation into whether he had been abducted or not.

Says FATE, "We checked out the story with the police and they confirmed to us that this was indeed the story."

A less happy tale is told by a one Ludovig Granchi who too had gone into the woods outside of the city of Rio de Janeiro. He'd gone into the woods because he was curious about a sudden sighting of strange lights in the woods. It was late at night and as he walked into the woods he began to hear what sounded like a hoard of crickets all around him. Without any warning he suddenly found himself in the middle of a group of 'men' of small stature who appeared to be wearing some kind of uniform. "They all had green eyes and blonde hair, white skin, and were very thin. They had wands with light coming from them."

He said they seized hold of him and took him into a cave in the woods where they forced him to lie on a slab of stone. The noise coming from them, like crickets he said, was "incessant," as they used their wands on him and 'inspected and examined' him. Sometime later he managed to find his voice and ask them if they knew who he was, and one of them replied in a high pitched voice that they did, and told him his name.

Eventually, after a thorough examination, they allowed him out of the cave, and he said that though he was safe, he felt 'strange and confused' for at least a week.

Those who follow Richard Sauder's work know he has chronicled alleged secret underground bases across the U.S. Along with the reporting of what he said are huge and sinister bases, he also chronicled the strange story of a man called George Haycock who, in the '60's, told him that he had found a shaft in a boulder field outside of Burley, Idaho. 'Native American legends tell of a demonic race who emerge from the caves and capture their families. George reported coming under strong psychic attack and being given the impressions of terrible 'evil activities' taking place under the ground. The shaft he discovered led to an ancient tunnel through a crawlspace with tunnels that branched off and a cave in which he attempted to dig. While in there he reported experiencing 'unusual resistance' when trying to dig. Later he would tell friends that 'someone' was trying to blast the tunnel to seal it up. The police classified him as "a druggist." He reported receiving a death threat by letter, which told him to 'cease and desist.' He was shortly after this found strangled in his home.'

In 'Project Red Book,' author Branton, who as outlandish as it sounds, claims to be a "sleeper agent" who was programmed with fractured personalities to serve the 'Bavarian-Gray collective,' alleges that in France, a woman Doctor told him she was abducted and taken into caverns where she found herself amid other human prisoners, who were being raped and tortured by 'cannibal beast-men.' She was held there for months, she claimed, until 'pale-skinned beings' in 'metallic' uniforms freed them all. She said that she learned the pale-skinned beings were sent to this planet to observe "the coming war between surface armies and the beasts of the caves, who have ancient technology which they use against humanity for their own pleasure."

The account was collected by him from 'The Hollow Earth,' by Warren Smith and was originally recorded by a German occultist who documented various similar accounts and put them into "The Messerschmidt Manuscript."

Also collected by Branton, according to the now defunct Search Magazine, in 1964, a woman called Ervin Scott wrote to them to tell of how she had heard a telepathic message, that it seems came to her as though she had somehow accidently picked up on it, and rather bizarrely, it appeared to be an urgent warning 'about a woman who was abducted into caverns beneath a Church in Boston 3 weeks earlier.'

Even more bizarrely, she then claims she heard another voice, which 'breaks into the transmission and says, "Don't believe her. Don't you know this is a trick and a lie?" and then warns her, "Keep quiet about this."

In an area of boulders, caverns and tunnels, the Black Mountain region in New South Wales, Australia, is said to be a site of supernatural phenomenon, with numerous accounts of mysterious disappearances of both people and animals.

There have been reports of people disappearing never to be seen again. Police and trackers who have set out to search for them have sometimes themselves also disappeared, giving Black Mountain the name 'Mountain of Death.'

It has a strange geography, comprising of enormous boulders that are black and formed from magma millions of years ago, and the indigenous population refuse to go near it. Just its appearance is sinister.

There have been a range of different types of reports, varying from strange sounds coming from beneath the ground, to sightings of human-like shadows. Even pilots flying over the area have reported disturbing air turbulence which has made flying difficult until out of the area. Alien researchers say it is a place with 'UFO activity.'

Underneath the boulders are numerous tunnels and caverns from which are said to come sounds of moans and crying. It could be the flow of air moving naturally through the place, but the indigenous people believe it is home to an ancient underground races. There are numerous tales of people seeing fleeting ghostly black shapes moving across the boulders.

One of the stories relates to a man named Harty Owens, who was out on the mountain looking for his cattle after they had mysteriously disappeared. He didn't return back to the farm so his farm manager Hawkins went to the mountain to look for him, taking with him some of the local police.

A pair of policemen went down into one of the caves to see if he had somehow fallen inside, but only one of them came back out. He was shaking and ghastly white and he was never able to talk about what it was he had seen down in the cave. Neither the other policeman who had gone down into the cave, nor the farm worker was ever found.

A Corpse in a cave? On April 15th, 1988, a High School senior left his Linwood home in Kansas, driving his mother's car en-route to a friend's party in a rural wooded area nearby. It's thought he disappeared around 2am, although no-one could confirm seeing him leave. On the night in question, Randy had left his parents' in the early evening and driven to a friend's house, then on to a garage where his soon-to-be graduation present, a car from his parents, was being restored.

He arrived at the bonfire party at a farm in the rural spot about 5 km from his own home, at around 10pm, where up to 150 other people were gathered. The mother of the boy whose party it was said that Randy 'had trouble walking but didn't appear drunk,' and also that she, and others, never saw him with a drink in his hand. He'd bought some soda at a gas store before arriving there. However, by the time he went to leave, one of his friend claimed he was too drunk to walk. His friend told him not to drive and amid the crowd they got separated after that. When his friend tried to find him again the car was gone and so was he. Neither the car nor the boy have ever been seen again.

His parents called the police by 2 am, worried as he had never before been late for a curfew. The police went to the site of the bonfire the next morning, but it had already been cleaned up and they couldn't find any evidence to suggest what might have happened to the boy. Then the farmhouse burnt down not long after.

Then a couple of months later, a man went to the police with a rather strange and disturbing story. He told them that he had been kidnapped by a satanic cult and held captive in a cave for fourteen days, and even worse, that he had seen a corpse hanging in the cave while he had been there. He thought it might be the missing young man. The man said his kidnappers had threatened to cut off his left arm and had then pointed to a dead man's body hanging in the gloomy cave. The

Police went to the location the man described to them and searched the cave but they found no evidence of any crime taking place there.

The conclusion the police decided to make was that the man had hallucinated the experience while under the influence of drugs. The police hadn't gone immediately to search the cave however; they had gone some time at a later stage. The cave has since been bulldozed, with some locals claiming it was at the demands of the police that it be done.

A close friend of the missing boy also went to the police to tell them what he had found. He took them to the banks of the Kansas River where a severed foot lay. The foot was not the missing boys however, and then this friend then died a few years later.

In 2002, the case was reclassified as a homicide and three men were arrested for his abduction. However, they were soon released without charge with the police saying they had made a mistake.

The case has many strange and unusual elements to it, with some claiming that his friend's death was suspicious, and then there are the internal police reports that kept turning up in the mailbox of his parents. The boy's father said he didn't know who they were coming from but felt it could be from a member of the investigation team who was trying to tell him something or show that the case was being botched.

In 1993, a man purporting to be a research journalist offered his assistance to the boy's parents and spent several months without pay interviewing those who had been there that night and others who might have known something about the case. The man went by the name of Terry. According to The Mirror, the local news journal for Tonganoxie, Kansas, in its article entitled List of Oddities, 'an independent investigator called Terry Martin was subsequently found shot to death along with his wife. Topeka police ruled it a "murder-suicide." Others are not so sure.... and there are still no answers about what happened that night, the alleged mysterious cave, and the fate of the young man.

Within the Bridgewater Triangle in Massachusetts is Freetown Forest. Bridgewater triangle is an area said to be rife with reports that range from alien activity to unidentified cryptids that lurk at night and frighten the unsuspecting traveller.

The Freetown forest is even darker, as it's believed a lot of the activities that occur inside of it are of a more human origin, but heavily linked to satanic worship.

The site of quite a few murders, there has been rumors of satanic cults using the forest as their conjuring and hunting grounds.

A teenage girl called Mary Arruda was found tied to a tree in the late 1970's. She had been left for dead after having been snatched and taken into the forest. Another time, a man was found terribly beaten inside the forest, and told investigators that he had been attacked by a group of Satanists who had tried to kill him. Another man was once found naked with an array of stab wounds. He had fled the forest and run to the nearest house for help.

Those who go into the forest, perhaps unaware of its black magic reputation are said to have experienced some terrifying things; of hearing demonic, disembodied voices near to them and yet there is no-one in the forest with them that they can see.

One man fishing in the nearby pool claimed that one day in early evening he saw a group of people walking toward him. He turned back to watch his fishing rod and when he turned back to look at the group of people they had gone but he saw them out of the corner of his eye, in a completely different location and one that would have been impossible to walk to in the amount of time he had turned his head.

Car drivers passing by the forest have also reported strange events, of not only seeing dark shapes in the forest but of those same shapes running alongside their car and keeping pace with them.

Back in 1972, in Springfield, New Jersey, Jeanette DePalma disappeared.

She had once had a drug and alcohol problem, but now she was clean and it was said that she dedicated her time to helping others struggling with the addictions, and had turned to the Church. She disappeared suddenly without any warning or indication that there was anything wrong in her life to make her leave town without telling anyone.

No sign of her was seen for nearly two months until a man was walking his dog in the local woods and his dog ran back to him with what looked like a large bone. On closer inspection it turned out to be a decomposed human hand and part of an arm.

The horrified man immediately called the police and the authorities set about searching the rest of the area for the remaining body parts with a team of bloodhounds.

It did not take long to find the rest of the body and it was a woman, laying face down and fully clothed in the woods.

Because she had decomposed so badly the forensic examiner was not able to determine how she had died, but obviously they believed it was a case of murder. She was positively identified as the missing girl, who had only just become a teenager that year.

There was no actual evidence left at the scene of the crime, except for what was at first dismissed; until the police looked at the ground more closely and realised that the logs and branches that surrounded her body, which looked like they were just natural forest debris that had fallen or gathered there quite naturally, were in fact not there by chance. According to the writers of Weird New Jersey, they looked as though they had been placed there in some kind of strange pattern almost suggestive of some kind of occult or black magic satanic ritual. Later, some of the police reflected that they were arranged around her almost like a trapezium that surrounded her, encasing her in a 'box' as though a coffin, with a cross formed at the top of her.

Was this some kind of altar or coffin formation that had been ritually created they wondered? Perhaps what also made them think in this way were the rumours in the area that it had been a site for witches and black magic and covens for many years.

Gossip started to circulate in the town of dead animals being found in mysterious ways in the same woods, and of cult activities happening there at night.

When reporters came to the town many local people spoke to them but did not want to be identified and gave vague accounts of possible covens and scarifies taking place. They seemed almost too frightened to go in to detail.

Was this just local rumour and superstition? Some even said they knew that human sacrifices took place in the area. Some even said they had accidently witnessed such things happening. The police received many anonymous letters and telephone calls but they never gave any names of suspects.

People began to speculate, was her new found religious belief and church attendance the motive? Had someone taken against her because she now went to Church? Had they felt affronted and provoked and as a gang, abducted her in revenge and to inflict their own warped beliefs on her?

Then there was the local library where the librarians had been forced to keep the occult books in a locked cabinet because so many of them on the subject had been stolen from the building.

With no suspects and no-where to turn, the crime eventually went cold and after that of course, new rumours started that the authorities knew who was involved and they were deliberately or quite possibly being forced to cover things up; being given orders from those higher up than them or by those they were in fear of.

The more level headed citizens agreed it was quite possibly a cover-up, but done so to preserve the good name of the area and not to alarm the people any more than they already were.

What is for certain, from the reactions of those living there at the time, they were definitely frightened of something.

Chapter 4:
Silence & Blood-curdling Screams in the woods.

Mysterious stone formations and circular trenches are embedded in the ground in Ballyboley Forest, in Larne, Northern Ireland, giving rise to beliefs that it's an ancient Druid site and a gateway to "the Otherworld," according to the Celtic tradition.

Although forest workers of the Park Service maintain the landscaped trails for visitors to use, there are other natural paths that never seem to need maintenance, that stay oddly clear of any foliage or branches, their paths always mysteriously remaining clear. It's said that the local people do not like to venture into the forest.

People who do enter it often return describing the eerie feeling that they were being watched. There are many tales of people seeing shadow figures standing amongst the trees, wearing dark robes, and their heads covered by cowls. There are ancient books which describe the mysterious disappearances of people who never returned after going in the forest.

In 1994, newspapers reported the strange incident of a couple who were walking through the forest when they suddenly heard screaming. Moments later a 'large dark shadow' appeared in front of them making them run off in terror.

In 1997 two men reportedly said they were walking through the forest when they heard a flapping sound that was very loud. They didn't know what it was so tried to ignore it and carried on walking.

Moments later they started hearing what sounded like a woman crying and moaning in pain or distress. Concerned for her state of health, they quickly tried to find her but could see no-one nearby.

What they did see however were trees smeared with blood all around them.

Running in fear, as they fled they both glanced behind them and to their horror both believed they could see a group of figures in dark cloaks standing where the trees were.

Found on Reddit ten years ago, one girl described how she had camped out in the forest for part of the Duke of Edinburgh Award scheme.

"On our last night there, we were camped in a clearing where there were no trees. As the light was fading someone in the group said they could see people moving around in the trees. We went toward the trees to check it out, thinking it was another group who'd got lost, but there was no-one there. We didn't think any more of it and went back and were having hot chocolate around the fire when someone else noticed there was some movement in the trees again. This time, the figures seemed to be holding torches, but this is where it got strange. Instead of modern flashlights the figures seemed to be holding branches on fire. There were four figures.

Later that night one of the group who lived on a farm and would therefore know a bit about this said that, after the figures had vanished, they could hear sounds like an abattoir; of cries and squeals.'

Posted to an outdoors forum in 2009, is another chilling and inexplicable experience.

"We were fishing on the shoreline of the river one night. We had a fire going, and we were talking and had some beers when all of a sudden we all stopped talking suddenly."

"We all felt as if something or someone was staring at us from across the river. We tried to shake it off with macho humor when the most bloodcurdling sound erupted from over there, that froze us all."

"The sound was unlike anything any of us had ever heard. It made every hair on my body stand up. The only way I can describe it is it sounded like a person being gutted alive. No words, just this high pitched bloodcurdling scream. Nobody moved or said a word. Just as suddenly a second scream came with even more force than the first."

"We sprinted to our firearms in the truck, then sat there in silence, our eyes fixed on the other side. We never did figure out or even guess what was there on the opposite bank."

The village of Pluckley and the woods surrounding it is the most haunted area in England, according to the Guinness book of records.

Frequent blood curdling screams coming from the woods are heard by the villagers but whenever they have gone into the woods to find out where the screams are coming from they never find anyone there.

People who have gone into the woods have said they were followed by an ominous black shadow and the sound of footsteps have suddenly been heard from behind them, but when they turn around no-one is there.

In one spot in the woods back in the 18th Century, a highwayman was once caught. He had attempted to hold-up a coach of passengers but it seems that some of the passengers fought back, and they used his own sword to impale him to a tree then tied him up and left him there to die of his wound. It's said that he now roams the woods in search of vengeance.

In one of the lanes in the woods, sometimes the apparition of a man's body hanging from the tree is seen and it's said to be that of an old school master who committed suicide there; or was taken there and killed. The true version is not known as one day he simply went missing and was never seen again until a few weeks later when his body was spotted hanging there in the woods.

At a disused clay pit in the woods, an industrial accident resulted in a worker being trapped by a fall of clay, covering him over and leaving him there to suffocate to death. Ever since then, walkers have spoken of hearing a man's screams and pleas for help.

In recent times, one female visitor was with a group of friends there when they had a strange experience.

'The atmosphere was a happy one and we heard all the birds and animals in the woods; but as we got deeper into the woods, it seemed that all the animals had gone quiet. In fact, it got so quiet you could have heard a pin drop. The girls in the group, including me, got spooked by this and we decided we wanted to go back to the car. We turned round and went out of the forest, but the boys carried on, going deeper into it.

About 15 minutes later they came back. They were running. They jostled with each other trying to get back in the car as quickly as they could and their faces were ash-pale. They started the car up and turned it to leave but it stalled suddenly and then we all saw this huge black mist coming from the woods, coming in our direction towards us. It looked like it was 'walking' toward us.'

S. Vince sent in her story to the *Haunted Writer* blog.

"In the summer of 2010, I was in the woods behind our parent's house with my brother in Butler County, Pennsylvania. I was 20, my brother was 18. We're both confident people, and I believe in logic. I don't get spooked easily because I think there's an explanation for everything; or at least I did.

We took an axe; we planned on having a bonfire and were on the quest for firewood. It was a warm sunny summer day and the wind was low.

We'd been in the woods about a thousand times. We started to venture deeper into the woods; something we'd done every time we had been there. We both said how loud the sounds were; the insects and birds and other animals scurrying around.

After about ten minutes, we found a few trees that looked dead and ideal for firewood and we went off the path into the thick.

As soon as we stepped off it things around us changed. I noticed straight away that all the sounds had changed. The birds had gone, and the insects and clouds came out of no-where.

Slightly unnerved, we kept working; but that did not last long. After maybe 30 seconds I started to get a sensation I had never felt before.

Every hair on my body began to stand up. I looked at my brother and could tell something similar was happening with him.

We looked around us but everything appeared to be normal; no other people, no animal. Our eyes met again and we sort of laughed it off, but we were not quite sure what was going on.

After what seemed like an hour, but was probably seconds of looking around again, we got back to work. No more than ten seconds later, the most frightening thing started. The wind stopped. All sound was gone. It was the kind of quiet where you hear your heart beat. The air was dead. I had pins and needles along my spine. I don't know what it was; all I know is that it was behind us. We could feel its presence and it did not want us there.

I exchanged a frantic look with my brother and we both get out of there and got back on the path. As we turned to look back around, a feeling of pure dread struck me. I felt like I was about to vomit. I felt like I was paralyzed in a vacuum, seeing everything around me frame by frame. I looked towards my brother and he snapped out of whatever trance we had been caught in, and we began sprinting towards home.

To this day, I don't know what happened. All I know is the next time I opened my eyes, I was running behind my brother on the way back to the house. I had no control over my body; it was just running, getting me out of there. To this day, I don't know what was out there.

Anonyn writes,

'I was not far from an area called Blood Mtn. I've camped and hunted in this area for 25 years. Never had anything like it before. I was hiking along a trail in the forest with two firearms. Suddenly I got really scared. All the hairs on the back of my neck stood up.

The ridge line of the hill was up about 700 yards ahead and something was up there tracking me. I turned back immediately, but even when I was back in the truck, I was still scared. I still felt something very close to me. I've never felt anything like it.'

Jim writes in forum *dcexposed*,

'While hunting in Georgia. In a familiar area, suddenly there were no normal sounds and no wind. Something came rushing toward me, pushing the plants aside.

I turned away before it reached me, had my gun aimed ready. Did this save me? There was a very bad feeling of danger. I pushed through a brier to get out of there. Something told me don't go back, just keep moving forward. To this day I feel I came close to something evil. My Brother and Dad had been calling me and sounding the car horn just 200 yards away. I never heard them.'

Among the foothills and pines of East Kentucky, on November 21st 2003, a University psychology professor and his two sons were driving home when they saw a bright light in the Western sky. There was a soundless aerial object, hovering over a nearby field. They stopped the car, and according to their testimonies, given to investigators Kenny Young and Donnie Blessing, something unexplained was in the sky. At the top of a hill ridge, not far away, they could see the white hovering object.

Getting back in their car with a growing sense of apprehension, unsure of whether the object had spotted them, they drove back to their nearby home and when they reached it, they all went to the second floor to look out of the window. The object in the sky hadn't gone anywhere.

At the same time, a woman in a nearby home was outside hanging up Christmas lights on the exterior of her house when she saw an object in the sky bobbing up and down. She became frightened and told her young daughter to go in the house. As she too turned to get back inside the house, the object began to lower and the lights coming from it turned to orange and red and as it touched down on the ground, dogs nearby began to howl. Suddenly the object shot off like a dart and disappeared into the sky. Immediately after it departed, blood-curdling screams could be heard from the fields or woods nearby. It was a woman's voice screaming, "Oh God, please somebody help me, Oh God, No!"

A man living in a house that was next to the field, called 911 immediately. He told the dispatcher he could hear a woman screaming and sounding like she was struggling. He told the dispatcher he'd gone outside into the field with his spotlight but couldn't see anyone in the field or the woods.

He later told the investigator Donnie, "It sounded like somebody being hurt; it sounded like somebody being ripped apart."

A police search yielded no answers. They searched the field and the woods. The witness described the area of his residence as isolated and surrounded by fields and woodland.

In UFO researcher Kenny Young's subsequent investigation of the incident, he did an internet search the following evening to find the telephone numbers of anyone who resided along the lane which was closest to the field and woods. He found one household and called them on the phone to ask them if they had heard or seen anything. The man who answered it was called Professor Virgil Davis and he was a British-born college lecturer at Kentucky Community College in Ashland.

The man told him, "I was here when the screams were heard; there were loud, blood-curdling screams but no-one could find anything."

The researchers asked him if he had seen anything, to which he replied that he was driving at the time with his two teenage sons. He said the object moved "like a humming bird," and was oval with white light and the size of a pea at arms length. As it was dark, approximately 9.30pm that winter, it could be seen very brightly against the night sky, and was quite high until it started to move, "coming down, and moving in increments."

He told the researcher that they stopped the car and got out to try to work out what it was, and they were sure it was neither an airplane nor the aurora borealis. "There was no explanation for this, and I didn't know what we were looking at. I had some concern that it could have spotted us, or that it might."

He told the researcher of their short drive back to their house and their observation of the object from their second floor window, during which time they watched it descend and settle in the field nearby as its color changed to red and it appeared larger. "Everything was real quiet, then everything went crazy."

He described how his dog tried to break its chain outside the house as it went into a frenzy, as did other dogs in the area. He said they became "dumfounded" when it suddenly shot off with great acceleration.

"I was very reluctant to call the police, and I wasn't going to report it," the witness continues, "but right after that my sons went outside and heard screaming. It was a woman's voice. They got in the car and called me within minutes saying the screaming was coming from the field where it had come down."

At that point, the witness called the police. "20 minutes later there were about twenty police officers and a rescue squad in the field. Others had heard the screaming too."

One of his sons repeated what he had heard coming from the field by the woods. He said it was "a desperate scream, blood-curdling. It was a female voice that kept saying; "Help me, Oh God, Help me!"

The witness told the researcher that he was not the one who made the report to NUFORC and that someone else must have. The NUFOCR report corroborated the sighting, the screams, and the search squad combing the field and woodlands. That report states: "report of a female crying for help x3. From two witness. The fire department was asked to begin searching with the thermal imaging camera. No results found.'

Says Young, "The report of desperate, blood curdling screams coming from a woman crying out, "Help me, Oh God, Help me," give this case a disturbing sense of dread. Clearly there was something taking place and this report raises the spectre of reported UFO/human abduction."

Chapter 5:
Non-humans in the woods

A report received by MUFON of an incident in February 25, 2011, was sent in by a witness who was in the Ansonia Nature centre, 150 acres of wooded hills, in Ansonia, CT.

"As I sometimes do, I was walking in the Ansonia Nature area late at night. This time, as I was on the way back through the woods, all of a sudden a deer ran frantically across in front of me, as if it had been spooked by something, and it skid and fell. I don't think it was me that spooked it. It felt like a weird quiet; like something is about to happen.

I walked on, taking a path on some open terrain next to the woods. While I was walking, I wasn't focusing on anything in particular, then suddenly my eyes focussed on some entity approximately 25 metres ahead, crouched slightly in a very aggressive stance and staring right at me.

When I first saw it, it was like I already knew subjectively that it was ET of some kind. Yes, there are many other logical explanations possible, of course, but I will elaborate on the strangeness anyway, even if it wasn't extraterrestrial.

The figure was glowing a blue-gray. It was as though it was naked. The head was over-sized, the arms and legs were skinny. It seemed human-like in form; athletic, ready, aggressive and focussed. I didn't see any eyes yet I could tell it was staring right at me and we were like two animals in the wild in a stand off, guarding our terrain.

It felt as though I'd stumbled into this entity too soon, like it was waiting for me but I'd noticed it too soon and was too alert, and it turned very athletically and ran at full speed into the woods. I heard the bushes as it took off into the woods.

I told a friend who said it was just a person. This is very possible but there was a strange energy involved in the encounter and I had the sense I might be ambushed by it. There was an extreme sense of danger and tension. I walk in the woods at night regularly and deer approach me or stalk, and all other kinds of sounds and I don't feel scared. If it had been a person, it would had to have had an eerie aura about it to scare me. And what on earth would cause him to stare at me overtly aggressively then run full speed into the woods. Crazy right? I went back the next day and looked at the exact spot. All the way along the path is very thick shrubs, trees, bushes; it's all tangled and I thought, how did it run full speed through this? It seemed impossible. It would have been impossible for me to go through it.

The strongest impression I get is that I felt it had been watching me, waiting for me, and I wasn't supposed to see it so soon. When it ran off, and this is very important, it was not in a scared manner but in a very confident and regimented way, and in a way that let you know it meant business and wasn't scared, but more that, it needed to get out of the area for some reason. Afterward, I was glad I went back the way I did, sure that if I had not I could have been ambushed. The feelings and impression I have is that this entity was something other than human.'

In Albert Rosales seminal work ufoinfo.com/humanoid, which lists sightings of entities of unknown origin worldwide since as far back as the 1870's to the present day, one of the accounts he has collected comes from John Colombo's book 'UFOs over Canada.'

It happened in a place called Onion Lake, in Wapiti Lake Forest, British Columbia, Canada, back in 1966. It was one evening in June that year, when a married couple were on a fishing trip with their son, who was a teenager. They were situated at the remote lake and were the only ones there. It was peaceful and quiet and exactly what they were hoping for; until something very disturbing happened.

Suddenly they found themselves engulfed in what they later described as "complete darkness and silence." The darkness came in an instant and was pitch black. The silence was disturbed only by a strange 'grinding' sound and what "smelt like metal burning." They clung to each other for comfort and reassurance but they suddenly realised that they couldn't feel their son. They reached all around for him in the blackness, but could not feel him anywhere, and despite their shouts for him, they received no reply back. He had literally disappeared while standing next to them.

Moments later, the absolute blackness 'evaporated' and their son reappeared as though out of no-where. He was stuttering and told them that he'd seen a 'disk-shaped airplane' and had gone towards it. He could remember nothing after that.

It was reported by his parents, in their letter to the Canadian Ufologist Mr Colombo, that their boy's state of amnesia quickly deteriorated into madness and that they had no choice but to confine him in a psychiatric facility, where he remained permanently.

Long since known for its variety of strange phenomenon including odd experiences of those hiking there, as well as strange lights and 'UFO sightings', anyone going into the woods of Ninham Mountain State Forest, in Carmel, New York State, may find themselves overcome by the feeling of extreme vertigo, hear voices calling to them in strange languages, or suffer bizarre feelings of unreality and unexplained visions.

Perhaps the most interesting incident on record is that of an ex-military intelligence officer who allegedly had the most disturbing of experiences. He was interviewed by Philip Imbrogo and Marianne Horrigan during their extensive investigation into the paranormal characteristics of the area, for their book 'Celtic Mysteries.' The man spoke to them back in 1992 and told them he was very familiar with the area, having camped and hunted there for many years.

The incident itself took place in January of 1992. He said he was walking through the woods until he reached the top of the mountain, where the wind was really strong. He estimated it was 40 below. He began to walk back down through the woods when it began to snow.

Already cold and with the sun now gone down, the temperature began to drop and he said it felt as though his feet and hands were already developing frostbite. It then began snowing very hard and it came down so thick and fast that he couldn't see more than ten feet in front of him. He said he was lost now, and could barely walk. He knew he was still pretty high up, and there were no trees or bushes to shelter him from the wind, since most of the tress were bare. The sky was very dark and the fog was surrounding him. He started losing orientation and had no idea what direction he'd started walking in. He said he felt dizzy and fell down and couldn't move once he was on the floor. He thought he was going to freeze to death up there and be found weeks later, dead. He couldn't feel anything; no pain, but he couldn't move either, he felt frozen already. It was as if all his joints had frozen. As he looked up into the sky right overhead ten or more lights of different colors appeared out of nowhere and started to come down. He heard no sound and the lights were in the shape of a circle. They were strange to see especially because they looked fuzzy through the mist and fog. Then he blacked out.

The next thing he remembers was when he woke up in the ranger's station at the bottom of the mountain. The ranger told him he found him at the bottom of the parking area lying down on top of the hood of a car.

Even more bizarre, the man says, "The ranger also told me he received a telephone call saying I was there! - I don't know how I got there; there was no way that I could have walked all that distance alone. Those lights must have been some sort of ufo. They must have been benevolent since they saved me. It seems that from the point I blacked out to the time that I woke up in the station I was missing for about 40 minutes. Whoever they were they didn't keep me for a long period of time. The only thing I remember is being in a room and seeing tall canisters with figures that looked like people in them.

Even more chilling, he says, "I know this sounds crazy, but in the dream I remember seeing a canister that was empty and I really feel that whoever they were they are going to come back for me because that's the canister I'm s'posed to be in."

Ufologist and ex-Navy man, Jorge Martin, in Evidencia OVNI, reported on a strange case that took place in El Yunque rainforest, Puerto Rico. It occurred in 1965, in a place that is rife with the weirdest of inexplicable encounters and experiences. An 8 year old school girl called Maria Figueroa was in the forest with her school class and their teachers, when they suddenly realized she had gone missing. Despite the most intensive of searches utilizing the military, who were based not far from the forest, the police, expert searchers, and trackers, she was never found.

It was only years later that a woman told newspapers of what had happened. She said she had been there that day as a young girl and had heard her school friend scream, and when she had gone to see where the scream was coming from she had seen the little girl trying to wrestle free from two tall men in 'gray-blue coveralls.' They had hold of her friend and wouldn't let her go, she said, and they warned the woman now telling her story that in no uncertain terms was she to tell of what she had witnessed or they would take her too. They told her to run fast, coming forward as though to snatch her, and she fled as fast as she could. She said she had not remembered this until she was older because she had blocked it from her mind until it resurfaced.

Was her memory serving her correctly? Did they seem tall to her because she was only small at the time, or were they unnaturally tall? Were they human, or 'other'?

In Brazil, the strange disappearance of a boy scout gripped the nation and led to one of the greatest mysteries Brazil has known. The case left a mark of fear and uncertainty because to this day no indication of what happened has been discovered. On August 6th, 1985, a small scout group went trekking in the forested mountain region near the city of Picket, Sao Paulo. The group consisted of Juan Cespedes Bernabeu, the scout leader, and four scouts all in their mid-teens. They were Marcus Aurelius Bosaja Simon, Ricardo Salvione, Osvaldo Lobeiro, and Ramatas Rohm. Only three of the four scouts returned.

Marcus Salvione disappeared in a way that would almost seem 'supernatural' when he disappeared without leaving any tracks or trail.

His father, a journalist called Ivo said, "At no time have I considered he is dead," but he also has no idea what happened to him.

While the mountain top reaches as high as 2420 metres above sea level, and is a rocky climb, it can be achieved without the use of specialist climbing equipment. The group had set up camp at the base and were in the process of trekking uphill on one the steep trails.

As the group were ascending the trail, one of the other boys, Osvaldo, slipped and dislocated his knee. Thinking that they may need to summon rescuers with a stretcher, the scout leader asked one of the boys to go back to the base to fetch medical assistance. Marcus volunteered to be the one to head back down to the base, and the scout leader agreed for him to go but told him to leave chalk markers of his route as he went back down. He was to leave markers saying "240" which was the number of their scout group. When the rest of the group got back to base later, having received no medical assistance, they found that the team there did not know of their predicament, as Marcus was not there. It appeared that he had never arrived back at the base.

For the next 28 days, civilian volunteers, the police, and the military went over the region with a fine tooth comb. They searched on foot and with helicopters. They found no body, no pieces of clothing, and just two chalk markings saying "240." There were no more markings after that, and no trace of the boy was found. It was as if Marcus had "evaporated".

The Police and military searched so scrupulously, covering every inch, that a soldier who had lost a knife in the middle of the forest found it the next day while searching again. That's how minute the searching method was in terms of scouring every inch of the forest and mountain. To this day however, Marcus Aurelius has never been seen again, and no clues about his mysterious disappearance have ever emerged.

Once a searcher asked the boys parents if they believed in 'flying saucers' and suggested they go to Brasilia to speak with an Air Force general, who was aware of extraterrestrial phenomena. The General said he could communicate with aliens telepathically. Desperate and willing to do anything to have their son back, his parents told the General to ask the aliens to return their child. They received no response from the General.

The tragedy that shook the family moved the entire country too, with the press and television following the desperate search. For a month, over 300 people including volunteers, fire-fighters and teams specializing in search and rescue had stayed in the forest, scouring the Pico dos Marins region without any success.

The boy's mysterious disappearance and the fact that they completely failed to find any trace of the Boy Scout left everyone who participated in the searches absolutely bewildered, as well as the authorities involved. There found none of his things, such as his knife, or water bottle. Nothing was found. It was like he was never there, and his disappearance remains an enigma to this day.

The scout party had set up base at the property of Afonso Xavier, who himself had five decades of experience as a guide in the area. Even he could find no clues about the boy's disappearance. He had gone with the scouts initially, but when the scout leader realised they could easily make it on their own, he said they could manage without him. The area itself is a common and popular spot for tourists and other hikers heading up to Pico dos Marins, and there was a clear trail to follow.

According to "Operation Marins" written by investigator Rodgrigo Nunes, the last time the scout Simon Marcus Aurelius was seen was at 2.40pm. The rest of the group had passed by two "240" marks made by Marcus, but after that they came to a fork, with tracks left and right. The group believed that Marcus had gone down the path on the left, but that path had obstacles, so that was not going to work for them, because they were carrying Osvaldo supported on their shoulders. The group leader decided to take the trail on the right. The leader later said he thought it would be no problem and that they would cross later and re-join with the trail the boy had taken.

The path they took however became longer than they expected and they didn't make it back to the camp until 5:30 in the morning, taking about 15 hours to accomplish their trek down, all the while carrying the injured boy.

Everyone thought they would find Marcus sleeping in the camp tent, but when they arrived, they found the tent empty with the belongings the boy had brought on the expedition still there, ruling out the possibility that he had made it back and, for some reason, left the base and gone home.

Officers of the Military Police, an Army Infantry Battalion, sniffer dogs, trackers, guides, and even parapsychologists, psychics, and clairvoyants arrived to participate in the efforts. It was one of the greatest searches ever held in the country, but nothing has ever been found.

Some of the assumptions made at the time were initially that the disappearance had to be tied to the scout leader, but he was easily ruled out after the other boys were questioned; he never left them alone at any point during the trek down.

Another theory was that the boy could have fallen into a hole, but if this had occurred, the decomposing body would have drawn the attention of the cadaver dogs who participated in the search, and that did not happen. The third hypothesis was that he could have been "abducted" by aliens. The Pico dos Marins is considered 'a region with very strong magnetic power,' which, according to mystics, attracts extraterrestrial craft. Accordingly, the family sought out Ufologists, but they also could not explain what had happened.

"We went to psychics and spiritualists including a famous medium Chico Xavier. Most say that he is alive," says the boy's father.

Xavier told his father, "I only communicate with people who disincarnated, not the living," and so because of this, the family believe the boy is still alive.

The only possible clue came on the second night of the search, when the scout leader and the other scouts were preparing to get some sleep after searching all day. They heard a scream, followed by the sound of a whistle. They were all astonished, as they knew the boy scout wore a whistle, as they all did with their scout uniform.

At the sound of the whistle, everyone ran out of the tent and with the guide Afonso, they headed toward the forest. Suddenly they saw a flash of blue light in the forest, followed by two more flashes.

The group leader, Juan Bernabeu, took hold of his whistle and started to blow it, hoping to hear the boy's whistle again but it didn't come and there was only silence.

That's what made Ufologists say that it was at that moment that the boy was 'taken.' The group reported the incident to the police and military searching for the boy, but they found no source for the blue lights and still no sign of the boy.

Chapter 6:
A case like Dyatlov

In a case that perhaps bears some similarities with the Dyatlov Pass incident, John Cooper & Jeannette Johnson tried to do something very few would attempt; they tried to climb South America's highest mountain during the worst month of the year; but they never made it to the top of Mount Aconcagua, Argentina. Their adventure was cut short by something that has baffled authorities for years.

The macabre mystery began in the summer of 1972. It was then that 8 climbers first got together to discuss scaling the 22,840 foot mountain. There was a lawyer, a doctor; a psychologist; a geologist, a policeman, and a farmer, as well as the couple formerly mentioned, Jeanette a teacher and John Cooper an engineer.

When the group arrived in the tiny town of Mendoza in the Andes to undertake the climb, local experts ominously warned them that January was a bad time of year to do it. The expedition however brushed their concerns aside, but they agreed to hire a local climber Miguel Angel Alfonso as a guide. Miguel told them to wait for better weather, but they were determined to begin as soon as possible, and on a freezing morning the party set out.

At first the climbing progressed relatively steadily, but very quickly several of the group found they were unable to continue in the weather conditions of ice and driving winds. First, two of the party dropped out, urging the others to give up but to no avail. Then one more of the party gave up too and the guide recalls that at this stage, they were 6,300 metres up. The man had mountain sickness and had lost control of his body. The guide took him back to base, leaving just four to continue the expedition.

"That was the last time I saw Jeannette and Cooper alive," the guide says.

"Three days later in the base camp there was a terrible storm and I was looking out of the cabin when I saw two figures in the far distance. Intending to go out and help them, I was forced back by the weather. The following day, I went back out and did succeed in reaching them. They were walking in circles and babbling, crying and blinded by the sunlight. There should have been four but there were only two of them. The two that did return were in a terrible condition from frostbite and they were both incoherent. They began shouting, "Cooper is where the road nears the trees. We're not men, not athletes ... They were ghosts. Jeannette has been taken by the women on mules."

He had no idea what the men were talking about. "The other two never returned. Later that year, another expedition came across the grisly remains of Cooper. There was a strange wound, in his stomach, perhaps caused by an ice-pick. But there were also multiple fractures in his skull and it was those that had killed him."

"It was to be another two years before a subsequent expedition found Jeanette's body, perfectly preserved in ice. She had been brutally beaten. No one has ever been able to find the reason for their deaths, and it seems it will remain a secret kept by the mountain."

Had the two men in their party killed them? How could "women on mules" have been there, up so high on the mountain and in such treacherous conditions? Had the men who said they had seen them been delirious with frostbite and hypothermia and hallucinated them? What did they mean, "They were ghosts?" Who are they referring to?

If it were possible for women to be up there on mules, why would they kill those two climbers and not the other two? Or had someone else killed them? Yet there were no other expeditions at the time they went up the mountain. All other parties had been wise enough not to attempt it in the weather conditions.

What had happened to them and how had they died?

The last time that Cooper had been seen by the other climber Zeller, he was not in the condition in which he was found, in that he was reportedly not fatally injured from a fall or lying down with serious fractures in his skull. The climber had said he had left him 'sitting.' Furthermore, the female climber was found on a section of the mountain where there was virtually no incline, which made it unlikely that she too had fallen. She was also found at quite some distance away from the other climber.

Both had sustained multiple fractures yet neither of the other two climbers, who did make it back to base, had said anything about them having a fall or accident, and where they were both found was not consistent geographically with them landing from a fall.

The authorities declared that murder had taken place, implying that Jeanette had killed her companion with an ice pick, and then had a fall. The forensics of the case however do not seem to add up to the geography, and it would appear that the mountain has indeed kept the secrets of their deaths.

Patrick N wrote into Sasquatch Chnonicles, "We'd been canoeing and camping along the lakes between Minnesota and Canada. This day we were going to canoe for a few hours but a storm started to blow and so we got out at a clearing and set up camp quickly to try and avoid the storm.

Next morning it'd cleared up and we started looking for a good fishing spot. We came upon another campsite, however it was completely wrecked. There was trash everywhere, there were clothes on the ground, the tent was torn and had collapsed. At first we were just like disgusted, but the closer we looked, the weirder things were. For one, their food was still tied high up in a tree to keep bears from it, but the bags were literally ripped open; despite being tied at least thirty feet up. Second, literally everything; rope, pans, hiking stuff, clothes, and food was all still there. Half of it was all torn up, half of it had not been touched at all.

We waited around for a few hours and then decided to call the helicopter crew who were to come and get us when we were leaving. We asked them if they'd heard any distress calls but they said they weren't aware of any. We were pretty upset by it. First we thought bear attack; but the food was still there not eaten. Why was half they stuff destroyed and not the other half? And the ripped bags at 30 feet up?"

A bird could reach the bags and rip them open perhaps, but not trash a complete camp surely? So what did the damage? And where were the campers?

David Brewster, writing for Seattle Magazine in August 1970, describes what was possibly a fatal Sasquatch attack; fatal in that the victim died in fleeing from the creature, or from something in Mount St Helens National Park.

'One of the eeriest encounters with Sasquatch may have occurred here in 1950. A well-known climber, Jim Carter, disappeared. Ski tracks indicated he had careered downward, taking the most risky chances, as one searcher later put it, "that no-one of his calibre would take, unless something was terribly wrong or he was being pursued." In his wild descent, this experienced man jumped several yawning crevices before going right off a steep canyon.'

'Neither he nor his equipment were ever found, and there were several members of the search party who reported that while they were searching they had the unnerving sensation of feeling they were being watched all the time they were there. Among the searchers was Bob Lee, who admitted that both he and some of the Mountain Rescue Council, came to the same conclusion; "The apes got him."

Brewster continues, 'In Indian tales, she (Sasquatch) is a cannibal and the Kwakiutl of Northern Vancouver have a singular theme; she kidnaps children, sometimes by disguising herself as their grandmother, seals up their eyes, and carries them off on her back.'

When the Danish explorer Knud Rasmussen arrived in arctic North America in 1921 to study the Iglulik Eskimos, he found a culture that revolved almost entirely around a multitude of unseen beings; "spirits that inhabited every person, animal and object, and spirits that were held responsible for seemingly inexplicable events, such as illness or bad weather. With the aid of an Eskimo shaman named Anarqaq, who drew for him pictures of the unseen spirits he saw, the explorer learned of invisible entities who were either kind and helpful or malevolent, aggressive, and evil.

The Shaman told him that the entire community worked together to try to keep the bad spirits at bay, by practising rituals and taboos, but it seemed that only the shaman himself was able to conqour the spirits and drive them out. Anarqaq said that he was helped in his endeavours by the benevolent spirits who came to his aid. Interestingly, he said that many of these kind spirits would often first appear as monsters or ferocious monsters, but once they were won over they remained steadfast and readily available to him to help him.

Anarqaq held the firm belief that an entity called Igtuk was responsible for the booming noises that were heard coming from arctic mountains. The shaman said he had seen this entity and it had just one huge eye which was set into his body at the same level as his arms. His mouth opened wide to disclose a dark abyss, and he was covered in thick dark hair. In a vision that appeared to the Shaman one spring day, a female spirit named Qungairuvlik tried to steal a child by concealing it in her parka.

Before she could accomplish the deed however, two well-armed helping spirits came to the rescue of the child, he said, and killed the kidnapper. One of the many spirits that Anarqaq claimed to have encountered during hunting expeditions was a monstrous being as big as a bear. With a mighty roar, the monster called the Kigutilik rose from an opening in the ice as the shaman was hunting seal. Anarqaq said he was so terrified that he fled without even attempting to try calling any spirit helpers.

With 7 million acres of primeval forest, this national park has no roads and access is usually by air. There's evidence of prehistoric humans being here. The Nahanni Valley in Canada's Northwest Territories has been called one of the few remaining unexplored places in the western world. Much of it remains unchartered, despite it being declared a national park four decades ago.

It's a place where bears and wolves reside, and possibly something else. The Genoskwa too are said to live there. The Genoskwa are a sub-species of the Sasquatch, and in Native American lore are called the 'Giant Stone Men.' They are rumored to be more aggressive than the Sasquatch, and are larger, estimated at between 9 and 11 feet and weighing at least 800 lbs.

In the 18th century, the fur traders came to the region, followed by the gold prospectors. It's the 200 mile gorge where most disappearances are said to have happened. Natives say that is where true evil lurks. It's been given the name of 'The Valley of the Headless Men' for good reason. During the gold rush there were a series unexplained incidents. Two brothers, Will and Frank McLeod seemed to disappear in the valley in 1906. It wasn't until two years later that other prospectors found their bodies. They had been decapitated. A decade passed quietly until another prospector, a Swiss man by the name of Martin Jorgenson was found headless too.

In 1940's, a Canadian gold miner was discovered dead in his sleeping bag. His head too had been removed. That same year a prospector called Ernest Sacabe was found without a head, decapitated.

They were just the ones who were found. In the '60's it was estimated that more than 50 men had gone into the valley and never come back out. Their bodies have never been found.

Here is an old newspaper account of a very grisly, disturbing and perplexing case.

"MAN ON MOUNTAIN SIDE FOR SIX DAYS," reads the headline from the Welsh Newydd Cymru Arlien Newspaper of 14th September, 1907.

The article says, "How the man got into the position in which he was found is enshrouded in mystery, and, although he was breathing when discovered, he was unable to give any account of himself. He had been idle for a week or so owing to a stoppage at a local quarry, and he left home on Thursday in last week for the purpose of seeking employment. It is said he arrived at Pont-neath-Vaughan during the morning of the 5th, but it is not known at what time he left for the return journey, though it is believed it was towards the evening. About half-a-mile from Pont-neath-Vaughan is an embankment, and Jones must have fallen down it. He was found by William and John Jones, who on Wednesday morning had proceeded to search for him. His disappearance was only notified to the police that morning, it being believed that he had secured work some-where away from home."

"A terrible spectacle met the searchers' eyes as they reached the spot. The man, who was embedded in fern, was still alive, and lifted up his left hand on the approach of his discoverers as if asking them to hasten to his aid. His skull was fractured, and his eyes, face, and that part of his body in contact with the ground had been devoured. It is stated that before he died early on Thursday morning he tried to speak, but his voice had lost all its power."

The report says that the man was "partly undressed," with the "flesh literally picked off his face, and the eyes eaten away. The man was still alive, but died soon after."

It was later said that he must have been eaten by vermin or birds, which is perhaps one possibility...

The Aberdare Leader Newspaper followed up on the poor man's inquest.

"Penderyn Tragedy. An inquest was held by the Coroner (Mr R. W. Jones) at the Lamb Hotel, Penderyn, on Friday afternoon touching the death of David John. Dr. Thomas of Hirwain, said that he was called to deceased about 11o'clock, on Wednesday night.

He found him in an unconscious condition. There were bruises on his legs. There were maggots in the cut on his head and also in one of his eyes. The bruises appeared to have been caused by accident. Elizabeth John, the widow of the deceased, who wept bitterly in giving her evidence, said that deceased was 41 years of age and the father of two children. He had left home stating that he was not sure whether he would go to look for work at a quarry or go and work on the hay. He promised to be back that evening. Her husband had been out of work owing to a strike at the quarry. He did not return that night. In the morning she told her neighbours of her husband having not returned home, whereupon they told her to let matters be because he would be sure to return shortly.

As he did not return on Sunday and on Monday she went to some men in the village and asked them to go in search of her husband. They declined because they were busy at the time. She did not inform the police until Wednesday. Her husband was brought home on Wednesday evening last and died the following day. The Coroner at this point said that there had been a serious neglect on the part of witness in not having taken steps earlier to find deceased as he had promised to be back on the same night. He sympathised with the widow but she ought to have reported to the police. William Kemys, Pont-neath-vaughan, said that he met the deceased on the 3rd in Pont-neath-vaughan. They went into the White Horse public house together. Witness gave him some beer and some bread and cheese. Deceased told him that he was in search of work. Witness then promised him two or three days' work on his farm if he came up with witness.'

'Deceased refused this offer on the ground that he promised his wife to be home that night. Witness, who was accompanied by Mrs Harris, the landlady of the White Horse, then left the deceased who proceeded to walk towards Penderyn. William Jones, of Green Cottage and Jn. Jones, of Gwalia House, spoke to finding deceased lying amongst some ferns. P.S. Davies said that he went to the place where deceased had been found. He found the clothing strewn about the ground.'

'They also came across a pool of blood among some ferns. The Coroner summed up, and said it was one of the saddest cases he had ever inquired into. According to the two discoverers' story, when John's wife became very anxious as to his whereabouts, they undertook to walk over the mountain from Penderyn in the direction of Pont-Neath-Vaughan. When they reached the Dinas Rock, "on Cilhepste Mountain, they found him. His trousers, boots, and stockings were lying some 50 yards away. When they got in sight the unfortunate man raised his hand as if making a signal for help, but when they reached him he was unable to articulate a word. His body was badly bruised as if by a fall, and there were several deep cuts on the head. His eyes were swollen, but whether they were gone or not is not known. One of the men at once proceeded to the village of Pont-Neath-Vaughan for some brandy and also to Glynneath, for a doctor.'

'Here Dr. Dyke at once accompanied him to the spot where the man lay: and he ordered him to be taken home. On the bank of the river was found a silver watch and chain and a man's hat, stick, and pipe at various points along the bank.'

Quite simply, the poor man most likely suffered a fall, and was then eaten by natural predators; but why were his clothes strewn 50 yards from his body? Why were his heavy work boots and his trousers no longer on his body? Why was his watch found further away by the stream? Why would he have been eaten while still alive? What happened to him out alone there on that terrible night? Was it simply a natural accident and natural predation, or was it something else?

Chapter 7:
Hunted by Humans?

The following letter was recently found in the woods in British Columbia;

"This message is for a certain young lady who has several terriers. I see you nearly every day in here. Every time I see you I want to approach you but I find myself overcome with shyness and jumping off the trail and watching you from afar, but yesterday I slipped up. I was too close and you could smell my cologne. I was close enough to hear you ask your friend if she smelled it. You seem to realize you are being watched. I know that your dog saw me because the hairs on its back stood up. I am very impressed every time I see you in the woods. Perhaps the bear spray and concealed knife I know you carry give you a sense of security. I realise others may find this creepy...'

The January 17 2014 issue of *The Times Colonist* displayed the very creepy letter found in the woods on Beaver Lodge trail in Campbell River, British Columbia. The police had requested it be released as a warning.

The writer of the letter ends by saying that he doesn't mean to scare her, that he just wants to say hello! The police are now looking for him, and have warned women to be careful when going into the woods as they are not sure what the unidentified man is capable of.

Daisey writes on Websleuths forum,

"My son was an avid hiker during college. His dream was to hike the Appalachian Trail. When he took off alone he had plans to meet up with other hikers at various points so none of them would be hiking alone too long. Two weeks into his trip, he called me to pick him up after getting an injury in a fall. Turns out he left camp in the middle of the night and was injured trying to evade several guys that had been stalking him for days."

'Anonymous' posts on a hiking forum, about an experience while hiking in Georgia, "It involved my hiking partner and I being followed. We had a scary experience one time on one of the trails. My hiking partner and I were being very closely followed and we were very frightened by these men. I believe we were saved only when we spotted other hikers and shouted out "Hey, here's some more hikers," because the men following us then took off up the hillside."

The Hour Newspaper reported on a case in November 1989, of a mid-twenties female student who'd got lost for two weeks in the wilderness of South Carolina, in Table Rock National Park.

She was found by a hunter, but what she told the authorities who'd been searching for her for a week with a party of over one hundred people, was quite alarming.

She said that she'd run off the main trail and into the woods when she sensed that she was being pursued by a group of men who she thought meant to do harm to her.

"There was no good intent involved," she told reporters.

Although she could see the search helicopters overhead, she said that she had been too frightened to create a fire to alert them because she believed if she had done so, then the men stalking her would also have been able to find where she was.

The authorities didn't believe her.

"From the very start, before the search was initiated she became paranoid that somebody was trying to run her down," said Walter Purcell of Emergency Preparedness in the county.

"We don't think anybody was chasing her," the deputy Sheriff commented.

The consensus of belief was that they think she saw hunters and panicked, thinking that they were after her, and that she then thought the rescuers were the same men too, hunting her.

Surely hunters look different to S&R teams?

Perhaps the authorities were right not to believe her. After all, they were probably irritated that they'd just spent exhausting and intensive man-hours over the period of week trying to find her.

Had she made the story up out of embarrassment because she'd caused everyone to come out searching for her after she'd accidentally got lost? Possibly, but the statement she made to the Press was very clear. She could tell that 'there was evil intent.'

Perhaps they were right to say that they didn't believe any men were chasing her and that there was no evidence to support this, given that they'd been covering the same ground looking for her; however if they couldn't find her for seven days because she managed to evade and elude them, wouldn't the men who were allegedly chasing her also have been able to evade and elude the searchers?

Eloise Lindsay herself was sure there were men stalking her.

Said to be one of the most intriguing and perplexing of mysteries in recent years, and one that has had thousands of people tying to figure out just what may have happened, is the vanishing of student Maura Murray.

A hard working student nurse at Amherst University, she had a busy schedule of attending lectures, doing nursing practice, and she had two jobs. She had a fiancé out of State and a Father who frequently visited her, and much of her childhood had been spent hiking with him in the countryside.

She had a security job at the dormitories and she been at her post there when she'd had received a telephone call that had upset her. Her supervisor even had to escort her back to her room because she was too upset to continue working that night.

What isn't known is who called her and what it was they said to her.

The next day she inexplicably invented a death in the family to use as an excuse to tell to her teachers, explaining that she had to leave college for a few days to get back for the funeral; but there had been no death.

After sending emails to her lecturers, she packed up some of her things, including some pictures from her wall, and about a week's worth of clothing, her gym kit, jewellery her fiancé had given her, and some of her study books.

She also took some alcohol, a book about true stories of hiking in the Mountains, and directions to get to Vermont.

Then she got into her car and drove off, but she crashed her car outside of Woodsville in New Hampshire. It was February of 2004 and it was a cold night.

She didn't seem to be hurt when a coach driver passed and stopped to see if she was ok, but he asked if she needed him to call the police. She said she didn't because she had already done so, but it seems he doubted her story because he knew that cell phone coverage was poor in that area and so, still concerned, when he reached his house only a minute or so beyond the crash site, he called them anyway.

The police arrived only minutes later and found the car was locked but she wasn't inside and they couldn't see her anywhere.

The front window was cracked and the air bags had deployed during the crash. The police were concerned for her well-being and after an initial search of the area they escalated the incident and instigated a full-blown search for the now missing girl.

Soon helicopters were flying overhead looking for her.

Her Father and her boyfriend were informed that they could not locate her.

Her boyfriend left Oklahoma to travel up and as he was travelling he received a voicemail message to his phone that came from a pre-paid calling card. He could only hear breathing and then crying, but he believes it was his fiancée.

The problem was that she hadn't told anyone where she was heading. Earlier that day, she had withdrawn most of her money, which was less than $500, and phoned a condo rental in another part of New Hampshire, but hadn't booked a rental.

She'd also stopped on her drive that night to buy some alcohol and when the police assessed the crash scene they believed that they found traces of spilt wine.

Had she fled the scene through fear of getting a DUI?

If she had, where had she gone on that cold night? Though she was used to hiking growing up, this was late at night and winter and she'd been drinking, which would only make her feel colder if she was outside.

Among the theories put forward over the years are that she fled for the Canadian border for some reason; or that she was taken by a serial killer who monitored the police scanners to get a lead on potential victims.

Others think she ran and hid from the police and suffered hypothermia and died.

But if she had died out there off the route, why couldn't even the cadaver dogs find her body? The police didn't find any tracks from the road into the woodland around the road.

How long could she have survived a new life without any money in her account, and no-where to go? Why would she leave her fiancé and Dad? It didn't make sense to them at all; and she'd packed her study books; indicating that she was intending to use them, and not leaving her old life behind.

Had someone taken her against her will? She'd spent three months as a cadet at West Point Naval Academy before transferring college and knew how to look after herself, but she had been in an emotional state and drinking that night. Then again, someone with a gun on a dark night could have taken her at will.

To this day, no word has been heard from her still. Maura Murray is still missing. It's possible she hid out in the woods, afraid of being arrested, but if she did, why couldn't the searchers find her? And why didn't she come out from where she was hiding after the police had left?

Another very strange case is that of Tara Calico and a young boy. In 1998, Tara Calico was a busy young woman. She worked at a bank in town, was studying for a degree in psychology, and fitted around this she regularly worked out or participated in sports.

She often went out for bike rides, and that day as she set out on her usual morning ride, she asked her Mom to look out for her when it got to midday, and if she wasn't back by then she wanted her Mom to come and pick her up. She was concerned because in the past she'd got a puncture on her bike and been delayed and she had a lot to do that day.

When midday came and went and her daughter didn't return home, her Mom duly set out in her car to go find her and bring her and the bicycle back home. But when she drove along the route her daughter always took, she didn't see her at all. Checking all the way, she then returned back home but her daughter still wasn't there and now concerned she immediately called the police.

A patrol car quickly arrived and started searching for her and the police found a cassette tape along the road that looked like it had probably come out of her Walkman stereo, but no other signs of her or the bicycle, just some bike tracks.

Where she was cycling was a straight route that cut through in a straight line, with very few cross sections, no buildings and no trees. There wasn't really anywhere for her to be if she wasn't on the road.

As the police extended their search area to a distance of nearly twenty miles away they came across a walkman lying in the road that her Mother identified as hers. She believed then that her daughter was trying to leave them clues and a trail to follow. This was close to a remote Campground called John F Kennedy. The trail ended there, at the base of the Mazano Mountain.

Witnesses had last seen her at close to noon, and less than two miles from her home. They'd also seen a pickup truck close behind her. The police were never able to trace the truck.

A year passed with no further leads or information or clues about the girl's disappearance. Despite the police searching everywhere for her, no other signs could be found and they were at a complete loss to explain what had happened to her.

Then, a year later and hundreds of miles away in a parking lot outside of a grocery store in Florida, a lady parked her car and walked into the store. When she returned, the white truck that had been parked next to hers was now gone, but what she found in the parking space on the floor was something terrible.

It was a Polaroid picture with a harrowing scene. Two children were lying on a bed, bound and gagged. A boy who looked to be in early adolescence, and an older girl. They were both staring into the camera anxious and scared and the image horrified the woman.

The woman drove quickly to the nearest police station, telling them that it must have been dropped by the man she had seen in the driver's seat; a man with dark hair and a moustache.

The police responded immediately, setting up road blocks to try to find him but it was too late and he'd already left the area.

When the mother of missing Tara was shown the picture, she was convinced it was her daughter. The parents and family of a missing boy were convinced the boy in the picture was their son too. He also went missing in New Mexico the same year. He'd been at a campsite in the Cibola National Park in the Zuni Mountains, less than fifty miles from where the girl lived. He had gone with his Dad and a friend of his Father to hunt turkeys.

They had only been at the campsite for a short while and were still setting up when they realised that young Michael had disappeared. They quickly started looking for him, thinking he must have gone off wandering but they couldn't see him anywhere nearby and quickly found a ranger and reported him missing.

The search was started but a sudden storm came and made it extremely difficult to look for him in the wilderness. Snow was falling fast despite it having been quite warm earlier in the day and the child had only thin clothing on. Nearly five hundred people searched for him, including the Rangers, the National Guard, the police and many volunteers, spanning out over a ten mile radius of the site. Even air searches were carried out.

Tracks thought to be his were seen in the snow but no-one could be absolutely sure they were his. Despite bloodhounds being used, there were just too many other scents from all of the volunteers and SAR teams, making it impossible for the dogs to distinguish the boy's scent.

Despite a week long search, the little boy was not found. What most involved believed had happened was that he must have wandered off, become quickly lost and disoriented, having only just arrived in the area and being completely unfamiliar with it, and become unable to find his way back to the camp ground.

Most of those involved in the search believed that what had happened to him was that he had then succumbed to the cold and died of exposure and eventually his body would have suffered natural predation. They also felt that when hypothermia began to set in and became severe he would possibly have burrowed and crawled into an enclosed area, which was what victims often did according to their years of search experience.

But still no remains were found.

And then came the Polaroid photograph, which both families said contained the bound images of their children. The boy's Father said at the time that even the boy's best friend said it was definitely the boy. Although the Father said he wasn't sure, he also didn't know if that was because he didn't want to accept that it was his child pictured in so vulnerable a position.

But then there was a new twist in 1990. The boy's remains were discovered approximately eight miles from the campground in the mountains. A horse rider had come across some human bones in a thick copse of trees that were identified as him. No-one could explain how he had ended up dead eight miles away.

It now seemed unlikely that the boy had been taken to Florida and then returned to the mountain.

But if it wasn't Michael, then who was the other boy in the photograph?

Between then and now, two other photographs were reported as possibly containing the missing girl. They were never released to the press or the public but it's known that one photo is an out of focus image of a girl with duct tape over her mouth, mysteriously found at a construction site. It was examined and it was discovered that the type of film was only manufactured after 1989. The second photograph was of a woman on a train, blindfolded.

Neither were positively identified as the missing girl nor were they ruled out either. Her Mom felt that it could be her, believing the images bore a striking resemblance.

Rivera, the local sheriff said that after twenty years, he was convinced some local boys, whose names he knows, had run her off the road and buried her, probably killing her by accident and then panicked and covered it up. He said that what he lacked however was a solid piece of evidence with which to prosecute them.

However, adding another twist to the mystery again was another photograph that materialised; sent to the police and the local newspapers in 2009, in which there is a young boy who has had a black pen drawn over his mouth, making it look as though his mouth has been gagged, just like in the original Polaroid photo from twenty years ago. Then there is a second photo of the original boy from 1989.

They were sent to the police and media around the time of the anniversary of when Tara went missing. Was it some kind of clue? What was the sender hoping to achieve by sending them? Was it some kind of sick hoax? But if so, how did the sender of them have the original picture of the boy? Was the abductor and possible murderer taunting the authorities, showing them that he'd got away with it?

There was nothing the authorities could do with the photos. There was nothing that would lead to helping them solve the case.

The letters containing the copies of the picture were posted in Albuquerque. The authorities were not sure if the boy in the new photograph was the same as the boy in the original photograph with Tara.

Again, there were no clear answers.

Chapter 8:
Taken, Held, and Drowned

This chapter concerns the rising number of young men who, for the last seven or so years, have disappeared in what can only be described as sinister and inexplicable circumstances. First mentioned in this author's 'Mysterious things in the Woods,' and continued in the books, 'Something in the Woods,' and 'Taken in the Woods,' it refers to the strange and disturbing phenomenon of scores of young men who have been vanishing without a trace, only for many of them to be found dead, weeks or months later, in remote rivers or creeks, shallow ponds or canals, in areas that search parties have thoroughly searched several times before, and their bodies then discovered as though placed there to be found.

As a quick recap before covering new cases, the strange deaths at first were given the meme 'The Smiley Face Killers,' when it was discovered that some of the locations had smiley face graffiti nearby. While this name continues to be used by some, the name has generally been ruled out as being a clue to the reason for any of the missing boys' disappearances and deaths.

Up to 300 young men, predominately in the Midwest, but State-wide, have completely disappeared or been found later, drowned, all under very similar circumstances, and all being of the same demographic victimology. Investigative Journalist Kristi Piehl was the first to publicize the cases back in 2008, through linking up with two detectives who had already discovered the rising number of young college-age men's deaths. Unknown to Piehl, at the same time as she was investigating one strange death, Kevin Gannon and Anthony Duarte, retired NYPD detectives, were already investigating the mysterious deaths of several college men from New York State.

Each of the deaths had been ruled as accidental drowning; then they learned of more student male drowning deaths in the Midwest. In all, the two detectives were able to connect unexplained drowning deaths of at least 40 male students across the whole country. The two detectives came to believe that in each of these cases, there was the possibility that the missing men had been drugged, and their bodies then placed in water, in order to make it appear as if they had drowned.

The two detectives were of the opinion that these deaths were highly likely to be the work of more than one killer, because some of them had taken place on the same day, in separate geographical states. Speaking to CNN, Gannon said, "I believe these young men are being abducted by individuals, taken out, and held for a period of time before they're entered into the water." He stated that he believed the victims were being mentally abused and sometimes physically abused, prior to being killed, though strangely, they usually had no marks on their bodies.

Both Senator Sensenbrenner of Wisconsin and U.S. Congressman McNulty of NY, submitted requests to the FBI for them to investigate the mounting number of disturbing cases occurring and to make efforts to stop them. Instead, the cases have continued and show no signs of abating.

The victim type is always the same; athletic, popular, high achieving white male college students who go missing after a night out drinking with friends. Choosing to go home alone, instead of walking back with friends, they disappear, only to be found some time later, drowned in nearby rivers or creeks.

Many will say they were simply drunk and disoriented and fell in the river. Many will say inevitably, that the reason they are all of a similar victimology is because more young men than women choose to walk off alone at night. They say that they are popular college kids who are letting off steam, drinking too much and then underestimating how much they have drunk, and as a result they then get into difficulty walking home. Others however will ask why they would choose to walk away from their direct route home, often for a long distance, to a remote river or creek, usually in the mid of winter, without coats, and go for a swim or 'fall in,' rather than go straight home?

This is the same scenario for almost all of the victims. The majority of them were former lifeguards or very active sportsmen and active outdoorsmen; and most of them were not known to be particularly heavy drinkers. They were all highly intelligent, and understandably not prone to jumping onto rivers and lakes in freezing temperatures, on their own, late at night.

To the detectives and to Piehl, it didn't make sense. Nor did it make sense to some forensic examiners. For the families, who knew their sons the best, the possibility of them drowning was something they found highly unlikely. The detectives, Piehl, many independent pathologists, and the families of the victims all disagreed that the young men had merely fallen prey to the outdoors and misadventure. Piehl and the detectives veered toward a much more sinister explanation; that a group of killers, identities yet unknown, were deliberately targeting these men, for reasons also as yet unknown. And it hasn't stopped.

Detective Gannon and Professor Gilbertson, a nationally acclaimed criminologist based at St Cloud University, Minnesota, were featured on News Channels in the early days of the investigation but Gannon was later accused of allegedly 'inappropriate behaviour' while investigating witnesses and this has probably not helped in furthering the credibility of their investigations. While the mainstream media have largely dismissed the cases as simple 'drinking &

drowning deaths' Gretchen Carlson of FOX News presented a documentary on the cases called 'Death at the Rivers Edge,' in August 2014.

Professor Gilbertson, Associate Professor of Criminal Justice, and involved in the organisation 'Nationwide Investigations,' as quoted by NBC, says, "This is a nationwide organization." I spoke to Professor Gilbertson 18 months ago, who at the time pointed out to me that he was concerned that the deaths appeared to have spread to the U.K.

I also spoke at the time with former federal drug enforcement agent Jerry Snyder's organization, a not-for-profit victim-search group called Find Me, composed of active and retired law enforcement officials and consultants. They too had been following the cases from the beginning, and are still investigating them now. "Look at all the names here and we think we've only scratched the surface; that's what's really scary to me,' Snyder said. I had also spoken with several family members of the victims, who were not of the opinion that these were 'accidents.'

Mystery enshrouds so many of these cases and on a side note, while I was looking into these deaths over the last couple of years, I was contacted by a woman who had a blog dedicated to charting and investigating these deaths. At her own request she has asked for anonymity, and while she gave me full access to the records of her blog if I desired, she also warned me that she had been forced to close it down after, in her words, "coming under extreme psychic attack," while running the blog and investigating the deaths, so bad she said, that she now wanted nothing more to do with the investigation. How does psychic astral attack come into this? Who would be behind doing something like that? And why?

She's not the first one to tell me they had been 'forced' to stop looking into things. Another man actively researching the deaths, JC Smith, has also told me of being 'warned off,' and being told 'something similar' to what happened to the victims could happen to him. Additionally, although Kristi Piehl appeared on Coast to Coast am a couple of times in an attempt to bring light to the mysterious events, it was not long afterward that she too closed down her blog about the deaths and refused to have any involvement in the cases. She also lost her job as an investigative reporter, though of course it's not known whether this had anything to do with her active investigations; but there are warning signs that keep flagging up for those who attempt to look into it, and this alone causes me to wonder why.

For those interested in learning more and following the continuing, mysterious, perplexing and possibly very sinister cases of missing college men who are being found later dead in rivers, creeks and even shallow ponds, there is an excellent blog, created several years ago by some of the concerned parents, called 'footprints at the river's edge.' It has very significant details of many of the cases. There is also an investigator called Vance Holmes, who runs the blog 'Drowning in Coincidence,' and who has been following these sinister cases from the very beginning, and again has much detailed information on his blog. There is also the very informative 'killing killers blog' too, run by crime investigator and writer Eponymous Rox.

Are all these people wrong in believing something bad is going on?

When Kristi Piehl first appeared on Coast to Coast radio back in 2008, she was joined by forensic pathologist Dr Michael Sikirica to discuss the tragic case of one of the victims, Todd Geib.

As already covered in my *Something in the Woods* book, in Casnovia, Michigan, 22 year old Todd was last seen at a bonfire party in June 2005. It was a marshy rural area. He left the party to walk back alone to his cousin's house, where he lived. He never made it back there. He had called a friend at 12:51 a.m., but all he had said was, "I'm in a field," before the phone call cut off. When the friend rang back, he answered but all the friend could hear was what sounded like the wind.

The area where he was last seen was thoroughly searched three times. During one of the searches, as many as 1,500 volunteers searched the area. Nothing was found. When his body was discovered three weeks later in a remote bed of water, his death was ruled as drowning; however when a new autopsy was carried out, he was discovered to have been dead only 2-5 days, despite being missing for 3 weeks. In other words, he had been somewhere, alive, for approximately two and a half weeks prior to his death. Where he was found had been thoroughly searched at least 3 times.

When the independent pathologist Dr Sikirica was allowed access to the autopsy files, he concluded through forensic analysis that Todd had been dead only between two to five days; and most crucially, he had no water in his lungs; *he could not have drowned,* and his body was not in the condition it would be expected to be in. He had not been in the water for the twenty or so days he had been missing; meaning that he had been held or kept alive somewhere for approximately three weeks, before being taken to the creek.

Dr Sikirica's opinion was backed up by around 200 other examiners, when he presented the case at an international convention of Medical Examiners.

Piehl said of the cases, "A lot of people have asked me, who is doing this? Whoever had Todd, is a sick individual. I think we're going to find a dark human being, of a kind we haven't met yet," said Piehl.

Recapping another case previously covered in my earlier books, Patrick McNeill was the case that first got the attention of the detectives who found the disturbing pattern. He was 21 when he walked out of a bar in New York City on a cold night in February 1997. He told his friends he was taking the subway back to Fordham University. His body was found near a Brooklyn pier nearly two months later. The Pathologist stated he was not drunk when he died of drowning, and two big questions arose. How did he end up dead in the water in Brooklyn? And where had he been for the last two months?

At his inquest, the Pathologist stated he was not drunk but he died of drowning. Another renowned independent Forensic Pathologist Dr. Cyril Wecht however, when reviewing the case for Kristie Piehl, stated, "There's no way this man is accidentally going to fall into a body of water, (and) the fly larvae (found) have been laid in the groin area. It's an indoor fly—not an outdoor fly. So we have a body that was already dead before it was placed in the water...I would call it a homicide, yes."

In other words, the young man had been kept alive for an extended period of time again, prior to being found in the water; long enough for indoor larvae to settle on his body. He had been kept alive somewhere. Kevin Gannon, investigating the McNeill case since

1997, said, "He was stalked, abducted, held for an extended period of time, murdered, and disposed."

Quickly recapping a couple more of the cases already featured in my earlier books before getting to new ones, Chris Jenkins was a very popular student at the University of Minnesota, and he was on the college swim team. He disappeared one night in 2003. When his body was discovered in the Mississippi river four months after he had disappeared, to the police his death looked like an accidental fall after a night of drinking; however, rather disturbingly, his body was found encased in ice, with his hands folded over his chest, in a manner that is wholly inconsistent with the official verdict of drowning. People drowning do not end up in this position. After justified protest from his family, his cause of death was eventually re-determined as a homicide.

Tyler Blalock, 19, was found in Kraut Creek, on Sept. 29, 2012, in the rural Appalachian State University's southeast side of campus, with police saying it looked like he hit his head and fell in. His mother however, could not understand how her son, a lifeguard, could end up dead in a creek in a cold month.

Honour student Jared Dion, again, like the other boys, a popular and athletic person, was discovered, five days after he disappeared, in the river near Wisconsin University in 2004. At a later autopsy, it was found that he had been moved ten hours prior to his death, and that because his body was still in rigor, he could not have been dead any longer than 72 hours, meaning he had been alive for some time prior to his death and had not died the day of his disappearance. That left 2 days unaccounted for, which again implied that he had been kept somewhere and placed in the water later.

Chillingly Piehl & the detectives found over 100 similar victims; Professor Gilbertson found 300; all young men, all very intelligent and high achievers, all actively fit and often even on the Swim Team. Some will say they were drunk and fell in the water, but for anyone looking into the cases and their autopsies, it's hard to believe this is what really happened.

Professor Gilbertson, talking about one of the cases, has stated that the victim's blood was completely drained from his body prior to him being found.

The two detectives think it's got to be more than one killer. Bodies have been found in different States at the same time.

Is it a gang of serial killers? A syndicate of some kind? A cult? An organised group of some kind that has criss-crossed America, travelling to rural college campuses in 25 different cities in a dozen different states in an ever increasing murder spree?

It's fair to say that young men are prone to misadventure after drinking, and there are tragically many documented cases of drowning worldwide; however, they are not usually found in this number or in these particular ways. It would almost seem as though the men are being deliberately targeted. It is hard to believe that so many educated and sporty men would choose to walk way off their usual route, toward rivers, in the winter, alone, and jump in, or fall in.

Why are the bodies returned to the area previously searched? Is it abductor/abductors? Or is it something less easy to define?

Is this all mere speculation, when the deaths could all be a combination of drink and inevitable accidents?

Some have commented that the victims clothes have been tampered with prior to being found, sometimes being put back on their bodies the wrong way, suggesting that they were removed by someone. Others have said that victims are being recovered with their clothes, wallets, and college ID cards, but that any religious necklaces, such as Crosses and St Christopher' they were wearing, were not recovered.

There are several theories being put forward by many interested in the cases, one of which points to the possibility of their deaths being ritual sacrifices, thought to be based on the ancient alchemy ritual of 'Killing of the Kings,' where the victim's life-force energy is said to be passed to the occult murder(s) at the moment of death, supposedly giving them greater power.

In alchemy ritual a solid substance is said to be 'disolved' in water in a 'slow and silent operation.'

Could this really be what is happening? Is some kind of elite group conducting ancient rituals to further enhance their desire for power, as described in more detail in my previous books when discussing the James Downard theory and the Killing of the Kings, and the 'occult line of tragedy,' in connection with the Jamison family water tower and the Elisa Lam water tower deaths?

Or, is this the work of a serial killer, or is it more likely that it's the work of some kind of organized gang? This is the belief of gang stalking expert Professor Gilbertson? That is his opinion, based on thorough scrutiny of the individual cases, the identical victim type, and what he believes is their abduction, confinement and subsequent death by drowning. But, why death by drowning? Why this particular method of killing?

What type of organized gang would be doing this? A group of travelling and highly organised serial killers? A weird fraternity-related cult? A fanatical religious or satanic group? An MK Ultra-style set up? An elite faction at the lower echelons of the illuminati?

And what is their purpose?

One link that really stands out, as previously discussed in my '*Taken in the Woods*' book, is that very often the young men who go missing have been kicked out of clubs and bars and left to wander the streets often without the means of getting home. Often their coats have been left inside the bars, with their keys and wallets inside. There is also very often the common factor that they have been talking on their cell phones when their calls have suddenly been cut off.

With reference to the victim's being kicked out of the bars, is this a case of negligence of duty of care in the case of doormen? Or is there something more sinister going on in terms of collusion and cooperation between them and the as yet unknown and unidentified gang allegedly stalking and abducting these men?

In several cases afterward, it has been found that although the young men were kicked out, there was no evidence of them causing a disturbance or fight, or even being that drunk. In other words, there was no real reason to throw them out. A reason seems to have been *created*.

As previously described in my other book as a clear example, take the case of Shane Montgomery, a student at West Chester who was escorted out of a Bar in Manayunk, PA, on Thanksgiving 2014, after accidentally tripping into the dj deck.

His body was found 5 weeks later in a part of the river close to the bar where search divers had thoroughly and repeatedly searched. The implication here then being that he was not in the river for all of the time that he had been missing. He was also found in water just three to four feet deep, which would seem a little shallow to drown in surely? Unusually in this case, the FBI quickly became involved in the investigation searching for him, and some have asked why they got involved.

Curiously, it has since been reported that the bar involved stated that there was no disturbance inside the bar and he was not escorted out.

And the other case, in March 2006 when an Ohio med student was having drinks with friends to celebrate spring break. During the evening he called his girlfriend to tell her he was looking forward to the trip they were going to take in a couple of day's time.

In the bar he was seen on the security camera at the top of the elevator, but then he moves out of shot. That was the last time he was seen. An emergency exit was covered by camera; he was not picked up on that either.

The only other route would have been to walk through an area of new construction, although tracker dogs did not detect his scent on searching that area. He has still not been found. Brian Shaffer seems almost to have vanished from inside a bar. Despite there being 3 surveillance cameras capturing all people entering and leaving the bar, he was not seen leaving.

Observers have suggested, 'Something else took him right in that bar.'

As also mentioned in 'Taken in the Woods,' in another case, in February 2015, the distraught parents of a young man went to the Newspapers to speak out about their distress, caused by having to endure listening to their son screaming down the phone to them one night in the last moments of his life.

Holding their phone to another phone which was connected to the emergency services operator, they were begging for help to find where there son was and what was going on.

Their son's last moments of life were heard by the emergency dispatcher but not recorded, contrary to standard operating procedure, due to the recording equipment not working.

The officer later resigned over the matter, upset that it had added to the parents distress. The parents do not feel that the subsequent disappearance of their son was investigated to the extent to which they would have found acceptable.

The police say they are still trying to piece together what might have happened to him, his body having been discovered dead in the Ship Canal three weeks later.

The 21 year old student and volunteer Civic Centre worker had been on a night out with friends. He was last seen at a music event at a racetrack in Manchester city centre, England.

In the early hours of the next morning, his parents were concerned that he had not come home and called him.

His Mother told reporters, "We rang him and when he answered he was incoherent. I could barely make out what he was saying. There was no noise in the background and it struck me that he was on his own. Minutes into the call he started screaming. He was howling and yelling. It was horrific."

While she called the police, her husband took over the phone. He was still screaming.

"It was a howl. I raised my voice at him to try to get him to snap out of it, but I couldn't get through to him. Then suddenly there was silence. There was a total silence, and it was so eerie."

The problem was that they couldn't really do anything because they couldn't find out from him where he was; they couldn't go to his aid.

That phone call was the last anyone heard from him. He was found dead three weeks later in the Canal.

It was later suggested that David Plunkett had been asked to leave the music event, where all alcohol had been free, for being inebriated. Indeed the coroner then wrote to the event organisers, admonishing them for simply evicting someone from an event which they were responsible for, rather then ensuring a duty of care was provided to someone if they became drunk.

When the police tracked his mobile phone records later, it was determined that he'd been a couple of miles outside of the City centre, not near the canals.

At the inquest, the police dispatcher who took the call from the parents described her own trauma from the night's events.

"I took a very distressing 999 call. He was in a distressed state but his parents couldn't hear anything other than his screaming. I stayed on with them for well over an hour, trying to provide assistance for them and him. The incident haunts me still and with each and every new death I see in the news I am more and more convinced that these are not accidents; these are murders."

The death was classified as accidental drowning. His parents clearly disagree with this verdict. They know only too well that he was terrified of something so horrifying he could not even articulate it to them. Whatever he saw was so chilling he could not find the words.

His mother, a former Head Teacher, spoke out, "It is not a case of 'young man drinks too much, falls in canal.' Someone is responsible for his death and the version of events that have been given are simply not adding up, and the case leaves many more questions than answers. He could have been attacked, he could have had his drink spiked; anything.."

This next case in the U.S., again also previously mentioned, bears similarities. Student Daniel Zamlen was reported as a missing person on April 5th 2009. He'd been at a party but his friends who were at the party said that he had left on his own to meet up with another friend at Minnesota University.

They say he was talking with them on his cell phone and was near the Mississippi River Boulevard and St Clair Avenue. Quickly bloodhounds, a helicopter and searchers covered the area where he had been walking, but found no trace of him.

Bloodhounds seemed to get partial hits on his scent near the river, but his father maintains that they kept stopping in the same place, and did but did not actually go near the river. He also said that his own job was as an open pit miner and he understood land, and when he walked that area, he did not believe that someone could just accidently slip into the water there; but if they did, he said it would have left marks and none were found.

In what is one of the most disturbing phone calls, reminiscent of the call received by the parents in Manchester, his friend Anna says she was talking to him when he began to become distressed. By then she says she had left the party and got in her car to go and find him.

'It took a really bad turn,' she told newspapers at the time, "Where are you?" she asked him.

"Oh, my gosh, Help!" – "This was the last thing I heard," she says. "His voice became distant as he said those words, as though he was moving away his phone, and then the line went dead."

She called him back but it just remained unanswered she claims.

It has to be said, his parents have spoken out about the accuracy of statements made by his friends, particularly disputing the content of his last known call.

Disturbingly his Mother also reported that there's significant evidence the drinks at the party had been spiked.

His body was found a month later in the river. A baseball was found near the scene with a smiley face on it, as well as a sign that was marked with smiley face graffiti near the edge.

It was discovered that some of the drinks at the party had been laced with the drug GHB.

His mother has stated "Victims of drowning usually surface within six and ten days after the drowning. The River was flowing four hundred times faster than normal yet Dan's body didn't surface for another 27 days and flowed only two miles."

She says, "The Coroner could not determine 100% that he did drown; just that that was where he was found."

Crucially, she also reports that the night before he disappeared, he was at a Club in the centre of town. He was thrown out because he was not wearing the right wristband.

She says, "He was separated from his friends and later he told his friends that he was approached by men outside. He said that he "ran" from these people. Sound familiar? Maybe he was supposed to have his 'tragic accident' that night, but even though "very intoxicated" he was able to out run these people."

In another bizarre case, college student Mike Knoll was celebrating his birthday with friends in a bar in

Wisconsin. It was November 2002 and just after 11.30pm when he walked out of the Bar. He'd been drinking but he wasn't thought by his friends to have been drunk, but for some indefinable reason he wandered into an old lady's home.

She asked him what he was doing and he quickly left her house; but one has to wonder, if he wasn't drunk when he left, how did he manage to become so confused and disoriented as to enter a person's home that he did not know, when he lived in college dorms?

When someone becomes suddenly confused and disoriented it's easy to blame drink but if that's the case why wasn't he like that in the Bar, before he left? Thoughts could then turn to the possibility of drugs being involved, but none of his friends knew him to be a drug taker. Were drugs somehow slipped in his drink perhaps? Or did he encounter someone after he left?

His body was found four months later in the frozen Half Moon Lake. He was half in and half out of the water, which in itself seems highly strange. Where had he been in all those months? The lake had been searched thoroughly several times when he disappeared. His body had no sign of injury. The location was no-where near where he lived or where he had been drinking.

There was a similar case again in Manchester, England, in June 2012. Chris Brahmy had been to a rock concert on the outskirts of Manchester with a group of friends and after it finished he decided to go into the City Centre to retrieve a new pair of trainers he'd hidden earlier in a car park rather than carry then at the concert all night.

CCTV this time captures over ten minutes of his journey, from retrieving the trainers in a shopping bag to carrying them through street after street in the city centre.

He can clearly be watched walking in a perfectly capable and coherent manner through the streets from around 1.45am until the last CCTV camera films him walking through a passage.

He is not stumbling or wandering around without co-ordination. In other words, he does not appear at all inebriated or under the influence of drugs.

Ten days later, his body is found in the Canal. What the police still do not know is how he ended up in the canal, which at the spot where he was thought to have entered the water, is a high railing that would have required climbing.

"While CCTV follows his movements, we still cannot say how or why he died," the police said.

The spot in which he died was not covered by CCTV. The police also made it clear they had no evidence leading it to be considered suspicious, despite the fact that the coroner found him to have a fractured cheekbone, bruising and cuts to his face.

There were traces of alcohol in his body, and indeed the drug MDMA. Clearly, one could argue the drug caused him to climb up the fence, and jump over it into the canal, although it does beg the question how he managed to find his shoes and walk so capably through the city centre for quite some time without any signs at all of being influenced and made incapable by a drug? Did he encounter someone in the canal area who offered him the drug? Did the drug then make him jump into the canal? Or was he placed into the canal?

Interestingly, the forensic pathologist Ms Carter stated that because the injuries he had sustained had no bruising, they would have happened *after* his death not prior to his death.

In other words, this ruling would imply that he died or was killed without these injuries, then suffered the injuries afterwards. He didn't experience the injuries as a result of throwing himself in the water in a desire to commit suicide. And if the injuries occurred after death, he didn't not inflict them himself.

When I was talking to Professor Gilbertson, he raised concerns that the unexplained phenomenon of identikit young men ending up dead seemed to have spread to England too. Professor Gary Jackson, head of Psychology at the University of Birmingham, England has also officially joined the growing number of people who are perturbed, alarmed, and feel there is something more sinister at play than accidental drowning after more than 65 men in the last five years have been found dead in the canals and ponds of the Northern City of Manchester.

Talking to the broadsheet The Telegraph, he says, "The number is far higher than one would expect and from the data I just don't believe these were suicides; canals are not a popular site for suicide, and people rarely choose this for their method; but they make for ideal grounds for predators. Many of the reports from the coroners are inconclusive."

Professor Jackson, having accessed freedom of information reports regarding many of the deaths, has come to a grim conclusion. He doesn't believe they were accidents.

Pointedly he adds, "If you're trying to commit suicide by drowning, it's very hard to do in a canal- unless you can weigh yourself down with something heavy."

Some of the deaths it seems have clearly indicated that something else might be going on other than an innocent accidental fall into the canals.

He also points to the very clear victimology - they were all young males. He says there is a clear connection between the cases from the fact that the in at least 48 of the cases, the bodies were so badly decomposed as to be impossible to identify. This links them together connectively in his opinion.

If these victims were being randomly pushed in by someone vindictive, they would not all be successful attempts. At some point, one of the victims would fight, struggle, and not drown. People would soon hear about it. No-one has come forward to say this has happened to them, although doubtless the dark and dimly lit canals are excellent places for drug deals, and muggings.

If they were all cases of criminal attempts and 'success' by psychopathic muggers, why is it not happening in Cambridge, another University town with canals, or Universities by the sea, of which there are many, such as Bournemouth or Brighton?

Not only that, but with Newspaper reports carrying images of police teams being able to walk through some stretches of the canals because the water is not even knee deep, it does beg the question how could they all so easily drown in shallow water?

The canals of Manchester run through parts of the city centre, mainly the old industrial parts but also quite close to very busy nightclubs and bars. Manchester is both a thriving University town and has a popular Gay Village, and every night, bars are packed with drinkers.

Many will inevitably on occasion drink too much, some will as a result have accidents, however the canals are not obvious routes to take. They are not renovated scenic canals; rather they are dimly lit, strewn with litter and damp.

They aren't a short cut to anywhere and they aren't a route home. They're not somewhere anyone would go for a pleasant walk.

Yet some of the deaths have clearly indicated that something else might be going on other than an innocent accidental fall into the canals.

In the next case, a swear word uttered in what was both surprise and shock was the last thing his father heard, ending a fifty minute telephone call as his father kept him on the telephone, trying to find him.

His son had called him late that evening to say he'd run his car into a dried mud bank and couldn't get it out; it was stuck and he'd asked his parents to come and get him.

It was May 2008 and student Brandon had been driving home to Marshall in Minnesota; a rural and mainly agricultural county comprised mainly of canals and wind projects. In fact, he'd just completed a technical college course in wind turbines.

After waiting for a while for his parents to turn up he became impatient when they told him on the phone that they were having trouble locating him. He told him he was going to walk toward the nearest town, whose lights he said were in the distance and said that he expected them to meet him en-route.

However, it would seem that perhaps Brandon was slightly off in his description of where he thought he was, because no matter how hard his parents looked for him, they couldn't locate him or his car.

He continued walking on toward the lights in the distance as his parents searched for him, now well after midnight, and they stayed in contact throughout, with his Father keeping him talking on the telephone.

Brandon was certain he knew where he was and he couldn't understand why his parents couldn't find him and he was becoming increasingly irritated; yet his parents had gone to exactly where he said he was and he was definitely not there. They continued to drive around the roads, unable to see him or his car, and then came the swear word in which he sounded suddenly surprised and shocked, and the phone cut off.

It didn't sound like he had fallen over or tripped up; it sounded like he was shocked by something, even horrified by something; but by what?

Whatever it was, Brandon did not answer his telephone again, despite his father constantly calling his number back. Now his parents were concerned. He wasn't answering his phone for some reason and they had no idea what had just happened to him, where he was, or what might be happening to him still.

Desperately they continued to drive around, urgently trying to find his location, and get him to answer his phone, and in fact they proceeded to spend several hours that early morning desperately looking for him, yet still they failed to spot any sign of him.

Around dawn they called the police and a search for the missing student was immediately initiated. It wasn't until the following day that the police were able to locate his missing car, by tracing signals received at cell phone towers from his cell phone.

The car was in fact nearly twenty miles from the town the boy had thought he'd been heading toward on foot. He'd told his parents that he was close to the town when he'd called them to come get him. That was why they couldn't find him that night. He'd been nearly twenty miles away from where he thought he was. He'd thought that the lights he could see on the horizon were the town but he was wrong, he was many miles from the town, and so while his parents had gone to that location, he had been wandering around miles away from them.

That explained why they couldn't find him, but it didn't explain why he could not be found now. The search party could not find him, or his cell phone.

What investigators started to believe was that he'd accidently walked into and then fallen into the river as he was talking to his father. That could explain his shock, they thought.

His father wasn't convinced. He said he may have had a drink, and according to the friends he'd been with that evening, he had been drinking but definitely not enough for him to have been drunk, and his father said he didn't sound drunk throughout the phone conversation that lasted almost an hour. It didn't seem plausible that he could fall in and not get out.

Despite an exhaustive search of both the water and the land however, he could not be found. Searchers said the river was flowing fast at the time and could have swept him away, but the water was extensively searched and they could not find his body.

The searches included aerial searches, horseback, ATV and many friends and volunteers on foot. They looked repeatedly over the ground. After the official searches ended, his family, along with volunteers didn't give up however, and continued to look for him for weeks.

The only clue came from the K9 search dogs that seemed to indicate that his scent had travelled in one particular direction, but that did not lead to finding his body as the scent stopped. However perhaps that was a clue that he couldn't have gone in the water after all.

What did hamper the search efforts, particularly the ability to track his scent, is that the area by its geographical nature is one of criss-crossing winds that break up the flow of scent.

It was possible that he'd succumbed to hypothermia, especially if he'd walked through wet grass and been out in the cold for hours, but it was May, not winter, and even so, they still should have been able to find his body.

Did his call, which ended so abruptly in shock, indicate that he had somehow become the victim of foul play? Had someone arrived there at the scene? Had they abducted him? Was that why his body was never found?

His heartbroken mother talked to news channels after the incident. "He wasn't injured. He said he was ok, no damage to his car. He felt confident about where he was and he was saying that we were lost. The minute the call dropped I became sick. I knew; I knew it was wrong and I knew it was bad."

Brandon Swanson is still missing.

Another man named Brandon, is Brandon Lawson, a 27 year old male who made a desperate call to 911 for help.

He was just off the highway outside of Bronte, Texas, when he called the police. It was August 2013 and just after midnight. He'd gone out for a drive to get some air, leaving his wife and children at home. Shortly after, he ran out of gas and he phoned his brother to ask him to come and help him.

While awaiting the arrival of his brother however, something happened that's hard to understand. He called 911, in some kind of trouble.

He tells them he's run out of gas and that he's in the woods just off the highway. It's hard to understand his exact words in the 911 call, but many who have heard it believe it's something along these lines;

"I got chased into the woods," or "There's guys chasing me in the woods."

He continues saying something that sounds like;

"Pushed some guy over. I accidently ran into them. I'm not speaking to them. I'm in the middle of a field. I ran into somebody. There is one car here. Got taken through the woods. Please hurry, please help."

He mentions other cars, other people, but again it's very hard to decipher although it's still on YouTube to listen to. Who were the other guys? What was going on?

That night, there was a lot of confusion. The police didn't turn up despite him saying he needed the police, not an ambulance, and asking them to "Please hurry."

A state trooper did arrive at the truck by chance, when he was driving by and saw it abandoned on the highway, but this was unrelated to the 911 call. His brother and his wife also arrived on the scene with a gas can.

The man in trouble called his brother while they were standing with the Trooper, but the signal was really bad and his brother could barely hear what was being said. He did hear the words, "I'm in a field," and that he said he was bleeding, but he automatically assumed that his brother was hiding out from the police because he'd just learnt he had an outstanding minor warrant.

Neither his brother and wife, nor the Trooper were aware of his call for help to the 911 dispatchers.

Obviously now in hindsight his brother realises that he was asking for help and was in trouble, but he didn't hear him properly at the time.

Since then there has been no sign of him. He has not been seen since.

The next day his family and the state troopers began searching for him when it was understood that he hadn't returned home.

An aerial search with infrared and a grid foot search were carried out. Later, cadaver dogs were brought in, but nothing was found of the man. Texas SAR did thorough and extensive searches in the area looking for any sign of him, in case he had got lost and lay injured, or had died out there.

According to his wife however, his last cell phone ping was received three miles from the area, and perhaps outside of the area at first searched. However, he still has not been found. No body, no clothes, no car keys or wallet; no trace of him.

His disappearance is truly a mystery, as is who was with him and possibly chasing him that night. He said in the 911 call that he was being chased by men in the woods. Who were the men and why were they chasing him?

When the Trooper and his brother arrived at his truck there were no other cars or trucks pulled over beside his. His own truck showed no signs of a collision or accident, so when he said he "ran into them," he didn't mean that he had an accident while in the car.

What does seem likely is that if he called 911 for help, he wasn't in fact hiding from the Cops in the woods. He'd called them himself asking for help.

Where did the car go that he said was near him when he called 911? Where did the men go? Why were they chasing him? What did they do to him? If he was bleeding, as he told his brother, why did the search dogs not pick up on his blood scent?

What happened out there in the dark that night?

His disappearance remains a complex and disturbing mystery, and his family have reportedly spent all of their savings trying to find him.

WISC-TV Madison Chanel 3000 reported on the disappearance of 22-year-old Josh Snell who vanished in June, 2005 in Eau Claire. His brother told reporters he had been in town to attend a wedding and that afterward, his brother had gone with friends to some bars in town. Four days later his brother's body was pulled from the Chippewa River. His brother said he does not believe his brother 'just wandered into the water.'

He went missing on the same day as Todd Geib, and Josh's last contact seems to have been when he called a friend late that night with a disturbing message.

In a phone call with a friend, "he said he was scared, that he was hiding in some brush, that he was running from someone. He said he didn't know who it was, or how he was going to get away. He said he didn't do anything, but he was terrified and he was scared for his life," Jon Snell says.

Another source quotes, "He called a friend to say that he thought unknown people were following him and that he might be in trouble with the police." The

Local police said they had no contact with Snell however.

Are these young men being hunted via their cell phones? Chosen somehow and tracked via the signals given out from their cell phones?

S. Ward's brother also died in mysterious and suspicious circumstances. "Walton was last seen alive at Landsharks Bar, Indianapolis, with a 'bouncer' at approximately 1:20-1:30 am on October 12, 2012. His last attempt to save his own life was at 1:30 am when he dialled 911 from his Phone for help. His killers interrupted his 911 call and murdered him...He knew he was going to be killed. His desperate call lasted for 1-second which was just enough to register to the nearest cell phone tower...but it wasn't not long enough to save his life."

"That was the last time we know him to be alive, until the Construction workers discovered his body on October 22, 2012, floating in the River a few blocks from the bar (less than a mile) 10 days after his desperate call to 911 on that night. His phone was found on the bank of the River behind a Restaurant. The police said he must have been 'drunk', 'fallen in' or 'gone swimming' in the dead of winter."

Interviewed by crime writer, Eponymous Rox of the Killing Killers Blog Spot, his mother said,

"Where he was found, the depth was two feet. He was going (to the Bar) to meet a young woman he'd been talking with on OkCupid.com dating website. She didn't show up. She said she was from Brownsburg, Indiana. He said that she was in college and planning to become a lawyer. One odd thing that he mentioned about her was that she told him she'd got a college scholarship for wrestling. Looking into this, I have not been able to find any school that has a women's wrestling program. The Indianapolis PD did not question her and still have not had their cyber unit complete that part of the investigation."

"He had met up with her in the week prior to the night (he disappeared) and said that she'd come to meet him with a few friends, to make it more of a laid-back group. They were not going on a dinner-type date, it was more of a casual situation where they could hang out and get to know each other. It seemed to make sense that she was probably being cautious, as a young woman meeting up with a man that she met online. That Friday night, I understood that he would be meeting her and her same friends he'd met the other night."

His mother's testimony would appear to offer a couple of very intriguing possibilities; while a glance at college scholarships offered for women at colleges shows there are some, the statistics given of the percentage of female high school Wrestlers who go on to compete in college is just 3%. That's a tiny number. In a post on IndianaMat.com, which is a place 'to give people involved with wrestling in the state of Indiana promotion,' there's a post which says, "I'm a coach for Brownsburg MS (the area which the girl online said she was in school) My 8th grader is looking for scholarship opportunities. I was wondering if you have any advice?" It would seem then that they are not easy to come by then perhaps?

It was an online correspondence initially between the girl wrestler and the victim, until they met in person. Was it really a woman he was talking to, or was it perhaps a man pretending to be a woman who had been corresponding with him, who had slipped up when he said he had a wrestling scholarship? Is this a vital clue of a 'group' involvement? If so; why? And if so, who is behind this group? It's extremely unlikely that a young group like this could be planning and carrying out nationwide abductions and murders, Remembering that sometimes young men have gone missing in different states in the same manner on the same night; were this group who showed up the first time to meet her son, somehow recruited to play a key role, possibly like some of the bouncers too?

His date and her friends never showed up. While he was seen in other bars in the street and on CCTV in the bars, and while he left alone, his father says to journalist Eponymous Rox, "I believe he was murdered on the basis of his 911 call being at 1:40 am, terminated within a second. He was in excellent physical condition, capable of getting out of three feet of water, and, he was visiting from California and was not familiar with the area and accessible paths to the canal." (In other words, his father means, why would he have gone down to the canal if he didn't even know it was there?)

His mother says, "My conclusion is someone, (probably more than one) was with him. It's very suspicious and illogical that a very healthy, strong, trained athlete 'fell' and drowned in three feet of water on his own."

The same family have also written an article on their website, dedicated to the mystery of their own son's death, with regards to another young man. "Coincidence?" they ask, of the circumstances surrounding the death of another boy, Joshua Swalls, (whose Toxicology reports later came back to show that he was not drunk nor under the influence of recreational drunks) when the 22 year old also vanished, not far from where their son did, and was subsequently found dead three weeks later in a retention pond that had already been searched by police divers after he went missing.

He disappeared three weeks after their son, and had vanished from outside of a friend's apartment, leaving his car keys, wallet and phone inside. Ward's family say, "So now there are 2 men that go missing within 3 weeks and 2 miles of each other and are later found dead in bodies of water. Obviously, the police have to consider the possibility that something is wrong here, right? Wrong. The police say again; a case of "drunk and fell in."

However, that night Josh had not had anything to drink before going to his friend's apartment. He stayed just over 35 minutes and did drink at his friends, but as the later autopsy shows, he didn't have enough alcohol in his system to be classified as drunk. The biggest problem his family see is how and why the young man managed to get to where he did.

Ward's family too say, "To get into that pond, he would have to scale a 6 foot fence. How then, after he had enough coordination and presence of mind to figure out how to get into that pond, did he become so incapacitated that he didn't realize he was walking into freezing water and suddenly forgot how to swim? Does this not sound crazy to anyone else?"

In 2011, Mike Shaw wrote of the grief, anger and sense of helplessness that he felt because he could not save his best friend. "Sly McCurry did not walk out onto the ice of Lake Superior (Wisconsin) that cold January (2010) winter night and fall through and drown. He was murdered. No one can ever convince me it was anything but murder. He would never have went from the Nightclub to that secluded area alone in 20 degrees below weather, with no coat, and drown. He had no car and after being thrown out of the club via the back door, on the alleged grounds that he was drunk, he was left in the alleyway."

Crucially, he adds that his best friend was not very likely to have decided to 'go for a swim,' not only because it was the middle of winter, but also because he had cut a finger the same day while at work as a junior chef. His finger was in a bandage and had a splint on it.

Tracker dogs traced his scent at an exit door of the hotel he was staying in but it led no-where after that. This was done two days after he disappeared.

Late in May, four months later, his body was found in the lake. Mike points out, "His hotel was two blocks from the club; his body was found in the Tower Bay slip, nine blocks in the opposite direction."

Clearly then, the overt implication again is that he did not voluntarily go to that destination.

Says Mike, "Like clockwork, I see this killer(s) strike all over the North-eastern United States."

There are so many cases that have been mentioned in my previous books and that could be covered in this book; and they continue to happen, and the links to all the cases seem to be that the victims are separated from their friends, and often make a distressed telephone call.

What are the young men seeing moments before their phone calls get cut off? Who is taking them? And why?

What is happening? Is some kind of elite group conducting ancient alchemical rituals to further enhance their desire for dark power? It's not beyond the realms of possibility, and we don't have to believe in this arcane power; it's whether others believe in it that matters.

There are also recorded cases of a catholic college harbouring convicted sex molesters within their own clergy in one part of the country where a disproportionately high number of cases have happened, and allegations that two boy's scents led to the doors of the college, despite one of the victim's not having been in the area at all before disappearing. However, this doesn't cover all the other cases state-wide and possibly internationally.

On the other hand, as Professor Gilbertson and the detectives feel, this is a more organised form of 'terrorism,' by some kind of group intent on sending a message. What exactly that message is, who the group are, and why this specific victim-type is selected no-one knows.

The likelihood is that it's not 'serial killers' in the most commonly understood meaning of the term, but rather, something more sinister, more organised, and perhaps at a much higher level. Again, if it were serial killers, they would need to be able to be in more than one location at the same time, as sometimes incidents occur in separate states on the same night. There have been suggestions that it has something to do with College fraternities; but the deaths take place nationwide. On the other hand, it would be possible to co-ordinate.

Are the bouncers or bar staff, nearby construction workers, or cab drivers involved? Some think the police are complicit or directly involved. Theories from speculators across internet platforms over the years, on social media and in articles, are wide and ranging, and perhaps it's all hysteria; but the families and the previously mentioned experts don't think it is. They think there are far too many commonalities.

There are elements in the cases which could lead to a conspiracy theory that it's organised by an MK Ultra-style project and that the killers are doing this under instruction, as part of either their initiation or on-going training as 'assassins' for their masters, who are well hidden behind the smoke and mirrors. Researchers such as David McGowan and his book 'Programmed to Kill,' clearly provided allegations of possible serial killer assassins who have been created, manipulated and programmed long before now.

On the other hand, a cursory glance on forums that talk about these drowning deaths will show that there are many who look into the numerology aspects of it, or the names of the victims. They indicate and attempt to prove for example, that these victims are chosen and that a combination of the letters in their names and the places they are either taken from or found in, often spell out very intricate messages from the killers, drawn from ancient texts, movies, art and literature. The suggested clues are complex and would require months and months of analysis to verify if there really is anything to this idea. Is it a possibility? Certainly, but it's hard to prove.

If that were to be proven however, it would indicate that the killers are both highly educated and very intelligent. Some have posited that the killers are therefore from an elite 'hunting' group; from elite secret societies along the lines of such groups as 'the skull and bones' or a sub-strata of the illuminati.

As just one example, in a wordpress blog no longer available, but quoted in various forums, 'someone' has pointed out that the word NEMEC can be found from the first letters of the location in which several victims were found;

New London, Daniel Newville, (August 2002)

Eau Claire, Craig Burrows, (September 2002)

Minneapolis, Chris Jenkins, (October 2002)

Eau Claire, Michael Noll, (November 2002)

Collegeville, Josh Guimond, (November 2002)

Why is this possibly relevant? Well, in their opinion, this could apply to the name of an actor, Colin Nemec. He played the role of the true story of a boy called Steven Stayner. Coincidently, he was mentioned in my 'Mysterious things in the Woods' book, for the reason that after he was abducted as a child, his brother turned into a serial killer, who hunted, abducted and killed women in the Yosemite national park. In 1999, three female tourists had vanished from their rooms at the Cedar Lodge while in the park on a hiking trip. A few months later, they were found, brutally murdered in the woods.

Five months later, Joie Armstrong, 26, a naturalist at the Yosemite Institute, also went missing. Her truck was still parked in the driveway of her home at her cabin. Her body was found in the woods, not far from the cabin.

A park employee had noticed a car parked near her cabin on the night of her disappearance, and police issued an alert for the car. A few days later, police spotted the car parked up near Merced River Canyon. They came across a man wandering naked. He said his name was Cary Stayner and that he worked as a handyman at Cedar Lodge. After the encounter, investigators compared the car tyres to tyre tracks found at the crime scene, and they matched. The police found Stayner and arrested him. He confessed quickly and readily to all of the killings.

His own family history astonishingly revealed a disturbing crime perpetrated against his younger brother, and perhaps was what shaped him into becoming a serial killer.

At the age of seven, his brother had disappeared without trace one afternoon in 1972, while walking home from school alone along the Yosemite Highway. Eight years later, Cary had heard an announcement on the radio that his brother had been found. It turned out that his brother had been abducted by a paedophile and former employee of the Yosemite Lodge, and kept prisoner for all of those years. Investigators wondered if Cary's homicidal behaviour had been caused perhaps by his own family's experience.

Colin Nemec played the role of the young brother in the subsequent movie. Nemec talks about Cary Stayner in the book The Yosemite Murders. Nemec is also mentioned in the book *I Know My First Name Is Steven*, which talks about the abduction.

In the case of the person who posted this NEMEC theory, they link it to the ATWA movement of Charles

Manson, with ATWA being the acronym he created standing for Air, Trees, Water, Animals and All the Way Alive; an ecological term the group designated to identify 'the forces of life which hold the balance of the earth.' With his small group of followers, prior to being imprisoned, it was Manson's attempt at eco living, though others say it was survivalist living.

In this case, the poster's theory, explained on themanyfacesofthezodiac.com/2013/04/07/charles-manson-link-to-smiley-face-murders/ follows through with the belief that the college killings are a continuation of the Manson group, and that they are examples of mind-controlled, programmed individuals. "The Manson Family through ATWA has grown to a point now where I am sure even the FBI does not know the number."

His implication is that the group never went away with Manson's imprisonment; it carried on. Interestingly, this does tie in with David McGowan's position and his alleged research findings. He says that Mason's house was at one point in the same neighbourhood as Boy's Town, which was identified as an underground paedophile abduction ring during the Franklin Scandal (as referenced in 'Taken in the Woods' with regard to the Johnny Gosh abduction case). According to McGowan, researcher Joel Norris makes the allegation that Manson was involved in a murder for hire ring and child pornography. He also alleges that he uncovered his association with a satanic cult involved in sacrifice and murder. McGowan also states that another researcher, Ed Sanders, on interviewing Manson's associates, alleges that he was involved in the production of snuff movies. The theories go further, claiming that Manson was allegedly mind-controlled by the CIA through the use of drugs and programming, but it's not for this book to go that deep into things related to this and go way off topic. However, the idea is that this 'group' are in fact 'mind controlled assassins' who hunt the selected targeted male college victims.

Is any of this at all in any way relevant? Or is it all just insane ramblings and attempts to form theories from random coincidences found in words and letters?

According to the person who found this connection, their belief is "'NEMEC' was being formed at the exact same time he (Stayner) was on trial for murder and making big headlines in the newspapers." In other words, it was pre-determined and being carried out now, if not much before these drowning cases came to be noticed. The chances are then, they go back a lot more than a few years.

Is this delusional? Or is it an example of what this alleged unknown organised group of killers could be, and their sending out a message, 'hidden in plain sight? Is this all an absurd over-stretch to even try to see connections where there may be none? Very possibly, and patterns can be found anywhere if you look hard enough among the statistics. Statistics can be manipulated to back up findings. Micro-patterns appear that can be misleading when viewed as a whole.

That is just one of the theories however, for what it is worth; but there are many more, such is the mystery of these drowning deaths. They could be entirely misleading, or they really could be a sign, a message, hidden in plain sight, as per the methods used by such enigmatic and elusive groups as the supposed illuminati or lower echelons of.

Could it be part of an ongoing MK Ultra? When investigated, the program had consisted of 149 'subprojects' which the Agency had contracted out to various *Universities* and institutions. Is it still going strong?

Is it some kind of water boarding hazing initiation? Which goes too far, deliberately, to implicate those involved and serving as a perfect blackmail tool to use to keep them in the 'frat' or secret society for life?

The theories go on and on, and could fill numerous books and still be complete nonsense, although they do show how many people are so convinced that something sinister is indeed going on that they are prepared to dedicate extensive amounts of time trying to solve it. Sadly for now however, there is no clear answer. Or is it just simply misadventure and drowning? That is for the reader to decide.

Why are there no unsuccessful attempts? Why are there never any witnesses? Or are there?

Worryingly, no-one has ever yet seen them being abducted, and there are never any witnesses to the crime. Or are there?

One possible 'witness' has written to killing killers website, "I didn't make much of it at the time and didn't still until I moved to Minnesota and met a friend of one of the victims. When I was in college, in October 2000 I was found blacked out and vomiting. My memory is hazy but I'd met this guy who wanted me to follow him to another party. We walked on for several blocks and I kept asking where we were going. At first I was expecting the TKE house (Tau Kappa Epsilon Fraternity) but he said no. I asked if he was on the football team and he said no. He wouldn't tell me our destination. After a few more blocks I said I'd had enough and went home. In retrospect, where we were walking was toward the river that cut across campus, before I'd left him and gone… Made me scratch my head a little.'

Again, is his story true, or accurate? Although why would he make it up? There are other similar posts about men who say they have been separated by a group of both young men and women who they have met in bars. One of them talks about thinking something had been slipped into his drink and then resisted being pushed inside a van while walking along the street afterward. Another describes a man following him and then a van driving up fast and blocking his exit. There are numerous potential stories like this if they are looked for hard enough. Are these people just jumping on the bandwagon? Are any of these accounts true? Possibly they are.

Another weird account reads as follows, from a while before the current killings started, implying they could have been occurring a lot longer than perhaps realized.

"I attended high school in 1960, 1961 and 1962 in New York City. I have a strange story. A school mate Michael who I had lunch with is what this story is about..

Some things I definitely remember but generally some facts are vague to me. I definitely remember standing in front of the academic building at lunch time and speaking to Michael.

He said he had a boat and wanted me to go for a boat ride with him. (He may have indicated he had some friend that would also be there). He and his friends..

I believe prior to this meeting he had asked me what religion I was and I said Jewish.

I believe he confirmed this (insistently) once or twice.. At some point I believe he asked me if I could swim, also was I good swimmer..I would have said yes a good swimmer.

Michael then asked me to meet them in a specific location by the water in Brooklyn or Queens (one or the other).He said you know where that is and how to get there, I said no.. Then he asked about one or two more locations. I said no; he said take this train and that train; I said no, I am from the Bronx and I would get lost. Well he asked me, do I know any desolate area in Brooklyn or Queens? I said no. How about the Bronx? I said yes City Island, Orchard Beach.

He thought about it but said he wouldn't know how to get home from there.

Here is where the story gets strange. Michael says to me "never mind, there's no boat," ... "we were going to lure you there and kill you! You are going to get me in a lot of trouble with my family" he said! "I was supposed to bring you there and kill you and now I am in trouble with my family." I was still trying to have lunch with him as he walked away mad at me because he was now going to get in trouble for not bringing the (prey) to the water edge!!!! and don't I understand. At the time other than losing a friend (lunch buddy) this immediately rolled of my back like water on a ducks back and I did not think about it (or talk about it) for over 50 years...until now."

His story doesn't make a lot of sense in terms of the victims now and why such a group, if it existed, would be hunting and killing them as prey; but then it doesn't have to make sense to us; just them.

'*TheyDontSee*' posted on a facebook interest group,

"It's a group, both men and women, and government involved. It's co-ordinated. Victims aren't snatched; they're tricked then forcibly pulled into a van and subdued. It's serious (spiritual/occult) yet it's a game too. They use the internet to communicate but not 'publicly' on it. They're kept alive and groomed; brainwashing, mental torture, (not physically). They have existed for decades. On the east it's killing with a gun, then they decided it was 'safer' to do it this way and they're right; we're still looking for them.."

Is this from an insider into some of the investigations? Or, just a guess? Of course, there's every chance that some of the messages and opinions posted on the internet are from those within the groups itself. They are probably monitoring and reading it all.

Tomich Carpenter, a former private detective, started a spreadsheet, gathering data to analyze for possible patterns. He believes he has found several similarities between the drowned men. 'I believe these students attended 'public' seminars and anyone interested were asked to stay after the meeting to learn more. That is where the recruitment started.

Later people turned up drowned to scare those already indoctrinated to remain in.' It's a good theory. (Or, alternately perhaps, those who wanted no part of it but now knew too much about the existence of this recruiting 'group' were the ones killed-off.) 'These young men would fit into any community they were assigned to, to await further instruction. Money could be enticement' (or perhaps, status and recognition of their abilities as scholars and sportsmen initially could have been the hook that attracted them) 'and death could be punishment. Those that did not turn up drowned are living in other communities with new identities. This is a national security issue and I believe black ops is involved.'

Well, again, it's not beyond the realms of possibility. The deaths and the subsequent theories will continue until something is done to stop them.

Another post from a recent graduate of engineering, writes, "I live in Wisconsin. The night I'm about to describe has nagged at me for almost two years now.. I tried to ignore it but as one who always trusts my gut..

While still in school I was at a bar one night not far from the house I was living in at the time. I used to like to go the bar and do my homework. I know this sounds odd but I can tune out my surroundings.

I always sat at one end of the bar and worked on advanced math. This night I could feel someone's eyes, and looking up I saw a man sitting across from me. He was dressed very nice. We made eye contact and shivers went down my spine, but I went back to my work.

A few minutes later I felt alarmed, as unbeknown to me the man had came and was sat right next to me. (There were other empty seats along the bar.) He attempted small talk. I told him I was in engineering school. This really got his interest, and he kept asking more and more questions. He seemed very impressed that I held a 3.5 GPA again it really aroused his interest. I presumed he must be gay and trying to hit on me. I answered his questions bluntly, trying to end the conversation. It did not end. He kept trying to make talk and buy me drinks. After I kept refusing my guard really started to go up. He'd told me he wasn't from round here but travelled through for business; then his story changed to having friends close-by and did I want to go to there and smoke pot with him. I did smoke pot; but I hadn't told him that and he looked real square. All my radars were going off.

Eventually, I went to the bathroom and slipped out the back door. A few months later I stumbled upon the murder theories and chills went down my spine. After much consideration I contacted the investigators and told them. I said I could give a good description for a police sketch, but nothing happened and they never contacted me again.

The guy was creepy on so many different levels...and on a side note, the bar is just down from a secluded park by the river....'

Another lead or just another strange story? Who was the smartly dressed man; and were there more like him waiting outside somewhere in the darkness?

Chapter 9:
Shape-Shifters & Missing Time

It's a chilling tale of abductions, mutilations, murders of adults and children, time slips and sorcery, and it ended in 'the world's last witch-trial.' It took place in 1880 on a remote Chilean island called Chiloe and was said to have been carried out in the name of 'La Provincia Recta', translated as the 'Righteous Province.' This was the term given to the rulers there; a sect of warlocks who lived in a hidden cavern.

Gruesomely, these warlocks were said to take to the sky and fly around the Island wearing magickal 'clothing' which was made from the flayed skin of their deceased victims.

Lying close to the 35th parallel, the island has a mysterious and sinister history. It was the spot in which at the beginning of the 16th century the Inca Empire ended, and according to the Smithsonian, 'a strange and unknown world began.'

A place of rain and cold and untamed forests, to the Incas, it was a place where the Warlocks lived and evil came from. English travel writer Bruce Chatwin unveiled the history of the Warlocks to the world, describing them as male witches, "who existed for the sole purpose of hunting people."

According to their own testimonies at their trial, they ran protection rackets on the island, and would dispose of their enemies by sajaduras: that is, by magically inflicting cuts to the flesh.

Their headquarters was located in a cave, the entrance of which had been camouflaged to maintain its secret existence. It was lit with torches fuelled by the burning of fat from their victims' bodies. The warlocks and other witnesses swore at the trial that the cave was guarded by two monsters who ensured that no-one could enter and seize the secret treasures they kept there, including an ancient leather spell-book and a bowl, which when filled with water was said to allow secrets to be seen in it.

Mateo Coñuecar was one of the Warlocks who gave testimony, and he described his first time visiting the secret cave when he was a young initiate.

He said that he had been ordered to go to the cave to feed the 'creatures' inside of it. He went with another Warlock, who, when they approached the destination of the cave, began to dance ritualistically in order to open the cave entrance. He used a "special alchemy key," to open it, and the layer of earth hiding it came away.

Two disfigured entities burst out of the darkness at them. One he described as looking like a 'goat, which dragged itself on four legs.' The other was a naked man. The man was an 'invunche;' a deformed man who had been abducted as a baby and taken to the cave to become its guardian.

After being taken from its home and brought to the cave, according to Chatwin, its arms, legs, hands and feet were purposely dislocated. Then the warlocks got to work on its head. This was a slow and methodical task whereby each day, the baby's head was twisted a tiny fraction more than the day before so that eventually it was rotated by a full 180 degree and the child could look straight down the line of its own spine.

Chatwin continues, "Once the child is able to do this, the final adaptation is done. On the night of a full moon, the child is laid prostrate and tied down and its head covered over. A 'specialist' then takes a sharp knife and cuts a deep hole under the right shoulder blade. Into this hole he places the child's right arm and then sows up the hole. The child has now become the cave guardian; the 'invunche.'

It is kept in the cave forever and fed with human flesh. It never learns to speak nor read or write. It responds only with guttural noises.

The tiny populace of the Island were terrified of the Warlocks and their supernatural powers. The Warlocks claimed they would fly at night, in the human skin they wore which glowed with shiny phosphorescence from the grease of the skin. They claimed they could turn themselves into any animal, being 'Shape-shifters.' They could magically transport themselves to a 'Caleuche,' a ghost ship. It was a glowing ship that today is still seen by islanders. Many of them believe that the ship is a harvester of souls.

In order to become one of the Warlocks, an initiate must wash away their sins in the freezing sea for night after night and then prove they are cleansed of all human emotions and feelings by killing a member of their own family.

It was claimed that once they had passed their initiation, the secret sect would then celebrate their new member joining, by feasting on the roasted flesh of a new-born.

According to the warlock named earlier, he carried out 'hits' for payment. When a woman on the island went to him because her husband had been seduced by another woman, he killed the love rival for payment of not money, but cloth.

Since the times of the witch trials, Chiloe has lost none of its mystery. It's said to be a place where it's almost as though a parallel universe exists with it or alongside it, for there have been many unexplained disappearances and bizarre events. Steeped in mythology and folklore, there have been sightings of a variety of odd creatures, including the 'brujos;' shape-shifters who are immortal and who can take the form of wolves, fish, or humans. They can even take the form of rocks. It has been said that when they take the form of a human they are always very tall, and blonde. Sightings of these beings go back to before the time of Columbus yet there were no Caucasian blond races in South America before Christopher Columbus. It's these Nordic looking human's who are said by the inhabitants to be behind the disappearances of people on the Island.

Along with the Nordic sightings are the reports of the Ghost ship, the Caleuche, which again is reported to be able to shape-shift. When described, it bears striking similarities to UFO sightings in terms of appearance, and those who have seen it have also often reported incidents of missing time and relocation from where they last were. Some have described it as without doubt a ship, while others have said it has glowing lights, and yet other witnesses talk of strange glowing rocks or trees.

Along with the sightings are usually the simultaneous reports of the most beautiful and ethereal sound of music. Those who have the sighting are often abducted; those who do not see it but hear the music have been reported to have become deranged as a result.

The Chilean newspapers have reported on cases of young men who have disappeared as youths, never to be seen again until decades later when they have reappeared as old men. One such case was reported by the journalist Antonio Cardenas Tabies, who spent many years obsessed by the strange accounts he kept hearing. In his book, 'Boarding the Caleuche,' he collected more than 50 testimonies of local islanders in the 1970's; all of varying ages and backgrounds. One man he interviewed as a boy of 16 had gone fishing alone one day when he suddenly disappeared. Two days later he was found alone and wandering aimlessly along the beach on the Island. He seemed to be in a complete daze when he was found, and when he was asked where he'd been, he said that when he got to a small hill that overlooked the ocean he began to hear a strange hum, like the sound of a generator running; but he said it was more like two generators running together at the same time. That was the last thing he could remember until he was found on the beach two days later.

When he was taken back to his home, his family were very concerned when they saw that under his shirt he had a large scar that he had not had before. It was a huge scar that was shaped like a hand with long thin fingers.

When they asked him how he had got it, he could not remember and he said that he didn't recall having been in any pain. Even stranger, the scar looked like it had been there a long time, not like it was a fresh wound. Antonio Tabies returned to interview the same man five decades later, when he was by then in his sixties. The grown man was reluctant to be interviewed again, and when asked about the scar he said that he could not reveal how he had got it or he would die.

The reason for Antonio's own obsession with interviewing people was that he too had a similar inexplicable incident when he was growing up, of missing time and then being 'returned' to the Island changed.

Conclusion

Sometimes Predators are animal or human....*and sometimes they are not.*

Something in the Woods is Taking People; Something unknown that we cannot define; something that others have had the misfortune to encounter. People snatched soundlessly, never to be seen again. Or returned; dead. A strange and highly unusual predator. Highly intelligent. Very successful. And able to overpower someone in an instant.

This is a puzzle. An often deadly one.

If you have experienced something strange and unusual like this, that's hard to explain, please feel free to let me know. I'm actively continuing to research and would be very interested.

Stephenyoungauthor@hotmail.com

Facebook; Steph Young Author

Also by Stephen Young:

Taken in the Woods

Hunted in the Woods

Predators in the Woods

Mysterious things in the Woods

Encounters with the Unknown

True Storied of Real Time Travelers

Demons: True Stories of Demonic Possessions & Demon attacks

Terror in the Night

Monsters in the Dark

Haunted Asylums, Morgues & Cemeteries; True tales of horror at the Asylum.

Made in the USA
Middletown, DE
29 September 2021